PLOTS AND CHARACTERS
IN THE FICTION OF
EIGHTEENTH-CENTURY ENGLISH AUTHORS

VOLUME I

THE PLOTS AND CHARACTERS SERIES

Robert L. Gale
General Editor

PLOTS AND CHARACTERS
IN THE FICTION OF
EIGHTEENTH-CENTURY ENGLISH
AUTHORS

Volume I
Jonathan Swift, Daniel Defoe,
and Samuel Richardson

Clifford R. Johnson

Archon Books
Dawson

Clifford R. Johnson 1977

First published in 1977

Archon Books, The Shoe String Press
995 Sherman Avenue, Hamden, Connecticut 06514 USA

Wm Dawson & Sons Ltd, Cannon House
Folkestone, Kent, England

Library of Congress Cataloging in Publication Data

Johnson, Clifford R   1945-
    Plots and characters in the fiction of eighteenth-century English authors.

    (The Plots and characters series)
    CONTENTS: v. l. Jonathan Swift, Daniel Defoe, and Samuel Richardson.
    1. English fiction—18th century—History and criticism. 2. English fiction—Stories, plots, etc. I. Title.
PR858.P6J6   823'.009'24   77-2572

Dawson ISBN 0 7129 0762 9
Archon ISBN 0-208-01498-5

Printed in the United States of America

To Nora

. . . that sort of Reading, which is but an earlier debauchery for young minds, preparative to the grosser at riper years, to wit, Romances and Novels . . .

Samuel Richardson, conclusion to *Clarissa*

The World is so taken up of late with Novels and Romances, that it will be hard for a private History to be taken for Genuine, where the Names and other Circumstances of the Person are concealed, and on this Account we must be content to leave the Reader to pass his own Opinion upon the ensuing Sheets, and take it just as he pleases.

Daniel Defoe, preface to *Moll Flanders*

CONTENTS

PREFACE

This two-volume handbook is designed to include plot summaries and character identifications for the narrative works of the most important eighteenth-century English novelists. This first volume treats in unified lists the works of Jonathan Swift, Daniel Defoe, and Samuel Richardson. The second volume will cover Henry Fielding, Tobias Smollett, and Laurence Sterne, plus *Rasselas* by Samuel Johnson and *The Vicar of Wakefield* by Oliver Goldsmith. Although the reader will not have all of eighteenth-century fiction at his fingertips, he will nevertheless have the narrative works of the great geniuses in the field.

For Richardson, the selection of books was easy; he wrote three novels and then stopped. For Swift, I have had to be rigidly selective and have excluded most of his writings. I include only those books which are primarily narrative in their method: *Gulliver* and the volume called *A Tale of a Tub*. The latter contains *The Battle of the Books* and a non-narrative satire, *The Mechanical Operation of the Spirit*, along with the *Tale*. I summarize *The Mechanical Operation* only for the sake of completeness.

Selection in the case of Defoe was much less simple. Since he is one of the most prolific writers in our language, to index all his works would be a task for a team of scholars, rather than for one man. Of course, I could have contented myself with only the five novels most frequently discussed: *Crusoe, Singleton, Moll, Colonel Jacque,* and *Roxana*. *A Journal of the Plague Year*, however, also has large narrative sections and is considered by some to be Defoe's best book, and the criminal biographies have begun to attract critical attention. Finally I decided to include arbitrarily all works in the Aitken edition of *Romances and Narratives*. I have excluded works such as *The Family Instructor*, which are not in Aitken and which are primarily didactic rather than narrative in intention, and works such as the *History of Charles XII* and the *History of the Union*, which do not belong in the realm of fiction. But there seemed to be no sense in leaving out *Captain Carleton, Robert Drury's Journal,* or *A General History of the Pirates*, which are now generally accepted to be Defoe's. Although they are mainly factual accounts, the material has been transformed by Defoe's novelistic skill. So the handbook treats all works by Defoe which are primarily fictional narratives and which are available to the reading public.

To summarize is to distort. This is particularly so in the case of eighteenth-century fiction, where I must necessarily omit some of the things we read the books for (for example, in Swift the humor, and in Defoe the vigor of the prose). Users of the Richardson summaries should keep in mind the penalty pronounced by Dr. Samuel Johnson for those who read with plot alone in mind. "Why, Sir, if you were to read Richardson for the story, your impatience would be so much fretted that you would hang yourself. But you must read him for the sentiment, and consider the story as only giving occasion to the sentiment" (James Boswell, *Life of Samuel Johnson*, April 6, 1772).

In the Richardson sections, I occasionally draw together into a paragraph plot elements which unravel themselves only over three hundred pages or so of text (the Everard Grandison episode, for example). I do so because otherwise the summary would be unreadable, but I pay the penalty of thus obscuring one of the chief beauties of Richardson. In drawing Defoe's books into neat summaries, I impart to them an appearance of order which those turning to the actual texts will not always find.

In listing characters, I have tried to be comprehensive, even to the point of triviality (every servant in Richardson is catalogued, for example). I make an exception, however, in the case of *A General History of the Pirates*, which contains a large amount of material of a purely documentary nature. Since Professor Manuel Schonhorn's edition contains a comprehensive index, I omit from my list some names mentioned in trial documents, and some ship captains who appear only once and who are not characterized. Nevertheless, I include everyone who influences the action. The characters in the *History* alone account for over a third of the total number of characters in Defoe, and for more than twenty per cent of the total for all three authors taken together.

The reader will find in the alphabetical character list a textual reference for each character, keyed to standard editions. I hoped in this way to avoid long prose sketches and to increase the usefulness of the handbook. The description itself often refers to the page cited, but by no means always. No effort is made to catalogue every appearance; so the reader will find more than one reference only in cases (1) where the character appears in more than one work, (2) where the character comes onstage before his name is actually mentioned, and (3) where the character's name is mentioned only in widely scattered volumes (in Richardson).

I spell characters' names as my authors have; so I list Robert Drury's captain as William Macket, even though the real captain spelled his name Mackett. The Duc de Vendôme appears as the Duke de Vendosme because Defoe spelled his name that way. I list named characters only, except in cases such as Defoe's "black prince," who appears throughout a hundred pages of action and is always referred to by the same title. Since Defoe was evidently trying to disguise his novels as factual narratives, the most important people in his book are exactly those he is most coy about naming, except by indirect reference ("the prince," "my Bath gentleman," etc.). But I include the most famous of these, under the rationale that readers will look for them. The most notable case of an unnamed character who plays a decisive role in the action is the Cavalier himself, who clearly could not be omitted.

In alphabetizing, I list something before nothing, and so "John, Sir" is followed by "John." Presumably Miss Bramber would have had a first name had Richardson given her one, but he did not; so I list her after her sister Sally. In the case of a large number of people with the same last name (e. g., the Porretta family), I first group all characters with first names, regardless of title, and then I group all characters without first names, arranged alphabetically by title. For the sake of consistency, rascals are entered under their real names rather than their aliases; so the familiar Dorcas in *Clarissa* is to be found under Butler, Deb; Blackbeard is under Teach, Edward. People whose names begin with de, D', and della are listed under the word that follows (de la Tour is under Tour).

I supply biographical data for characters in Swift because his works are satiric and frequently can be understood only by referring to the historical personalities behind them. I identify the person first, then note what the character does in Swift's narrative. I omit dates of birth and death for characters in Defoe, even though the majority of them were real people on the stage of history, because to include such information would generally not add to understanding the work and would turn the list into a handbook of European history.

I refer to standard editions, but with *Gulliver's Travels* and *A*

Tale of a Tub paperbound reprints are in far wider use than the
corresponding volumes in the Davis *Prose Works;* so I cite characters in these works by chapter. For characters in Richardson,
the Roman numerals refer to the volume number of the multi-
volumed novel in question, rather than of the whole set. (The
first volume of *Grandison* is thus I rather than XIII). My reasoning
here is that the volume arrangement was evidently part of
Richardson's plan in writing (he was a printer by profession) and
features prominently in Richardson scholarship.

For Defoe, all references are to *Romances and Narratives by Daniel
Defoe,* ed. George A. Aitken, 16 vols. (London: Dent, 1895), with
the following exceptions: *Captain Carleton* is from *The Novels and
Miscellaneous Works of Daniel De Foe,* 20 vols. (London: Tegg, 1840),
VIII. *A General History of the Pirates* is from the fine edition by
Manuel Schonhorn (Columbia, S.C.: Univ. of South Carolina Press,
1972). *Robert Drury's Journal* is from *Madagascar; or, Robert Drury's
Journal,* ed. Capt. Pasfield Oliver (London: T. Fisher Unwin, 1890).

For Swift, all references are to the *Prose Works,* ed. Herbert
Davis, 14 vols. (Oxford: Blackwell, 1939-1968).

For Richardson, all references are to *The Shakespeare Head Edition
of the Novels of Samuel Richardson,* 18 vols. (Oxford: Blackwell, 1931).

Finally, without writing a critical dissertation, I would like to
point out some directions for future scholarship that this sort of
systematic consideration suggests. I think that anyone who goes
through all of Defoe will notice an enormous sameness in the
narrative voice. The reader may be forced to entertain doubts
about his supposed dramatic technique and the ironic distance
which he is sometimes said to maintain from Moll and Crusoe,
since these characters come out sounding remarkably like Capt.
Carleton and Robert Drury. Secondly, one is struck by the great
extent to which *Moll* and *Colonel Jacque* should be read as companion
pieces to the criminal narratives, which employ the same widely
praised particularity and thinly disguised admiration for the
clever rogue.

A fair reading of all of Richardson leads one, I think, to give
him high marks for planning and to question the allegation that
he made up his books as he went along. His consistency in the
treatment of his minor characters (to cite one example) is enormous. In *Pamela,* Jane and Nan maintain their personality traits
across many volumes of text, while Defoe forgets the name of
Col. Jack's tutor within thirty pages (he is first Robin, then Will).

Richardson also has enormous control over a great mass of material, most notably in *Clarissa*, and is clearly working in large plot units, sometimes a volume in length. We cannot fail to be struck again by the relative planlessness of Defoe, and may be nudged toward the unmodish conclusion that he is something of a primitive.

At the same time, much of Defoe's best work is clearly going unread, untaught, and undiscussed. *Robert Drury's Journal* and many chapters in the *History of the Pirates* may be far better fiction than most of *Captain Singleton* and large portions of *Colonel Jacque* and even *Moll Flanders*.

A number of things in Swift become reminiscent of Defoe when one considers the two authors together. Scholars have already noticed the similarity between *Crusoe* and *Gulliver*. Furthermore, Swift's use of pirates and mutinies and his love of fantastic names clearly appealed to the same audience that was reading Defoe's tales of pirates and castaways. There should be more comparison between Swift's best-known works and Defoe's least-known ones.

List of works treated (the Roman numerals refer to the volume of the standard edition where the work is to be found).

Swift:

The Battle of the Books, 1704 (I).
Gulliver's Travels, 1726 (XI).
The Mechanical Operation of the Spirit, 1704 (I).
A Tale of a Tub, 1704 (I).

Defoe:

The Apparition of Mrs. Veal, 1705 (XV).
Captain Carleton, 1728.
Captain Singleton, 1720 (VI).
Colonel Jacque, 1722 (X, XI).
Due Preparations for the Plague, 1722 (XV).
The Dumb Philosopher, 1719 (XV).
Duncan Campbell, 1720 (IV).
Farther Adventures of Robinson Crusoe, 1719 (II).
A General History of the Pirates, 2 vols., 1724, 1728.
John Gow, 1725 (XVI).
Jonathan Wild, 1725 (XVI).
A Journal of the Plague Year, 1722 (IX).
The King of Pirates (Captain Avery), 1719 (XVI).
The Life of John Sheppard, 1724 (XVI).

Memoirs of a Cavalier, 1720 (V).
Moll Flanders, 1722 (VII, VIII).
Narrative of John Sheppard, 1724 (XVI).
A New Voyage Round the World, 1724 (XVI).
Robert Drury's Journal, 1729.
Robinson Crusoe, 1719 (I).
Roxana, 1724 (XII, XIII).
The Six Notorious Street-Robbers, 1726 (XVI).
Richardson:
Clarissa, 7 vols., 1747, 1748 (V-XII).
Pamela, 4 vols., 1740, 1741 (I-IV).
Sir Charles Grandison, 7 vols., 1753, 1754 (XIII-XVIII).

Clifford R. Johnson

University of Pittsburgh
Pittsburgh, Pennsylvania

CHRONOLOGY OF EVENTS

1660?   Daniel Defoe born in London, the son of a merchant.

1667   Jonathan Swift born Nov. 30 in Dublin, the son of a lawyer and a distant relation of John Dryden; raised partly in England and partly in Ireland by a nurse and by his uncle Godwin.

1673   Swift enters grammar school at Kilkenny, Ireland.

1674   Defoe attends the Dissenting academy at Newington Green kept by Charles Morton.

1680   Esther Johnson ("Stella") born.

1682   Swift matriculates at Trinity College, Dublin.

1684   Defoe marries Mary Tuffley.

1685   Defoe goes into the hosiery business; joins Monmouth's rebellion.

1686   Swift granted the B.A., *speciali gratia*, by a special dispensation.

1688   Samuel Richardson born in Derbyshire, the son of a carpenter, his mother "not ungenteel." He is intended for the church, but financial considerations cause him to be put to a trade. The troubles in Ireland cause Swift to travel to England.

1691   Swift becomes secretary to Sir William Temple at Moor Park, Surrey; writes first poems.

1692   Defoe's first bankruptcy.

1695   Defoe establishes a pantile factory at Tilbury in Essex. Swift ordained as a priest of the Church of England; serves in the parish of Kilroot, near Belfast.

1696   Swift's flirtation with Jane Waring ("Varina").

1696-   Swift returns to Moor Park; writes *Tale of a Tub, Battle of*
1697   *the Books*; friendship with Esther Johnson begins. Defoe begins to write in defense of the policy of William III.

1700   Swift becomes vicar of Laracor and prebendary of St. Patrick's, Ireland; lives in Dublin.

1701   Swift becomes Doctor of Divinity of Trinity College, Dublin; Stella joins him in Dublin; visits London in 1701, 1702, 1703-1704, 1705; wins the favor of leading Whig politicians for his *Contests and Dissensions*.

1703   Defoe imprisoned and forced to stand in the pillory for *The Shortest Way with the Dissenters*, an ironic attack on the Tory High-Fliers.

1704   Defoe released from prison, apparently on the condition that he write for the government; writes *The Review* (1704-1713). Swift publishes *Tale.*

1705   Defoe's second marriage, to a daughter of Samuel Annesley, the Dissenting minister.

1706   Richardson apprenticed by John Wilde, the stationer. Defoe goes to Edinburgh about the proposed union with Scotland.

1707-   Swift in England to petition (unsuccessfully) for certain
1709   financial favors from the crown for the Church of Ireland; friendship with Addison begins. His sympathies become alienated from the Whigs because of their church policy.

1710   Death of Swift's mother; he writes moving epitaph on her death.

1710-   Tories in control of the government; Swift works as a
1714   propagandist for the Oxford ministry; edits *The Examiner*, writes *The Conduct of the Allies, Journal to Stella*; friendships with Gay, Pope, Arbuthnot, Bolingbroke; flirtation with Esther Vanhomrigh ("Vanessa").
        Having earlier defended the war, Defoe now defends the peace; becomes permanently alienated from the Whigs.

1713   Swift made Dean of St. Patrick's; £300 reward offered for the arrest of the author of his *Public Spirit of the Whigs*. Defoe prosecuted for libel for writing three anti-Jacobite tracts.

1714   Death of Queen Anne, accession of George I. Swift returns to Dublin to exile. Defoe supports the new ministry.

1716   Swift's secret marriage to Stella?

1716-   Defoe works as a double agent for the administration;
1720   infiltrates opposition journals, the *Newsletter, Mist's Journal.*

1719   Richardson sets up in business as a printer in Fleet Street; later moves to Salisbury Court, where he remains for the rest of his life.

1719-   Period of Defoe's novels, beginning with *Robinson Crusoe.*
1724

1720   First of Swift's Irish tracts, urging the Irish to use goods manufactured in their own country. During the 1720's, Swift is working on *Gulliver's Travels.*

1723   Richardson, previously known for being a Tory, obtains a lucrative contract to print the journals of the House of Commons; his business flourishes.

1724   Swift becomes a hero of the Irish people for his *Drapier's Letters*, attacking English plans to alter the Irish currency; he has a price on his head for the second time in his life for the fourth letter. Richardson marries Martha Wilde, a printer's daughter; none of their six children survives to adulthood.

1724- Period of Defoe's criminal biographies; lives genteelly in
1725   a large house in Stoke Newington with his wife and three daughters. Mist attacks Defoe with a sword (having found out about the infiltration?).

1726   Swift visits England, anonymously publishes *Gulliver's Travels*, a huge success.
       Defoe is blacklisted by numerous journals; engaged in the sale of cloth.

1727   Swift visits England for the last time; returns to Dublin because of Stella's illness.

1728   Death of Stella, Jan. 28; many of Swift's famous gloomy letters begin appearing at this time.

1729   Defoe's daughter Sophia marries Henry Baker.

1729- Swift writes some of his most biting satires, most notably
1736   the *Modest Proposal* (1729).

1730   Defoe very bitter about the conduct of his son, Benjamin Norton Defoe, whom he accuses of not supporting his mother and sisters with the money Defoe has placed at his discretion.
       Richardson's first wife dies.

1731   Defoe dies Apr. 26 in Ropemaker's Alley, London.

1739   Two publishers persuade Richardson to undertake the project of writing a volume of model letters for country people to imitate; this project proves to be the germ of *Pamela*.

1740   *Pamela* published, becomes a sensation. Richardson composes his novels in his country house in Hammersmith.

1742   Richardson deeply hurt by *Joseph Andrews*, Fielding's spoof of *Pamela*.
       Swift is suffering very much from giddiness (Menière's syndrome); declared unsound of mind by a court.

1744   Richardson begins to write *Clarissa*; resists pleas that it have a happy ending.

1745 Swift dies in Dublin, Oct. 19; buried next to Stella; leaves over £10,000 to found a hospital for the insane.

1747- Publication of *Clarissa* makes Richardson an international
1748 sensation; extravagantly praised by Diderot and Rousseau. Correspondence with Lady Bradshaigh begins.

1751 Richardson working on *Grandison*.

1753 *Grandison* published; Richardson idolized by a circle of admirers.

1754 Richardson chosen a master of the Stationer's Company; sets up a country residence at Parson's Green, Fulham.

1755 He turns his old warehouse into a dwelling; his wife's dissatisfaction with the project distracts him from future literary efforts.

1760 With Miss Catherine Lintot, Richardson becomes law printer to the king. In his later years, he becomes hypochondrial; communicates with his workmen by means of notes; plants coins in the types for the earliest riser to find. A nephew succeeds to his printing business.

1761 Richardson dies of an apoplexy, July 4, in London.

Source: *Dictionary of National Biography*.

CHRONOLOGY OF PUBLICATIONS

Books not summarized in this handbook are included in parentheses.

1725   *Jonathan Wild*; (*Tour through the Whole Island of Great Britain*,
       Vol. II); *John Gow*; (*Complete English Tradesman*, Vol. I), Defoe.
1726   *Gulliver's Travels*, Swift.
       (*Tour through the Whole Island of Great Britain*, Vol. III, Defoe.)
1727   (*The Complete English Tradesman*, Vol. II; *Conjugal Lewdness,
       or Matrimonial Whoredom*, Defoe.)
1728   *Captain Carleton; General History of the Pirates*, Vol. II, Defoe.
1729   (*A Modest Proposal*, Swift.)
       Robert Drury's Journal, Defoe.
1739   (*Verses on the Death of Dr. Swift*, Swift, composed 1731).
1740   *Pamela*, Vols. I and II, Richardson.
1741   *Pamela*, Vols. III and IV.
1747   *Clarissa*, Vols. I and II, Richardson.
1748   *Clarissa*, Vols. III and IV (April).
       Clarissa, Vols. V through VII (December).
1753   *Sir Charles Grandison*, Vols. I through IV (November),
       Richardson.
       Sir Charles Grandison, Vols. V through VI (December).
1754   *Sir Charles Grandison*, Vol. VII.

(NB: The Shakespeare Head edition of Richardson's novels, used in this handbook, contains *Clarissa* in eight volumes and *Grandison* in six.)

For more exact information, the reader may consult the following bibliographies:

Moore, John Robert. *A Checklist of the Writings of Daniel Defoe.* 2d ed. Hamden, Ct.: Archon Books, 1971.

Sale, William M. *Samuel Richardson: A Bibliographical Record.* New Haven: Yale University Press, 1936; reprinted 1969, Hamden, Ct.: Archon Books.

Teerink, H., and Arthur H. Scouten. *A Bibliography of the Writings of Jonathan Swift.* 2d ed. Philadelphia: University of Pennsylvania Press, 1963.

PLOTS

The Apparition of Mrs. Veal, Defoe, 1705. (Original title: *A True Relation of the Apparition of One Mrs. Veal the Next Day After her Death, to One Mrs. Bargrave at Canterbury, the 8th of September, 1705.*)

This most famous of Defoe's short sketches is supposedly narrated by a justice of the peace of Maidstone in Kent to his friend in London. Mrs. Bargrave and Mrs. Veal were friends in childhood and consoled each other when they were neglected by their fathers. Mrs. Bargrave married a man who abused her terribly. Mrs. Veal in the meanwhile moved to Dover, where her brother obtained a post in the Customs Office. At the time of the story, Mrs. Bargrave has been living alone in Canterbury for six months when there is a knock at her door, one Saturday just as the clock is striking midday.

Mrs. Veal enters in a riding habit and says that she has come to pay her respects before departing on her journey, and to apologize for neglecting her old friend of late. Mrs. Bargrave offers to kiss her, but at the last moment Mrs. Veal draws back her face. They discuss the beauties of a future state, and Mrs. Veal asks her friend to fetch Drelincourt's book on death, which she especially likes. She advises Mrs. Bargrave not to be concerned about present suffering since this will be as nothing compared to her heavenly reward. Mrs. Bargrave then strokes the sleeve of Mrs. Veal's dress, and the latter says that it is made of scoured silk. After declining a cup of tea and asking that a few gold pieces be given to her cousin Mr. Watson, Mrs. Veal leaves.

Mrs. Bargrave is indisposed the next day with a cold and sore throat. Monday she goes to the Watsons', finding to her astonishment that Mrs. Veal died Friday at noonday! Mrs. Watson is immediately convinced that Mrs. Bargrave has truly seen an apparition, since only Mrs. Veal and Mrs. Watson herself knew that the dress she wore was indeed made of scoured silk.

The justice closes with protests of Mrs. Bargrave's absolute reliability. Mr. Veal has been trying to suppress the story, for what reasons the justice cannot imagine, since the spirit was clearly benign and talked only of the loftiest and most heavenly matters.

Mr. Bargrave, Mrs. Bargrave, old Mr. Breton, Mr. Veal, ghost of Mrs. Veal, Capt. Watson, Mrs. Watson.

The Battle of the Books, Swift, 1704. (Published with *A Tale of a Tub*; original title: *A Full and True Account of the Battle Fought last Friday, Between the Ancient and the Modern Books in St. James's Library*.)

The *Battle*, which is really an appendix to the *Tale*, deals with the value of modern learning compared to that of the ancients. In particular, Swift was writing a spoof of the literary war between the adherents of Sir William Temple (the "Christ Church wits") and those who impugned his scholarship, William Wotton and Dr. Richard Bentley. Temple (Swift's former patron) had cited as examples of the excellence of the ancients *Aesop's Fables* and the *Epistles of Phalaris*. Wotton and Bentley defended modern achievements, and Bentley went so far as to prove that Aesop was later than Temple had thought and that the *Epistles* were a modern forgery. Charles Boyle, Earl of Orrery, and Francis Atterbury had denounced Bentley and Wotton as plodding dunces, and Swift joined the fray with his satire (written 1696-1697). Swift uses the controversy only as a taking-off point to comment on the faults of his contemporaries. By "ancient" culture, we should understand not only Greek and Roman authors, but also well-read gentlemen of the present, as opposed to pompous pedants and half-educated hack authors.

The piece opens like the *Tale*, with a mock passage from the publisher to the reader and a preface glancing at the ineffectiveness of satire. In the narrative proper, we are told that the moderns inhabit the lower of the twin peaks of Mt. Parnassus, while the ancients have always inhabited the higher. The moderns demand that the ancients either give up their peak or allow it to be torn down to a level below that of the moderns. The resulting controversy fills many books and occupies much space on the shelves of the "regal library." Unfortunately, the royal librarian (Bentley) is a partisan of the moderns. He shelves the moderns promiscuously in among the ancients, which leads to a falling out among the books. Here, "Virgil" stands not for the poet himself but for his works, and so on. The moderns plan an attack on the ancients but are at a heavy disadvantage because the only armor they have is what they have plundered from their antagonists. Several moderns, including Temple, have spent much time among the ancients and go over to their side before the fight.

While the conflict is brewing, a bee flies into the library through a broken pane and becomes entangled in a spider web. Having freed himself, he is berated by the spider. This little argument is Swift's fable of the difference between modern and ancient literature. The ancient like the bee gathers his material from an observation of human nature and produces works which are both pleasant and edifying, while the modern thinks all literature depends on self-expression and as a result produces works which are malignant and poisonous. He excels at the sciences of architecture and mathematics, but when put to the test, modern constructions fall apart like the spider's web.

The books now draw themselves up in battle array, with the ancients far outnumbered. The moderns have trouble choosing their leaders. A council on Olympus is called, as in the Homeric epics (throughout the *Battle*, Swift makes mock use of epic conventions). Momus, the spirit of stupidity, is on the side of the moderns and so flies to the mountain home of Criticism, the daughter of Ignorance and Pride, who lives with her sister Opinion. Criticism flies to help her son Wotton. She transforms herself into a book (Wotton's *Reflections on the Ancient and Modern Learning*, 1694) and enters his body, thus squeezing out his eyeballs and overturning his brain.

The battle begins, heavy with references to seventeenth-century literature. The ancients easily defeat their modern counterparts. Dryden calls Virgil (whom he has translated) to a parley and appears as a tiny shrunken head within a helmet much too large for him. He changes horses with Virgil but is then afraid to mount.

Abraham Cowley was the author of verses he believed to be imitations of the great odes of Pindar, but the latter cuts Cowley in two with his sword. Venus takes half of the corpse and transforms it into a dove, which is then attached to her chariot. (Most readers of the time thought Cowley's love poetry better than the Pindarics on which he prided himself.)

Bentley and Wotton now enter. Bentley is a misformed figure whom humane learning has merely transformed into a pedant. He spatters his antagonists with ordure and turns against friend and foe alike (Bentley loved controversy). In a parody of Ulysses' night attack in the *Iliad*, Bentley and Wotton sneak out to assault the sleeping ancients. Bentley finds Phalaris and Aesop sleeping and prepares to daub them with manure, but the goddess Affright causes him to withdraw.

Meanwhile, Wotton has been attempting to drink out of the brook of Helicon, but Apollo makes the water draw back from his lips (true poetic inspiration is denied to dunces). He sees Temple drinking copiously from the spring and throws a lance at him, which rebounds harmlessly and unnoticed by Temple. But Boyle notices Wotton's impudent attempt and rushes to the attack. Bentley arrives on the scene only to flee from Boyle's wrath, but the latter impales both his enemies with one throw of his lance. Swift breaks off the narrative at this point with the pretense that the manuscript has been left in a fragmentary state.

Aesculapius, Aesop, Afra, Apollo, (St. Thomas) Aquinas, Aristotle, (Sir Francis) Bacon, (Roberto) Bellarmine, (Dr. Richard) Bentley, (Sir Richard) Blackmore, (Charles) Boyle, (George) Buchanan, (William) Cambden, (Abraham) Cowley, (Thomas) Creech, Criticism, (Enrico) Davila, (John) Dennis, (John) Denham, (René) Descartes, (Nicolas Boileaux) Despréaux, (John) Dryden, Dulness, Duns Scotus, Euclid, Evander, (Bernard de) Fontenelle, Galen, (Pierre) Gassendi, Gondibert, (Francesco) Guiccardine, (William) Harvey, Herodotus, Hippocrates, (Thomas) Hobbes, Homer, Ignorance, Ill-Manners, Impudence, Jupiter, (Sir Roger) L'Estrange, Livy, Lucan, (Juan de) Mariana, Mercury, (John) Milton, Momus, Noise, (John) Ogleby, (John) Oldham, Opinion, Pallas, Paracelsus, Pedantry, Phalaris, Pindar, Plato, Positiveness, (Charles) Perrault, Pride, Regiomontanus, (Joseph Justus) Scaliger, (Torquato) Tasso, (Sir William) Temple, Vanity, Venus, Polydore Vergil, Virgil, (Gerard) Vossius, (Samuel) Wesley, (John) Wilkins, (George) Wither(s), (William) Wotton.

Captain Avery, Defoe. See *The King of Pirates.*

Captain Carleton, Defoe, 1728. (Original title: *The Memoirs of an English Officer, Who serv'd in the Dutch War of 1672, to the Peace of Utrecht in 1713. By Capt. George Carleton.*)

These supposed military memoirs cover the wars in Holland briefly, but are devoted mainly to the exploits of the famous Earl of Peterborough in Spain in 1705 and 1706. They are interlarded with Carleton's observations on Spanish scenes and

Spanish life. In the year 1672, George Carleton enlists with the Duke of York to fight the Dutch and takes part in the naval engagement off Sole Bay on May 28. He strenuously contradicts reports of the Duke's cowardice; in fact, the Duke spent the entire battle on the quarterdeck with cannon balls whizzing around his head. The Earl of Sandwich (Pepys's patron) is killed, and his corpse is later picked up by the captain of a packet boat as the gulls are feasting on it. One Hodge Vaughan is carried below badly wounded, only to be devoured by ravenous hogs. A gentleman volunteer has himself tied to the mast to keep from fleeing below, and Carleton reflects that courage under fire is another matter from the dueling field.

After peace is made with the Dutch, Carleton joins the army of the young Prince of Orange in Holland in 1674. The Prince was one of Defoe's heroes, and he dominates the first part of the *Memoirs*. Once he stumbles into the French lines but through his perfect command of French is able to pass himself off as one of their own officers. He later is forced to raise the siege of Oudenarde because of the sluggishness of his reinforcements. All of Holland is alarmed when the Prince falls ill with smallpox, but fortunately he recovers. During this campaign Carleton lives through a hurricane in which so many soldiers' hats are blown into the air that they resemble flights of rooks at evening.

In 1676 Carleton takes part in the assault on a Dutch city called the Grave. The Dutch forces panic when a soldier unskillfully throws a hand grenade and it comes rolling back down the parapet at them. Carleton is promoted to ensign because of combat attrition. Immediately after the assault is resumed, he receives a bullet wound in the hand and a broken collarbone from the stroke of a halberd. The Prince's conduct is extremely gallant; when he is wounded he waves his hat to show his troops that he is still all right. He again must raise the siege because his subordinate Count Souches is tardy in coming to the field.

The country people are not altogether friendly. One day Carleton discovers the burnt corpse of a soldier who wandered into a farmhouse and was murdered by the farmers. Finally the Prince goes to England to marry the Princess Mary, and in 1678 the Peace of Nimeguen is concluded. During the lull between wars Carleton learns the science of siege engineering, which he is to use later in Spain.

Carleton frets until 1685, when he is recalled to England to help repel Monmouth's rebellion and to accept King James's commission. When the Glorious Revolution of 1688 occurs, the Prince of Orange becomes William III of England and Carleton gladly shifts his allegiance to the new king. He is sent to Scotland to suppress rebellions there and conceives a low opinion of the wretched Scots economy. He is pleased only when he visits Forrest, the scene of the witches' dialogue with Macbeth.

After crossing the river Spey, Carleton's regiment engages some rebellious Highlanders at Cromdale Hill. Carleton flushes out a nest of the enemy by throwing grenades in among them and discovers one of the Highlanders to be his old friend Brody from the Dutch wars, now missing a nose as a result of one of Carleton's grenades.

War has now been declared against the French, and Carleton's regiment is sent to attack Dunkirk. They have to be diverted to Ostend, however, because the clacking tongue of a female politician has revealed their military secrets to the French. In the battle of Steenkirk (1694) the English are defeated because the Dutch refuse to come to their aid. One Dutch officer declares, "Damn 'em, since they love fighting, let 'em have their bellies full!" (p. 32).

At Dixmuyd Carleton experiences his first earthquake. He is back in London when a floor in the Tower of London collapses under twenty thousand barrels of gunpowder. Only the interposition of Providence, explains Carleton, prevented the powder from being ignited by a stray spark. Meanwhile King William is besieging Namur, and the French are trying to create a diversion by bombarding Brussels. They lay a great part of the city in ruins, but before beginning the bombardment, the Duc de Villeroi politely inquires of the Duke of Bavaria where in the city his duchess is residing, so that they may not shell that quarter. The French diversion fails to distract William from his goal, and finally Namur surrenders.

The year 1696 sees the notorious Assassination Plot against the life of King William, and Carleton helps round up the suspects. He saves the government a thousand pounds by capturing one suspect (Cassels) the evening before the reward is proclaimed. For this service he receives not the slightest acknowledgment, and most of his friends feel that he has made a sacrifice beyond the call of duty.

Carleton is dispatched back to Shoerbeck in Holland, where he finds that the soldiers under his command have been drinking while on watch. He quickly brings the garrison into proper order. That very night they are awakened by what they think is a party of the enemy, but it turns out to be only a mock raid from the neighboring English garrison to see if Carleton's men are on their toes. Later during this campaign Carleton notices a suspicious figure hanging around the ammunition wagons. He has the man arrested, and when he is searched, he is found to have matches and kindling. He is executed as an incendiary.

In 1697 the Peace of Ryswick is signed and Carleton fears he will be assigned to the West Indies, where he may die of fever. To his great relief, war is declared again in 1702, the War of the Spanish Succession. The English want to prevent Louis XIV's grandson Philip of Anjou from inheriting the throne of Spain; instead they back the Austrian candidate, Charles III. Unfortunately King William dies after a fall from his horse, but the war is gloriously prosecuted under the honest English queen, Anne. Carleton ships with the Earl of Peterborough (real hero of the *Memoirs*) on his expedition into Spain.

Peterborough is ordered against his better judgment to attack Barcelona, in Catalonia, far from his sources of supply. He manages to conquer the town against all odds by a night march and surprise attack on Monjouick, on the western side of town. At one point during the assault, the Lord Charlemont unwisely allows the soldiers to persuade him to retreat. Carleton rushes with the news to Peterborough, who in turn charges to the front and leads the men again to the attack, thus saving the day. The English finally conquer Monjouick when a lucky shot blows up the Spanish powder reserve.

When Barcelona finally capitulates, Peterborough gives sanctuary to the Spanish commander, Don Valasco, and to the duchess of Popoli, who are threatened by the vengeful mob of Catalonians. (Among the Spanish people, only the Catalonians support the English interests; the others prefer Philip of Anjou as king.) The victory celebration includes the Earl's throwing out handfuls of dollars to the crowd and releasing a flight of birds, symbolizing the liberation from French oppression. During this fiesta, Carleton is mortified to see the mob laughing at a drunken English soldier.

Peterborough continues to conquer against heavy odds by a combination of daring and cleverness. He raises the siege of Santo Mattheo by making the commander think that the English army is far larger than it really is. He also procures the surrender of the town of Nules by allowing the city fathers only six minutes to consider before surrendering; otherwise he threatens to put the entire garrison to the sword.

Peterborough undertakes a daring march toward Valencia, despite the fact that he has only the tiny force of six hundred horse and two thousand foot. He negotiates with the defender of Molviedro, Brigadier Mahoni, and makes elaborate promises ("taxing even the faith of a Catholic," as Carleton comments) to induce him to defect. The Earl meanwhile sends double agents into the other Spanish force marching to reinforce Mahoni, who tell the Duke of Arcos that Mahoni is in the pay of the English. Accordingly, when Mahoni marches to a juncture with Arcos, he is arrested as a traitor. Arcos then marches off in the direction opposite to the one Mahoni wanted to go in, opening the way for Peterborough to capture Valencia! (Carleton comments on the beauty of the women and the recklessness of the bravos there.)

Peterborough rushes back to Barcelona to save the skin of Charles III, who is besieged there. The earl has been empowered to act as admiral; so he daringly slips out to sea in an open boat to join the fleet. He then outmaneuvers the French fleet under the Duc de Toulouse and relieves his allies in Barcelona.

Peterborough shows a combination of firmness and tact in dealing with the Spanish people. At a villa near Campilio, the peasants murder a group of English officers and their wives by throwing them down a well. Peterborough's vengeance is swift. He captures the ringleader and hangs him in front of his own front door. Then he burns the villa to the ground. A second incident occurs when two English officers seduce a pair of nuns. The irate townspeople (even the nuns' parents) want to wall the nuns up and starve them to death, but Peterborough persuades them to pardon the girls. In Valencia, he ingratiates himself by staging a "tawridore" (bullfight) for the populace.

Carleton inserts here an account of the religious fervor of the Valencians. During carnival time the greatest excesses are committed; pedestrians are spattered with water, ink, and ordure. But during Lent, the people scourge themselves with thongs. "He that is most bloody is most devout," comments the sturdy Protestant Carleton. He also describes the idyllic life led by the hermits of Montserat, and contrasts it with the base superstition prevailing in the cloister church. The description of Montserat is completed by an account of a plague of locusts.

Carleton is sent in his role as military engineer to aid in reducing Requina. Unfortunately the commander of the engineers (a Dutchman) takes a nap too close to the cache of powder. One of the soldiers takes a pot shot at a stray pig and detonates the entire powder stock along with the commander; only an arm with a ring clinging to a finger is found. Carleton tells how General Gorge swindled the inhabitants of Alicant out of their possessions under the pretense of protecting them from looting sailors. Carleton gets the credit for a cavalry victory, since he warns his commanding officer Captain Matthews that the Spaniards are preparing an ambush. Peterborough rewards Carleton for his diligence by making him the sole engineer of the castle at Alicant.

Peterborough's military genius does not obtain for him a deciding voice in the English councils of war. Instead of being allowed to block up the northern approaches into Spain so as to prevent the French from re-entering, he is required to secure Aragon so that Charles III may make a triumphal procession to Madrid. During the winter he goes to Genoa to negotiate a loan to the English of a hundred thousand pounds. While he is gone, he is superseded in his command by the Earl of Galway, whose advance into Spain from Portugal has been made possible only by Peterborough's phenomenal successes.

Without Peterborough at the helm, the war takes a turn for the worse. Lt. Col. Bateman's cavalry squadron is decimated by a handful of Spaniards. In 1707, the English army is smashed at Almanza. Carleton has moved on to Denia, where he is included in the surrender of the English garrison. Major Percival capitulates to the Spanish only in order to preserve his own personal horde of money. Carleton is now *hors de combat* and passes two years pleasantly under gentleman's arrest at San Clemente de la Mancha, the setting of *Don Quixote*. He only has to be extremely careful to avoid trouble with the spies of the Inquisition, who are everywhere. He drives one of these spies into a rage by his bland evasion of doctrinal questions. During his stay he learns of how the pigheaded English were blown up with a mine at Alicant, despite the open warnings of the Spanish that the mine was ready to be detonated.

Contrary to English prejudices, perfect order is maintained in the nunneries. False rumors of the sisters' sexual obligingness are created by a trick of the city fathers. They hide the real nuns away from the invaders and supply prostitutes in the cloister. The English soldiers, filled with stories of goings-on in the convents (vintage 1588) run pell-mell to throw trinkets over the convent walls. Only when they begin to develop venereal diseases does it occur to them to doubt the purity of their paramours.

The English win victories at Almanar and Saragosa, and Philip thinks of retiring into France. But at the decisive moment he is reinforced by French troops under the Duke de Vendosme. At the same time, Charles III enters Madrid instead of proceeding to Pamplona to block the French troops. This mistake decides the outcome of the war. Stanhope's army is smashed at Breuhiga, and Staremberg is forced to retreat to Barcelona. This double French victory is celebrated at San Clemente by a bullfight, which Carleton finds cruel. Some of the bulls have more "humanity" than the bull-fighters.

The remainder of the *Memoirs* is made up of a series of anecdotes of Spanish life, concentrating on Spanish dignity and popish superstition. When the ave bell rings, people go down on their knees immediately for prayer, even if they are standing in the gutter. Franciscans' habits are much sought after as shrouds. Carleton is particularly displeased by the music of guitars, which the English sailors call "strum-strums." He finds a Spanish lady overtly friendly toward him, but his landlady warns him that she may be a decoy for robbers. He decides not to take a walk to Minai because of the picaroons, highway maurauders who even rip open the intestines of travelers in a search for their money. When a criminal is executed, the hangman embraces the victim and throws himself through the trap with him to make sure that the neck is snapped. Carleton is surprised that the victim is not torn apart.

An Irish priest named Murtough Brennan visits Carleton, ostensibly to convert him. But one day Maria, the landlady's daughter, runs screaming to Carleton for help, pursued by Brennan in his shirt. Carleton throws Brennan into the street. When the Irishman complains to the corregidor, Carleton carries his case to the dean of the Inquisition in Madrid and Brennan is defrocked.

When a truce is reached in 1712, Carleton returns home by way of Madrid, telling us what sights he sees. While waiting at Bayonne for passage, he is invited aboard an English ship to drink beer, but the gangplank collapses and he is almost sucked under by the strong current. The captain later tells him the plank had been booby-trapped to surprise thieves! After being driven back to port once by a storm, Carleton arrives home on March 31, 1713, after an eight years' absence. He has been out of touch with English politics for so long that the conflicts of Whig and Tory seem utterly incomprehensible to him.

Alberoni, Count D'Alfelt, Duke of Arcos, Duke of Auverquerque, Anthony Barnwell, Gen. Basset, Lt. Col. Bateman, Duke of Berwick, Blackburn, Brigadier Bourgard, Bouflers, Maj. Boyd, Murtough Brennan, Brody, Capt. Bush, Mons. Calvo, Capt. George Carleton, Gen. Carpenter, Cassels, Charles II, Charles III, Sir John Chicheley, Maj. Collier, Mr. Crow, Curtisos, Lord Cutts, Davison, Pedro de Dios, Sir Robert Douglas, Father Fahy, Sir John Fenwick, Lord Galway, Cardinal Giudici, Gen. Gorge, Count Guiscard, Col. Hales, Maj. Harding, George Harris, Gen. Harvey, Prince of Hesse, Col. Jones, Col. Killigrew, Sir John Leake, Mr. Le Noy, Sir James Lesley, Sir Thomas Levingston, Capt. Littleton, Duke of Luxemburg, Brigadier Mahoni, Maria, Capt. Matthews, Mr. Mead, Paul Methuen, Duke of Monmouth, Count de Montery, Col. O'Guaza, Duke of Orleans, Maj. O'Roirk, Don Pedro de Ortega, Earl of Ossory, Don Felix Pacheo, Maj. Percival, Earl of Peterborough, Philip of Anjou, Duchess of Popoli, Capt. Porter, Gen. Ramos, Gen. Richards, Marquis of Risburg, Col. Rivet, Don Ronquillo, Mr. de la Rue, De Ruyter, Col. Salter, Earl of Sandwich, Duke Schomberg, Cloudsley Shovel, Slunt, Count Solmes, Count Souches, Col. Southwell, Edward Sprage, Gen. Stanhope, Gen. Staremberg, Col. Syburg, Count de Tholouse, Conde de los Torres, Col. Tufton, Princess of Ursini, Don Valasco, Sir Walter Vane, Admiral Van Ghent, Prince Vaudemont, Hodge Vaughan, Duke de Vendosme, Prince Waldeck, Capt. Daniel Weaver, White, William Prince of Orange (William III), Gen. Windham, Duke of York, Mons. Zoulicafre.

Captain Singleton, Defoe, 1720. (Original title: *The Life, Adventures, and Piracies of the Famous Captain Singleton.*)

Bob Singleton is a typical Defoe character. He begins as the innocent waif and later becomes the world traveler and the goodhearted rogue who reforms. He knows practically nothing about his origin. At the age of two he is taken on an airing to Islington and entrusted to the care of a little girl while his nursemaid goes to have a drink with her boy friend. He is then kidnapped by a vagrant woman and sold to an old gypsy.

When the gypsy woman is hanged for her misdeeds, Bob goes to the parish school, where a parson tells him that if he minds his book and serves God he may grow up to be a good man, even though he is poor. A ship's captain takes a fancy to him and takes him on several Newfoundland voyages. Their ship is captured by an Algerine pirate and young Bob is given a bastinado on the soles of his feet so that he cannot stand for several days. Finally the ship is recaptured by two Portuguese men-of-war and taken to Lisbon. Here the captain dies of his wounds and young Bob is in danger of starving to death, until an old Portuguese pilot who speaks broken English takes him on as his body servant.

Together they ship for Goa, and among the profligate Portuguese Bob learns to be "an arrant thief and a bad sailor." However, his personal charm draws the captain's attention and he is made an assistant to the steward, which enables him to steal food. But all does not go well. His master pilot keeps Bob's wages for himself, and when Bob complains the pilot threatens to turn him over to the Inquisition as a Turk. Only the ship's priest saves him from the fate. He strips Bob and, finding that he is uncircumcised, concludes that he cannot be a Turk.

Singleton (now seventeen or eighteen years old) lays plans to murder the pilot, but he is also involved in a mutiny plot off the coast of South Africa. When the captain discovers the plot, he is furious at Singleton's betrayal of his trust. He executes two ring-leaders and maroons five others, including Singleton, on the coast of Madagascar. Some other crewmen later sneak away and join them, bringing their number to twenty-seven. Alone on the island, the men pool their money, and Bob chips in two pieces of eight and a moidore of gold. (He does not reveal that he has twenty-one other stolen moidores in his pockets.) Singleton unsuccessfully attempts to persuade the other men to turn pirate. At this, the gunner looks at the young man's palm and pronounces that he is born to be hanged.

The castaways discover they can buy food from the natives and pay with trinkets beaten out by the ship's cutler. Money is unknown on Madagascar, but for a few shillings' worth of metal they can buy an entire cow. They hollow out a canoe from a tree trunk but are unable to undertake a long voyage because of the danger of high seas and the difficulty of carrying fresh water. They start north along the western shore and round a cape which they dub "Point Desperation." There the natives tell them they must wait

until September for easterly breezes to blow them over to the mainland. While waiting they find a shipwrecked Dutch ship with an
abandoned ship's carpenter's yard, with which they are able to
build an ocean-going vessel. In February they sail over to Africa
and decide to strike out for Angola and the Atlantic coast, an overland journey of between two and three thousand miles.

The men decide to provoke a quarrel with the natives and take
ten or twelve slaves to carry baggage, but a quarrel occurs without
their having to provoke it. During a wrangle over a cattle purchase,
a number of blacks are shot and the whites take sixty slaves, most
importantly a black prince, whose broken arm they set. The blacks
are terrified by firearms and swear by the sun eternal loyalty to
the white men. This is Singleton's first real encounter with any
sort of religion, and he thanks God he was not born among such
heathen. The Portuguese now prove to have no staying power
unless led by an Englishman; so Singleton is chosen co-captain,
along with the gunner.

The entire party strikes out for the great lake of Coalmucoa,
from which the Nile springs (Lake Victoria). They reach the edge
of a great desert and set out, allowing the blacks a quart of water
per day apiece and themselves three pints, even through the blacks
are carrying the baggage. They narrowly avoid being trampled
in an elephant stampede. In the desert episode Defoe tells some
tall stories, such as finding elephant skulls made out of solid ivory,
and the black prince's being pursued at breakneck speed by a
bulletproof crocodile.

The trek continues into a fertile region, where one day the black
prince comes in innocently with lumps of gold he has found along
a riverbank. The white men feverishly gather up eighty-four
pounds' worth. To prevent quarrels they agree to share alike and
to forbid gambling in camp. The rainy season overtakes them; so
they surround themselves with a palisade against wild beasts and
remain in camp from June to October. (Defoe describes the most
improbable mixtures of lions, wolves, and tigers attacking the
stockade.)

As they approach the coastal regions, they are increasingly fear-
ful of hostile blacks who have been exploited by white men. To
their astonishment they come upon an Englishman living among
the savages, his naked skin burnt into black scales by the sun. He
fled inland after his trading post was despoiled by the French. He
embraces Singleton tearfully. Despite the men's haste to reach the

coast, the Englishman (he is a good scholar and speaks four languages) persuades them to tarry for six months to gather up the gold dust which lies abundantly along the streams in the region. The ship's cutler is able to trade his elephant cut-outs for whole handfuls of gold.

They all travel to a Dutch trading post or "factory" on the Gold Coast. They free the black prince, paying him well, and the Portuguese set off for Portuguese factories in Gambia. The scholarly Englishman dies of grief when the ship bearing his wealth back to England is captured by the French.

Singleton returns to England, but in two years he has squandered all his money and has to sign aboard a ship bound for Cadiz. A rogue named Harris leads him and eleven others in a mutiny plot. They then decide to "go upon the account," or turn pirates. Cruising in the West Indies, they capture a Spanish ship and make a very important acquisition, a Quaker named William Walters. Quaker William is glad to become the pirates' advisor, as soon as they give him an affidavit certifying that he was carried along against his will, so that he can exonerate himself in any future investigation. William proves particularly useful in sea battles, where he directs the cannon fire as tranquilly as though he were mixing a bowl of punch.

The pirates one day discover a vessel with most of her sails disabled and driving helpless before the wind. When they go aboard they find that she is a slaver full of blacks, but where are the white men? The blacks can't explain since they don't speak English, and William has to dissuade the pirates from murdering the lot. He then cures one of the blacks of an infected wound and teaches him enough English to tell his story. The blacks became enraged at the rape of one of their women, it seems, and slaughtered and drove out their white masters. Having done the blacks these favors, William takes them ashore in Brazil and sells them, making a profit of sixty thousand pieces of eight.

In October, 1706, the pirates set sail for the Cape of Good Hope. They take prizes in the Red Sea until a merchant whom they rashly free alarms the whole Arabian coast against them. In Somaliland Quaker William, guided by a dream, discovers a party of their old comrades, from whom they were separated in a storm at Tobago. The group joins forces temporarily with the pirate colony of three hundred men set up by the famous Captain Avery on the shore of Africa. The pirates then split up, and Singleton takes two ships to Ceylon (1707).

On the way to the Spice Islands the ship is struck by a great bolt of lightning and partially disabled. Singleton is driven to think momentarily on his sins, but after a while he is back to his old hardened ways. During their voyage back to India, they land on an island and are attacked by savages, who then hide in an immense hollow tree. Repeated stink bombs fail to drive them out; so Quaker William deduces that the tree must be hiding the entrance to a cave. The pirates pack the tree with gunpowder and blow the natives to bits.

In describing the pirates' course back to India, Defoe has them sail directly through the continent of Australia (he was writing before the discoveries of Captain Cook) and into the Indian Ocean. On Ceylon again, the sailors molest some of the native women, and Singleton comments that his shipmates must have pretty strong stomachs. The usual fracas ensues with the natives. Seventeen whites are wounded, and William is able only with difficulty to prevent the pirates' taking a bloody revenge on innocent islanders.

On their way south the ship is buffeted by a hurricane and driven aground on the coast. An embassy of natives comes down to the shore with a white flag, but William notes how heavily armed the blacks are and advises against going ashore. To their surprise, a white man (a Dutchman) invites them ashore, but William sounds him out and finds him to be the unwilling servant of the king, whose job it is to entice unsuspecting sailors ashore so they can be enslaved. The natives attack with fire arrows, but the pirates escape, taking the Dutchman with them. Defoe here interpolates the story of Robert Knox, who was captured in this fashion in 1657. He died of an ague, but his son and a friend finally made their escape after nineteen years' captivity.

The pirates travel to the Coromandel coast, where William begins to worry about Singleton's soul and advises him to think about what may lie after death. The worm of conscience begins to gnaw, and the two friends decide to desert. They make their way to Bassorah and set themselves up as Persian merchants, letting their beards grow and adopting Persian garb. Singleton wonders whether they ought not to abandon their stolen goods, but William prudently points out that doing so would not help the original owners one bit. Singleton becomes obsessed with guilt and dreams that the devil wants him to commit suicide. He even begins to talk in his sleep and quiets down only when William threatens to murder him if he doesn't stop blathering.

The two friends travel to Venice, where they remain incognito, speaking a sort of bastard Armenian with each other. William thinks of his relatives in England and writes his sister to learn if she is still living. It turns out that she is widowed and living with four children, keeping a rooming house in the Minories. She even sends William five pounds. Singleton is so moved with this sacrifice from a poor widow that he resolves to make her rich with his ill-gotten gains. He and William agree to live together in England, but never to speak English before other people lest they attract suspicion. Singleton returns and marries the widow. At the close of his narrative, he is living a reformed life in his native country and keeping a weather eye out for the law.

Padre Antonio ("Father Anthony"), Capt. Avery, John Burford, Don Garcia de Pimentesia de Carravallas, King of Ceylon, Thomas Chambers, the cutler (later "the silversmith"), the dissauva, Dutchman on Ceylon, George the reformade, Gordon, gunner's mate ("our gunner"), Harris, "young Capt. Kidd," Capt. Robert Knox, Robert Knox, John Loveland, the black prince, Stephen Rutland, Capt. Bob Singleton, William's sister in England, Vandergest, William Walters ("Quaker William"), "Capt." Wilmot.

Clarissa or, the History of a Young Lady, Richardson, 1747-1748.
Volume one—Clarissa's family attempts to force her into marriage with Roger Solmes.

Clarissa Harlowe is the beautiful young daughter of a wealthy country family. The opening letter is from her friend Anna Howe, asking for particulars about a sword fight between Clarissa's older brother James and Richard Lovelace, who has been paying Clarissa many attentions. Anna also asks for a copy of the will of Clarissa's grandfather. Clarissa had brought such joy to the old man in his last days that he left his estate to her, thus frustrating James's plans for getting it himself. He and sister Arabella fear that Clarissa, because of her sweet Christian character, will alienate their uncles from them and further frustrate their dynastic ambitions. Clarissa sweetly entrusts the estate to her father and her cousin Morden, the latter currently in Italy.

Robert Lovelace is heir to a title and hence an important step in the social ladder above the Harlowes. Clarissa's Uncle Antony brings him to see Bella as a possible suitor, but his reserved behavior contrasts oddly with his reputation as a wild rake. Nevertheless, Bella swells at the possibility of out-doing her sister and winning such a handsome young man. In order to punish Lovelace for his reserve, Bella acts more bad-tempered than usual during his next visit. But Lovelace surprises her by popping the question, and the demands of eighteenth-century decorum are such that Bella must refuse (albeit with "consenting negatives"). To her dismay, Lovelace pretends to take her refusal seriously; so Bella is in the position of having denied the lover she would secretly like to have. She declares that she didn't want to marry him anyway.

On his next visit, Lovelace is struck with Clarissa's beauty. At the request of her Uncle Hervey, Clarissa agrees to cor-respond with Lovelace. He is to supply accounts of Europe for the benefit of Uncle Hervey's ward, who is planning to take the Grand Tour. Lovelace secretly includes love letters to Clarissa, but she refuses to read them. She confides to Anna that she does not like Lovelace at all. He is conceited, and she glimpses haughtiness and pride behind his smooth exterior. Further-more, his servants are afraid of him, which bodes ill for his future wife.

The first important interview between Clarissa and Love-lace occurs when he asks if she has been receiving his secret letters, and she forbids his writing further. He manages to swallow his rage, but Clarissa is too quick-sighted to miss it.

Lord M., Lovelace's uncle, offers handsome terms for a mar-riage alliance between the families; but James and Bella join in opposing any alliance between Clarissa and Lovelace, allegedly on the score of Lovelace's faulty morals. In reality, James has been nursing a grudge against Lovelace because when they were at college together Lovelace was more clever and popular than James. It is shortly after this that James provokes the fight at a neighbor's house. Lovelace disarms James easily, and, to make things even more irritating, helps him to bind up a wound in his arm.

The Harlowe family breaks out in righteous rage against Lovelace. When he pays them another visit, Clarissa's father must be physically restrained from assaulting him. James exploits his bandaged arm to tyrannize over Clarissa, accusing her of a predisposition in favor of the rake. Clarissa's mother is sweet-tempered and objects to the family's bullying of

Clarissa, but she allows herself to be too easily overruled by her husband. Clarissa is granted permission to visit Anna, on condition that she receive no visit from Lovelace.

When Clarissa returns to Harlowe House, she finds the whole family arrayed in solemn conference against her. She is accused of having received the visits of the rake at the Howes'. Clarissa protests that she merely sat quietly by while Lovelace visited Anna, but her defense is ignored and she is treated like a criminal. James brings the odious Mr. Solmes home as a suitor for Clarissa. Solmes is physically repulsive but very rich, and he plans to disinherit all his own relations in order to conclude a marital alliance with the Harlowes. James has won Mr. Harlowe over to his side, and Clarissa perceives that James and Bella are deliberately behaving in a highhanded fashion in order to drive her to resistance. If James can force Clarissa to marry Solmes, he will have revenged himself on Lovelace. If she refuses, then he will have alienated her from her two rich uncles.

Clarissa's tyrannical father informs her, "Clarissa Harlowe, know that I will be obeyed." She is forbidden to go to church lest she meet Lovelace, nor may she correspond with anyone. Nevertheless, she hides letters behind the rotting boards of the chicken house in the Green Lane, whence a servant carries them to Anna. "You are all too rich to be happy," declares Anna, adding that Clarissa is really in love with the dashing Lovelace but doesn't know it. Clarissa responds indignantly that she is not in love with the man at all, but she must concede that he is generous toward his tenants in refusing to rackrent them, especially in contrast to her niggardly Uncle Antony. Meanwhile Mrs. Howe is trying to persuade Anna to marry the sententious and proper Mr. Hickman.

Clarissa goes down to breakfast and finds that the splay-footed Solmes has been invited. He obtrusively sits by her, his weight pressing on her hoop. Clarissa behaves civilly to him only because of the intimidating presence of her father. Upstairs in Clarissa's room, her mother pleads that she marry Solmes. At this point her father bursts in. Clarissa will not be considered his daughter or allowed to come downstairs to sit with the family unless she agrees immediately to the match. Mrs. Harlowe's real sympathies lie with her daughter, but her pride as a parent has come into play, and she has given up her will to the men in the family.

Clarissa privately admits to her mother that she is still corresponding with Lovelace despite being prohibited from doing so. She insists that she has been forced to do so to prevent Lovelace from assaulting James, and that she has said nothing indecorous.

Mr. Harlowe and James go off to dine at Uncle Antony's so that Mrs. Harlowe may have one last chance to persuade Clarissa. Her mother threatens her with breaking her grandfather's will, accuses her of a prepossession in favor of Lovelace, and informs her that the silks have already been ordered from London for the wedding garments. Clarissa's objection to Solmes's intellectual inferiority goes unheeded.

When Clarissa goes downstairs to make a final plea, she finds Solmes there and concludes that a trap has been laid for her. Nevertheless, she voices her objections to him in his very presence. Shocked at this boldness, her mother takes her out and expostulates with her. Mr. Harlowe and James return from Uncle Antony's. Clarissa's keys are taken from her, and her father refuses to look again upon her face until she complies with his will.

At this juncture, Clarissa receives a letter from Lovelace. Somehow he has exact intelligence of everything that goes on at Harlowe House. He offers her asylum should her family proceed to compulsion. Clarissa shrewdly notes that she has been driven by her family into a more intimate correspondence with Lovelace than she would have otherwise chosen. (This is part of Lovelace's plan.) Clarissa is now ordered to refer all requests directly to her brother James. The same day her beloved servant Hannah is discharged in disgrace, since the family suspect her of spying and of carrying letters for Clarissa. The pert Betty Barnes is set over Clarissa and feels free to taunt her for being disobedient.

In the first of Lovelace's letters to his rakish friend John Belford, he avows his true motives in pursuing Clarissa to be desire of conquest and love of revenge. He loves Clarissa but not matrimony. He wants to revenge himself not only on the Harlowe family but also on the entire female sex, since in his first love affair he was jilted by a lady of quality. He grants that he has been free in his morals, but argues that the only difference between himself and other men is that he does not hide his immoralities under a hypocritical exterior. Most importantly, he concedes that Clarissa's coldness to him comes

from her virtue rather than from either pride or lack of sensi-
bility.

Clarissa's appeals to her two paternal uncles fall on deaf ears.
Uncle Antony's reply is comic, full of narrow-minded "prudence"
and anti-feminine pomposity. Clarissa then writes Solmes asking
him to desist, but this request brings a denial apparently written
with the help of James.

Lovelace asks Belford to come down from London to help
him and describes the family at the White Hart, where he is
staying. The innkeeper's daughter he has nicknamed "Rosebud." He has promised her grandmother not to seduce her,
but this is from motives of policy rather than of principle. To
atone for his other enormities, he will give her a hundred
pounds for her marriage with Johnny Barton the carpenter.
Lovelace also explains how he has planted an agent at Harlowe
House, a certain Joseph Leman. This man has told Clarissa's
family that she is attempting to correspond with Lovelace,
thus hardening them against her. He has also obtained keys
for the Harlowe's garden gate.

The next evening Lovelace uses this key and surprises
Clarissa going to hide a letter to Anna. He argues cogently
that her only option is to seek refuge with him and asks her
to accept a letter from his highborn kinswoman, Lady Betty
Lawrance. Clarissa is taken in by Lovelace's seeming openness.

She is interrupted at her pen by her beloved old nurse Mrs.
Norton, who has been enlisted by the family to change Clarissa's
mind. She finally comes over to Clarissa's side, and James
accuses her of being in the pay of Lovelace. Clarissa is forbidden
further contact with her.

Mrs. Harlowe attempts to bribe Clarissa by offering her six
new suits and an ample financial allowance. When she persists
in her refusal, her father flies into a rage and threatens to
carry her off to her Uncle Antony's house within the week,
where she will be forcibly married to Solmes.

Bella comes up and provokes a furious quarrel, in which
Clarissa stings her into a rage by reminding her of her earlier
infatuation with Lovelace. The next morning Clarissa's Aunt
Hervey joins Bella in another assault. Bella taunts Clarissa
by flaunting specimens of the silks for the six wedding dresses.
Aunt Hervey says that she admires Clarissa's steadiness but
that she should marry Solmes nevertheless for her own best
interests.

Volume two—The central event of this volume is Clarissa's running away with Lovelace.

Anna reveals that James Harlowe's ascendancy over the Herveys is due to his having paid off a debt for Mr. Hervey, which he exploits in a small-minded fashion. Hickman has been in London to talk with Lovelace's dissipated companions, and Anna is now in no doubt about his bad character. At this point, who should visit Anna but Lovelace? He threatens violence should Clarissa be forced to marry Solmes. He speciously urges that Clarissa take refuge at the Howes', at the same time he has so alarmed the Harlowes through his agent Joseph Leman that they dare not let Clarissa leave the house. This is all part of Lovelace's plot to reduce Clarissa to dependence on himself.

After more exchanges of letters at Harlowe Place, Clarissa overhears her brother and sister laughing with Mr. Solmes over the cleverness of James's last reply. They admit that they must force Clarissa into marriage before her cousin Morden arrives from Italy to take her part. Clarissa writes James again, asking that she be allowed merely to live on her grandfather's estate. This letter enrages the whole family and brings Bella upstairs to accuse Clarissa of trying to be independent of them all and wishing her father dead.

Lovelace advises Clarissa to resume her estate, but she suspects his motives. He knows that she cannot resume it without being dependent on him for legal aid. True, he has promised to keep his distance from her if she puts herself into his protection, but he has offered nothing that she would not have demanded of him anyway. She has contempt for his bravado, along with the whole dueling ethic.

Anna reports a conversation which Sir Harry Downeton has had with Solmes, in which the latter alleged that fear is better than love for a good marriage. He will rely on Clarissa's famous virtue for her remaining faithful to him. Meanwhile, Clarissa learns from Betty Barnes that Solmes has threatened to make Clarissa sorry for her resistance until the last day of her life.

Clarissa receives a secret letter from Lovelace, deposited in the woodhouse. He writes more like a spurned protector than a suppliant lover and objects to being reduced to skulking around Harlowe Place like a thief. Clarissa replies tartly that it is his vices which have reduced him to a level with common men, and hints that if he and Solmes were to fight and eliminate each other, her situation would thereby be much more amiable. Anna sends a lively account of the quarrels which she and her mother engage in about Clarissa's situation. Mrs. Howe argues strategically that people who marry for "love" are seldom as happy as those who marry for convenience.

When her father returns a letter of hers unopened and torn in two, Clarissa writes James offering to make her estate over to Bella so that Bella can marry Solmes, of whom she apparently thinks so highly. But this request is denounced as mere trickery; presumably Clarissa thinks she could resume the estate in the future if she wants. Clarissa is driven to open a new letter from Lovelace, which she kept unopened until she could learn the result of her most recent offer. He says her family has already written to Clarissa's cousin Morden to win him over to their side. Her only chance is reliance on him. He will wait for two nights in the Haunted Coppice in the hope that she will come to the garden door.

The next day he writes again that he has caught cold by waiting all night in the dew. He confesses that he has a spy planted in the Harlowes' midst. Clarissa regrets that Lovelace has suffered inconvenience for her but resents the presence of the spy, whom she concludes to be her brother's most trusted agent, Joseph Leman. Despite her resentment, Clarissa agrees to meet with Lovelace the following night. When she thinks better of it and goes back to retrieve the letter, it has already disappeared.

Clarissa procures a week's delay of her trip to Uncle Antony's by agreeing to meet with Solmes in the company of her Uncle Harlowe. She revokes her appointment with Lovelace, meanwhile asking Anna to make inquiries about his behavior at the White Hart. Soon she receives a distraught reply from Lovelace and sees that his gentleness was feigned. She sends him a tart reply; he has no right to feel insulted.

Anna sends Clarissa an alarming report of how Lovelace has financially aided "Rosebud" at the White Hart. Anna assumes that Rosebud's innocence has already been sacrificed. Clarissa reacts with shock. When Anna next writes, she must admit that she has done Lovelace an injustice. Clarissa is then inclined to think rather well of Lovelace. (Richardson warns his readers in a footnote against being won over by Lovelace's actions here. He was kind to the girl because her grandmother appealed to his pride and because he hoped the story would make a good impression, should it get abroad.) Clarissa meanwhile has discovered a love affair going on between Joseph Leman and Betty Barnes.

Writing to Anna, Clarissa wins great credit with Mrs. Howe for urging Anna to marry Hickman. The favored suitor arrives at the Howes', plump and stroking his ruffles. The Harlowe family suddenly starts behaving sweetly to Clarissa, seemingly without reason. Dr. Lewen, the beloved pastor, visits but does not allude to Solmes. Even her brother and sister are mannerly, although Bella can hardly conceal her malice. Clarissa is puzzled.

On the day of the long-awaited interview with Solmes, Clarissa finds out the reason for this change in the wind. Her Aunt Hervey visits her and pretends to think that Clarissa has really changed her mind and is diminishing her hostility by degrees only to save face. Clarissa now sees the family's kind behavior as calculated, so that they can pretend they genuinely thought she was coming around.

Just before the interview with Solmes, Betty Barnes comes rushing upstairs to discompose Clarissa with reports of how her whole family is assembled, waiting for the outcome of the meeting. She goes downstairs to confront Solmes alone. He is abashed, and she intimidates him by saying that she would prefer death to marriage with him. Then Uncle Antony barges in and asserts that, by God, he shall have her. Her brother joins the fray, but Clarissa shows herself to be his equal in repartee. She then withdraws to the garden for an hour.

In the second phase of the interview, James seeks to join Clarissa's hand by force with Solmes's. When she refuses, James hurls her hand away and hurts her shoulder. Mr. Harlowe is heard from the adjoining room, commanding her to prepare immediately to go to her uncle's. Clarissa tries to go to him, but the door is locked. She bursts in, only to find the room deserted.

Just as Clarissa is reduced to despair, she finds in the garden wall a letter from Lovelace urging her to escape with him. He will carry her to one of his rich aunts and will promise not to come near her until she is reconciled with her family. Clarissa promises to meet him at four o'clock, Monday afternoon.

The Harlowes are terrified because Joseph Leman has told them that Lovelace will attempt a rescue while Clarissa is being carried to her uncle's moated house. Accordingly, Aunt Hervey informs Clarissa that she is to be forcibly married in her own room on the Wednesday following. She even brings the marriage settlements, already engrossed on parchment, for Clarissa to sign, but she refuses even to look at them.

She has begun to have dark forebodings about the escape plan. She has an ominous dream that Lovelace pushed her into an open grave, which he then filled with earth and stamped on. Anna opposes the plan and laments that Mrs. Howe will not give Clarissa sanctuary, for fear of undermining the cause of parental authority. Clarissa should either run away with Anna to London or marry Lovelace immediately upon fleeing with him. Once she is out of her father's house, all punctilio will immediately become impossible. Everyone will assume that Lovelace is her lover, and her reputation will be a shambles. When the alternatives are put this starkly, Clarissa realizes that deciding to flee with Lovelace was a mistake. She writes Lovelace canceling the appointment and leaves the letter in the garden wall.

The Harlowes proceed full steam ahead with the wedding plans. Worthy old Dr. Lewen has declined to perform the office; so the pedantic young Mr. Brand will do so, in return for which Clarissa's Uncle Harlowe will make his fortune.

To Clarissa's chagrin, the letter she has left for Lovelace revoking the appointment has not disappeared from the hiding place. So she decides to meet him only to say that she has decided to remain at Harlowe Place. While her family is searching her room for letters from Lovelace, Clarissa steps through the garden gate at the appointed hour and finds him waiting for her. He takes her hand and begins to draw her away. She resists, but he terrifies her by threatening to accompany her into the house and confront her relations. Suddenly a pounding is heard on the other side of the gate and a voice calling, "Pistols! Your gun!" Terrified, Clarissa is unable to help herself from being carried away in Lovelace's coach-and-six. As they drive away, she looks back and sees a figure pursuing them. It resembles Joseph Leman. Her next letter is dated from St. Albans, bemoaning her rash and inexcusable error.

The final two letters in the volume are an exchange between Lovelace and Joseph Leman, revealing that everything was prearranged between them. After Clarissa fled, Leman was to place Lovelace's new key on the ground on the inside of the garden gate, so that it would look as though Clarissa had collaborated in the escape plan.

Volume three—The main action of this volume is Lovelace's maneuvering Clarissa into an evil house in London.

Lovelace first carries her to an inn at St. Alban's, where he gives out that she is his sister, whom he has carried away to prevent her marrying a "confounded rake." His revengeful and treacherous character reveals itself in his letters to Belford. He must make Clarissa believe that there is great danger of pursuit so that she will remain under his protection. He will regard any resistance to him as a challenge to do his worst. He makes a great parade of obeying the stipulations Clarissa made about his maintaining his distance from her. Thus he renders it impossible for Clarissa to make him marry her, as Anna advised her to do.

The pair have a long interview in the inn. He offers to take her to his relations, but she refuses to go there, since any association with him would render reconciliation with her family virtually impossible. Lovelace knows that she will react this way and hints that she will be safe from recapture only in London (where he knows she will be in his power). She accuses him of making a young creature sacrifice her duty and conscience to his selfish love. He blazes out with injured innocence, but she knows that his anger is managed in order to intimidate her. She feels that she must show anger at him to justify her earlier refusal to go off with him. Were she not to appear resentful, it would seem that her earlier conduct had merely been coyness.

Lovelace steals a kiss, which he declares he enjoyed more than sexual consummation with many other women. Clarissa resents his forwardness. He confesses to Belford that the force of her personality makes him feel that he is falling more and more into her power, rather than vice versa.

Hickman has arranged to convey Anna's letters to her friend, thus winning Anna's heartfelt appreciation. Clarissa's family is full of rage, except for her brother and sister, who are triumphing in the success of their schemes and who are keeping up the uncles' resentment against their fallen sister. Clarissa writes her family but perceives herself to be in a dilemma. She must pretend that she ran away willingly with Lovelace, or her parents will demand that she return home to marry Solmes. But how then can she request their help? She urges them to send her clothes and money, lest they widen a misunderstanding into a public disgrace.

During an angry interview with Clarissa, Lovelace proposes marriage, knowing that the demands of decorum will require her to refuse, as she does. He feels that to marry her would be to lose the opportunity of revenging himself upon the Harlowes. He thinks he can persuade Clarissa to live in sin with him. "Once subdued, always subdued," is his motto. He believes that he can always marry her if he so chooses. Virtue is not virtue unless it can withstand temptation, after all, and since women should follow a higher moral standard than men, there is nothing wrong with his being the one to test her.

She demands that he confess the full extent of his contrivances. He does so, suppressing only the fact that he ordered Joseph to alarm her into fright. To exonerate himself, he produces a letter allegedly from Joseph (but really dictated by Lovelace) confessing that he was frightened into making an outcry. Anna is unimpressed by Lovelace's seemingly open confessions of wrongdoing; he admits only to things that Clarissa already knows or could find out for herself. Clarissa in turn blames Anna for being too harsh with Hickman. At least he is virtuous.

Lovelace supposedly goes to Windsor to look for lodgings but returns saying he could find nothing suitable. He makes pious asseverations about reformation, even claiming that he has written a drama on the subject of the Prodigal Son. To Belford he confides that all this pious talk is only a "stalking-horse." Finally, to Lovelace's joy, Clarissa herself inquires about the possibility of going to London. He feigns indifference, but she imagines that she can see something in his eye. The next morning he writes a friend of his called Thomas Doleman, asking him to seek out a variety of possible lodgings in London among which Clarissa can choose.

Lovelace admits to Belford that he has never even gone to Windsor. He learned that James Harlowe is raking up the embers of Lovelace's past bad conduct with a certain Miss Betterton. James is also planning to have Clarissa abducted by a Capt. Singleton and carried away to Hull or Leith. The letter arrives from Doleman. It is phrased so that Clarissa will be drawn to accept lodgings allegedly occupied last by a dignified clergyman (really the lodgings are in a house of ill repute). Joseph Leman writes that James Harlowe wants the Bettertons to prosecute Lovelace for rape. Joseph, in his self-centered way, hopes Lovelace will set him up as promised as an innkeeper before he is hanged. Lovelace responds that Miss Betterton indeed died in childbirth, but he by no means raped her.

He even went into mourning for her, as he does for all his mistresses who die in childbirth.

Anna approves of the decision to go to London, since a city is the ideal place for anonymity. She has soured in her evaluation of Lovelace. Nevertheless, Clarissa cannot afford to stand on ceremony and must marry him. At the same time, Lovelace's friend Belford writes advocating the lady's cause. Should Lovelace succeed in seducing her, he would end only in making himself miserable. But Lovelace responds that an illicit relationship keeps passion alive, unlike bourgeois marriage.

Clarissa receives two brutal letters from her family. Her Aunt Hervey writes that Wednesday's trial was to have been her last. Her father would have begged her on bended knee to marry Solmes, but if she had refused, she would thenceforth have been left alone. (Anna says that no one in the neighborhood believes these claims, and everyone condemns the Harlowes' treatment of Clarissa.) Even worse, Bella writes telling Clarissa that her father has cursed her both in this world and in the next. Upon receiving Bella's letter, Clarissa falls into fits. Lovelace arrives and, moved by his own measure of responsibility for her state of mind, proposes immediate marriage. But Clarissa is too ill to accept. Anna reminds Clarissa that only God can curse; they all should pray that her father be forgiven for his unnatural conduct. But the curse continues to weigh heavily upon Clarissa's mind.

Clarissa and Lovelace set out for London and arrive at the widow Sinclair's in "Dover Street." The manlike madam claims to be the widow of a colonel; two prostitutes, Sally Martin and Polly Horton, pretend to be her nieces. Lovelace tells Clarissa that "Dorcas," her personal maid, is illiterate. Thus he hopes Clarissa will leave her correspondence with Anna out unguarded.

To Clarissa's dismay, Lovelace announces that they are actually married and that they have agreed not to consummate the marriage until an alleged family quarrel is reconciled. Clarissa must submit to this charade, and the "widow" and her girls play the part of urging her to an immediate consummation. Clarissa is misled into trusting Mrs. Sinclair by a group of edifying books that Lovelace planted in her chamber. But she takes an instinctive dislike to Dorcas and discovers that no one in the house meets her glance happily.

In reality, Lovelace's old mistresses Polly and Sally are jealous of Clarissa and urge Lovelace to rape her. Lovelace dangles before

Clarissa the possibility of finding other lodgings for her and allegedly goes to rent a house from a widow, a Mrs. Fretchville. He
extracts from Clarissa an agreement to attend a dinner party for a
friend of the widow Sinclair's, Miss Priscilla Partington.

The group of rakes are all to attend the dinner party and, carefully drilled by Belford, are to make the best impression possible.
Lovelace is willing to run the risk of exposing his low friends to
Clarissa's sharp and critical eyes because he wants Clarissa to be
maneuvered into publicly acknowledging herself married. Then
in case she should run away, she could be compelled by a court of
law (Lovelace thinks) to return. He also hopes to coax her into
accepting Priscilla as her bedfellow, thus opening the door for
himself.

The dinner is duly held, and Clarissa sees through Lovelace's
frothy companions. Belton's forced gaiety fails to hide his con-
sumptive cough. Mowbray is clearly a ruffian, Tourville affects
sprinkling his speech with French and Italian words, and Belford
refers too obtrusively to Clarissa's alleged marriage. Priscilla
Partington is clearly not sufficiently embarrassed by the gentlemen's *double-entendres*. That night Clarissa steadfastly refuses
Mrs. Sinclair's request that Priscilla be permitted to join her in bed.

Volume four—This volume builds up to Lovelace's great attempt
on Clarissa in the fire scene.

Before going to his dying uncle, Belford joins the other rakes
in expressing his reverence for Clarissa and beseeching Lovelace
to give up his designs. Lovelace treats the plea cavalierly. He
merely want to reduce Clarissa to a passive dependence on him,
and this is no worse than girls do to their pet birds. In the clothes
which Clarissa's family sends her, she finds a letter from her cousin
Morden (the only person on whom she can depend for support).
He makes severe observations on libertines in general and on
Lovelace in particular. He sides with her family in the Solmes
affair, since he has drawn all his information from James's one-
sided account.

Lovelace is determined to have a look at Clarissa's correspondence. In a bold attempt, he snatches one of Anna's letters from
the floor where Clarissa dropped it. She sees what he has done,
plunges her hand boldly into his bosom, and retrieves it. She is
now thoroughly alarmed at his aggressiveness. In order to retrieve
his fortunes, he decides to terrify her with James's plot to have her
abducted. He pays a seaman to impersonate one of Capt. Single-

ton's crewmen and make inquiries after her. Anna writes with an important change of attitude. She now urges Clarissa to leave Lovelace instead of trying to make him marry her. However, Anna is playing into Lovelace's hands without knowing it, since she informs Clarissa that a mysterious seaman has been snooping around asking questions about her.

Since Lovelace cannot allow Clarissa to move out of Mrs. Sinclair's house to Mrs. Fretchville, he invents the story that the prospective house is infected with smallpox. While Clarissa is at church, he breaks into her file of letters and discovers that Anna has been keeping up Clarissa's resistance to him. He plots to kidnap Anna and her mother, and rape them.

Belford warns Lovelace against keeping mistresses and tells the cautionary tale of poor Belton, who was deceived by his mistress Thomasine. But Lovelace scorns all advice. He must keep Clarissa from running away to Anna's London friend Mrs. Townsend. He contrives to keep her hopes alive for a reconciliation with her family by having a rogue impersonate "Capt. Tomlinson," allegedly an envoy from her uncle. "Tomlinson" (really a smuggler named Patrick McDonald) and Lovelace carry on sham negotiations for Clarissa's forgiveness by her Uncle Harlowe. Lovelace actually has marriage agreements drawn up and engrossed for Clarissa's perusal and attempts to obtain a marriage license.

While the Tomlinson plot is afoot, Lovelace takes ipecacuanha to make himself ill and has the prostitutes tell Clarissa that he has broken a blood vessel. This stratagem has the desired effect of arousing Clarissa's concern. When he has recovered, he behaves with freedom toward her and even dares to kiss her on the breast, but she spurns his advances.

Believing that Clarissa loves him in her heart, Lovelace decides on a "master-stroke" to precipitate her into his arms. Late one night he has the girls start a minor fire on the third floor. Dorcas then rushes to Clarissa's door with cries of "Fire! Fire!" Clarissa panics and rushes out partially dressed, only to find Lovelace waiting to sweep her up into his arms. But the trick does not bring the anticipated surrender. Clarissa feels disgraced by his embraces and threatens to stab herself with a pair of shears. Lovelace gets the shears away from her, but she beseeches him on her knees to leave her. Intimidated by her steadfast resistance, he agrees to leave her on the condition that she not resent his forwardness. She bolts her bedroom door and collapses into hysterical sobbing.

Volume five—This volume contains the Hampstead episode and the rape.

Lovelace goes off to Doctors' Commons to apply for a marriage license. When he returns, he is horrified to find that Clarissa has escaped. While he is desperately dispatching messengers to find her, a letter from Anna arrives. Lovelace opens it and finds that she has penetrated his entire plot. He receives word from his servant Will Summers that the lady is hiding at the widow Moore's in Hampstead under the name of Miss Harriot Lucas.

Arriving at Hampstead, Lovelace borrows a large cloak and disguises himself as a gouty old man. In a scenically rendered passage, he goes to the widow's and rents lodgings for himself and his "aged wife." He then asks to be shown Clarissa's chamber. By disguising his voice he is able to lure her out of her closet. However, she recognizes him and he throws off the disguise, only to send her into a screaming fit.

Lovelace tells the women of the house that he is really married to the lady and that she has laid him under a vow of chastity until she is reconciled with her relations. He has dinner with Mrs. Moore, the prudish Miss Rawlins, and the sprightly young widow Bevis, who has a roving eye and finds Lovelace very attractive. He convinces them that Anna Howe is the villain of the piece and is trying to spoil his marriage out of jealousy. Thus he is able to win over their romantic hearts to his side; he gains the sympathy of Mrs. Moore by renting out all her rooms for a month. Miss Rawlins actually tries to persuade Clarissa to share Lovelace's bed.

Anna's messenger, old Farmer Grimes, arrives. Will Summers gets him drunk, spirits Anna's letter away from him, and substitutes a forged letter for it. The version Clarissa receives is full of talk of Lovelace's reformation and advice to marry him. Tomlinson arrives, allegedly to further Clarissa's reconciliation with her uncle. He and Lovelace agree on a set of signals so that he will know how to respond. Clarissa comes down, and Tomlinson pretends to be shocked that all is not going well with the supposedly newly wedded pair. Clarissa first confounds Tomlinson by seeing through the signals. She then moves him to tears by remarking that she no longer has a mother and father, and that she is being punished for her error by the agency of the rake in whom she had put her trust. After this experience, Tomlinson tries to dissuade Lovelace from his evil purpose, and Lovelace must promise him to marry Clarissa if the attempt should miscarry.

Lovelace prevails on Clarissa to await a visit from his aunt, Lady Betty Lawrance, and his cousin, Miss Charlotte Montague. Clarissa has been planning at any rate to wait at Hampstead until she receives Anna's next letter. Lovelace knows that the success of his entire scheme depends on intercepting it. To his great good fortune, the lady is at church when the messenger arrives. Lovelace persuades the widow Bevis to pose as Clarissa and to receive the letter. As he anticipated, it would have exposed his entire scheme. Anna is even planning to have a gang of sailors break Lovelace's bones and carry Clarissa away to safety.

Lovelace now steels himself for revenge. He goes to Westminster to fetch the marriage license with which to beguile Clarissa. He then procures three courtesans to impersonate his highborn relatives and returns with them to Hampstead. Clarissa is prevailed upon to accompany the "ladies" back to Westminster to pack up her things, preparatory to accompanying the pretended Lady Betty Lawrance down into Oxfordshire. Once she is back at Mrs. Sinclair's, the courtesans abandon her.

On her knees, Clarissa implores Lovelace's mercy. He pretends to send for a coach to carry her back to Hampstead. The grotesque Sinclair upbraids her for her lack of respect for her house. Clarissa is reduced to hysterical despair. Lovelace's next letter to Belford relates starkly, "The affair is over."

Belford rails at Lovelace, imploring him to do himself the honor of marrying Clarissa and threatening him with a duel if he allows the wicked women to reduce her to a prostitute. Lovelace refuses to take him seriously. He admits he stooped to drugging her to have his will of her and reports that she is still in a state of stupor. When he first sees her after the rape, she pathetically holds up the marriage license which he speciously procured. Belford's uncle has died in the meantime and left him a considerable fortune. Belford is away from the scene because of a fall from his horse.

Lovelace expects that when Clarissa returns to normal, his lack of modesty will enable him to look her into confusion. But the sequel is otherwise. In their first interview, Clarissa completely routs him and makes him stammer like a guilty criminal. He promises marriage, but in a series of stormy interviews, she indignantly refuses. She astonishes him by three escape attempts. At one point she throws up a window and cries out for help to the passersby. A constable comes to investigate, and Lovelace is forced to have one of the prostitutes pose as Clarissa with a plausible

story. Lord M.'s steward arrives with word that the old peer is ill
and that Lovelace must leave London to visit him. He prepares to
go, fully expecting that upon his return he can either cajole or
terrify Clarissa into his favorite scheme of cohabitation.

Volume six—Penknife scene; Clarissa's second escape and confinement in the sponging house.

Dorcas reveals to Lovelace that Clarissa is attempting to bribe her.
She shows him a note offering her an annuity of twenty pounds a
year if she will help her escape. Lovelace decides that no holds are
barred. He stages an elaborate scene, pretending to discover
Clarissa's letter. He wants to use his assumed outrage to put Clarissa
on the defensive. He also wants an excuse for breaking his promise
that she may return to Hampstead. While he is pretending to upbraid Dorcas, Clarissa emerges from her chamber and announces
that she sees through the entire shabby plan. The prostitutes sneak
away in shame. When Lovelace makes an advance, Clarissa draws a
penknife and threatens to stab herself if not left alone. As he nears
her, she bares her bosom and raises her hand to strike, but he hurls
himself at the last instant to the other side of the room. Clarissa's
life is saved.

Lovelace goes to M. Hall in Berkshire to attend his uncle. From
there, he besieges Clarissa with letters asking her to name the
date and place of the wedding. But to his consternation, Tomlinson reports that the lady has escaped in the clothes of Mabell, the
chambermaid. To make things worse, Lord M. does not die after
all; so Lovelace cannot inherit any money.

Clarissa finds sanctuary with the Smiths, glovers in King St.,
Westminster. She tells Anna her side of the rape story: how she
was taken in by Lovelace's alleged relations, brought back to Mrs.
Sinclair's, and abandoned. She was given tea that had an odd taste.
She threw herself at Lovelace's feet but received no mercy. She
asks Anna to conceal the rape so that she will not have to appear in
court. She has lost her will to live and is pleased to find herself
declining.

Lovelace is grilled by his relatives, especially since Clarissa has
revealed to Lady Betty the full extent of his rogueries. By cheek
and impudence he comes off unscathed. He teases his pretty young
cousins out of their anger. His old uncle is partly in sympathy with
a young man's sowing wild oats, and the old aunts are mollified by
Lovelace's admitting his faults and promising to marry the lady if
she will have him.

Anna is alarmed when Clarissa stops answering her letters. She learns that Will and Mrs. Sinclair have actually had Clarissa arrested for debt, allegedly because she bilked her lodgings. Belford is on the scene in London and sends Lovelace detailed descriptions of Clarissa's arrest as she came out of church and the shabby room at the bailiff's where she is confined (the "sponging house," where debtors were kept till their debts were settled, or "sponged"). He says that her linen is still white beyond imagination, despite all she has gone through. Polly and Sally, the prostitutes, come to taunt her and reduce her to absolute misery. She has no desire to eat. Belford breaks off to torment Lovelace with suspense.

He in turn raves at the misguided actions of his accomplices and commands Belford to have Clarissa discharged. She is accordingly released and carried back to the Smiths'. The worthy Dr. H. attends her and pronounces the malady to be spiritual rather than physical. He fears that her heart is broken. Her attitude toward the doctor is almost filial, notes Belford. He describes to Lovelace the dying agonies of their old comrade Belton, who has been cuckolded by the girl he thought was his kept mistress. (Lovelace proposes to drown her.)

Lovelace is torn between the desire to have Clarissa for his own and his aversion to marital shackles. He writes Anna that he will marry Clarissa, but in such a jesting tone that she sends Hickman to him to find out his true intentions. In the ensuing scene, Lovelace first scandalizes Hickman by telling him that Clarissa is in love with a greedy, bald old gentleman. Then he reveals that this gentleman is none other than Death himself.

As she is composing herself for heaven, Clarissa writes Bella, asking that the part of her father's curse relating to the afterlife be removed. The part cursing her in this life has already been fulfilled. Clarissa will not allow Dr. H. to inform the Harlowes of the true state of her health until she has received Bella's answer. Unfortunately, Anna is writing just at this time with news of Clarissa's approaching demise. The Harlowes conclude that Anna's letter is part of a stratagem of Clarissa's to gain sympathy. A bitter exchange between Anna and Bella results in the Harlowes' hardening their hearts against Clarissa.

Lovelace is still busy. He goes to a ball at Colonel Ambrose's, where he encounters Anna Howe. She is indignant at his effrontery and at the ease with which the other girls allow themselves to be charmed by him. They find his reputation as a rake titillating. She at first refuses to speak to him, but Mrs. Howe insists that she listen to his proposal, which is one of marriage to Clarissa. Anna accordingly writes, reminding Clarissa that if she refuses this chance, she will never have another. Clarissa responds with a letter to Lovelace's kinswomen, explaining that marrying him would be to sanctify his treachery. She can bring herself to forgive him on condition that he promise not to molest her during her last days on earth.

Volume seven—The death of Clarissa.

Lovelace cannot believe that Clarissa's heart is really broken; the real problem (he thinks) is that she is pregnant. His family has turned against him and avoids the part of the house where he is, but he claims not to be affected by this isolation. Clarissa continues to hope for her father's last blessing until Bella responds to her letter with brutal disbelief and lack of sympathy. The Harlowes will send their toady, the pedantic Rev. Elias Brand, to find out whether Clarissa is really sick or not, and whether she is genuinely repentant.

Clarissa decides to entrust the execution of her will to John Belford; the members of her family are too prejudiced to be trustworthy. Belford gratefully accepts the honor of the executorship. He offers to inform the Harlowes of Clarissa's health, but she declines.

In London, Brand believes a lot of conjectural hearsay from the neighbors, to the effect that Clarissa is receiving Belford's visits. His letter to Uncle Harlowe is so full of innuendo that the Harlowes conclude her to be totally abandoned. She is afflicted by a letter from Bella, saying that she is the talk of the neighborhood. (Bella omits to say, however, that the talk is composed exclusively of condemnation of the hardhearted Harlowes.) She is then thrown into hysterics by letters from her uncles inquiring whether she is pregnant by Lovelace.

After recovering from a period of acute depression, Lovelace comes up to town to talk to Clarissa in person. Belford warns her so that she is able to be absent the day he comes. He arrives at the Smiths' and literally takes over their shop, taunting Mr. Smith with not mastering his wife sufficiently and threatening to pull the teeth of Joseph, Mr. Smith's journeyman. That night he has a dreadful nightmare, in which he attempts to embrace Clarissa but is stopped by Col. Morden, and then in which Clarissa rises into the heavens, while he falls into a deep pit. The next day he revisits the Smiths but is again frustrated. He agrees to return into Berkshire but only after he receives a letter from Clarissa, announcing that she is going to "her father's house" after the interposition of a "dear blessed friend" and that she hopes to meet him there. He fails to perceive that the letter is allegorical and that she is referring to her own death. He concludes simply that she must be pregnant.

Belford is in Epsom Wells tending to Belton on his deathbed. He and Mowbray have driven out Belton's parasitical mistress Thomasine and have beaten up her boy friend, the hostler. Belton finally expires in agonies of remorse for his sins, including having done away with his uncle. The brutal Mowbray is utterly unmoved by Belton's and Belford's mingled tears.

Both the worthy Dr. Lewen and the implacable Bella want Clarissa to prosecute Lovelace for rape. Dr. Lewen feels that not to do so would be to encourage villainy, while Bella simply wants revenge. But Clarissa responds in a Christian spirit that she wants the merit of forgiving Lovelace. Once her correspondence is published, it will serve as a better warning than a public legal process.

Col. Morden finally arrives in England. He visits M. Hall, and has a talk with Lord M. and Lovelace in order to ascertain the latter's true intentions toward his cousin. As Lovelace acknowledges to Belford, the badness of his cause puts him at a disadvantage, and he is forced to resent the Colonel's justified indignation. The gentlemen are upon the point of drawing their swords, but Lord M. manages to mollify their tempers. Lovelace conceals from the colonel the depth of his villainy and insists on his willingness to marry Clarissa. The two men part on relatively good terms, Morden still hoping for a reconciliation.

After Belford has read Brand's censorious letter (seasoned with pompous Latin tags), he berates the neighbors for spreading such unfounded gossip. Clarissa, however, takes Brand's letter in a philosophical spirit and observes that young people must be very careful of their reputations. She has her coffin delivered to her chamber, where she uses it as a writing desk. It is decorated with scriptural quotations and designs of her own choosing.

In a tumultuous scene with the Harlowes, Col. Morden discovers that James is continuing to keep the hostilities alive and preventing Mrs. Harlowe from contacting her daughter. Mr. Harlowe declares that he would sooner see his daughter dead than Lovelace's wife. Morden stalks out of the family conference, swearing that he will leave his entire fortune to Clarissa. This threat alarms the Harlowes, especially the venal uncles.

Back in London, Clarissa makes her will and prepares for death. Dr. H. finally writes Mr. Harlowe on his own initiative that the worst must be expected. Lovelace tells Belford that when Clarissa actually dies, he must simply advise Lovelace to "take a tour to Paris," so as to avoid actually mentioning the dread event. Tormented by conscience and appalled at the unforeseen results of his actions, he moves his base to Uxbridge and spends his time riding frantically back and forth on the road between Kensington and Piccadilly, waiting for word.

Brand writes a creeping letter to Uncle Harlowe seeking to be reinstated in favor. He thinks that in the future he may become Clarissa's private chaplain and even have a chance of marrying her. Clarissa writes her last letters to Anna and to Mrs. Norton, in which her Christian spirit soars the highest. She freely forgives Lovelace. Her cousin Morden arrives, cursing himself for having delayed so long, to find Clarissa sleeping with her head on Mrs. Lovick's breast. When she awakens, she makes him promise not to avenge her death and hides from him all details of the rape. She declares that her isolation is ultimately for her good: "God Almighty would not let me depend for comfort upon any but Himself."

Lovelace's servants meanwhile are in a fever. If they fail to bring Lovelace news, he is frantic; but no one wants to be the bearer of the fatal tidings. Belford sends Mowbray and Tourville to be with Lovelace so that he doesn't do violence to himself. Finally the message comes that Lovelace had best take a tour to France. Mowbray describes Lovelace's frenzy at the news, but he for one is unable to understand how anyone could make such a fuss over a woman.

Volume eight—Clarissa's funeral and the death of Lovelace.

Clarissa dies blessing everyone, an angelic smile on her lips. The onlookers give "flowing testaments of their humanity." Shortly after she expires, the letters of reconciliation arrive from her family, but too late. Mrs. Norton arrives and faints on the spot. Clarissa has left a series of posthumous letters to all her relations, calculated to soothe rather than revile; but the effect, of course, is to heap coals of fire on everyone's head.

Before the body is cold, Sally Martin arrives to summon Belford to the bedside of Mrs. Sinclair, who has broken her leg and is lying at death's door. Sally is shocked upon learning of the lady's death. Belford sends Lovelace an account of Sinclair's death ravings and vivid descriptions of the prostitutes, their streaming make-up hideous by daylight.

Belford's servant carries the news down to Harlowe Place, where it spreads consternation. Mrs. Harlowe has a series of fits, and Mr. Harlowe's gout is thrown into his stomach. James vows vengeance on Lovelace. When Clarissa's hearse reaches home, the people she called "her poor" are on hand to mourn her. The family reproach themselves and each other, and all join in shunning James. Anna Howe arrives to kiss Clarissa's dead face and take a last farewell. Mr. Morden is so moved at the curate's funeral eulogy that he presents him with a ring before giving himself up to a "repeated fit of humanity."

James objects to having a friend of Lovelace as Clarissa's executor and asks Belford to give up the post. Clarissa's uncles will agree among themselves which points in her will they will undertake to perform. Belford refuses to resign, however, since he sees it as his sacred duty to perform every point of the will in full. When it is read, James complains about her generous presents to the servants. This penny-pinching costs him thousands of pounds, since it leads Col. Morden to exclude James from his own will.

Clarissa's will contains a dark hint about Lovelace's having once seen her "in a manner dead." Morden realizes for the first time that Clarissa was not simply seduced, but no doubt drugged and raped. He considers himself released from his promise not to wreak vengeance on Lovelace. He argues that if he doesn't take Lovelace on, James Harlowe will, with possibly disastrous results. Lovelace has already demonstrated his superiority to James once. Belford, fearing a confrontation, writes the Montagues to hurry Lovelace out of the country. But Lovelace must not discover that his friends are trying to put him out of the way of a duel, or else he would seek out the colonel.

Even though Clarissa is dead, her personality continues to dominate. Her letter to Lovelace forgiving him drives him to distraction with the hint that she actually could have loved him. He is actually insane for a few days and is full of remorse, until his normal buoyancy returns and he resolves to pursue "the sex" with as much zeal as ever. Belford feels that a sort of retribution is working. Mrs. Sinclair is dead, and Patrick McDonald ("Tomlinson") has been apprehended in a smuggling attempt and has died of gunshot wounds. Despite Lovelace's raillery, Belford sets up annuities for people whom he has injured during his rakish career.

Belford manages to keep Lovelace from meeting Morden, even though both men are in London at the same time. The rakes (sans Belton) celebrate until the morning hours, and the next day Belford takes a tearful farewell from his friend as the latter sets out for France. Belford also meets Morden on his way to the Continent; he says he cannot answer for the consequences should he and Lovelace meet.

A long interlude is taken up with Anna Howe's character of Clarissa. She was perfect in all things, even her spelling. She had every day perfectly scheduled, with her time apportioned between business and good works. She kept books on time as businessmen do on money (e. g., debit fifteen minutes to "Good Works").

Lovelace hears from Joseph Leman that Morden has been threatening him behind his back, but Belford urges him not to let Leman be an agent of the Harlowes' revenge. No matter which gentleman should fall in a duel, the Harlowes would benefit. But Lovelace receives Belford's cautions too late; he has already written Morden, giving him the opportunity of a meeting. The letter is phrased in such a way as to give the colonel the option of refusing a duel, but Lovelace confesses that he, in the circumstances, would feel himself called upon to fight.

The two finally come together at Trent and agree to meet outside the city. On the night before the duel, Lovelace is tormented by thoughts of his ingratitude to Clarissa. He admits that it is he who has sought out the colonel, because he cannot stand suspense. He deplores the colonel's skill only because it may make it impossible for him to spare his life. But events turn out otherwise. After slightly wounding the colonel, Lovelace is run through the body and dies the next day. On his deathbed, he looks up to Clarissa in heaven, and his last words are "Let this expiate!"

In the conclusion, Anna marries Mr. Hickman and continues to care for Clarissa's poor folk, while James and Bella make unhappy marriages. Of particular interest is an account of the early lives of Sally Martin and Polly Horton. Sally was the daughter of social climbers; and in trying to marry above herself she was entrapped by Lovelace. Polly's mind was corrupted by an early reading of plays and novels. In later editions of the novel, Richardson added an interesting postscript in which he defended his decision to allow Clarissa to die, his use of the epistolary mode, and his allowing the novel to grow to such a length.

Mr. Ackland, the Allisons, Fanny Alston, Mr. Alston, Col. Ambrose, Sally Anderson, Anderson, Andrew, Andrew,

Mr. Arnold, Mrs. Barker, Betty Barnes, Johnny Barton, Arthur Bedall, John Belford, Miss Bell, Hal Belton, Thomas Belton, Tom Belton, Mrs. Benson, Miss Betterton, Betty, the Widow Bevis, Rachel Biddulph, Sir Robert Biddulph, Dr. Blome, Blomer, Elias Brand, Sir Josias Brookland, Mr. Brown, Hannah Burton, Deb Butler (alias "Dorcas Wykes," "Dorcas Martindale"), Mr. Byron, Miss Cartwright Campbell, Miss Campion, Betty Carberry, Mrs. Carter, Catharine (also called Katharine), Clements, Simon Collins, Sir George Colmar, Mr. Secretary Craggs, Fanny Darlington, Jack Daventry, Counsellor Derham, Mr. Diggs, Thomas Doleman, Mrs. Doleman, Mr. Dormer, Mr. Dorrel, Miss Dorrington, Sir Harry Downeton, Miss Drayton, Mrs. Drayton, Empson, (Miss) Farley, pious Mrs. Fetherstone, Filmer, Mr. Finch, Mrs. Fortescue, Mrs. Fretchville, Jenny Fynnett, Ganmore, Mons. Garon, Mr. Goddard, Johanetta Golding, "the Governor," Rosebud's grandmother, Greme, Mrs. Greme, Grimes, Dr. R. H., Mother H., Dr. Hale, Uncle Antony Harlowe, Arabella ("Bella") Harlowe, Mrs. Charlotte Harlowe, Clarissa Harlowe, James Harlowe, Sr., James Harlowe, Jr., John Harlowe, Sen., Uncle John Harlowe, Aunt Harman, Harriot, Harry, Mr. Hartley, Lady Hartley, Johnny Hartop, Miss Hatton, Anna's cousin Herbert, Dolly Hervey, Dorothy Hervey, Uncle Hervey, Charles Hickman, Mrs. Sarah Hodges, "Sir Edward Holden," "Lady Holden," Sir Antony Holmes, Mary ("Polly") Horton, the hostler, Anna Howe, Mrs. Annabella Howe, Mr. Hunt, Archibald Hutcheson, Tony Jenyns, Joel, Jonas, Jonathan, Joseph, Kit the hostler, Kitty, Mons. Klienfurt, Mrs. Knollys, Miss Lardner, Grandmother Larkin, Lady Betty Lawrance, Mrs. Leeson, Joseph Leman, Dr. Lewen, Mr. Lilburne, Biddy Lloyd, Miss Lockyer, John Loftus, Mrs. Lorimer, Robert Lovelace, Clarissa's grandmother Lovell, Mrs. Lovick, Lady M., Lord M., Mabell, Mallory, Margaret (also called "Peggy" and "Margery"), Mons. Margate, Mr. Martin, Mrs. Martin, Sarah ("Sally") Martin, Patrick McDonald (alias "Capt. Antony Tomlinson"), Mr. Melvill, Tom Metcalfe, Miles, Charlotte Montague, Patty Montague, Mrs. ("Goody") Moore, Col. William Morden, Mr. Morden, Susan Morrison, Richard Mowbray, Mr. Mullins, Newcomb (alias "Capt. Mennel"), Mrs. Judith Norton, Tommy Norton, Nelly D'Oily, Biddy D'Ollyffe, Mr. Osgood, Mrs. Osgood,

Simon Parsons, Peter Partrick, Dr. Perkins, Peter, "Priscilla Partington," Miss Playford, Mr. Pocock, Pritchard, Mr. Rawlins, Miss Rawlins, Robert (also called Robin), Rogers, "Rosebud" (real name: Betsy), Rowland, Mrs. Rowland, Dr. S., Lady Sarah Sadlier, Col. Salter, Mrs. Sambre, Widow Sanderson, Miss Savage, Dame Anne Shelbourne, Shorey, "the widow Magdalen Sinclair" (alias "Aunt Forbes"), Capt. Singleton, Mr. John Smith, Mrs. John Smith, Col. Solcombe, Sir Oliver (Solmes), Roger Solmes, Betty Sorlings, Miss Sorlings, Mrs. Sorlings, Anna's cousins Spilsworth, Mr. Spurrier, Stedman, "Stella," Elizabeth Swanton, Will Summers, Mr. Symmes, Edward Symmes, Mrs. Thomas, Thomasine, Thompson, Titus, Mr. Tomkins, Tomkins, F. J. de la Tour, James Tourville, Mrs. Townsend, Lucy Villars, "the old Viscount," Lady Bab Wallis, John Walton, Mrs. Walton, Maj. Warneton, Dolly Welby, Paul Wheatly, Counsellor Williams, John Williams, Mrs. Williams, Wilson, Baron Windisgratz, Dr. Wright, Wycherly, Mr. Alexander Wyerley, "Dorcas Wykes" (alias "Dorcas Martindale," real name: Deb Butler).

Colonel Jacque. Defoe, 1722. (Original title: *The History and Remarkable Life of the Truly Honorable Colonel Jacque, Commonly called Colonel Jack.*) Colonel Jack claims to have sprung from a good family since, according to the nurse to whom he was entrusted as a bastard child, his mother always kept good company. Concerning his father, Jack knows only that the nurse was strictly charged to raise the boy in the knowledge that he was a gentleman. The boy is raised with two other Jacks. He is called Colonel, the nurse's own son is called Captain Jack, and the youngest of the three is called Major Jack. When the Colonel is ten, the nurse and her husband die, leaving the three boys desolate. They must turn to picking pockets for a living. To keep from freezing at night, they sleep in the ashes from Dallow's Glasshouse. Captain Jack is rude and surly, but Colonel Jack is fair-spoken and wins the friendships of the neighbors in Rosemary Lane, and particularly of the soldiers and sailors, whose stories he loves to listen to.

With his first booty the Major takes the Colonel to Rag Fair, where they outfit themselves with the first warm stockings they have had in their lives. The Captain in the meantime is arrested with a gang of kidnappers and whipped at Bridewell. The sight of the Captain howling under the lash horrifies the Colonel and keeps him honest for awhile. But soon he falls in with a celebrated "diver," one Robin, who takes him to the Long Room at the Custom House, where they steal a merchant's pocketbook. The Colonel is unable to sleep that night for fear his money will be stolen. The next day he walks into the fields and drops the money high up into a hollow tree. To his dismay, the whole booty slides down inside the tree. Jack tries to get it back with a long forked stick, but without success. Just when he has given himself up to despair, he finds that the tree is open on the other side near the base, and there sits his money on the ground. He falls into tumults of joy.

Robin learns that the merchant has offered a reward for the lost purse. Since the Colonel has a good heart (and since at any rate some of the bills are so large that the boys dare not try to cash them), he carries the merchant's pocketbook back to him. He collects the reward, but since he is illiterate he can't even count the money. The merchant sympathizes with the Colonel's sad story and agrees to invest his reward money for him.

Jack has the luck to steal a Jew's pocketbook which he sees sticking out of a pocket. The boys find in it a packet of diamonds in the rough. After superciliously lecturing the Jew about taking better care of his valuables, Jack's tutor (his name has now changed to Will) promises to get the packet back from the thief. Will gladdens the heart of his poor old mother with the reward.

Colonel Jack robs a poor old woman named Mrs. Smith of Kentish Town of 22s. 6d. The old woman cries, and Jack feels very guilty. But the other members of the gang feel no compunction at all. Will's dream is to become a highwayman so that he can "live like a gentleman." Finally Will's gang breaks into a house in Hounslow and kills the gardener. One of the boys turns state's evidence, and Will is arrested. Later that same day, Colonel Jack (who did not participate in the housebreaking) is arrested by the constables, who are looking for a boy named Jack who lives in Rosemary Lane. Jack pleads his own case before the justice in Newgate and is released because the officers have arrested the wrong Jack. The justice compliments the Colonel on his forensic ability and comments that he seems meant for better things than the life of the streets. The Colonel resolves to learn to read so that the next time he will be able to read the arrest warrant.

After Will is hanged, Captain and Colonel Jack (aged seventeen

and eighteen) decide that London is too hot for them and set out
for Scotland. But before leaving, Colonel Jack goes to Kentish
Town and returns Mrs. Smith's 22s. 6d. (He says that "the thief" is
a friend of his.) He is moved when the old woman prays for the
thief's repentance. Captain Jack, however, is unredeemed, and on
the way north he insists on stealing a horse, laundry hanging out to
dry, and as many purses as he can manage. In Edinburgh they see
a pair of pickpockets being whipped through the streets. This
sight gives the Captain unpleasant memories, and so he disappears
for eighteen months.

During the Captain's absence, Colonel Jack is taught to read and
write by a poor scholar. He works for a custom's agent but is
bilked out of his twelve pounds' wages when the agent is turned
out of his place. When the Captain returns, the two young men
enlist in the army. Colonel Jack seems to take naturally to the
profession of arms, and the sergeant remarks that he must be an
officer's bastard. But when the regiment receives orders to ship
for Flanders, Colonel Jack has no desire to be knocked on the head
for 3s. 6d. a week, and so the two desert. The Colonel wants to go
to London, get his money, and buy a commission.

They sneak away to Newcastle and go to an inn, where they meet
a hearty ship captain who promises to take them to London. That
night the beer is strong and the boys are carried aboard ship. They
awaken the next morning to learn that the ship is already under
way, not southward toward London, but northward around the
Orkneys and to Virginia, where they are to be sold as bondservants.
In thirty-two days they reach "Virginia" (in fact, Maryland) and
learn that after five years of servitude they will each be awarded a
plot of ground and be allowed to set up for independent farmers.
Captain Jack has no interest in hard labor and runs away, but the
Colonel proves such a good worker that his master, Mr. Smith,
makes him an overseer.

Colonel Jack is unable to bring himself to whip the Negro slaves.
Consequently the other overseers resent him and report to Smith
that the farm is falling into disorder. One morning two Negroes
are brought in for punishment, having stolen liquor and attacked
an overseer. At this very moment Smith arrives to investigate the
charges against Jack, who is able to win Smith over to a policy of
merciful treatment and appealing to the slaves' consciences. As a
result of this kind treatment, Mouchat, one of the most brutal
Negroes, reforms. He becomes so loyal that he offers to give up his

life for the Colonel when he hears a false rumor that Jack is to be hanged.

Smith offers to manumit Jack after only three of his five years' indentured servitude. But Jack, still after the main chance, confides, "I was too cunning for him," and insists on staying in Smith's service. Smith sets Jack up as a farmer and even builds a house for him. Jack sends back to his merchant-friend in London for a shipment of farm equipment, but the ship is cast away at the entrance to the Chesapeake. Upon reflection, Jack decides that this is for the best, since goods purchased with dishonest money might pollute wealth lawfully gained.

Twelve years after Jack's arrival, Smith dies. In the meantime Jack has been reading history books and learning Latin from a transported Bristol felon who happens to be something of a scholar. Jack's tutor was converted to Christianity as a result of his being saved from the gallows, and his conversation arouses in Jack a sense of his own sinful nature. But since he has no religious background at all, the reformation doesn't last. Jack's estate has grown to three plantations, and he decides that he is tired of living in a remote part of the world. Leaving his property in the hands of his erstwhile tutor, he ships several large cargoes of tobacco for England and, at the age of thirty-three, embarks for home.

After being captured by pirates and soldiering in the Lowlands, Jack reaches England, where he is comfortably off from the sale of his tobacco. He learns that both his brothers have been executed for highway robbery (the Captain has been hanged in England and the Major has been broken upon the wheel at Paris). Jack poses as a French merchant and is entrapped into marriage by a woman who lives across the way. (Up until now he never thought about women.) After the birth of their first child, the lady turns out to be addicted to gambling. When Jack refuses to support her extravagances, she leaves him. One day a rude fellow comes to demand payment of a bill of thirty pounds which the lady has run up and, when Jack declines to pay, a heated argument occurs. That evening Jack goes for a walk and is approached by what seems to be a cripple. To his surprise, the cripple attacks him with his crutch and knocks him unconscious. When Jack regains consciousness his nose has been slit and one ear almost cut off. Jack recovers from his injuries; but, learning that his wife is pregnant by another man, he divorces her and enlists in the Irish brigade in the service of the king of France.

Jack takes part in the campaigns of 1701 and 1702 between the French and the Germans in northern Italy, where he is captured. While under house arrest in Trent he marries a burgher's daughter. When he is exchanged, he takes his wife with him to Paris to recruit troops for the Irish brigade. There he enlists in the abortive attempt of the Chevalier de St. George (the "Old Pretender") to invade England. Unable to land on the Scottish coast, the fleet returns and Jack finds that his new wife has been misbehaving. He thinks about murdering her but instead becomes involved in a duel with her lover, a certain marquis. The marquis falls (as Jack thinks) mortally wounded, and so Jack runs back to England, feeling he has finally vindicated his manhood. Later he hears that the marquis has recovered but has lost his commission in the army as a result of the affair. His wife has become the marquis's mistress.

Jack lives for a few years at Canterbury, passing as a French merchant under the name of Mons. Charnot. He marries a ship captain's widow whom he meets in the London coach. They are happy for six years until she takes to drinking. Her alcoholism leads to sexual promiscuity, and Jack finds himself a cuckold for the third time. He canes the offending gentleman, leaves his wife to drink herself to death, and moves to Lancaster with his three children.

For a year Jack remains thoroughly soured on women, but finally he decides to remarry for the sake of his children. He pitches upon Margaret ("Moggy"), a plain but industrious servant girl who has befriended his children. He overwhelms her one night with a proposal, and they are secretly married by a local doctor, who is really a papist in disguise. They remain happily married for four years until smallpox carries away three of their children and Moggy dies in childbirth.

Jack leaves his daughter by Moggy with her grandfather and returns with his son to Virginia, where he finds his estate flourishing. One day while riding out he discovers that one of the woman laborers has been overcome by heat and strain. This woman seems to be of gentle birth, and so Jack has her assigned to light labor. To his astonishment, she turns out to be none other than his divorced first wife. After she left the Colonel, she fell in with a band of robbers to support her extravagance and was eventually convicted of theft and transported. She humbles herself to him utterly, and he compares her to the returning Prodigal. The steward-tutor becomes Jack's rival for the hand of his own ex-wife, but she prefers Jack and so they are married again.

Trouble enters the picture in the form of a number of transported rebels, convicted of supporting the Chevalier de St. George in the rebellion of 1714. Jack tells us in a flashback that, despite Moggy's warnings, he joined the rebel army for a brief period of three days just before the battle of Preston. He was known only as "the French gentleman," but he now fears that the transported Scots will recognize him and give him away. His wife hides him in the house, giving out that he is suffering from the "rheumatic gout." Then she has him smuggled out of the country to Nevis or Antigua in the West Indies, while she writes to a friend in England asking for Jack's pardon, for which he declares himself willing to pay three or four hundred pounds. When the news comes that King George has extended a general pardon, Jack bursts out with gratitude and reconfirms his stand that mercy is a more effective method of reform than punishment.

On the voyage back to Virginia, Jack's ship takes refuge from a storm under the lee of the island of Cuba. They are captured by five *barcolongos*, accused of trying to trade in the Spanish dominions, and imprisoned. Fortunately Jack speaks fluent Spanish and is able to prove that he has served the Spanish king's allies in Italy, and so he is allowed the freedom of the streets. He must ransom himself and his crew, but the corregidore senselessly refuses to allow him to send for the money, since all contact with foreign nations is forbidden by his commission. Finally the governor of the fort brings the corregidore to reason, and Jack has a ship, handsomely laden, sent from Virginia. When it arrives, he not only ransoms himself, but carries on a handsome under-the-counter trade with the Cuban merchants for textiles.

Finding contraband trade profitable and the Spanish merchants willing, Jack makes two voyages from North America to Mexico, where he meets a rich merchant living "like a sovereign prince." While he is on shore with the merchant, his flotilla is chased away by some Spanish men-of-war, and Jack is temporarily isolated. (One of his sloops is forced ashore at Pensacola, which Defoe thinks is at the mouth of the Mississippi.)

While he is admiring the efficiency of the Spanish warehouse system, Jack also indulges in reflections about his misspent life. He has lived a dissolute life for twenty-four years after the reformation he made as a bond servant. Finally Jack is able to obtain passage on board a Spanish ship for Cadiz. The homing instinct again manifests itself, and he makes his way back to London, where his wife joins him and where he sets about writing his memoirs. Alcade Major, "Bullet-Head," Sir George Byng, Mons. Catinat, the Chevalier de St. George, the Prince de Commercy, the Marquis de Crequi, Cullum, Lord Derwentwater, Prince Eugene, Sir Stephen Evans, Sir Henry Furness, King George I, George, Capt. Jack Gilliman, Gen. Herbeville, Capt. Jack, Col. Jack, Maj. Jack, "the marquis," "Moggy" (or Mrs. Margaret), Mouchat, Jack's nurse, Pennico, Duke of Savoy, Mrs. Smith of Kentish Town, Smith, Sir John Sweetapple, Count de Tesse, Tom, Sir William Turner, the "tutor," Duke de Vendome, Duke de Villeroi, Will (first called "Robin"), "Wry-Neck."

A Discourse Concerning the Mechanical Operation of the Spirit, Swift. See *The Mechanical Operation of the Spirit*.

Due Preparations for the Plague, As Well for Soul as Body, Defoe, 1722.

This book is mainly a handbook about piety and hygiene in the face of plague, but it contains two narratives. The occasion was the reappearance of bubonic plague on the Continent and the groundless fear that it might again spread to London, as it had done in the terrible year 1665.

Part one—The plague, Defoe believes, is spread by "poisonous effluvia," especially in merchandise imported from infected regions. He particularly deplores smuggling since it makes the purity of the merchandise impossible to regulate. When Provence was infected the French authorities succeeded in sealing it off, but such measures would not work in England because the militia can be so easily bribed. Defoe opposes removing sick people into pesthouses because of the risk of spreading the infection. Instead, the sound people should be quarantined for their own safety.

While this prescription would be effective for a village, it would obviously not work for a gigantic city like London. London should be emptied of exactly those elements of the population most subject to infectious diseases, that is, the rabble. The poor should be given a supplement to remove themselves. Apprentices, pensioners, and prisoners for debt should be sent out of the city, along with the Blue Coat boys and girls. All loose animals, especially rats and mice, should be exterminated, and stable refuse should be collected.

In particular, open sewers, which are periodically (and ineffec-
tually) washed out by the tides, should be purified.

An even worse jakes than the open sewers is the bodies of the
Londoners. Every citizen should purify himself by purges and
salivation a good six months before the onset of plague. People
should also leave off drinking so much liquor and eating so much
meat, since these substances load the blood with impurities. Defoe
dismisses scornfully the suggestion that the plague might be carried
by insects.

The first narrative portion recounts the fortunes of a grocer's
family that kept itself locked up in their house from July 14 until
December 1, 1665. They are a family of ten, but the grocer dismisses his two apprentices before their time is out and keeps his
porter in employment only as a message carrier. His only com-
munication with the outside world is through a third-story window
equipped with a tin shutter (poisonous effluvia cannot cling to
tin). Before sticking his head out, the grocer always burns a great
quantity of gunpowder so that the sulphur will singe the air and
purify it. Nor does he neglect spiritual preparation; they fast
two days a week and have prayers three times a day.

Abraham, the faithful porter and errand boy, succumbs to the
plague, and the grocer hires one of the watchmen to serve in his
place. Finally toward the end of the plague summer, the grocer
himself is taken sick, and his family fears the worst. But he takes
sweating medicines, and his illness turns out to be only a stress
reaction. On the first of December when the plague has abated,
he walks out of his house like Noah out of the ark.

Defoe now returns to his discussion of the causes of the infection.
Some allege that the plague is not carried by human contact, since
in 1665 poor people working around the corpses are said to have
escaped unscathed. Defoe denies that this was generally the case.
If it were so, why would the French have shot down people trying
to escape from Marseilles? He recommends running up and down
stairs to sweat unhealthy humors out of the body, and carrying a
bunch of rue in the mouth as a prophylactic measure.

Part two—Having described preparations against the plague,
Defoe proceeds to discuss preparations for the plague, that is, how
one should prepare one's soul to face death. In 1665 there was a
family in London, composed of an aged mother, two brothers, and
a sister, called "the Governess," a pious and beautiful young
woman. The elder brother hardens his heart against his mother's

pious warnings. He argues that discussing plague is bad for business. The younger brother, however, is moved by his sister to
repent of his sins. Together the two of them undertake daily ses-
sions of Bible-reading and prayer. The sister reels off a string of
obscure Old Testament texts which apparently she knows from
memory.

Just as the dead carts have begun their grim work within the
walls of the City, the family, by great good fortune, makes a bargain with a ship captain to remain aboard his ship anchored in the
Thames until the plague goes away. But just before embarking
the sister is taken ill. Even now the younger brother refuses to
leave her side. Fortunately she proves not to have the plague, and
so the little family moves safely on board ship, along with the
captain's wife and son. The ship drops down-river to Bugsby's
Hole. They decide against sailing for Harwich, since so many
Dutch packets land there and the plague originally came over from
Holland.

At last they receive the glad news that the bills of mortality have
decreased. At the end of November, the weekly death toll is down
to 210. They cautiously sail up to Deptford Reach and finally back
home, where the brothers have all their internal furnishings burnt,
for fear they retain any of the "noxious effluvia." Defoe closes his
narrative by remarking that Christians should always be in a
proper frame of mind for death, so that a sudden calamity may not
catch them unawares, as it did the elder brother.

Abraham the porter, older brother, younger brother,
Thomas Molins, sister ("the Governess").

The Dumb Philosopher; Or, Great Britain's Wonder, Defoe, 1719.

Dickory Cronke, a Cornishman, is born mute, although perfectly able to hear. The day before his death in 1718 he miraculously
obtains the power of speech and delivers an inspiring discourse
to his hearers.

Young Dickory is nicknamed "Restoration Dick" because he is
born May 29, 1660, the day Charles II returns to England. Despite
his handicap he learns to read and write but is physically too weak
to work in the Cornish coal mines. He works for twenty-four years
as a servant and then returns to Cornwall with some sixty pounds
which he has saved. He lives in St. Helen's with his widowed
sister, eating only bread and milk and going for morning and
afternoon walks.

After fourteen years he suffers a stroke on one of his walks and is found the next morning lying under a tree. While resting in bed he begins to speak, predicting his own death and declaring his loyalty to the church of Christ (some doubts have been raised about his faith since he never attended church). He then loses the power of speech again, but before he dies he selects from his papers a series of religious meditations and predictions of political events to come in Europe between 1720 and 1729. (The meditations are conventional, the prophecies couched in vague symbolic language.) The pamphlet closes with an elegy and an epitaph, allegedly by different hands but sounding rather similar, and suspiciously like Defoe.

Anthony Barlow, Dickory Cronke, Mrs. Mary Mordant, Owen Parry.

Duncan Campbell, Defoe, 1720. (Original title: *The History of the Life and Surprising Adventures of Mr. Duncan Campbell.*)

In this book long narrative portions are interspersed with discursive sections on clairvoyance and spirit lore. The preface is a compendium of eighteenth-century beliefs about how to induce dreams revealing future marital partners. The introduction is a curious blend of credulity and Enlightenment willingness to investigate new psychological phenomena.

Archibald Campbell is born and grows up in the Shetland Islands. The islanders devise a cable car so that the boys can gather birds' eggs from the crags. On one occasion night falls before young Archibald can return to the mainland, and he has to spend the night on the rocks. The next morning a Dutch ship is blown into the cove and agrees to carry Archibald away to Holland. When the islanders find him missing, they assume the eagles have carried him away.

A storm blows the Dutch ship to the coast of Lapland, where Archibald meets and marries a landowner's daughter. The Lapp maiden is gifted with "second sight." When she is pregnant with Duncan she predicts by observing the moon that he will be a boy. He is born with a caul and with three teeth already descended, signs of an unusually gifted child (1680). When his mother dies (having predicted her own death two years in advance), Duncan's father carries the boy back to Scotland, remarries, and moves to the Western Islands. At four the boy has still not begun to speak and is evidently deaf, but a professor from the University of Glasgow teaches him to read and write. There is a long extract from Dr.

Wallis' book on the subject, explaining how words can be grouped under subject headings for the deaf student. The chapter provides insights into the sorts of items that would be considered household words to an eighteenth-century family; for instance, breeds of horses and a number of tools.

In 1685 Duncan's father supports the Earl of Argyll's invasion of Scotland. When the rebellion is put down, Archibald Campbell abdicates his estate; soon he pines away and dies. (At this point, the elderly "author" of the volume claims that his personal acquaintance with young Duncan began.) His mother brings Duncan to Edinburgh to live, where he is already showing an ability to predict the results of children's games. Nubile maidens and squeamish widows pamper him and shower him with presents to find out their future mates. One day our narrator surprises Duncan in a state of trance. When he comes to, he describes a beautiful curly-haired boy whom he sees in visions and who entrusts to him the knowledge of future events.

A full chapter recounts examples of famous men who have seen spirits, such as John Donne and Torquato Tasso. The Earl of Orrery's Irish butler was almost abducted by spirits. The Duke of Buckingham was warned of his imminent assassination by his grandfather's ghost.

In 1692 Duncan's mother dies, and soon his relatives send the young man up to London. Our narrator discovers him as a beautiful long-haired youth of eighteen, surrounded by admiring young ladies in a tavern. He divines the future of beautiful young Miss Welwood. At first he is reluctant to speak out, and the company imagine that he himself is in love with her. Under pressure, he predicts her disfigurement and death from smallpox, an event which follows a few years later. Miss Irwin, the hostess of the tavern, wants to know the fate of her little boy. Duncan predicts a dishonorable death. The young fellow is indeed hanged at Tyburn in 1713 for stealing a cheese in the Haymarket.

Two other incidents have more cheerful outcomes. The popular maiden Christallina and the pretty young widow Urbana come to learn if they will gain their trueloves. While sitting in Duncan's waiting room, they are at first cold to each other. Then they warm up and unburden all their secrets. Finally they end up by slandering each other. But as Duncan predicts, Christallina obtains her beloved Secretarius, while Urbana marries Alderman Stiffrump.

A merchant is anxious about his fortune. To talk with him Duncan dismisses a young woman, two rich old maids, a bouncy widow, and a woman anxious for the death of her husband. Duncan tells the merchant to disregard rumors of the ruin of his ships. His wife will prove extravagant, but if he resists the temptation to despair, all will come right in the end. Everything falls out as predicted.

Not all the citizens of London believe in Duncan's powers. A brassy lady comes to laugh at him but is confounded when Duncan reveals that she has birthed a bastard in Leicestershire. Duncan warns a young woman against marrying a swaggering army captain, and the officer along with three bullies decides to take revenge. Duncan is easily lured to a tavern, where a fight ensues and he is wounded. Finally Duncan vindicates himself against skeptics by seeing through the disguises of a lady of quality and her servants who are scheming to trick him. He predicts that the footman will rise one day to be a fine gentleman but that the lady herself will throw herself away upon a servant. These events come true, as we expect them to.

Chapter seven deals with second sight and is essentially a digest of Daniel Martin's *Description of the Western Isles of Scotland, called by the ancient geographers, Hebrides.* Even cows and horses and children in the Western Islands are gifted with second sight. This assertion is used to document the existence of clairvoyance, for indeed how could cows and horses be drawn into a plot to deceive the public? When a shroud is seen next to a person it signifies his imminent death; a wraith seen standing by a person's side is his future spouse.

By 1702 Duncan is weary of the public and decides to lead an idle life. His elderly friend (the narrator) warns him against dissipation, but nevertheless Duncan falls in with a crowd of wealthy heirs. Soon he is bankrupt and is attacked by bailiffs in a tavern for nonpayment of debts. While he is defending himself, the creditor's wife lays hold of his genitals and almost squeezes the life out of them. Fleeing, he is run down by Lord Rivers' servants, who think he must be a murderer. After six days his rich friends procure his release from the Marshalsea prison. He then decides to enlist in the army in Flanders.

After a series of misadventures on the Continent, he is jailed and examined by a group of English Catholic friars on the charge that he is in league with the devil. By his learned arguments he is able to exonerate himself. Returning to England, he borrows money of an old barber-friend, Tobit Yeats, and sets up business again at the old stand. His financial condition is mended when he marries the rich widow, Mrs. Digby. He is now at the summit of his fame and in 1712 is the subject of several *Spectator* papers.

He cures Miss Susanna Johnson of Essex, who is forced to bend double under a witch's curse. Duncan enables her to stand up again and (with the help of a glass of wine) to break wind for the first time in months. He cures Mr. Coates, a tobacco merchant in Fenchurch St., of an intestinal ailment brought on by witches. For Mr. and Mrs. Saxon he not only finds six pounds' worth of lost Flanders lace, but also reveals that they have been unwittingly swindled out of an inheritance in Kent. The family travels out to Sevenoaks and finds a house corresponding exactly to the one Duncan saw in a vision.

Mr. Amandus brings his ward to Duncan and, for a test, asks him to guess her name. The trick is that the girl's usual name is not her true one. But Duncan discovers after intense concentration that the young woman is not really Adeodata, but Amanda, the bastard daughter of her "guardian."

In the appendix Defoe summarizes the laws against witches and fortunetellers to exonerate Duncan from the charge of being the devil's agent. Two related tracts are included. *A Remarkable Passage of an Apparition* is an account by the Rev. Ruddle of Cornwall of the appearance of Dorothy Dingley's ghost. *The Friendly Demon* purports to be a letter from Duncan describing the marvelous cures wrought by a certain white powder discovered by Sir Kenelm Digby.

"Adeodata," Amabella, Amanda, Amandus, Earl of Argyll, Mr. Barnard, Daniel Bow (alias Daniel Black), Sir Archibald Campbell, Duncan Campbell, Sr. (Duncan's grandfather), Duncan Campbell, Mrs. Campbell, "one Cantle or Cantlow," Mr. Coates, Count Cog, Christallina, Lady Delphina, the Widow Digby, Dr. John Donne, Sir Robert Drury, Mr. Greatrix, Mrs. Irwin, Susanna Johnson, Capt. Leathes, Miss Lee, Archibald Macdonald, Sir Donald Macdonald, Sir Norman Macleod, Manso, Capt. Meek, Maj. Gen. Middleton, John Morrison, Daniel Nicholson, Parker, Perkin, Mrs. Pight, Earl Rivers, Mr. Saxon, Mrs. Saxon, Secretarius, Mrs. Anne Stephens, Mrs. Stephens, Alderman Stiffrump, Torquato Tasso, Mr. Toland Toler, Urbana, ghost of old Sir George Villiers, Sir George Villiers (the Duke of Buckingham), Dr. Wallis, Miss Welwood, Mrs. Welwood, Tobit Yeats.

Farther Adventures of Robinson Crusoe, Defoe, 1719.

At home again after his island sojourn, Crusoe, now aged sixty-one, is still obsessed with thoughts of his island. His wife's willingness to follow him wherever he may ramble touches him so that he moves to Bedford and sets up for a farmer. But her death sets him a-hankering again after a wandering life. He returns to London, where he leads an idle and bored existence until his nephew, a sea captain, returns from a profitable voyage to Bilbao. The nephew is planning a voyage to the East Indies and offers to take Crusoe along for a visit to his now-famous island. So on January 8, 1695, Crusoe leaves his three children with his old friend the captain's widow and sets sail. He is accompanied by the faithful Friday, two carpenters, a smith, a tailor, and a jack-of-all-trades, along with supplies and tools to strengthen the colony which he planted.

On the way across the Atlantic they rescue sixty-four Frenchmen from a burning ship. Crusoe notes that the extravagant joy of these people upon being saved is typical of the mercurial French temperament. He makes friends with a young French priest, who has none of the narrow bigotry Crusoe associates with the Roman Catholic church. They set most of the people ashore at Newfoundland but take the young priest with them.

On March 19 they sight a crippled vessel which has lost most of its yards in a storm. The passengers and crew are almost starved to death, having drifted for weeks with no provisions. In the main cabin are an English gentlewoman, her seventeen-year-old son, and waiting maid Susan. The mother has given her last morsel of food to her son, and so she dies soon after Crusoe comes aboard.

Crusoe takes the young man and girl to his island, where he finds a flourishing colony composed of the shipwrecked Spaniards and the marooned English mutineers. Crusoe's friend the Spaniard tells them what hard times they have had with the Englishmen. Crusoe left the three incorrigible mutineers on the island, and they were soon joined by two deserters. These two turned out to be sturdy and reliable farmers, but they were harassed unmercifully by the three rogues, led by the rascal Will Atkins. After a murder attempt the three were driven out of the encampment and starved into submission.

One night the Spanish governor (Crusoe's friend) was unable to sleep. He got out of bed to find that two parties of savages had landed. The next day the savages staged a ferocious battle among themselves in which thirty-two were killed. The Spaniards made

slaves of three wounded ones, but they made the error of not con-
verting their slaves to Christianity and so they had three potential
traitors in their midst.

One day one of the three roguish Englishmen flew into a rage
and attempted to murder one of the slaves, crippling his arm with
a hatchet. A brawl ensued in which two Spaniards were wounded.
The three rogues were tried and convicted of attempted murder,
and their two countrymen thought that they should be hanged. But
the Spanish governor was unwilling to execute an Englishman,
since their benefactor Crusoe was of that nation, and so the three
were simply banished to another part of the island. Shortly there-
after the three took a *barcolongo* and set off for the mainland.
When they returned they brought with them three savage men and
five women. The latter have been parceled out as wives among the
Englishmen, and ironically the worst rogues got the best wives.

The Europeans had to repel two attacks by the savages. Once
the Englishmen sprang an ambush from a tree, routing the enemy.
On a second occasion they were attacked by twenty-eight canoes
full of savages. Atkins fought bravely and led an attack from the
rear which drove the natives back to their canoes. The worst of the
English rogues was killed. The savages who did not get away were
then gradually hunted down and exterminated by the whites until
only thirty-seven were left. The two remaining English rogues
have now thoroughly reformed and have constructed wickerwork
houses for themselves.

Crusoe and his friend the French priest are concerned for the
spiritual state of the colony. In good Enlightenment fashion
they agree to ignore religious differences between themselves. The
priest touches Crusoe's conscience by pointing out to him that the
Englishmen are living with savage women without benefit of clergy,
that the savage women are still totally ignorant of Christianity, and
that the thirty-seven fugitives are in the depths of paganism. In
response Crusoe persuades his countrymen to be properly married
by the priest (they conceal the fact that the priest is a papist) and
urges them to evangelize their wives. Susan the servant girl is
married to Crusoe's jack-of-all-trades from England.

The priest decides to remain on the island and convert the thirty-
seven savages with the help of Friday's father as interpreter. Among
the Englishmen only Will Atkins sets thoroughly about the work of
reformation. It turns out that Atkins is the son of a clergyman gone
astray and now has a deep consciousness of his sin. His wife is at

first skeptical of the power of a God who could allow such a rogue as Atkins to keep on living, but at length she lets herself be baptized with the name of Mary. Crusoe brings tears to the eyes of the couple when he gives them a Bible to strengthen them in the faith.

At this point Susan tells her story of being almost starved to death. She had to drink the blood which gushed out of her nose to keep from dying of thirst. On May 5, 1695, Crusoe departs for Brazil, having been twenty-five days on the island. In his absence Atkins dies and the colony gradually disintegrates. The priest returns to Lisbon. Meanwhile Crusoe's ship is attacked by 126 canoes of savages near the coast of Brazil. When Friday tries to negotiate with them, they shoot him dead with their arrows. Crusoe in his grief destroys a number of the savages with the ship's guns and takes one prisoner, whom they attempt to teach a little English. In Brazil they recruit as potential colonists some fugitives from the Inquisition.

The ship sets out for India round the Cape of Good Hope. On Madagascar they land a party of men who pitch camp on the beach and make a truce with the natives. Crusoe, however, is wary and goes to sleep just offshore in the ship's boat. That night the camp is abruptly attacked by several hundred natives. The crew members all escape except for one Thomas Jeffery. When the supercargo interrogates the crewmen, it comes out that Jeffery abducted and raped a native girl who had come innocently with her mother to sell the Englishmen milk, roots, and herbs.

Three nights later Crusoe accompanies a party of twenty men ashore to take a body count and to look for Jeffery. Against the protests of Crusoe and the supercargo, the crew members go through the jungle to the native village, where they find Jeffery's body hung up by one hand with the throat cut. In a rage the crewmen set fire to the village and massacre the inhabitants as they flee from the flames.

After the ship sets sail again, Crusoe denounces the crime with such vehemence that the crew, especially the boatswain, fear he will make trouble for them when they return home. So when they reach the roads in Bengal, the men refuse to sail further if Crusoe continues on board. The captain is forced to leave him there with only his body servant and the purser's clerk to attend him. Crusoe proves as resilient as ever and quickly moves into a boarding house kept by an Englishwoman for European merchants. During a six years' stay he and another Englishman make two lucrative trading voyages in the opium trade.

Crusoe and his friend buy a ship from one "Emanuel Closter-hoven," but without inspecting the papers very closely. They sail for Siam and anchor in the Cambodia River to career the vessel and stop a leak. Other ships are anchored nearby, and that evening an English gunner's mate and a Dutchman come aboard and warn Crusoe that he is in possession of a stolen ship. The previous owner had turned pirate, and now every English and Dutch ship in the Far East has his description and is out to exterminate the thieves. Crusoe finishes caulking his ship just in time to escape down-river from an attack by five longboats full of incensed English and Dutch sailors. The gunner and the Dutchman go along with Crusoe, since they secretly think he really is a pirate and would like to "go on the account" themselves.

Crusoe is in a panic because he remembers the massacre of Amboyna and fears that if he falls into the hands of the Dutch he will be tortured to death. In a dream he smashes his fist against a bulkhead and breaks two knuckles. He narrowly avoids three Dutch merchantmen, repels an attack of Indo-Chinese natives with buckets of hot pitch, and puts in briefly at Formosa. There he takes on a wily old Portuguese pilot who regales him with the story of the stolen ship. He is astonished when he learns he has signed aboard that very ship. Convinced of Crusoe's good intentions, he steers them past Nanking (too full of Dutch) to Quinchang. Here they sell the vessel to a Japanese who is planning a voyage to the Philippines.

Crusoe, the English merchant, and the pilot now travel with a Chinese mandarin to the Imperial Court at Peking. Crusoe has a low opinion of the Chinese empire. Why, any English artilleryman could easily blow a hole in the Great Wall. They join a caravan of Muscovites on the way back to Russia, repelling attacks by the Tartars as they go. Crusoe makes the mistake of commissioning a Chinese to buy a camel for him. During the transaction they are attacked by Tartars, Crusoe is clubbed unconscious, and the camel is stolen; but a Chinese justice of the peace rules that Crusoe must pay for it anyway.

Crusoe rejoices when he enters Russia because he thinks that he is again in a Christian country. But he is soon disillusioned by the idol worship among the peasants, whom he finds only slightly more civilized than the naked savages of South America. Near Nerchintsk he sees an idol to the god Cham-Chi-Thaungu and learns that the natives have tortured to death a Russian soldier who was bold enough to interrupt their sacrifices. Crusoe is enraged and (somewhat inconsistently) resolves on the same sort of revenge the crewmen took on Madagascar. Under cover of night he and two Scots sneak out to the village, tie up the village priests, and force them to look on while they blow up the idol. The next day the Russian provincial governor has to face a virtual insurrection, but Crusoe and his friends disclaim all knowledge of the affair and go innocently along their way.

They fight their way through more Tartars and winter in Tobolsk, the provincial capital of Siberia. After devising a system of central heating for his hut, he meets a Russian prince who has been exiled by the Czar. This prince has a fine contempt for the tinsel and intrigue of court life. He declines Crusoe's offer of rescue, but asks him to take his son with him to western Europe. He rewards Crusoe with a gift of sables (Crusoe is to sell them in London for two hundred pounds). Crusoe has also been able to sell his Chinese cloves and nutmegs in Siberia for a good price.

In the beginning of June the weather breaks, and Crusoe sets out for Archangel with the prince's son. From there they take ship for Hamburg, where Crusoe sells some of his Oriental wares for an immense profit. The prince's son goes to Vienna, where he will seek the protection of the emperor. Crusoe returns to London via the Hague, arriving home January 10, 1705, after an absence of ten years and at the age of seventy-three.

Will Atkins, "Emanuel Closterhoven," Robinson Crusoe, Mrs. Crusoe, father of Friday, Friday, Jack, Thomas Jeffery, Mary, Capt. Richardson, Father Simon, Susan, Mr. Thompson.

The Fortunate Mistress, Defoe. See *Roxana*.

The Fortunes and Misfortunes of the Famous Moll Flanders, Defoe. See *Moll Flanders*.

A General History of the Pirates, Defoe. Volume one, 1724; Volume two, 1728. (Original title: *A General History of the Robberies and Murders of the Most Notorious Pirates*.)

(The *History* is a massive compilation of biographies of English pirates who were active in the West Indies and around Africa

during the early years of the eighteenth century. Allegedly
compiled by a Capt. Charles Johnson, it is based almost entirely
on contemporary journals and pamphlets. The most famous
lives are those of Blackbeard and Capt. Kid (*sic*) (volume one,
chapter three, and volume two, chapter three). Only the life
of Misson (volume two, chapter one) is fictional. The two
volumes have appeared in countless versions and selections,
each one different from the next. I follow the fine recent edition
of Manuel Schonhorn [Columbia: Univ. of South Carolina Press,
1972.]

Volume one—In the introduction, Defoe tries to show how
dangerous pirates can be if allowed to increase unchecked by
the civil authorities, and tells of notable men in history (Caesar,
Pompey) who have had encounters with them. Also included
here is an account of the English pirates in the West Indies,
who prey not only on the Spanish but also on their own countrymen. Then King George I issues a proclamation that those
who turn themselves in by September 5, 1718, can receive a
pardon. Capt. Woodes Rogers invades their stronghold on the
island of Providence in the Bahamas to implement the decree.
The great bulk of the pirates accept the pardon, but one John
Augur "goes on the account" again immediately after being
pardoned. He and his crew are run down and hanged. One of
his men says on the scaffold that he regrets only that all the
others are not being hanged as well (see the appendix).

Chapter one—Capt. Henry Avery. The highly overrated
Avery is reputed to have commanded a pirate empire, but really
his famous colony on Madagascar consisted only of a handful
of renegades. At the time he was supposed to have been worth
millions, he didn't even have the money to buy a coffin. After
hijacking an English ship commissioned by the Spanish *guarda
del costa*, Avery establishes his base on Madagascar and becomes
famous by capturing a ship of the Grand Mogul. He absconds
with his shipmates' share of the booty and returns to England,
where he rashly entrusts his diamonds to a group of supposedly
upstanding merchants. They expropriate his investment and
threaten to turn him over to the law if he complains. He dies
penniless. (See the summary of *The King of Pirates* for a fictionalized life of this figure.) His men left on Madagascar make
themselves into Oriental monarchs, with slaves as subjects.
Their cruelty almost provokes the blacks into insurrection.

After twenty-five years on the island, their number has shrunk to only eleven.

Chapter two—Capt. John Martel. He carries on a vigorous career of plundering until he is cornered on the island of St. Croix by an English man-of-war. Trying to escape, Martel goes aground and burns his ship, leaving twenty captive Negroes to their fate. He and his men take to the jungle, where presumably they perish.

Chapter three—Capt. Edward Teach, alias Blackbeard. He is born in Bristol and begins his career of piracy under Capt. Benjamin Hornigold. Later he captures a French ship and renames her the *Queen Anne's Revenge*. Upon encountering Stede Bonnet, he replaces him in command of his own ship with one Richards, declaring Bonnet too halfhearted to be a pirate. The gang blockades Charleston harbor, where they capture all ships going in or out. They hold certain prominent citizens hostage, and so the pirates feel free to flaunt themselves ashore. Then they sail northward, and Blackbeard takes Ocracoke Inlet in North Carolina as his lair. He has a cozy working relationship with the governor, Charles Eden. The merchants of the region finally appeal to Gov. Spotswood of Virginia, who sends Lieut. Robert Maynard to capture Blackbeard. Maynard has to go into the inlet with shallow-draft boats, since the water is so shoal. Blackbeard is shot to death, but only after twenty of Maynard's men are killed. One of the pirates is barely restrained from blowing up the ship.

Before his death, Blackbeard married a total of fourteen women. Once he fired pistols indiscriminately beneath a card table, crippling one of his own men. On another occasion he closed up the hatches and lit brimstone below to see which of the crew could stand the hellish condition the longest. When boarding ships, he would stick lighted matches into his hair so as to look like the devil incarnate. Satan is actually rumored to have been seen once among Blackbeard's crew.

Chapter four—Maj. Stede Bonnet. He is basically a decent man but is the victim of some sort of personality flaw which drives him into crime. After being deposed by Blackbeard, he goes to Bath-Town in North Carolina, turns himself in, and (it being before the September 5 deadline), receives the king's pardon. He is commissioned as a privateer to prey on the Spanish, but, once on the high seas, he is unable to resist temptation and turns pirate again.   Finally Col. William Rhet, under the commission of the governor of South Carolina, hunts Bonnet down along with his crew.

Chapter five—Capt. Edward England.   He captures a sloop off the coast of Africa, commanded by a Capt. Skinner.   Unhappily for Skinner, some of his former crew members are among the pirates, and they remember that he once bilked them of their wages.   They tie him to the mast and pelt him with glass bottles; then they shoot him in the head and throw him over the side.   England and his crew are eventually pardoned by the king of Spain.   Defoe compares them to the directors of the South Sea Company, much to the disadvantage of the directors.   (There was a notorious scandal about the sale of stock in this company in 1720.)

Chapter six—Capt. Charles Vane.   He is the only pirate at Providence Island who refuses to avail himself of the royal amnesty.   Later he declines battle with a French man-of-war, and so his men depose him for cowardice and elect John Rackam captain (see chapter seven).   Vane is later shipwrecked on the island of Barnacko.   There he is found by his old privateering friend, Capt. Holford, who declines to rescue him since he would probably lead the crew to mutiny.   When Vane is finally rescued by another English ship, Holford accidentally discovers him on board, claps him in irons, and delivers him to be hanged.

Chapter seven—Capt. John Rackam.   In 1720 Rackam is cruising the coast of Hispaniola, where he invites nine men from a turtling vessel to come aboard for a drink.   At this moment, a man-of-war heaves into sight, sent by the governor of the island.   Rackam's gang is captured, and not only the pirates, but also the nine guests are condemned to death, the court assuming that they went aboard with intent to commit acts of piracy.   The most incriminating circumstance is that the guests helped to man battle stations against the man-of-war.

Included in chapter seven are the lives of the two women pirates, Mary Read and Anne Bonny.   The latter is Rackam's lady love.   After being raised by her mother as a boy, Mary Read becomes an intrepid pirate.   She is so ruthless that she once fires a brace of pistols down the hold into the midst of her own cowering shipmates to force them to come topside and fight the enemy. Mary successfully passes herself off as a young man until Anne Bonny falls in love with her and Rackam's jealousy forces her to reveal her true sex. She approves of the death penalty for piracy, since it keeps cowardly rogues from going on the account and crowding brave men out of the business. She falls in love with one of her shipmates and fights a duel for him to prevent his being killed. She is captured with Rackam and condemned, but she "pleads her belly" and receives a stay of execution. Ironically, she dies in prison of a fever.

Anne Bonny is the illegitimate daughter of a lawyer from Cork. There is a long and amusing story of how the lawyer's wife tricks her husband into going to bed with her by pretending she is the maid Mary (Anne's mother). The lawyer and Mary finally take their bastard daughter to North Carolina, where they prosper. Anne marries a seaman, James Bonny, but deserts him to run off with Rackam and turn pirate. She shows a total lack of sympathy for Rackam when he is condemned to death and says if he had fought like a man he would not have to die like a dog. The jury finds Anne's having deserted her husband especially incriminating and condemns her to death; but she pleads her belly and, at the time of writing, has dropped out of sight.

Chapter eight—Capt. Howel Davis. He distinguishes himself by his daring and clever tricks. When he happens to have a large number of captives on board, he bluffs a French sea captain into surrendering by leading them all on deck, thus giving a grossly inflated impression of his strength. At Sierra Leone, Davis passes himself off as an honest merchant and procures an invitation to dinner by the commandant of the fort. At the crucial moment, one of his men claps a pistol to the commandant's breast and makes him a prisoner. The pirates then lock the soldiers up in the guard room and take over the fortress. Davis then goes to the Island of Princes, where he plans to abduct the Portuguese governor. But the governor is warned of the plan by a Portuguese Negro, and when Davis goes ashore he is ambushed and shot down. With his last strength, he fires his pistols at his assailants so that he will not die unrevenged.

Chapter nine—Capt. Bartholomew Roberts. He takes over after Davis' death and wreaks as much revenge on the Portuguese as he can. When he attacks the fort, the Portuguese run away in panic, as is their habit, comments Defoe. While he is out chasing a prize in the sloop, his lieutenant, one Kennedy, runs away in the large ship, abandoning Roberts' portion of the crew to their fate. The pirates then draft a series of articles of confederation, explicitly excluding all Irishmen from their company. Kennedy goes eventually to London, where his sister in a fit of pique betrays him to the law.

After raiding Newfoundland, Roberts cruises back and forth in the Atlantic. Because of an incredible lack of foresight, his crew is without water and comes close to dying of thirst. They are even forced to drink sea water and urine. Finally they reach the coast of Surinam and procure water, but they are totally without gratitude to God for their salvation and rely on Providence to provide them with something to eat.

Harry Glasby attempts to desert the flotilla and, according to the piratical articles, is tried for his life. One of the judges, Valentine Ashplant, declares, "Glasby is an honest fellow, and I love him. By God, Glasby shall not die, damn me if he shall." Then, taking two pistols in his hands, he persuades the other judges to come around to his way of thinking.

Roberts sails to Africa to plunder the Portuguese. They capture a parson and think of taking him along as ship's chaplain but finally decide against it, since he would do nothing but make punch and pray all day. When the blacks refuse to trade with the pirates, they burn out their village in senseless retribution.

In Whydah Roads, Roberts extorts protection money from eleven ships. When one captain refuses to co-operate, Roberts sets his ship on fire; and since it is too much trouble to unchain the Negroes within, eighty of them either are burned to death or leap overboard to be torn to pieces by sharks. Meanwhile two royal ships of the line have been dispatched to run him down. The *Swallow* is detained along the coast by tropical illnesses among the crew, and so Roberts' evasive maneuvers actually bring him into contact with the man-of-war. Roberts receives a grapeshot charge in the throat and dies instantly, sword in hand. His two ships surrender. Some of the pirates attempt to blow up the powder room but are restrained by their shipmates. They are confined on board the *Swallow*, where the pirates' surgeon Scudamore attempts to foment an insurrection among the blacks.

The trial documents provide a number of interesting capsule biographies. Robert Johnson pleads that he did not join the pirates voluntarily. This claim is true, strictly speaking, since he was so drunk at the time that he had to be hoisted aboard with a block and tackle. However, he was afterwards among the most ruthless of the desperadoes. William Davis, it seems, was once married to a Negro, but sold her into slavery to buy liquor for himself. He blames his career of crime on alcohol. In all, fifty-two men are executed outside the gates of Cape Corso castle. Only Scudamore seems truly repentant and recites the 31st Psalm.

Chapter ten—Capt. Thomas Anstis. Anstis, in the *Good Fortune*, breaks off from Roberts before his capture. He and his men are guilty of a gang rape of a woman captive, after which they break her back and throw her overboard. After this they have the nerve to petition the king for a pardon, meanwhile hiding out on an island near Cuba and subsisting on turtle meat. Here they hold a series of mock trials. Members of the crew take turns playing judge, sitting on a tree limb with a tarpaulin about the shoulders and a thrum cap on. The "felon" is invariably ordered hanged.

The pirates set to sea again, but through carelessness they run one of their ships aground. At this moment they are attacked by two men-of-war. They escape narrowly, but while careening the ship they are surprised again. Anstis gets away, only to be murdered in his hammock by his own men.

Chapter eleven—Capt. Richard Worley. He leaves New York in 1718 in an open boat and with only eight men. After a brief but dramatic career, they are all captured at the order of the governor of South Carolina. In a bloody battle, Worley and one other man are the only ones among the pirate crew who are not killed. They are quickly taken ashore and hanged, lest they die from their wounds before suffering the full rigor of the law. Along with Worley are captured a large crew of transported felons, including a number of women who were planning to set up a colony of prostitutes in the West Indies.

Chapter twelve—Capt. George Lowther. He ships with the Royal African Company to garrison James's Island off the coast of Africa. He persuades the commander of the contingent of troops, Capt. Massey, to run away and turn pirate. But Massey later has a guilty conscience. He restrains Lowther from plundering French settlements in the West Indies and then takes passage for London, where he turns himself in. The government is unimpressed with such noble behavior and has him hanged. Lowther continues to raid the American coast until his crew is surprised while careening the ship. Most of the men are captured and hanged. Lowther himself flees into the jungle and blows his own brains out.

Chapter thirteen—Capt. Edward Low. This mad dog among the pirates grows up in the streets of Westminster. His brother was celebrated as a child for riding in a peddlar's pack and snatching the wigs and hats off gentlemen when their backs were turned. Ned himself murders all New England captains because he feels that he was badly treated while working as a rigger in Boston. He massacres the entire crew of a Spanish vessel because English goods have been found aboard. He makes one captain eat his own severed ears with pepper and salt. Finally he is attacked by a man-of-war, the *Greyhound* out of New York. One of the ships in his flotilla is disabled, and so Low sails away, abandoning his messmates to their fate. After torturing the crews of several whalers, he falls sick and dies. As a result of his activities, English ships obtain such a bad reputation that the Portuguese begin to jail any English captain they capture, dishonest or not.

Chapter fourteen—Capt. John Evans. He is noted for his practice of interrogating the crew of each ship about whether or not they have been favorably treated by their captain. In a quarrel, Evans is shot through the head by his own boatswain. The crew decide to torture the boatswain to death, but one of them becomes impatient and guns him down. After this the pirate band disperses.

Chapter fifteen—Capt. John Phillips. Initially in Anstis's crew, Phillips and five companions run away with a Newfoundland vessel. The first quartermaster, Fern, is displaced by another former pirate who has the prestige of having served with Blackbeard. In a pet, Fern runs away with one of the pirate vessels and has to be run down by Phillips. In the resulting sea battle Phillips is wounded in the leg. The ship's carpenter saws off the wounded limb as though it were a log of wood and cauterizes the wound with a hot axe.

Phillips is on his way back to Newfoundland to replenish his crew with poor fishermen when there is a mutiny on board. Edward Cheeseman, who was forced to join the rogues, and

Andrew Harradine, a captured ship's master, attack the pirate officers and either throw them over the side or butcher them with axes. The ship is then taken ashore and the four pirates still alive (including Phillips) are condemned to death.

Chapter sixteen—Capt. Francis Spriggs. He is known for his ingenious tortures. A group of Portuguese captives undergoes a "sweat," being forced to run around between decks until they are exhausted. A Capt. Hawkins has to eat a plate of candles before being marooned. Other prisoners are hoisted as high as the maintop and then dropped to the deck, breaking all their bones. Spriggs then makes the mistake of capturing a load of slaves, who eat up his provisions. Finally he is so bold as to capture a sloop off Port Royal, which brings two men-of-war out to chase him. One of his ships is run aground on the coast of Florida, where the crew is eaten by cannibals. Spriggs himself is chased ashore on the Spanish Main.

Chapter seventeen—Capt. John Smith, alias Gow. Defoe first published an account of this pirate in the third edition of volume one of the History, which appeared the same month Gow was executed (June, 1725). He later expanded this account and published it separately on July 1. (See summary of John Gow for details.)

At the end of volume one is an account of five men who set up for a company of pirates. Defoe blames the Portuguese governors in Africa for being willing to trade with such scoundrels. There is also a sketch of the career of Philip Roche, an Irishman. He and his henchmen charter a French vessel, murder the crew, and then go on the account. Roche's handsome appearance belies his gruesome crimes. He is captured while trying to collect on his insurance benefits in London. Finally, Defoe includes an abstract of the civil and statute laws relating to piracy.

Volume two. Chapter one—Capt. Misson. (This is the only totally fabricated chapter in the History.) Misson is the younger son of a good French family and serves on board the Victoire, a French privateer in the war with England. His morals are corrupted in Rome by a lewd Catholic priest named Caraccioli, who before enlisting himself on the Victoire convinces him that Christianity is merely a pious fraud. Caraccioli also has a great effect on the crew, many of whom are Calvinists from Rochelle. In battle with an English ship, Capt. Fourbin is killed, and Caraccioli persuades Misson to take command. The crew joins enthusiastically in the pirating enterprise, since it is passed off as a stroke for human liberty. When they capture an English privateer off St. Christopher, they treat their prisoners with courtesy.

Misson captures the Dutch ship *Nieuwstadt* and takes forty hands on board, but the Dutchmen begin to corrupt the pure morals of Misson's men by their profane language, and he has to read them a stiff lecture. The Dutchman also carries seventeen slaves, whom Misson liberates and distributes among the various messes so that the blacks can learn French more quickly.

The *Victoire* rounds the Cape of Good Hope and lands on the island of Johanna, where the Frenchmen help the queen repel an attack by the king of Mohilla. Against the queen's advice, Misson and Caraccioli attend a peace banquet given by the king. There they are suddenly ambushed and wounded by the treacherous Mohillians, although their friends inflict terrible losses on the enemy. The Europeans are impressed when the widow of one of the slain Johannians refuses their offer of gold and insists on killing herself on the bier of her husband. With the queen's help, Misson plants a colony on Madagascar called Libertalia, and a number of his men intermarry with the natives.

Chapter two—Capt. Thomas Tew. (Defoe intertwines the fortunes of this historical figure with those of the fictional Misson.) Misson has just captured a Portuguese ship when he is in turn attacked by a strange vessel, which turns out to be Tew's. An Englishman, Tew was originally commissioned as a privateer by the governor of Bermuda but persuaded his men to turn pirate. A group of twenty-three has already defected with the quartermaster and settled elsewhere on Madagascar. Tew joins forces with Misson's colony, of which he is elected admiral, and Caraccioli secretary of state.

Misson grants the captured Portuguese their liberty, but first makes them swear not to take arms against him or to lead other Europeans back in an attack on Libertalia. But the Portuguese break their word, and the Libertalians must soon repel an attack. Two of the perfidious Portuguese are captured and hanged as examples, despite Misson's preference for mercy.

After capturing a boatload of Moorish girls on pilgrimage

to Mecca, Tew visits his old quartermaster and tries to persuade his former messmates to join the well-organized and
harmonious Libertalians, but to no avail. During this visit
a storm arises and, while the distraught Tew looks on, the
Victoire is driven ashore and wrecked with all hands. He remains
with the quartermaster for three months until Misson comes
in a sloop to say that the entire colony of Libertalia, including
Caraccioli, has been massacred by the natives.

Misson returns to civil life in France, but Tew goes on the
account again and is killed by a cannon shot while engaging
a ship of the Grand Mogul's near the Red Sea.

Chapter three—Capt. William Kid. In 1696 Lord Bellamont,
the governor of Barbados, procures a privateering commission for Kid, by which he is to root out the pirates plaguing
English commerce and prey on the French enemy. But once
in the Indian Ocean, Kid persuades his crew to turn pirate
and prey on all nations. He shows a curious lack of resolution
and once refuses to attack a Dutch ship, even though he has
already committed enough acts of piracy to hang him. When
one of his crew berates him for this trepidation, he brains
the man with a bucket. He then has a rendezvous with the
notorious pirate Culliford near Madagascar.

Meanwhile the merchants in England are alarmed and have
Kid specifically excepted from a proclamation offering amnesty
to pirates. Ignorant of the proclamation, Kid audaciously sails
to New York, evidently expecting that the law will wink at
his crimes. He is sent to England, where his plea that the ships
he captured had French papers proves ineffective. He is condemned and hanged along with five other pirates, and his
body is exposed to rot.

Chapter four—Capt. John Bowen. (This chapter begins a
series of seven dealing with the pirates on Madagascar.) Bowen
begins as an honest seaman, but is forcibly detained aboard
a pirate ship for his skill in seamanship and later goes on the
account himself. On Madagascar he and his men seize the
Speedy Return, from Edinburgh, and take her a-pirating, joining
forces later with Thomas Howard (chapter seven). Next is an
account of the trial and execution of Capt. Thomas Green, who
arrives at Edinburgh with his ship the *Worcester* shortly after
the disappearance of the *Speedy Return* (1704) and is blamed
for its capture. On the fragmentary and hearsay testimony

of an Indian boy and a surgeon, Green and two of his crew are executed for the crimes committed by Bowen. Much of the blame for this outrage lies at the door of the furiously anti-English Scottish mob and the bigoted Presbyterian clergy. (Bowen's story is continued in chapter ten, the life of North.)

Chapter five—Capt. John Halsey. He starts as a privateer but like many others turns pirate. He intends to rob only Moorish ships. On Madagascar he trades with a group of English merchants, come especially from Madras in the *Greyhound* to buy stolen goods at a bargain price. The Scottish ship *Neptune* arrives to trade also, and the Madras merchants instigate Halsey's men to seize their competitor (see chapter nine). As just deserts for their chicanery, their own *Greyhound* is seized as well. Then the pirates' fleet is decimated by a hurricane and Halsey himself dies of a fever. He is buried in a water-melon patch with the full ceremony of the Church of England, and his grave is fenced in to prevent his body's being rooted up by wild hogs.

Chapter six—Capt. Thomas White. His career follows the familiar pattern: he is first forced aboard a pirate ship and then finds the life attractive. On the island of St. Mary's (off Madagascar) he falls in with Bowen. They are attacked by an English merchantman, the *Speaker*, under a young and rash captain, Thomas Eastlake. The result of the affair is that the pirates storm the *Speaker* and take possession of her, after which she is commanded by Bowen. White puts together his own pirate band. He displays generosity to a group of children on board one of his prizes, whose considerable fortune he persuades his crew to spare. On returning to Madagascar, White dies of diarrhea.

Chapter seven—Capt. Thomas Howard. The son of a Thames lighterman, Howard runs out his father's inheritance, turns his mother out-of-doors, and then runs away a-pirating. The crew in which he is serving as quartermaster captures a Portuguese ship and whips the captain about the decks for his cowardice in refusing to fight them. Off Madagascar the ship strikes a reef, and Howard with the bulk of the crew abandons his captain and sets up for himself. He eventually marries a native girl in India but is murdered by her relations for his bad treatment of her.

Chapter eight—Capt. David Williams. This morose and

illiterate Welsh shepherd runs away to sea. He is accidentally abandoned by his ship on Madagascar and enslaved by a native king. Here his history resembles that of Robert Drury. He is made prisoner-of-war by several successive tribal leaders, until a chief named Dempaino, who is friendly to Europeans, demands that he be delivered up into his custody. Eventually Williams is rescued by the pirate North. In the course of their excursions around Madagascar, two of the crew members fall into the hands of the Arab governor of a town called the Boyne and are tortured to death. The native king, who wants to stay on good terms with the whites, does not distinguish between upstanding and criminal Europeans, and so has the Arab governor put to death.

Chapter nine—Capt. Samuel Burgess. Another privateer-turned-pirate, Burgess is captured by an East Indiaman and carried to London, where he is convicted of piracy but pardoned. He ships on the *Neptune* and is instrumental in betraying the captain into the hands of Halsey. He is finally poisoned by a Madagascar king for his arrogance in a slaving transaction.

Chapter ten—Capt. Nathaniel North. He begins in the privateering business in the West Indies against the French, but discovers that when he captures a French ship which originally sailed under an English flag, the original owner is usually awarded a share in his former vessel by the court. So North turns to piracy, where he can keep 100% of the profits. On Madagascar, North accepts the king's amnesty brought by Commodore Littleton, but then thinks better of his action (since the deadline for the amnesty has already expired) and swims ashore, where the natives are terrified by the sight of a naked white man. He sails on the *Speaker* with Bowen.

In the Gulf of Tonkin, the entire crew comes close to death by heedlessly eating a fish called the Red Snapper, even though Bowen has warned them that it is poisonous. They escape death only by drinking a large amount of liquor (the only antidote). Upon the death of Bowen, North becomes captain. The pirates return to Port Daupin on Madagascar, whereupon their Moorish prisoners run away with their ship. Marooned, they set up an ideal commonwealth. Since perfect unity is necessary in the face of potentially hostile natives, North decides all quarrels with an even hand.

North leads his men in certain native wars as allies of the Mangorians. They capture an enemy village by filling a tree with gunpowder and placing it against the gate. Having enriched itself with slaves, North's colony is reinforced by Capt. Halsey and is shifted twice, to Maritan and then to Ambonavoula, both locations on Madagascar. On the island of Mascarenas, North participates in the seizure of the *Greyhound* and *Neptune* (chapter five).

Finally North is murdered at Ambonavoula by the natives. In his will, he asks his friend J. B. to take his children by his various native wives to the island of Mascarenas, where they can be raised by priests. (Better to have them papists than not Christians.) But the pirates prevent J. B.'s leaving because the man never really participated in their piracies and they are afraid of his betraying them.

Chapter eleven—A Description of Magadoxa (the sixteen years' sojourn of a mulatto in that kingdom). (This account is taken almost verbatim from a manuscript, now in the Sloane collection of the British Museum. The details of the salt and fish net are Defoe's own.) In the year 1700 the *Albemarle*, Capt. William Beavis, anchors off the coast of Somaliland and sends the third mate ashore to ask the natives for fresh water. As interpreter he sends a "mulatto" (actually a Chinese) who speaks both Turkish and Arabic. The mate rashly consents to go inland to receive a present from the prince of Magadoxa. When the party does not return, the captain sends the first mate to stick a mast up on shore with a note, but the only response from the natives is a volley of musket fire. Assuming that his men are dead, the captain sails away.

In Magadoxa meanwhile, the crewmen have been seized and confined in a dungeon until the return of the Accabo, or king. Later the mulatto is transferred to a jail reeking with human excrement. An old man speaks with him through a window and shows him a two-ounce chunk of bleeding human flesh, a souvenir from the bodies of his comrades, who have been torn to pieces and devoured. The two officers have been thrown to wild beasts. But the mulatto is spared because of his color and becomes a trusted servant of the Accabo. He pleases the king by demonstrating the use of birdshot and is made a member of the honor guard appointed to the magnificent royal tombs, the Moorzacks. When one guard leaves his post at night, the Accabo orders his brains to be beaten out, and so the mulatto is careful about sticking to his duty. He shows the Magadoxans how to manufacture salt and how to use an improved fish net, but since these revelations do not bring him any favor at court, he ceases to share European technology with them.

After sixteen years at his post, the mulatto is sent with a detachment of guards to subdue the rebellious town of Saeni with great slaughter. He hears that a European ship has been sighted off the coast near Bandon and flees under cover of night to reach it. To elude his pursuers he has to swim a swift river and dodge an alligator. Finally he is picked up by Dutch sailors and taken home, where to this day he is enlisted in the service of the East India Company.

Chapter twelve—Capt. Condent. He escapes from Woodes Rogers' attempt to round up the pirates at Providence Island. As a good English Protestant, he makes a captured Portuguese captain say mass at the mainmast, and then rides him about the deck. Finally he purchases a pardon from the governor of Mascarenas (near Madagascar) and settles down to be a respectable merchant in France.

Chapter thirteen—Capt. Bellamy. He and his fellow-captain, Paul Williams, are caught in a terrible storm off the Virginia coast, but the danger moves them not to repentance but to even more desperate blasphemies. When Bellamy captures a sloop off South Carolina, he reads a lecture to her captain, to the effect that the only fellows resisting the tyranny of rich men are the pirates. Life on board is enlivened by a strolling actor who portrays himself as Don Quixote and who recommends the founding of a pirate kingdom on Newfoundland, which would have at least as much legal sanction as France and England. A play enacted on board ship is taken so seriously by a drunken gunner that he throws a lighted grenade into the midst of it, blowing up two men.

Bellamy presses a New England captain into service as a pilot, but the fellow slyly runs Bellamy's vessel aground, and Williams follows suit. The pirates murder their captives to eliminate witnesses against them, but they are nevertheless captured by the New Englanders and executed.

Chapter fourteen—Capt. Lewis. He speaks French, Spanish, English, and the language of the mosquito Indians, and it is unknown whether he is French or English in nationality. He whips a captured commander about the decks for surrendering so readily and for not taking better care of his employer's property. In Trinity Harbor, Newfoundland, his quartermaster John Cornelius is lured ashore and captured, but Lewis secures his release by taking hostages and threatening to put them to death. While chasing a prize off the coast of Guinea, Lewis has his topmasts blown away; but he climbs to the maintop and, tearing out a handful of hair, makes a pact with the devil, and so is able to overtake the prize anyway. When the French members of his crew want to set up on their own, Lewis treacherously gives them their own ship and then sails alongside and scuttles them. His master the devil warns him that the Frenchmen will murder him in his cabin, which indeed comes true that very night.

Chapter fifteen—Capt. John Cornelius. He assumes command of the *Morning Star*, Lewis's ship, and engages in a hard-fought battle with an English slaver. Joseph Williams leads the resistance, having inspired the slaves to fight by telling them that the pirates are all cannibals. Finally the slaver is sunk and Williams must promise to join the pirates before they will fish him out of the water. On Madagascar, Cornelius's men are cordially received and provided with a cargo of slaves by the local king, Chimenatto, who was formerly set up in his kingdom through the aid of English allies. But a number of the pirates die of diarrhea brought on by the native liquor, and Cornelius is deposed by a slave revolt led by Williams. He eventually dies on Madagascar.

Chapter sixteen—Capt. William Fly. Ignorant of most seamen's skills, Fly is distinguished only by his cruelty and profanity. He and his accomplices murder their captain and mate in a gruesome fashion, chopping off the captain's hand as he tries to cling to the taffrail. Fly later presses into service the mate of a captured sloop, Mr. Atkinson, along with a number of other sailors, and goes cruising along the American coast. He suspects Atkinson of deliberately steering them wide of Martha's Vineyard and threatens to pistol him. Finally, while most of the crew is off in the sloop chasing a prize, Atkinson leads an uprising of the pressed sailors and captures Fly. They take him to Boston, where he is executed.

Appendix to volume one—We read here particulars of the arrival of Woodes Rogers at the island of Providence in the

Bahamas, along with further details of the careers of Vane, Rackam, and Anne Bonny. We also learn the saga of Phineas Bunce and Dennis Macarty, who revert to a criminal life and maroon their honest shipmates on Green Key. They then attack what they innocently think is a group of three merchantmen. Unfortunately, these turn out to be heavily armed Spanish privateers, who give them a thorough trouncing, killing Bunce. Gov. Rogers mops up the remnant and hangs them, including Macarty. A detailed account of the trials and executions of this group, sent anonymously to "Capt. Johnson," is also appended.

The Accabo, Capt. Airs, Mr. Annesley, Capt. Thomas Anstis, Don Antonio, Armstrong, Valentine Ashplant, Mr. Atkinson, John Augur, Capt. Henry Avery, Ralph Baldrick, Mr. Baldwin, Mr. Baldwin, the Bamzau, Barbarouse, Isaac Barnet, Capt. Barnet, Capt. John Beal, Capt. William Beavis, Capt. Beer, Lord Bellamont, Capt. Bellamy, James Benbrooke, Jonathan Bernard, Jean Besace, Capt. Bird, Robert Bland, Maj. Stede Bonnet, Anne Bonny, James Bonny, Mr. Boone, George Booth, Capt. John Bowen, Capt. Bowles, Capt. George Bradley, James Bradshaw, Bridds, Capt. John Brown, Bruce, Phineas Bunce, Stephen Bunce, Capt. Samuel Burgess, Burgess, Nicholas Butler, Julius Caesar, Capt. Canning, Seignior Caraccioli, James Carr, Capt. Cary, Capt. Chandler, Edward Cheeseman, Mr. Child, Chimave, Andian (or Deaan) Chimenatto, Robert Clark, Capt. Cock, Cocklyn, Coggershall, John Colquhoon, Adam Comry, Capt. Condent, John Cornelius, Mr. Courser, Capt. Cox, "Crackers," Edward Crisp, Andrew Cullen, Pierce Cullen, Capt. Culliford, William Darling, Capt. Howel Davis, William Davis, Robert Deal, Andrew Delbridge, Dempaino, John Dennis, Capt. Diamond, Capt. Dill, Capt. Dittwitt, James Douglas, Capt. Drummond, Capt. Durfey, Capt. Thomas Eastlake, Capt. Eastwick, Charles Eden, Benjamin Edwards, Capt. Edward England, Conde Ericeira, Estwell, Selim Eutemi, Capt. John Evans, Capt. Evans, George Fenn, John Fenn, Antonio Ferdinando, Thomas Fern, Capt. Fin, James Flecker, Samuel Fletcher, Capt. Fletcher, Capt. William Fly, Claude Comte de Fourbin, Capt. Fourgette, Charles Franklin, William Frazier, Capt. Fulker, Anne Fulworth, Capt. Gee, Harry Glasby, Mr. Glyn, Capt. Goulding, George Grant, Capt. Graves (two), Capt. Thomas

Green, Capt. Green, William Greenaway, Capt. Gwatkins, Fayrer Hall, Capt. Hall, Capt. John Halsey, John Haman, Capt. Hamilton, Gen. Hamilton, the Hamman, John Hance, Israel Hands, Hardy, Andrew Harradine, David Harriot (also Hariot), Charles Harris, James Harris, Capt. John Headland, Capt. Hill, Capt. Hingstone, Holford, John Hood, Benjamin Hornigold, Capt. Thomas Howard, Capt. Hume, Capt. Hunt, Hunter, Benjamin Jeffrys, Thomas Jenkins, Capt. Jennings, "Turn Joe," Queen of Johanna, "Capt. Charles Johnson," Col. Robert Johnson, Robert Johnson, Seignior Jossee, the Kasboo, Lieut. Walter Kennedy, Capt. William Kid, Capt. Kirby, Mr. Knight, Capt. Knot, La Bouse, Sir Nicholas Laws, Capt. Laws, Capt. Lawton, Capt. le Barre, Robert Leonard, Matthieu le Tondu, Capt. Lewis, Lilly, Commodore James Littleton, Capt. Loane, Capt. Loversiene, Capt. Edward ("Ned") Low, Capt. George Lowther, Andian (or Deaan) Lyfouchy, Dennis Macarty, Capt. Mackray, Mafaly, Magnes, Malpa, John Mansfield, Peter Manwaring, Mare, King of Maritan, Mr. Marks, Capt. Marston, Capt. John Martel, Mary, Capt. John Moor, Capt. Montgomery, Moody, Morasab, Humphrey Morrice, Samuel Morwel, the mulatto, Neal, William Noakes, Capt. Nathaniel North, Norton, Mr. Nyn, Samuel Odell, Capt. Chaloner Ogle, Col. Otley, Joseph Palmer, Parker, Payne, James Pease, Ignatius Pell, Maj. Penner, James Philips, William Philips, Philips, Frederick Phillips, Capt. John Phillips, Gen. Phips, John Pinkham, Capt. Plumb, Capt. Plummer, Mr. Plunkett, Pompey the Great, Thomas Porter, Porter, Punt, John Rackam, Harry Ramsey, Mary Read, Thomas Read, Mr. Read, Mrs. Read, George Redding, Col. William Rhet, John Richards, Richards (two), Capt. Roach, Capt. Bartholomew Roberts, Black Robin, Philip Roche (or Roch), Rodrigues, Woodes Rogers (Sr.), Capt. Woodes Rogers, Capt. Rogers, Capt. Rolls, George Rounsivil, Charles Rowling, Mr. Rowry, Charles Russel, Mr. Sale, Capt. Saunders, Capt. Scot, Scot, Peter Scudamore, Capt. John Sharp, John Shattock, Shivers, the Shubander, Simpkins, Simpson (alias "Sim. Tugmutton"), John Sims, Nathan Skiff, Capt. Skinner, Skyrme (or Skyrm), Capt. Smith (two), Capt. Peter Solgard, Thomas Spenlow, Jack Spinckes, Gov. Alexander Spotswood, Capt. Francis

Spriggs, Richard Stanny, Staples, Capt. Stephenson, Ste-
phenson, Isaac Sun, Sutton (alias "Aaron Whifflingpin"),
John Tarlton, Thomas Tarlton, Peter Tartoue, Edward
Teach (alias Edward Thatch or "Blackbeard"), Capt. Thom-
as Tew, Capt. Thomas, Capt. Thompson, Capt. Tillinghaft,
Hosea Tisdell, Capt. Trahern, Elizabeth Trengrove, Capt.
Trengrove, Capt. Trevor, Nicholas Trot, Capt. Tucker,
Tuckerman, Richard Turnley, Capt. Tyzard, Charles Vane,
Ort Van Tyle, Walden, Capt. Wallden, Robert Walter,
Henry White, James White, Capt. Thomas White, Jonathan
Whitfield, Col.. Whitney, Wickam, Capt. Wicksted, Capt.
Willard, Capt. David Williams, Joseph Williams, Capt. Paul
Williams, Paul Williams, William Williams, George Wilson,
Capt. Wilson, Wincon, John Wingfield, Francis Wise, Capt.
Wooley, Capt. Richard Worley, Samuel Wragg, Capt. Wyar,
Yeats, Don Joseph de la Zerda.

Grandison, Richardson. See *Sir Charles Grandison*.

Gulliver's Travels, Swift, 1726. (Original title: *Travels Into Several
Remote Nations of the World*.)
The volume is prefaced by a letter from Captain Lemuel
Gulliver to his cousin Sympson expressing surprise that the
herd of Yahoos has not immediately reformed upon the publication of Gulliver's memoirs.
Part one—"A Voyage to Lilliput." Lemuel Gulliver is educated as a surgeon and settles with his wife in London. On
May 4, 1699, he sets sail as ship's surgeon on the *Antelope*. In
the East Indies the ship is driven by a violent storm to the northwest of Van Diemen's Land, where it is wrecked. Gulliver
swims until he is exhausted, but, just before he gives up, he
discovers that his feet can touch bottom. He makes his way
to shore and falls into an exhausted sleep. When he awakens,
he finds himself tied down by many little threads and discovers
himself beset with hundreds of little people six inches high.
He is addressed in pompous terms by a *Hurgo* (a Lilliputian
lord), and when he tries to free himself he is punished by a
shower of hundreds of little arrows. Finally the little people
feed him and he makes water, to their great astonishment.
The medical men of Lilliput have mingled a sleeping potion

into the hogsheads of wine Gulliver drinks, and while he is
asleep he is conveyed on a flat-bed wagon to the capital,
Mildendo. There he is quartered in an old temple west of the
city (Westminster Abbey?), in which he is once forced to move
his bowels. The emperor, a majestic creature six inches high,
visits him. Gulliver is tormented by the rabble, and the soldiers
push six of them toward him with their pikes. His mercy
towards them wins him favor at court. His pockets are searched,
and the Lilliputians conclude that his watch must be his God,
since he consults it upon all occasions.

In order to obtain a place in the administration, the ministers
of state must cut capers upon a tightrope. They win special
honors by creeping back and forth under a rod held out by
the emperor. Gulliver contrives a little parade ground for the
Lilliputian cavalry by fastening his pocket handkerchief tautly
to nine stakes driven into the ground. The army passes in
review under his legs, and his trousers are in such poor repair
that the soldiers can marvel at the size of his genitals.

Although the vindictive Skyresh Bolgolam opposes it, a
treaty of peace is signed between Gulliver ("the Man-Mountain") and the emperor. Gulliver's friend Reldresal tells him
about court politics. The Tramecksans (Tories) are in the
majority and are truer to the old constitution, but the Slamecks-
sans (Whigs) are more favored by the emperor. The kingdom
of Lilliput is engaged in a bitter war with the neighboring
kingdom of Blefuscu (France) as a result of a religious controversy over whether people should crack their eggs at the
small or the large end.

In order to help the emperor, Gulliver wades over to the
neighboring island of Blefuscu and brings away their fleet,
to their great despair. The emperor of Lilliput makes him a
Nardac on the spot. However, when the emperor asks Gulliver
to subdue the Blefuscans utterly, he refuses, and this action
incurs the emperor's undying enmity. To make things worse,
a fire breaks out in the royal palace and Gulliver, at a loss for
what to do, puts it out by urinating on it. It is illegal to make
water within the precincts of the palace, and the queen refuses
ever to live there again; secretly she vows revenge.

Next follows an account of the social and legal institutions
in Lilliput. The law operates by reward as well as by punishment, and law-abiding citizens receive a cash reward along

with the title of *Snilpall*. In the choice of candidates for public offices, morality is considered more important than talent, since a clever dishonest man can do far more harm to the state than a well-meaning dullard. Parents are not entrusted with bringing up their own children lest they spoil them. Instead, the children are raised in public nurseries, and young noblemen are strictly forbidden the company of servants lest their manners be corrupted. Nursemaids caught spreading old wives' tales are whipped, imprisoned, and banished.

Gulliver describes the ingenious methods by which the Lilliputians feed and clothe him. On one occasion the emperor visits to watch him eat, and Flimnap the treasurer takes the opportunity to hint that Gulliver's tremendous feeding is a prodigious strain on the treasury. Flimnap hates Gulliver because he suspects him of having an affair with his wife (Gulliver denies it) and because Gulliver is a *Nardac* while Flimnap is only a *Clumglum*.

A court friend visits Gulliver to tell him that articles of impeachment have been adopted against him. Flimnap and Skyresh Bolgolam pressed for Gulliver's execution; but because of the merciful interference of Reldresal, the punishment has been reduced to blinding and starvation. Shocked, Gulliver plans his escape, although he says that if he had been more inured to the treachery of courts, he would have submitted with alacrity and readiness to so easy a punishment. He wades over to Blefuscu, where he is cordially received by that emperor.

Gulliver declines to become a Blefuscan ally. Instead, he finds an abandoned ship's boat with which he sets sail, taking some Blefuscan cows and sheep as souvenirs. He is picked up by an English ship and rejoices at the opportunity of returning to England. He moves to a good house in Redriff, helped by a legacy from his uncle John. Soon the wanderlust overcomes him again and he sets sail on June 20, 1702, for Surat.

Part two—"A Voyage to Brobdingnag." The *Adventure* reaches the Pacific and is blown far off course to the northward by a storm. The crew land on a mysterious shore for water, and Gulliver becomes separated from his shipmates. He returns to the beach only to see them rowing madly away before a gigantic figure who is wading after them. Gulliver makes his way into a field of wheat that towers over his head. He is picked up by a husbandman as tall as a church steeple who

is astonished to see such a tiny insect of a man. He is carried
home to the farmer's family, where he sports on the dinner
table. The baby takes him and promptly sticks him in its mouth.
He is disgusted when the nurse suckles the child, since her
nipple is as big as his head.

Gulliver goes to sleep on the wife's bed and is attacked by
two rats as big as mastiffs, one of whom he kills with his sword.
He must ask to be carried outside so he can relieve himself,
which he says he takes note of for the particular benefit of
English scientists, who delight in such anatomical details.

A miserly neighbor hits upon the scheme of exhibiting Gulliver, and so he is taken on an exhausting tour of the neighboring villages, accompanied by the farmer's daughter. This
girl, whom Gulliver calls his *Glumdalclitch*, or "little nurse,"
takes care of him and teaches him the language. Eventually,
after a journey of only three thousand miles, they reach
Lorbrulgrud, the capital. The farmer gives a command per-
formance at court. Gulliver flatters the queen so grossly that
she decides he must be extremely intelligent and asks the farmer
if he will sell him. Since the farmer expects Gulliver to die
soon anyway, he sells him for a thousand pieces of gold.
Glumdalclitch continues at court as his nurse.

The king's learned men refuse to admit that such a creature could
have been produced in the normal course of things and so pro-
nounce Gulliver a "wonder of nature," or exception to all rules.
Gulliver becomes a favored plaything at the king's dinner table.
The king remarks what a contemptible thing human grandeur
is, if humanity can appear in such a ridiculous form.

Life in Brobdingnag proves less than entirely pleasant.
Gulliver is disgusted by a close-up view of the beggars in
the street, with gigantic lice rooting like swine in their flesh.
He also observes a public execution, and the spurt of blood
from the severed carotid artery is as high as the great fountain
at Versailles. The court dwarf (only thirty feet high) conceives
a hatred for Gulliver. He drops him into the cream pitcher,
crams him into a marrow bone, and releases a handful of
gigantic flies under his nose. Gulliver engages a number of
wasps in battle and kills some (their stings are an inch and a
half long).

Gulliver is pelted with falling apples, almost killed by hailstones, and unwillingly retrieved by a cocker spaniel. He falls over a mole hill. He manages to overcome a linnet, but only by great exertion. The maids of honor make him their pet, and one sets him astride one of her nipples (he is repelled by the scent of her skin). He sails a model boat in a contrived horse trough and is attacked by a frog, which he beats with one of his paddles. His most dangerous adventure is being carried away to a rooftop by a court monkey, which stuffs his mouth full of partly digested food. He is narrowly saved by a brave lad who scales the roof. Even more ignominious, Gulliver falls into a cow dung while trying to display his prowess in jumping over it.

The king is a type of the enlightened monarch and questions Gulliver carefully about English institutions. Gulliver gives a detailed description of Parliament, the education of young noblemen, the law, the management of the treasury, the standing army, and the sects in the church. He concludes with a summary of recent English history. The king asks a number of probing questions and concludes that the English legislature is venal, the nobility depraved, and the ministry dominated by jobbery. Laws are written by those who then make a business of distorting them. Recent English history is a spectacle of senseless strife and bloodshed. He concludes that Gulliver's countrymen are "the most pernicious race of little odious vermin that Nature ever suffered to crawl upon the surface of the earth."

Stung to the quick, Gulliver tries to impress the king by describing gunpowder. He offers to impart this secret to the king so that he may become absolute master of the fortunes of his people, but the king declines in dismay. How could such a contemptible race propagate such evil? Gulliver concludes that the king is prejudiced by a provincial education. Indeed, what could be expected of a people such as the Brobdingnagians, whose learning consists entirely of such low subjects as history and morality? They have no notion at all of abstract philosophy. The king even refuses to entrust the government into the hands of specialists. Their laws are limited in length to twenty-two words, and it is a capital offense to write a comment on a law. Nothing could be more different from England.

Gulliver finally makes his escape when the king and queen

make a progress to the country palace at Flanflasnic. Thus he is spared the ignominy of breeding up a race of tame humans as pets (the king is on the lookout for a female of Gulliver's species). Gulliver becomes ill and asks to be taken down to the seaside. Glumdalclitch has a foreboding of evil and weeps at parting from him. Gulliver is set down in his travelling box on the beach and suddenly feels himself being carried away into the air. Overhead he hears the beating of wings and concludes that a gigantic eagle has carried him off. Finally he is let fall and descends with tremendous momentum into the sea. Fortunately his case is of wood and consequently buoyant. Finally he is sighted by an English ship and towed alongside.

Gulliver is astonished at the smallness of the ship's crew. Only with difficulty does he persuade the captain that he is not raving mad. He arrives back in England on June 3, 1706, and almost gets his head broken for yelling at people to get out of his way.

Part three—"A Voyage to Laputa, Balnibarbi, Luggnagg, Glubbdubdrib, and Japan." Gulliver's desire to see foreign parts leads him to enlist on the *Hopewell* as surgeon. They depart August 5, 1706, to trade on the coast of Indochina. While the ship is waiting at Tonkin, Gulliver leads a party of men in the sloop to trade along the coast. They are captured by Japanese pirates, among whom is a rascally Dutchman who urges that the English dogs be tied back to back and thrown into the sea. Fortunately the heathens prove to be more merciful than this alleged Christian. Gulliver, however, is abandoned to his fate in a small boat. He sustains himself by rowing about among small rocky islands and eating birds' eggs.

Suddenly the sun is darkened, and Gulliver sees that a flying island is hovering directly overhead. He is taken up into it by a chain, where he discovers that the inhabitants of Laputa are totally absorbed in abstract speculations about mathematics and music. One of their eyes is permanently pointed upward, the other turned around and directed straight inward. Each Laputan gentleman must have a "flapper," a man with an empty bladder full of dried peas who recalls him to attention when it is time for him to speak. Since Gulliver knows nothing about their two favorite subjects, Laputans form a very low opinion of his intelligence. The Laputan women do not share the interests of their husbands, however, and they carry on with the servants, unnoticed by their ivory-tower spouses. The wife of the prime minister once slipped down to the subject island of Balnibarbi, where she lavished her fortune on an old deformed footman who beat her every day.

The island is able to fly because of the operation of a gigantic magnet mounted in a cave deep in the bowels of the island. The entire practical side of life is neglected, and their buildings are all lopsided because of their contempt for any applied science. They spend their time worrying about whether the earth will fall into the sun. Finally Gulliver has had enough and goes down to Balnibarbi. When the inhabitants of this island refuse to pay their taxes, the king either deprives them of sun and rain or lowers the island to crush them. (Many readers see in this passage an allegorical treatment of England's Irish policy.)

The entire economy of Balnibarbi has been wrecked by modern managerial science. Only the estate of Lord Munodi (Swift's friend Robert Harley) is flourishing, but soon he too will have to tear down his ancestral mansion and redesign his farming methods according to current theory. The government experts have already forced Munodi to relocate his grain mill high on a mountainside, under the theory that water pumped up to that height will descend with greater force and drive the mill better.

Gulliver visits the great Academy of Lagado (a parody of the Royal Academy in London), where he finds a crew of mad scientists busy with many projects. Swift is attacking two aspects of modern scientism here. The first is crazy laboratory schemes, the second the distortion of traditional literary culture. One "projector" in the Academy is extracting sunlight from cucumbers; another is resolving human ordure into its original ingredients. A blind man is distinguishing colors by feel and smell, and an agricultural expert is planning to have fields plowed by hogs; first acorns are buried in the earth, and then hogs are turned into the field to root about. One projector is feeding brightly colored flies to spiders so that they may spin colored cloth, while a medical man is attempting to revive a dead dog by blowing air up its anus with a bellows.

In the linguistic division, a famous professor has constructed a "language frame," a device by which many little dice with words printed on the sides are arranged arbitrarily to form sentences. Thus books can be produced without the fatigue

of studying.   A team of linguists is making language more
succinct by leaving out all the words except nouns.   A scheme
is also afoot to replace words altogether with things, and the
most advanced practitioners carry around immense sacks of
objects with which they hold silent discourse.   (This passage
is Swift's dig at the Royal Society for its attack on eloquence.)
An educational expert is carrying on instruction in mathematics
by printing formulas on wafers and having the students eat
them.

The most absurd projects of all, says Gulliver, are the
political ones, that is, schemes to inject honesty into public
affairs.   Some planners want to strengthen the memory of
public officials so that they will keep their promises, reconcile
party differences by brain surgery, and raise money by taxing
sexual prowess.   Conspiracies against the state can be detected
by examining the fecal matter of politicians, say the scientists.
Gulliver responds by revealing the security measures in the
kingdom of "Tribnia" (i.e., Britain), where seemingly harmless
private correspondence is seen to conceal a mass of dangerous
information.   (This passage was considered so sensitive po-
litically that the printer omitted it from the first edition.)

While waiting to depart for Luggnagg, Gulliver makes a
side trip to Glubbdubdrib, where the king is a magician and
the servants are ghosts summoned up from the dead for a
three-months' stay.   After conquering his initial squeamishness,
Gulliver has many of the great men of history called up for
his pleasure.   The Senate of Rome appears like an assembly of
demigods, compared to a degenerate modern parliament.   Gulliver also learns about the unreliability of the approved historical
traditions; great national heroes were often in reality the worst
scoundrels of their time.   He amuses himself with inspecting the
entire lineage of some noble families and observing how often a
diseased line has been renewed only by secret liaisons with coach-
men and page boys.

Gulliver proceeds to Luggnagg, where he is favored with a
special audience before the emperor.   He is required to crawl upon
his belly and lick the floor as he advances toward the throne, but
as a special favor the floor is swept before his arrival.   The most
striking feature of Luggnagg is the Struldbruggs, or "Immortals,"
of whom there are only eleven hundred in the whole kingdom.
From time to time a child is born with a red spot over the left
eyebrow, a sure sign that it will never die.   Gulliver is enraptured

with the blessed state of a kingdom with such a supply of venerable counselors. He spins fantasies how, if he were a Struldbrugg, he would amass great wealth and master all the arts and sciences. He is heavily disillusioned, however, when he meets some of these immortals. They are subject to all the infirmities of age, but added to this is the curse of never being able to die, but sinking deeper and deeper into senility. They are barred from holding property, and their greed and peevishness makes them despised. After they reach eighty, their marriages (should they be married to another Struldbrugg) are dissolved, since those who are condemned to remain forever on earth should not have their misery doubled by the load of a wife. Because of the Struldbruggs, Luggnagg is the only land on earth where the people are free from an irrational clinging to life.

Having traveled to Japan, Gulliver goes to see the emperor. He passes himself off as a Dutch merchant, since no other nationality is allowed into Japan. He asks to be allowed to dispense with the usual ceremony of trampling on the crucifix. This request arouses the emperor's suspicions, since no Dutchman has ever made such a request. He begins to suspect that Gulliver is no Dutchman, but rather a Christian. However, the emperor grants the request as a special favor. Gulliver sails safely to Amsterdam and from there to London, arriving in the Downs on April 10, 1710.

Part four—"A Voyage to the Country of the Houyhnhnms." On September 7, 1710, Gulliver sets out again, this time as captain of his own ship. While he is cruising in the West Indies, several of his men die of fevers; so he takes on extra crewmen. This decision turns out to be a disastrous error, since the new men are former buccaneers and corrupt the rest of the crew. In the South Seas, the men mutiny and set Gulliver ashore.

While making his way upland, he sees in the fields certain repulsive creatures which look oddly human. When one approaches too close, Gulliver whacks it with the flat of his sword, whereupon a number of them climb trees and drop turds on his head. Fortunately they are frightened off by the approach of a dapple-gray horse. Another horse, a bay, approaches, and Gulliver sees that they are actually speaking to each other. To his astonishment, Gulliver finds that the rational creatures in the country are in fact horses (called *Houyhnhnms*, or "perfection of nature"), while the disgusting beasts he at first encountered are degenerate humanoids called Yahoos.

The horse family with which Gulliver stays is unsure whether he is a Yahoo or not, since he wears clothes, a thing they have never seen before, and refuses to eat rotten ass's flesh like the Yahoos. Finally a servant-nag discovers Gulliver sleeping partly undressed, and the horses see that he is a true Yahoo. He must now explain how European society can be managed by such degenerate creatures as Yahoos. How can Gulliver explain the treachery of his crew, when the Houyhnhnms have no conception of evil? His Houyhnhnm master constantly suspects him of "saying the thing which is not" (they have no word for "lying.") Only with great difficulty can the Houyhnhnm understand either crime or law. If men claim to be reasonable, laws should be unnecessary, since nature and reason alone should be enough to direct a rational creature.

Gulliver explains war to his master and the various pretexts under which it is waged. When the Houyhnhnm professes disbelief at the number of people killed in European conflicts, Gulliver is forced to explain guns and bombs, which gives the horse an "uneasy feeling in his mind." He is equally confused at hearing that men can be "ruined at law," and so Gulliver explains the knavish practices of lawyers and judges, who are so used to injustice that they will refuse a bribe from the side on which justice lies rather than run the risk of disobliging their colleagues.

Gulliver goes on to explain money and greed, and how thousands of men must labor to support the luxury of one. He describes the depraved appetite in England for exotic foods and wines and the diseases of over-indulgence brought on by them. The Houyhnhnm assumes that Gulliver is a nobleman because of his healthy complexion, but Gulliver assures him that the true mark of the European nobility is physical degeneracy, brought on by hereditary venereal disease.

The Houyhnhnm admits that European Yahoos may have a pittance of reason. Hence they are even worse than the bestial Yahoos, since they can devise new methods of aggravating their natural vices and even create new vices. He then describes the behavior of the Yahoos in Houyhnhnmland, which corresponds in every detail with what Gulliver has just finished saying about the Europeans. The Yahoos love to heap up shining stones, and they suck on the juice of a certain root to drive them out of their senses. They hate each other, as no other animals do. The Yahoo king is the most deformed of the herd, and the Yahoo chief minister, upon being discharged from office, is covered with the dung of the entire tribe. The Yahoos even experience depressions (the only remedy is hard work) and diseases of repletion (the best cure is a mixture of dung and urine forced down the animal's throat). They have every vice except homosexuality, which Gulliver admits is a European innovation.

Gulliver at length is brought to realize that he also is a Yahoo, since while bathing he is attacked and passionately embraced by a young Yahoo girl. Nevertheless, he wants to remain forever in the land of the Houyhnhnms, because their commonwealth is so perfectly governed by reason. They have intercourse often enough to produce only one child of each sex, and they come together again only in the case that one child dies. They show other people's children as much affection as they show their own. They cannot imagine how a conflict of opinions can exist, since where one is unsure one must remain silent. Every four years they hold a congress, at which the only point debated is whether or not to exterminate the Yahoo race.

Gulliver lives happily in Houyhnhnmland, subsisting on oatmeal and free from European corruptions, but the Houyhnhnm assembly decides he must leave lest he become a leader of the Yahoo herd and foment a rebellion. In great sorrow, he builds a canoe out of Yahoo skins and Yahoo tallow, using the skins of young Yahoos for the sails. His fellow-servant, the sorrel nag, wishes him farewell, and his master is so good as to raise his hoof for Gulliver to kiss.

Gulliver makes his way to the shore of New Holland, where he is attacked by savages and wounded with an arrow. Having paddled out to sea, he sights a European ship and hastens back to the island, preferring the company of savages to Europeans with their refined vices. The sailors capture him, however, and bring him on board. Gulliver churlishly rejects the kind attentions of the Portuguese captain, Pedro de Mendez. The ship reaches Lisbon, and Gulliver can only gradually accustom himself to looking out of doors at Europeans. Mendez eventually persuades Gulliver to return home, and so he takes ship and arrives in London on December 5, 1715.

He can hardly bear the sight of his wife, still less the thought that he has actually copulated with a Yahoo and produced cubs. He buys two stallions and spends four hours a day talking to them. The only Yahoo whose company he can bear is the groom, because of the agreeable odor that clings to him. Gulliver justifies himself

for not having laid claim to his new-found lands, since the plantation of colonies is normally accompanied by a massacre of the
natives. Finally he insists that any Yahoo having the least trace
of the idious vice of pride should remain out of his sight.

Agrippa, Queen Anne, Aristotle, Balmuff, James Bates,
John Biddle, Emperor of Blefuscu, the Bliffmarklub of Lugg-
nagg, Skyresh Bolgolam, King of Brobdingnag, Queen of
Brobdingnag, Edmund Burton, Mary Burton, (Julius)
Caesar, Clustril, Ferdinando Cortez, Dampier, Drunlo,
Dutchman, the queen's dwarf, farmer in Brobdingnag,
Flimnap, Lady Flimnap, Clefren Frelock, Marsi Frelock,
Glumdalclitch, Golbasto Momaren Evlame Gurdilo Shefin
Mully Ully Gue (Emperor of Lilliput), Betty Gulliver, John
Gulliver, Johnny Gulliver, Capt. Lemuel Gulliver, Mr. Gul-
liver, Homer, Emperor of Japan, Lalcon, King of Laputa,
Prince of Lilliput, Queen of Lilliput, Limtoc, King of Lugg-
nagg, Pedro de Mendez, Herman Moll, Lord Munodi, Capt.
John Nicholas, Abraham Pannell, Calin Deffar Plune, Capt.
Pocock, William Prichard, Robert Purefoy, Reldresal, Wil-
liam Robinson, Richard Sympson, Theodorus Vangrult,
James Welch, Thomas Wilcocks, Peter Williams.

John Gow, Defoe, 1725. (Original title: *An Account of the Conduct
and Proceedings of the late John Gow.*)

This narrative is mainly concerned with the capture of a
pirate band by a group of private citizens. The Scotsman John
Gow is frustrated in his first attempt to foment a mutiny while
on a Lisbon cruise. He then ships with Capt. Ferneau on a
voyage to Barbary. He joins with two desperate rogues named
Petersen and Winter to spread discontent about the food among
the men. They first affront the captain while he is entertaining
merchants on board. Repeated defiance from Petersen alarms the
captain and makes him resolve to barricade himself in the great
cabin, but unfortunately he relies on Gow for help. Five of the
mutineers surprise the surgeon, chief mate, and supercargo in
their hammocks and cut their throats. They then overwhelm the
captain, murder him, and throw his body over the side. They persuade or compel the remainder of the crew to join them and "go
on the account."

After capturing a few fishing vessels and extorting provisions
on the island of Madeira, they encounter a French merchantman

who is too strong to attack. Lieut. Williams goes beserk, accuses Gow of cowardice, and attempts to persuade the crew to attack the Frenchman anyway. He snaps a pistol at Gow and then runs into the powder room to blow up the ship. Finally the men subdue him. He is already roundly hated because of his bloodthirstiness, and so they deliver him up to a Bristol vessel so that he can be taken back to England and hanged as a pirate.

The crew are undecided where to sail; so Gow persuades them to go to Scotland, where he intends to plunder his own country. They arrive at Carristown in the Orkneys. While the ship is being careened, one of their captives escapes and alarms the countryside; ten other prisoners make away with the longboat. The pirates attack the house of the sheriff of Grahamsey, Mr. Honnyman, but his wife escapes with the family gold. They sail to the island of Eda at the opposite end of the part of the archipelago where the alarm has been raised, to plunder the estate of Mr. Fea, an old school chum of Gow's.

The ship goes aground, and Gow is forced to ask Fea for a boat to bring them off. Fea is shrewd enough to have his boat staved. Five men and the boatswain go ashore to search for another boat, but Fea entices them to an alehouse where they are captured by some of his tenants. Meanwhile Gow's ship is blown even harder aground, and he has to come ashore and negotiate with Mr. Fea for help. Fea's retainers rashly allow Mr. Scollary to go aboard the *Revenge* as a hostage, but Fea nevertheless takes Gow prisoner. The pirates remaining on the ship are demoralized and have lost the will to resist and so they go ashore and give themselves up, not even taking revenge on Mr. Scollary. Defoe remarks that Heaven must have marked out the rogues for destruction, since it made them so stupid that five or six country fellows could capture the whole crew of twenty-four.

When the frigate *Greyhound* carries the band to London, they find their old crony Williams waiting for them in chains. Five of the crew turn state's evidence. The men who went along only out of compulsion are acquitted. Gow himself is sullen and is induced to plead only by the threat of being pressed to death. He and Williams are both hanged. The rope breaks under Gow's weight, and so he has to be hanged twice before his body is displayed on the river-bank to rot.

James Belvin, William Booth, Capt. Bowler, Capt. Cross, George Dobson, Mr. Fea, Mrs. Fea, Mr. Fea of Whitehall,

Capt. Oliver Ferneau, governor at Porto Santa, John Gow,
Mr. Honnyman, Mrs. Honnyman, James Laing, Lumsdale,
Macauley, Melvin, Timothy Murphy, Panton, Petersen,
John Phinnes, Robert Read, Rowlinson, Scollary, John
Somerville, Archibald Sutor, Lieut. Williams, Winter,
Thomas Wise.

Jonathan Wild, Defoe, 1725. (Original title: *The True, Genuine, and
Perfect Account of the Life and Actions of Jonathan Wild*.)
Wild was the most notorious fence and informer of his age and
was called the "thieftaker-general of England." He was born in
Wolverhampton, Staffordshire, in 1683 and hanged in 1725 at the
age of forty-two. After being apprenticed to a buckle maker, Wild
comes up to London as a servant and falls in with a prostitute and
thief, Mary Milliner, whom he takes as his consort, although he
already has one wife and child. (Eventually Wild has six wives, all
living simultaneously.) He goes with Mary "upon the twang" (on
her rounds as a streetwalker) to protect her from obstreperous
customers. He drifts into a career as a fence but soon finds he can
make more money from honest citizens by getting back their stolen
goods (for a price). Since his clearinghouse for hot items performs a
public service, he is countenanced by the public and government
for ten years. He leads young men into careers of crime so that he
can live off their winnings, and from time to time he puts the finger
on one of them for the reward. He is believed to have the blood
of 120 men on his hands.

One of Wild's most skilled employees is "Skull" Dean, who is
finally arrested and hanged despite an attempt to escape while going
to the "necessary-house" (bathroom). Wild takes up with Mrs.
Dean, and Defoe forbears suggesting that Wild was behind Skull's
arrest. Soon Mrs. Dean has the misfortune of having lost two
husbands on the gallows, first Dean and then Wild himself.

Defoe introduces two dramatized incidents to illustrate Wild's
knowledge of the underworld, his method of maneuvering the
customer into paying a higher price for his own goods, and his
seeming disingenuousness. The first incident is Defoe's own visit
to Wild to recover a silver-hilted sword; a longer incident recounts
a lady's visit to get back a diamond watch.

Finally Wild's crimes begin to catch up with him. Joseph Blake,
alias "Blueskin," assaults him in court and cuts his throat, almost
killing him. Then Parliament passes a law which is aimed specifically at Wild and which makes it a felony to accept a reward for

returning stolen goods, knowing them to be stolen. Wild refuses to restrain his operation. He is arrested and condemned but continues to direct his criminal empire from within Newgate prison. Although he is curious about life after death, he seems utterly unaffected by religious reflections. In a fit of sudden despair he attempts suicide by taking liquid laudanum, but the guards make him vomit it up again. On May 24, 1725, he makes his journey to Tyburn. The London mob usually sympathizes with condemned criminals, but today they pelt Wild with filth and threaten to tear him apart on his way to the scaffold.

Councillor Daniel, Mary Dean, "Skull" Dean, M(o)ll K(i)ng, Lynx, Elizabeth Man, Mary Milliner, Judith Nun, Sarah Parrin, Katherine Stetham, Mr. Tidman, Andrew Wild, John Wild, Jonathan Wild.

A Journal of the Plague Year, Defoe, 1722.

This book is allegedly the diary of Mr. H. F., a saddler who lived just outside of Aldgate during the plague. The first rumors that the plague has reached Holland are heard in September, 1664. At the beginning of December two Frenchmen die of plague in Drury Lane; but the infection does not spread, and the fears of the city are quieted. Disquieting signs continue, however. An unusual number of deaths occur in January, 1665, and the month of April brings the first plague death within the walls of the city itself. By May it is apparent that many deaths have been concealed by knavery and collusion. June brings hot weather and a dramatic upsurge in the death toll.

The better sort now begin to flee the city in droves, and many streets are totally deserted except for a watchman guarding the abandoned houses. By summer 200,000 people have fled and 10,000 houses stand empty. The saddler at first wants to flee too and is advised to do so by his brother, who has already sent his wife and children into Bedfordshire. But his attempts are repeatedly frustrated, first by difficulties in hiring a horse and then by the disappearance of a servant. He interprets these events as signs from God that he should stay and mind his shop. One morning he turns by accident to the 91st Psalm: "Surely He shall deliver thee from the snare of the fowler, and from the noisome pestilence." So he decides to remain.

This outbreak of plague is particularly severe because of the mushroom growth of London after Charles II's restoration in

1660. The city has 100,000 ribbon weavers alone (according to the saddler) to supply the luxury of the court. The saddler thinks that the plague may be a judgment of God for the sinfulness of Charles's court, which removes to Oxford for safety.

Before the plague truly breaks out, the common people are disturbed by a comet in the sky and by dreams of old women. In March an angel clothed in white with a sword is seen in the sky threatening the city. (The saddler sees only a cloud with the sun on one side.) In Bishopsgate churchyard a ghost is allegedly seen indicating that many plague victims will be carried there for burial. Astrologers note an ominous conjunction of planets. Quack doctors prey upon the people, and later the plague sweeps many of these swindlers away since they have been so foolish as to depend on their own remedies. One physician relies so heavily on liquor as a prophylaxis that he has remained a sot to this day. The saddler scornfully rejects the theory that the disease is caused by microorganisms; instead he favors the theory that the effluvia from sick bodies spread the infection.

Meanwhile the city administration is at work. Days of fasting and prayer are proclaimed, and the churches are jammed. The College of Physicians publishes recipes for cheap plague remedies for the use of the poor. Large coal fires are kept burning to keep off the infection. Some experts oppose this practice since plague spreads best in warm weather, but the saddler agrees with those who think that the fires help to dry moist and unwholesome humors out of the air. In July the Lord Mayor and Aldermen issue an order for shutting up houses in case even a single person living there is infected. A red cross with "Lord Have Mercy Upon Us!" is to be painted on the door.

This last regulation causes much dispute and suffering since remaining in an infected house may mean death for every member of the family. People are driven to breaking out and running about the streets spreading the infection. A number of watchmen appointed to guard the houses are assaulted, and one is even blown up with gunpowder. Terrible rumors fill the city about patients smothered by their nurses, but the saddler dismisses these as unfounded. Finally in the month of July the deaths come so frequently that the parish churches leave off tolling the bells and the corpses have to be gathered up in large carts appointed for the purpose.

The saddler keeps healthy by remaining at home and living off his provisions rather than sending his servants out frequently to shop. But sometimes his curiosity drives him out. He visits the great burial pit at Aldgate Church. (His friend the sexton procures admission for him.) There he finds a man walking about and moaning. The dead cart approaches loaded with bodies, and the man faints on seeing the corpses of his family shot indiscriminately into a mass grave. He must be carried into the Pie Tavern across the way to recover. The saddler accompanies him and finds a group of rowdies there, drinking and mocking the people going to prayer service. The saddler rebukes them for their impiety in such a terrible time but receives only abuse for his trouble. He goes home and prays that their hearts may be moved to repentance. A few days later he hears the news that the entire party of revellers has died of the plague.

Efforts to contain the plague to London are not entirely successful. One infected man breaks out of his house and makes his way to Islington, where he takes lodging in an inn. The next morning he is found dead in his bed, and several employees at the inn soon succumb. The most dangerous form of the infection is that which remains hidden until it suddenly brings death. People are overcome in the streets and sink down and die in doorways. But the sick person has a much better chance if the infected matter draws together into a bubo in the groin or armpit. This sore may break and run, thus relieving the patient. One man driven mad by pain jumps naked into the Thames and swims across. The cold water and violent exercise make his buboes drain so that he recovers.

Life in time of plague is not all grim, of course. Once the saddler goes to visit his absent brother's warehouse in Swan Alley. On the way he notices a large number of women in new hats, and upon arriving he finds that the warehouse is being looted. Everyone in the neighborhood is wearing one of his brother's hats. The saddler also tells the story of the piper who used to beg his way about the pubs but who has fallen upon hard times with the plague. One evening he has a drop too much and lies down to sleep on a bulk, only to be taken up and put into one of the dead-carts. Before he can be shoveled into a grave pit he wakes up and cries out from the middle of the pile, sending the men dashing madly off in terror.

After fourteen days' confinement in his house, the saddler goes out for a walk. He sees a purse of money lying abandoned in a courtyard. Three men take it up but only after burning it with gunpowder and dunking it into a bucket of water to remove the contagion. Continuing his walk through the eastern suburbs, he comes to Blackwall Stairs. Here he encounters a poor waterman forced to remain in the city to support his wife and two children. The man's wife and only child are already ill, and so he dare not come into their presence. The saddler is moved by the waterman's loyalty and realizes he himself has been presuming upon the protection of Providence. He gives the man four shillings and has himself rowed out to view the vast number of ships full of refugees anchored in the Pool. He sees some floating coffins driven back and forth by the tide.

There is a long story of three brothers, Thomas the sailmaker, John the baker, and Richard the joiner, all from Wapping. Since business is bad and they are still in health, they leave the infected city and go tenting until the plague subsides. In the fields they are joined by thirteen other refugees. They are barred from passing through Walthamstow (then far out in the country) by anxious constables. John is a former soldier and has the people make dummy rifles and plant campfires far apart so they can pass themselves off as a host three hundred strong. They bluff the townspeople out of provisions and make their way toward Epping, where they encamp. Their singing psalms on the sabbath makes a good impression on the country people, who supply them with food until December, when the infection slackens and they can return home.

Not all fugitives prosper so well; many of them die miserably in holes and huts, and many villages around London come to be infected by the higglers who carry goods up to London. Consequently many country people treat Londoners with great cruelty, even though they make their living from the city. There are reports that plague victims behave like mad dogs, willfully infecting others. One plague sufferer forcibly kisses a young gentlewoman, literally scaring her to death. Another man goes visiting an unsuspecting family in his delirium, forcing them to fill the house with smoke to disinfect it. The only man who can sense whether the plague is among a seemingly healthy company is an old soldier whose wound begins to smart when a sick person is near.

The city fathers appoint examiners to find out infected houses, but this policy has little success. In August the saddler himself is assigned the disagreeable job of examiner but manages to buy a substitute within three weeks. One man ingeniously eludes the examiners by making a red cross with "Lord have mercy upon us!" and affixing it to his door himself.

The plague finally rages with such fury that the people give up all efforts to check it. Rumor has it that three thousand people die in one night between the hours of one and three in the morning. The total official body count for the plague year is 68,590, but the saddler estimates it nearer 100,000, since the number of people taken up at night was probably never recorded in the official Bills of Mortality.

Since all efforts are unavailing, people again return to public worship. Since some pulpits have been left vacant by the official tenants, Dissenting ministers deprived by the Act of Uniformity are recalled to preach. The saddler remarks that another year of plague would "scum the gall from our temper" and make us again united in religion. When the plague ends, the Church-of-England preachers return and begin anew to persecute the Dissenters. The Dissenters likewise blame the priests, and many doctors are taunted for having fled the city. The saddler disapproves of all such wrangling. No one need be ashamed for having fled from the avenging hand of God, and some who appeared brave may have been merely rash or ignorant. The common people who carted off the dead are the only ones who should be commended, since they alone understood the full extent of their danger.

The suffering caused by the disease is so intense that one man burns himself up in his bed to escape the torment and others dance deliriously in the streets. Sometimes even the drivers of the dead-carts and the bellmen drop down dead in their work and the carts overturn, spilling the corpses into the street. And yet trade continues. The richer employers keep their men working right through the infection, anticipating an upsurge in demand after it subsides. And the Fire of London the following year creates an unprecedented demand for replacement goods, so that the seven years after these twin disasters are extremely prosperous for England.

During the last week of September the plague abruptly begins to subside. The saddler's friend Dr. Heath notes that whereas before two out of three patients died, now it is only two out of five, and whereas before the plague killed in two to three days, now it takes eight to ten, if indeed the patient dies at all. As soon as this news spreads, the poor begin to behave with great abandon, crowding together into public places. People from the country flood back into the metropolis, disregarding the warnings of physicians and ministers. Accordingly the death rolls lengthen again, and even many of those who do not die fall ill and curse their recklessness. John Cock the barber comes back to town prematurely and is wiped out along with his entire family. The court begins to return at Christmas, but many of the nobles don't come up to town until much later. The citizens sweeten their houses by burning perfume or even gunpowder. Some people accidentally burn their houses down, and one man blows up his own roof.

The common poeple greet one another again in the streets and shout the good news back and forth across the narrow alleys. Many actually reform their ways for the time being, and the saddler notes less public drunkenness. With time, however, the people return to their old ways; they sing God's praise but soon forget his works.

Alderman of Portsoken Ward, Dr. Berwick, Dr. Brooks, brother of the saddler, Sir Robert Clayton, John Cock, Constable of Walthamstow, Sir Charles Doe, Solomon Eagle, Mr. H. F. (the saddler), Ford, John Hayward, Mrs. Hayward, Dr. Heath, Dr. Hodges, John the biscuit maker, Sir John Lawrence, the piper, Rachel, Richard the joiner, Robert the waterman, sexton in Aldgate Church, Thomas the sailmaker, Dr. Upton, Sir George Waterman.

The King of Pirates, Defoe, 1719. (Often called *Captain Avery.*)

The story is told in two letters from Avery. He has been bred to the sea and is cutting logwood in Central America when he falls in with a pirate named Nichols, nicknamed "Capt. Redhand" because of his bloodthirsty treatment of prisoners. They set out to plunder the Spanish Main and soon capture a large ship with a Quaker skipper off Florida and a sloop off Santo Domingo (1690). They sail south to avoid the sultry weather and lay in a cargo of penguin meat off the Penguin Islands. Having sailed round the Horn, they find slim pickings because a band of English desperadoes under one Guilotte has alarmed the whole coast. Finally they capture a Spanish treasure ship. A friar on board tries to dissuade them from taking the silver plate since it has been consecrated to the Blessed Virgin, but the English heretics are hardly moved by such a plea. In this battle Capt. Redhand's head is torn off by a cannon ball, but none of his crew is sorry.

On the island of Juan Fernandez they fall in with the pirate Guilotte, with whom they make common cause. In order to prevent fights they rule that whoever gambles shall forfeit his share of the booty, which Avery duly puts up in little chests. The pirates discover that none of them can trust the others; if anyone returned to civilization, he might betray the others to save his own skin. So they decide to start a colony on Madagascar, which according to an old sailor is well suited because the climate is good and the blacks are easily terrified.

Guilotte's band has meanwhile departed in the frigate (Redhand's original vessel) to seek more plunder, and so Avery leaves a lead tablet on Juan Fernandez to direct him and sets sail around the Horn with the large ship and the sloop. On April 7, 1693, they reach Madagascar. The large ship is wrecked on the rocks, but the men all land safely. Once the encampment has been made Avery lays plans to leave his men and "go on the account" again, but he hides his intentions behind a seeming desire to stay on Madagascar and guard his share of the booty. At length he "allows" himself to be talked into taking the sloop along with forty picked men to fetch another ship. On January 3, 1694, he sets out.

Some of the men make their way to the English colonies in North America, where they disperse. Avery gets to London, where he tries to use his ill-gotten gains to buy another ship. He has almost closed the deal on *The Griffin* when the owner decides not to sell because his wife has bad dreams about the transaction. At last Avery has to ship as first mate on another vessel along with his men. Off the coast of Spain they mutiny, set the captain ashore, and set out for Madagascar, which they reach after a three years' absence. There they find that other pirates have come to swell the colony. Soon the raiders in the frigate from the Spanish main arrive, directed by the lead tablet.

Avery goes to cruise in the Bay of Bengal. Off Sumatra they learn that the daughter of the Grand Mogul is on her way to marry the King of Pegu. They sight the ships and capture them easily, since the Indian sailors are terrified by the pirates. Avery bursts into the princess's cabin with his saber but denies reports that he ravished her. She was certainly terrified, but he took only her jewels, not her virginity. He admits that each member of the princess's large retinue was lain with four or five times by the pirates, but asserts that the young ladies were quite willing. Unfortunately the ship is loaded with arrack punch, and the pirates stay drunk so long that six or seven either fall overboard and drown or fall into raging tropical fevers and die.

Avery returns to Madagascar. His men have now become even more ruthless and are willing to prey even on their countrymen. One day Avery sees a large party of English and Dutch sailors coming ashore. He emerges suddenly from the bushes with his men and gets the drop on them. They have, of course, heard a great deal about the famous Capt. Avery. He tells them that he has thousands of men at his disposal and expects to be offered a pardon by the queen, which he would gladly accept and even pay handsomely for. He then lets the sailors go, confident that the tale will not lose in the telling. From this incident springs the false tale that the pirates once offered the queen ten million pounds for a pardon and were turned down, asserts Avery. In fact his peak strength was six hundred and the colony was down to 108 by the time he left.

In a second confidential letter Avery tells how he sneaks away from his own colony with a picked crew of thirteen. Seven of the band leave the main group and are eventually picked up by a Portuguese ship. Back in Lisbon, they are swindled of their booty by the knavish captain, who threatens to turn them in as pirates if they complain to the authorities.

Avery and the rest of the men make their way laden with immense wealth to Baghdad, where they disguise themselves as Persian merchants. Avery and a trusted companion buy a cargo of European goods and set off with Indian guides for Ispahan, in Persia. The Persians despise Indians, however, and so Avery finds himself ill-received. He and his friend dismiss the guides with three dollars apiece, but the guides in revenge set the village afire. Avery would have been torn apart by the angry villagers if he had not captured one of the arsonists and turned him over to the people. He is enormously impressed by the even-handed justice of the Persian official, the *cadi*, who prevents a lynching. Then the Indian escapes from prison, and the *cadi* levies a heavy fine on the town for allowing justice to miscarry.

Avery and his comrade make their way across Persia, staying at fine inns set up by the Shah. They decline the trip through Russia because of the barbarity of the natives there and instead make their way across terrible deserts to Constantinople, where Avery is still residing incognito.

    Capt. Avery, Capt. Goignet, Capt. Guillaume, Guilotte,
    Capt. Hawkins, Mr. Johnson, Macmow, "Capt. Redhand"
    (Nichols), Capt. "Bat" Sharp, Snelgrove.

The Life of John Sheppard, Defoe, 1724. (Original title: *The History of the Remarkable Life of John Sheppard*.)

Sheppard was one of the most notorious criminals and escape artists of Defoe's day. This pamphlet was published after Sheppard's

second escape, when any story about him had high news value.
Sheppard was born in 1702 and was later apprenticed to a good old
carpenter, Mr. Wood, from whom he learned the skills he later
needed for his escapes. As a very young man he turns bad and
fells Mrs. Wood with a stick. He then takes up with a prostitute,
Elizabeth Lyon, alias "Edgworth Bess." He robs some of Mr. Wood's
customers and then goes on to burglary with such notorious felons
as Joseph Blake, alias "Blueskin," and James Sykes, alias "Hell and
Fury." Defoe provides abundant detail about Sheppard's crimes,
with the names of his victims and his manner of robbing them. One
Mr. Kneebone sets the thieftaker Jonathan Wild on Sheppard's trail.
Sheppard and Bess are captured, confined to New Prison, and condemned to death. When the guards advise him to use his remaining
time well, he promises that he will. He files the bars of his prison
and perpetrates an almost miraculous escape, taking Bess along
with him. Mr. Kneebone is naturally terrified for his life.

Sheppard is soon back in business. This time he is apprehended
by Newgate officials with stolen goods on his person. He is again
condemned to death, but the jailers make the mistake of leaving
him alone in his cell. He opens a series of padlocks with an ordinary
nail and passes through a series of six heavily bolted doors, one
of which has not been opened for seven years. He then makes his
way over the rooftops, through the window of a nearby house,
downstairs, and out the front door. The Newgate officials are
scandalized and are naturally suspected of bribery. "One file's worth
all the Bibles in the world," quips Sheppard, who at the time of
publication is still at large.

William Austin, Mr. Bains, Ballard, Mr. Barton, Benson, Mr.
Bird, Justice Blackerby, Joseph Blake (alias "Blueskin"), Mr.
Brown, Mrs. Brown, Mr. Carter, Mr. Charles, Mr. Cole-
theart, Mrs. Mary Cook, Lumley Davis, Mr. Dobbins, Wil-
liam Field, Mr. Figg, Sir Frances Forbes, Stephen Fowles,
Capt. Geary, Mr. Gough, Charles Grace, James Harman,
Mr. Ireton, Mrs. Kendrick, Mr. Kneebone, Anthony Lamb,
Langley, Elizabeth Lyon (alias "Edgworth Bess"), Mr.
Marten, Justice Newton, William Page, Mr. Panton, Mr.
Pargitter, Justice Parry, William Phillips, Mr. Pitt, Mr.
Price, Mr. Purney, Quilt, Mr. Robins, Sarah, John Sheppard,
Thomas Sheppard, Tabitha Skymmington, James Sykes
(alias "Hell and Fury"), Anthony Upton, Rev. Mr. Wagstaff,
Justice Walters, Joseph Ward, Jonathan Wild, Mr. Wood,
Mrs. Wood.

Madagscar; Or, Robert Drury's Journal, Defoe. See *Robert Drury's Journal*.

The Mechanical Operation of the Spirit, Swift, 1704. (Published with *A Tale of a Tub* as *A Discourse Concerning the Mechanical Operation of the Spirit*.)

This piece is not a narrative, but should perhaps be seen as one of the treatises Swift had promised at the beginning of the *Tale*. It is another attack on the claims of the Dissenters to a special inspiration and follows the popular "letter to a friend" formula. The first section opens with a comparison between Mohammed's mounting to heaven on an ass and the Dissenters' pretending to be inspired by God. They have been laying claim to "inspiration" so long that the fraud has become second nature, and they almost believe it themselves. As in the *Tale*, Swift goes through the forms of a learned discourse, laboriously (and ironically) refuting those divines who assert that the Spirit cannot be truly present among the Dissenters. He compares them to a group of Irish peasants nodding over a pipe of tobacco.

Section two traces the true origin of enthusiasm. In fact, fanatic preaching is nothing else than a lucrative trade. We need not concern ourselves with the long arguments about whether this state comes from God or the devil; it comes from neither one. Why should some droning, driveling mortal assume that either one of the two presumed supernatural beings concerns himself with his carryings-on? Swift compares the Dissenters' brains to a large mass of tiny insects imbedded in the skull. They are excited by heat to gnaw upon the nerve centers in the brain and thus set the tongue and right hand in motion.

The nasal droning characteristic of fanatic preaching is really caused by venereal disease, which destroys the bridge of the nose and obstructs the nasal passages. Swift then fancifully traces the ancestry of modern "saints," finding predecessors in the Greek orgies, the early heretics, and wherever piety has been used as a cover for lewdness. The eye motions and sighings in a conventicle are indistinguishable from those among lovers, and the preachers often ejaculate at the high point of their sermon.

Swift closes the letter with an injunction that it should be burned as soon as it has been read. Thus the entire mass of matter that makes up the 1704 volume comes to an end which is as anticlimactic as the opening was pretentious.

Memoirs of a Cavalier, Defoe, 1720.

For many years this work was thought to be the genuine memoirs of a Col. Andrew Newport. It is now agreed to be a fictionalized history by Defoe, compiled largely from published sources (A. W. Secord, *Robert Drury's Journal and Other Studies* [Urbana: Univ. of Illinois Press, 1961], pp. 72-133). Part one deals with the Thirty Years' War in Germany (1618-1648), part two with the English Civil Wars (1641-1648).

Part one—Before the Cavalier is born his mother dreams that she has given birth in a field, escorted by a troop of cavalry, and that the infant sprouts wings and flies away. Then she dreams that as she is giving birth a man is standing under her window beating a kettle drum (a seventeenth-century recruiting technique). The Cavalier is born in 1608 in Shropshire; although he is a second son, his father gives him a good education, including three years at Oxford. When his father offers to set him up in life, he opts instead to roam the world. With the blessing of his father and accompanied by his Oxford schoolfellow, "Captain" Fielding, he departs from Dover on April 22, 1630.

In Amiens they walk once into the "Great Church" but see "nothing very remarkable there" (the vogue of cathedrals as art monuments had not yet set in). In Paris the Cavalier gets into a fight at the tennis court. He kills his opponent, but sustains a serious thigh wound and has to be smuggled out of the city by night. Although he suffers greatly from his wound's opening, he and Fielding make their way to Lyons. There they witness a riot diplomatically quieted by the Queen Mother, and the Cavalier wishes that Charles I of England had later been so diplomatic as the French queen on this occasion. Later he and his companion are roughed up by mutinous troops, which inspires him with a lasting dislike of popular agitations.

After serving briefly in the French army, the Cavalier tours Italy but is unimpressed. "All the diversions here ended in whoring, gaming, and sodomy." The ruins of Rome hold no charm, for "I had no gust to antiquities." The naïve young man is enticed to the apartment of a courtesan but beats a hasty retreat when he discovers her intentions. The next morning he is surprised to see her piously returning from Mass.

In the spring of 1631 the Cavalier journeys through southern Germany, intending to go down the Danube; but he changes his

mind when he hears that the Protestant champion, King Gustavus
Adolphus of Sweden, has landed in Pomerania and is plans to relieve
the oppressed German Protestants. He hurries northward and is
present at Magdeburg to witness the sack of the city and the massacre of the inhabitants by the Imperial army under General Tilly.
He reaches the Swedish outposts and is so impressed with the
discipline and morality among the troops that he and Fielding join
a regiment of Scots volunteers serving the Swedish king. Sir John
Hepburn takes the Cavalier to see the king, who wants to know
all about Tilly's army. The Cavalier says Tilly has two armies, one
of soldiers and the other of prostitutes who follow along.

The Cavalier distinguishes himself for bravery at the Battle of
Leipzig on September 7. Tilly's army is defeated. Fielding is dan-
gerously wounded, and the Cavalier stays behind to nurse him.
Meanwhile George, the Cavalier's servant, poses as a Swedish
officer and makes an immense haul of plunder from a party of
retreating Croatians. Later the Cavalier discovers his captured
horse being galled by a purse of 438 gold pieces hidden under
the saddle, and this too he presents to George, urging him to set
himself up as a gentleman-soldier. But George begs to be allowed
to remain in the Cavalier's service.

Leaving Fielding in Leipzig, the Cavalier joins in the storming
of Würzburg in Franconia, receiving a painful halberd-wound in
the arm. The king gives him a position on his personal staff and
goes to winter near Frankfurt am Main, having conquered two-
thirds of Germany like a whirlwind. The Cavalier's father offers
to raise a regiment of men at his own expense for his son to command, and Charles I himself writes kindly of the Cavalier to King
Gustavus.

In the spring of 1632 the king marches along the Main into
Bavaria. At the crossing of the river Lech a brave sergeant of dragoons disguises himself as a peasant to find out the depth of the
river. As Gustavus is crossing the river in the face of the Imperial
army, gallant old General Tilly is mortally wounded in the thigh
and the enemy must retreat. On the approach to Augsburg the
Cavalier is heavily engaged with the enemy and barely comes off,
having lost a hundred men.

The war enters an important new stage when Wallenstein, the
new Imperial commander, enters Bavaria and besieges the Swedish
king in Nürnberg. During this siege the Cavalier leads a raiding
party to attack the Imperial magazine. His band is routed and he

is captured, not to be exchanged until after the Battle of Lützen in November. The Protestants win this battle but at an immense cost, for the king of Sweden is killed in the front line. From this time on the Protestants begin to suffer reverses.

The Cavalier's promised regiment lands in Emden; but they soon suffer heavy losses, and the Cavalier resigns his command in favor of Fielding. Before leaving Germany, however, he witnesses the heavy Protestant defeat at Nördlingen on August 17, 1634. The Baron Offkirk provokes Gustavus Horn into a rash attack, and the Protestant army is decimated. Thinking the Protestant cause doomed, the Cavalier journeys into Holland. · He observes Prince Maurice's war of attrition against the Spanish occupation force and finds it lacking in *élan*, but he is forced to concede that the prince's tactics may have more lasting effects than the king of Sweden's rapid marches.

The Cavalier returns to his father's Shropshire estate. In 1641 the king personally asks him to aid in the Northern War to impose the Prayer Book on the Scots. The king's army is in a very beggarly condition and overrun with priests, who keep urging the king to take such rash steps as imposing Episcopalianism on Scotland. The Cavalier accompanies a reconnaissance party into Scotland but feels disgraced when his men run away in the face of the enemy.

Part two—While a truce is being negotiated, the Cavalier visits the Scots camp and is impressed with the rugged strength of the Highlanders. He feels that the king is making far too many concessions to the Scots and that he is always either too rigid or too conciliatory, never finding a mean between extremes. The following year is even worse for the king. Urged by the bishops, he sends another force against the Scots which is promptly smashed, after which the Scots occupy Newcastle and Durham. The king takes the mad step of fitting out a fleet, although the Scots have virtually no navy. At first the Cavalier is reluctant to join the royal forces because of their poor discipline, but when the king begins to suffer reverses he rallies to the cause and is honored with carrying the king's offer of peace to the Scots at York. He is antagonized by the insolence of the Scots.

After the king is forced to call the Long Parliament, the Cavalier comments that the bishops' tyranny has been succeeded by a Parliamentary tyranny. When the king raises his standard at Nottingham on August 22, 1642, the Cavalier goes down to Shrewsbury to raise troops for him. His father recruits a regiment at his own expense in which the Cavalier serves, and when his father is wounded he takes command himself.

Now follows a detailed account of the marches and counter-marches during the Civil War. The most important event of the campaign of 1642 is the Battle of Edgehill. The king steals a march on the Parliament forces and would have captured London if he had only continued his march, but he allows himself to be talked into giving battle for the sake of military glory. Because the royal army retreats after the battle, the Roundheads are able to claim the victory. The Cavalier's father bitterly condemns the king for letting slip the opportunity of seizing the capital, since it is a Puritan hotbed.

The comments of the Cavalier illustrate his royalist point of view. He deplores the sanguinary fury of the fighting but observes that the war was thus brought more quickly to an end. The king has lost some of the people's sympathy because of Prince Rupert's depredations in Buckinghamshire, although the Cavalier insists that these raids were extremely mild compared to the devastation he had witnessed in Germany.

During 1643 the king makes an even worse mistake by marching away from London and besieging Gloucester. He does this in response to the western landowners, but by doing so he allows the Puritan preachers to whip up the London rabble and rally recruits. In the north an obscure Lincolnshire farmer named Oliver Cromwell begins to win victories for the Roundheads against great odds. In January, 1644, the Scots invade the northern counties at the invitation of Parliament. In response the king enlists some of the Irish to help him; but since the Irish have recently been guilty of a number of Protestant massacres, this action brings down on the king the opprobrium of the nation and a number of his most loyal supporters leave his cause to sit the war out. The Cavalier blames the Parliament for reducing the king to such a stratagem but admits that it was poor policy.

The Cavalier goes with Prince Rupert to raise the siege of York. This task accomplished, the prince hazards all on one throw of the dice by engaging the Parliament men at Marston Moor. The prince brings on disaster by recklessly dashing off to pursue one part of the enemy army, leaving the rest of the royal forces to their fate. The Cavalier with a troop of men retreats westward across England, eventually joining the prince in Westmoreland. The Cavalier disguises himself as a farmer, and two of his men dress up as a cripple

and a country woman. In this garb the Cavalier becomes involved
in a brawl with three North-Country fellows and knocks one down
with his pitchfork. By coincidence they put up the next night with
a loyalist farmer who turns out to be none other than the man
the Cavalier disabled and whose horse he stole. He makes amends
as best he can. Eventually the Cavalier's party rejoins Prince Rupert,
but only after three of them have died of fatigue and exposure.

The winter witnesses the reorganization ("new-modelling") of
the Parliamentary army and the rise of the implacable Independents
to dominance in the Parliamentary councils. Incidents of rape and
murder by royalist soldiers cause the king to lose popular support
even further. In 1645 the king captures Leicester and rumors of a
massacre are spread abroad. The Cavalier denies the rumors,
although he admits killing some civilians who ambushed his men.

The king marches northward but is overtaken by the Parliamentary army and decisively defeated at Naseby, June 14, 1645,
losing his entire body of foot soldiers. He retreats into Wales. The
Cavalier leaves the king's army on the eve of battle, an action for
which he later blames himself. On the march from Ludlow to
Chester the king's army is again defeated and the Cavalier's regiment dispersed. From now on only mopping up is left. After unsuccessfully attempting to rally the king's friends at Worcester, the
Cavalier flees to Cornwall, where he is later included in Sir Ralph
Hopton's capitulation to Lord Fairfax. (The Cavalier has a high
opinion of Fairfax's military genius, ranking him second only to
Gustavus Adolphus himself.)

The king surrenders to the Scots, who carry him to Newcastle
and hand him over to the Parliament. (The Scots will do anything
for money, is the Cavalier's jaundiced comment.) The king escapes
briefly from Hampton Court but is later run to earth. Before a
treaty can be drafted, Parliament is taken over by the Independents,
who have the king condemned and executed. The fateful day is
January 30, 1649. "The devil is always master where mischief is
the work." But these bloody-minded villains later also perished
by the sword, and at the time the Cavalier is writing, Charles II
has been happily restored.

King Gustavus Adolphus of Sweden, Gen. Altringer, Mr.
Ashburnham, Sir Jacob Ashby, Sir Arthur Ashton, Sir Jacob
Astley, Sir William Balfour, Sir John Baner, Col. Bellasis,
Mr. Bennet, Duke Bernhard of Weimar, the King of Bohe-
mia, the Duke of Brandenburg, Sir William Brereton of

Cheshire, Sir John Byron, Earl of Callander, Earl of Carnar-
von, the Cavalier, Lt. Gen. Cavendish, King Charles I of
England, Prince Charles of Bohemia, Earl of Cleveland,
Lord Conway, Col. Cratz, Lord Craven, Lord Crawford,
Sir Nicholas Crisp, Oliver Cromwell, Col. Cullembach,
Earl of Denbigh, Earl of Denby, Countess of Derby, Earl of
Derby, Lord Digby, Col. Dubalt, Baron Dyvel, Maréchal
D'Effiat, Lieut. English, Earl of Essex, Sir John Evelyn, Sir
Thomas Fairfax, Lord Fairfax ("old Fairfax"), Lord Falk-
land, father of the Cavalier, Capt. Fielding, Col. Fielding,
Col. Nathaniel Fiennes, Capt. Forbes, Col. Forbes, Duke of
Friedland, Sir John Gell, George, Col. Gerard, Sir Thomas
Glemham, Col. Charles Goring, Capt. Gourdon, Col. Gray,
Sir Bevil Grenville, Col. Grey, Carolus Gustavus, Capt.
Hacker, Col. Hall, Col. Hammond, Mr. Hampden, Col. Hast-
ings, Sir John Henderson, Princess Henrietta Maria, Sir
John Hepburn, Marquis of Hertford, Earl of Holland, Sir
Ingram Hopton, Sir Ralph Hopton, Gustavus Horn, Sir
John Hotham, King of Hungary, Commissary-Gen. Ireton,
Col. Jones, Cornet Joyce, Bishop Juxon, Sir Peter Killigrew,
Baron Kronenburg, Col. Lambert, Archbishop Laud, Sir
Marmeduke Langdale, Maj. Gen. Langhorn, Gen. Leslie
(later Earl of Leven), Earl of Lichfield, Earl of Lindsey, Sir
Charles Lucas, Gen. Ludlow, Col. Lumsdell, Col. Lundford,
Earl of Manchester, Col. Marrow, Massey, Prince Maurice
of England, Prince Maurice of Holland, Lord Maxwell, Sir
Thomas Middleton, Col. Mitton, Earl of Montrose, Sir John
Morley, mother of the Cavalier, Grave Noels, Marquis
(later Earl) of Newcastle, Baron D'Offkirk, Earl of Ormond,
Commissary Osta, Axel Oxenstiern, Pappenheim, Maj. Gen.
Porter, Maj. Gen. Poyntz, "the Queen" (Henrietta Maria of
England), Commissary-Gen. Ramsey, Sir James Ramsey,
Lord Reay, the Rhinegrave, Col. Rossiter, Prince Rupert,
Lord. St. John, Col. Sandys, Duke of Saxe-Weimar, Duke
of Saxony, Lord Say, Dr. Seigensius, Skippen, Sir Nicholas
Slanning, Capt. Smith, Maj. Gen. Sparr, Col. Spencer, Col.
Spezuter, Sir Philip Stapleton, Sir Edward Stradling, Earl of
Strafford, Earl of Sunderland, "Goody Thompson," Good-
man Thomson, Maj. Gen. Tillyard, Col. Tortenson, Sir Wil-
liam Vaughan, Sir Edward Verney, Prince of Wales (later
King Charles II of England), Wallenstein, Sir William Waller,

Whalley, Lord Widdrington, "Duke William," Lord Willoughby, Marquis of Worcester.

Moll Flanders, Defoe, 1722. (Original title: *The Fortunes and Misfortunes of the Famous Moll Flanders.*)

Moll is born in 1614 in Newgate prison, where her mother has "pleaded her belly" to escape execution for stealing three pieces of Holland linen. Her mother's sentence is then commuted to transportation; and Moll, aged six months, is left in the hands of a relation. She falls into the care of roving gypsies who abandon her in Colchester, leaving her a ward of the state. A good Christian nurse raises her, teaching her good manners, plus spinning and sewing. Moll now takes it into her head to become a "gentlewoman," by which she means she wants to be like a certain seamstress in the neighborhood who earns an independent living. Bur her nurse reveals that this "gentlewoman" is the mother of two or three bastards. Even the Lord Mayor brings his lady and daughters to see this orphan who wants to become a gentlewoman.

When the nurse dies her daughter turns Moll out, confiscating her small supply of money in the process. Moll, now fourteen, is taken into the home of a wealthy family in the neighborhood as a servant. She is called "Mrs. Betty," and soon outclasses the daughters of the house in singing and dancing as well as in beauty. When she is seventeen the older son of the family turns her head with flattery, fuddles her with money, and seduces her. At the same time the younger brother Robin falls in love with her. The older brother tells Moll in confidence he will never marry her and urges her to marry Robin instead. In the ensuing family fight, the mother suspects Moll of trying to entrap Robin, and the sisters vent their spleen for being outclassed. In reality it is Robin who wants to marry Moll and not vice versa. A bribe of five hundred pounds from the older brother helps Moll to swallow her lovesickness. She consents to marry Robin but continues to commit adultery with the older brother every night in her mind.

Robin dies and Moll leaves her two children by him with her in-laws, never to see them again. She marries a linen draper who after a brief career of extravagance flees to France, forcing Moll to seek sanctuary in the Mint to escape her creditors. Defoe inserts here a lecture on the evils of extravagance. (The Mint was a section of the city where debtors were free from arrest.) Moll has had one child by the linen draper, who dies.

Moll meets the widow of a ship captain and sets up housekeeping with her. She is disillusioned with romantic love and sees marriage as a market where women are valued only for their fortunes. The widow is jilted by another captain; so she and Moll circulate rumors that he is in desperate financial straits and that he has a wife in every port. Accordingly the captain is dropped by all his female acquaintance and is eventually brought to marry the widow after all. The widow spreads the false rumor that Moll has an immense fortune. She is courted by a gentleman with whom she writes love verses with a diamond on a window pane. Through this verse-writing game she disingenuously confesses that she is really poor; but the gentleman, thinking that she means only to test him, marries her anyway (her third husband) and is then stuck with his bargain.

Moll and her husband emigrate to Virginia, where her husband's mother is living. By listening to this woman tell of her Newgate experiences, Moll deduces the horrible truth that she is listening to her own mother and that she is married to her half-brother, to whom she has born two children and by whom she is now pregnant with a third. She shuns her husband's bed ("I could almost as willingly have embraced a dog"), telling him she is not legally married to him but keeping back the whole truth. As a result of their estrangement and a suicide attempt on his part, she is sent back to England after eight years in Virginia, taking with her a cargo of tobacco to sell and leaving her children in America.

Moll arrives safely, but the tobacco is lost in transit, and so she takes up residence in Bath with a lady of independent means and loose morals. She attracts the attention of a "Bath gentleman" whose wife has been put away in a madhouse. After she nurses him through an illness, they become such good friends that they sleep in the same bed without having intercourse, although Moll confesses that she has had her eye on him from the first moment she saw him. Their relationship remains chaste for two years; but one evening after too much wine, they overstep the barrier. They then live in sin for six years, during which time she bears him a child and they move to Hammersmith near London. The Bath gentleman has a serious bout of illness; having again faced death, he repents and casts Moll off, but only after she has procured a hundred pounds from him. (Their child now inexplicably disappears from the novel.)

Moll lives once again under the pretense of being a wealthy gentlewoman, meanwhile looking for someone to marry. She meets a North-Country woman who promises to take her to Lancashire to live at small expense. Before leaving London Moll entrusts her money to a banker who has fallen in love with her and wants to divorce his wife in order to marry her. Leaving this affair to hang fire, Moll goes to Lancashire and meets a man who calls himself an Irish lord. Genuinely in love again for the first time since the affair of the older brother in Colchester, she marries him (fourth husband), only to discover that he is penniless and that he paid the North-Country woman five hundred pounds to procure him a wealthy wife. They have duped each other. (" 'Tis something of Relief even to be undone by a Man of Honour, rather than by a Scoundrel.") Jemy deserts her but returns because by some supernatural agent he has heard her voice calling after him from miles away over the fields. After a brief sojourn he leaves her to seek his fortune and she returns to London.

Moll finds herself pregnant by Jemy. This is a particular inconvenience since the banker's wife has done away with herself and the way is clear for Moll. She goes into a home for unwed mothers run by "Mother Midnight," later called "my Governess." Moll refuses the Governess's offer to bring about an abortion, and a son is born who is given to a Hertfordshire woman to raise. Moll first lectures us on how terrible it is for women to give their children away to God knows who, and then bargains the Hertfordshire woman down from ten to five pounds a year support money.

Moll takes a coach into Staffordshire so that she can fool the banker into thinking she is returning from her stay in the country. He leaves London for their rendezvous. They meet at Brickhill and are married, after many sham protestations of reluctance by Moll (fifth husband). The next morning Moll looks out the window of her bridal chamber and sees none other than her Lancashire Jemy going into an inn across the street. Jemy proves to be a highwayman on the lam, but Moll swears to the constable that she knows him to be a gentleman of a large estate in Lancashire, thus putting the pursuit off the scent and saving Jemy's life.

Moll lives happily with the banker for five years and bears him two children (never subsequently mentioned) until one of the clerks decamps with all the money, after which the banker sinks under melancholy and dies. Moll is now forty-eight years old (1662). She lives on capital for three years until she is bankrupt. She supports herself with her needle until the devil tempts her and she turns to theft.

The second part of the novel now begins as Moll performs a series of thefts. She gains her famous nickname of "Moll Flanders" and falls in with her old Governess, now turned "pawnbroker" alias fence. Moll is put apprentice to a seasoned pickpocket and shoplifter who shows her how to jostle pedestrians and steal their watches. Once she entices a little girl into a dark alley and steals her necklace. For a moment she is tempted to kill the child, but she refrains and then delivers a lecture on the folly of parents' sending their children to walk the streets alone. Moll goes to a house on fire, pretends to be a neighbor, and helps the lady of the house to secure her goods, only to march away with a goodly share of them herself. She steals smuggled lace from a warehouse for a customs officer but then keeps much of the goods herself. During one attempt to steal a gentlewoman's watch, another pickpocket is apprehended by mistake and delivered up to the terrible vengeance of the London mob. During these thefts Moll assumes false names and even dresses as a man so that her accomplices are unable to identify her when they are apprehended.

Moll's only real experience as a prostitute occurs when a drunken gentleman picks her up at Bartholomew Fair. While he is seducing her, she picks his pocket. The Governess finds out where the gentleman lives, and despite his allegedly high moral character he supplies Moll with money in return for sexual favors. But to Moll's disappointment he will not go so far as to keep her as a mistress.

Among Moll's other "pranks" are procuring a merchant's goods with a false bill of lading and taking the trunk of a sleeping Dutchman in Harwich. Once she is falsely accused of theft by a journeyman who mistakes her for someone else. With a great parade of self-righteousness she has the journeyman imprisoned, and she and the Governess extort five hundred pounds from the shopkeeper to make up for Moll's injured reputation. Once she is almost apprehended by a neighbor when she has stepped into a shop to steal, but fortunately she sees the neighbor approaching and has just time enough to call out for the shopkeeper so that she can pretend her intentions were honest. Finally two "hard-mouthed wenches" catch her with the goods in her hand and she is committed to Newgate. She undergoes a false repentance; she is sorry, not because of her life of crime, but rather for getting caught. While she is in prison Jemy is committed for highway robbery, to Moll's intense distress, since she realizes that she is implicated in Jemy's crimes and the deaths they caused.

Moll is tried, convicted, and in spite of a moving speech to the judge condemned to death. In her despair she is visited by a minister and undergoes what she says is true repentance, even though she continues to assert that she should have been acquitted and even though she later sets herself up on the proceeds of her life of crime. Since Moll has repented the minister persuades the judge to commute her sentence to transportation. She persuades Jemy to be transported too.

(The circumstances of Jemy's transportation are unclear. At one point we are told that Moll's Governess procures his release and that he is not to be sold as a bond servant since he is going of his own free will. A second passage says that Jemy is found guilty and sentenced to transportation to the colonies; later in the narrative, both he and Moll must buy their freedom from an obliging planter when they reach Virginia.)

In Virginia Moll discovers from a Mrs. Owen that her brother is almost blind and her son Humphry still living. She and Jemy, who has become submissive and dependent on Moll, settle on the Eastern Shore of Maryland. She tells Jemy only as much of her former life as she wants him to know and writes to her brother, knowing that he will be unable to read her letter and that Humphry will read it instead.

Moll goes back over Chesapeake Bay to Virginia and is tearfully reunited with Humphry, who tells her of an estate her mother has left her. She wishes for a moment she had not brought Jemy with her to the colonies. She returns to their Maryland estate, however, with a purse of fifty-five pistoles. Jemy is so moved at God's generosity to him that he too undergoes a reformation. Moll manages the farm while Jemy spends his time hunting. Moll at the age of seventy returns to England with Jemy, where they plan to spend the rest of their days in a prosperous state of remorse.

Bath gentleman, Lady Betty, older brother in Colchester family, Mrs. Chime, the Devil, Moll Flanders ("Mrs. Betty"), "my Governess" ("Mother Midnight"), Humphry (Sr., Moll's third husband), Humphry (Jr.), Lancashire Jemy, Anthony Johnson, Mayor of Colchester, mother of Moll, Mistress Nurse, Mrs. Owen, Robin.

Narrative of John Sheppard, Defoe, 1724. (Original title: *A Narrative of All the Robberies, Escapes, &c. of John Sheppard*.)

This account purports to have been written by Sheppard himself while awaiting execution. It is dated November 10, 1724, from the

Middle Stone Room of Newgate prison and covers much of the same ground as the earlier *Life of Sheppard*. Less detail is supplied of Sheppard's crimes, but more of his famous escape from Newgate. There is considerable self-justification in the narrative. Sheppard denies that he felled his mistress Mrs. Wood with a stick, and, if he did, he hopes it did her no harm. He admits stealing a piece of fustian from Mr. Bains but alleges that he returned to clear an innocent chambermaid from suspicion.

Sheppard escapes in turn from St. Anne's roundhouse, St. Giles's roundhouse, the New Prison, and Newgate. He admits chafing his legs with his manacles in Newgate (even though he had already found out how to get them off) to win sympathy and alms from visitors to the prison. On October 15, 1724, he uses the occasion of Blueskin's murderous attack on Jonathan Wild to break out of Newgate. Free in the neighborhood, he tells people that he was in Bridewell only for siring a bastard child (Bridewell was a prison for social offenders, as opposed to felons). Having rid himself of his chains, he proceeds to celebrate with his doxy and his mother, until he is again arrested in a state of total inebriation. The narrative closes with protestations of penitence and expressions of thanks to a number of London clergymen for coming to visit him in prison.

William Austin, Mr. Bains, Rev. Dr. Bennet, Joseph Blake (alias "Blueskin"), Rev. Mr. Edwards, Will Field, Rev. Mr. Flood, Mr. Garret, Capt. Geary, Rev. Mr. Hawkins, Joseph Hind, Mr. Kneebone, Elizabeth Lyon, Mr. Lyon, Justice Parry, Mr. Pitt, Rev. Mr. Purney, Mr. Rawlins (two), Mr. Rouse, John Sheppard, Thomas Sheppard, William Sykes (alias "Hell and Fury"), Rev. Mr. Wagstaff, Mr. Owen Wood, Mrs. Wood.

A Narrative of the Proceedings in France, Defoe, 1724. (Full title: *A Narrative of the Proceedings in France, for Discovering and Detecting the Murderers of the English Gentlemen, September 21, 1723, near Calais.*) Four English gentlemen and their servants are murdered by highway robbers, and the Duke of Orleans weeps upon receiving the news. Extraordinary efforts are put forth to apprehend the criminals and redeem the honor of France. Finally the lieutenant of police in Lisle catches two cronies of the highwayman Cartouche, but even torture fails to extort a confession. Luckily one of the servants of the English travelers, Spindelow, has recovered from his wounds and comes over from England. Upon hearing themselves picked out from the lineup, they exclaim, "We are dead men!" But the braver of the robbers, Bizeau, still refuses to name his accomplices.

Defoe now fills in the history of the band. Mons. Cartouche is a low street robber who accidentally attains fame as a highwayman and so attracts many desperadoes to his standard. Bizeau is actually more intrepid. Among his adventures are the robbery and rape of an entire coachful of ladies. During the frenzied speculation around the Mississippi Bubble, Cartouche plants his men on the roads around Paris, and there is a pitched battle with a band of Germans. In the city itself, gentlemen with stock certificates (which are as good as cash) are even followed into their lodging houses, robbed, and murdered. Their bodies are then thrown into the Seine.

Bizeau's band is drawn to join Cartouche because of his ill-gained fame. One of many stories narrated is the robbery of a young gentleman of his gambling winnings. The robbers follow him to a house of ill repute where they surprise him with his mistress. After the robbery, they strip everyone in the house stark naked, tie all of them up belly to belly, and go upon their way. The other thief apprehended at Lisle is Peter le Febvre, who began his career as a sutler, looting corpses after a battle. He even strangles wounded men for their money. Bizeau on the contrary has a certain magnanimity. After he has robbed a party of Jewish horse traders, he returns a large sum of money to one, which (comments Defoe) the Jew valued more than his life.

Bizeau skulks about the northeastern part of France, between Paris and Lisle. Once the band is careless enough to leave some witnesses alive, and their prostitutes berate them so much that they resolve to be more ruthless in the future. On September 23, 1723, they hear that our party of English merchants has set out from Calais for Paris with three hundred pistoles in silver. When attacked, the Englishmen surrender their purses without resistance, after which the robbers order them to lie down on their faces. They are then murdered in cold blood. Only Spindelow and Mr. Mompesson remain alive.

Later the local peasants come to rifle the bodies, and when Spindelow and Mompesson plead for help, the peasants refuse to stop looting. Finally the two men make their way to the coach and a peasant drives them to a farmhouse, where Mompesson dies. For this dreadful deed, the robbers get only 120 pistoles, the rumors of a great fortune proving false.

The band is forced to scatter. Bizeau disguises himself as a Wal-

loon silversmith and with le Febvre continues his depredations.
When captured, the two are examined separately so that each can
be led to believe that his crony has peached. Spindelow's testimony
makes their guilt certain, and the judges condemn them to death.
Bizeau is broken upon the wheel and lives for twenty-four hours
in agony until he dies, while le Febvre is granted the *coup de grace*
by the executioner.

> Joseph Bisseau or Bizeau (alias "Gratien Devanelle"), Mary
> Frances Beausse de Caron, Col. Cartouche, Mr. Davies,
> Laurence Hennelet, Jean Baptist le Febvre, Lewis le Feb-
> vre, Peter le Febvre, Mr. Lock, Catharine Moffat, Mr.
> Mompesson, John Pouillard, Mr. Seabright, Spindelow.

A New Voyage Round the World, By a Course Never Sailed Before,
Defoe, 1724.

Part one—Our unnamed narrator captains a ship setting out from
London in 1713 to prey on the French South Seas trade (despite
the fact that the war with France is almost over). A certain merchant underwrites the voyage in the hope that new lands can be
discovered and opened up for exploration. They take along a crew
of Frenchmen and a pretended French commander, "Capt." Mirlotte, so that they can pass for a French ship when they enter the
Spanish dominions (France was Spain's ally in the War of the
Spanish Succession).

On December 20, 1713, they leave the Thames. By March 30 they
have landed in Brazil, where they add to their expedition a Spanish ship that mistakes them for a French vessel. They pass the
Strait of Magellan, and the captain comments sardonically on the
undeserved reputation of Sir Francis Drake for shooting this
strait. Contrary winds hinder their voyage westward, and so they
turn back and sail for the Cape of Good Hope. When they have
anchored in the roads off the Dutch fort, the crewmen plan a
mutiny, unhappy about rumors they are going to sail to the South
Pole. Fortunately the captain's black cabin boy, Spartivento,
overhears the plot and warns the captain that a seemingly innocent
trip ashore for fresh water will really be used to plan the mutiny.

With this warning the captain and Mirlotte arrange to have the
men arrested by the Dutch authorities. The mutineers go ashore
and are promptly locked up. The captain now confronts the rest
of the crew on the quarter-deck. He makes them ashamed of themselves, and they sneak below one by one. The three ringleaders

(the second mate, the gunner, and the cockswain) are whipped and "pickled" (that is, their raw wounds are doused with salt and vinegar). The second mate is also condemned to death but is first confined in the hold to contemplate his sins.

The ship stands away for Java, bound for the Philippines. On the way they capture a sloop; their flotilla now is comprised of three ships. On Madagascar they discover a large colony of pirates living on the northern end of the island. The now-repentant second mate is forgiven and taken back into the captain's confidence. He is sent ashore to recruit new crew members among the pirates. It turns out that every pirate wants to be included among the sloop's crew, but the gunner can take only twenty-two of them and drives the rest off at gunpoint. As they are preparing to set sail, the other two mutineers (the gunner and the cockswain) prove incorrigible and try to spark another mutiny, and so the captain is forced to set them ashore.

The little flotilla lands on Ceylon for victuals, but the natives prove treacherous. One of them tries to steal a crewman's shoes and, when apprehended, stabs the crewman with a pair of scissors. He is whipped bloody and then sent ashore, where the captain is sure he will die from lack of medical attention. A second fight occurs when the natives try to defraud the English on a shipment of chicken. All in all, the expedition is glad to leave Ceylon.

They sail through the straits of Malacca and punish some hostile Malays by plundering and burning. They then make their way through Indonesia toward the Philippines. They have trouble with their Dutch pilot, who suspects them of being pirates and threatens to run the ship aground; but he quickly becomes more tractable when the boatswain hauls him around the ship with a halter around his neck. They land at Manila and bribe the Spanish governor to relax the laws forbidding trade with foreigners. They even trade with some "ill-looking" Chinese and Japanese who come on board.

The captain contemplates striking out for the "island" of California and perhaps discovering the Northwest Passage, where the Great Lakes are presumed to empty into the Pacific. But since they are unsure that the Passage even exists and since they would almost certainly perish for want of supplies, they choose a more cautious route along the equator through Melanesia.

Here the English discover two new islands, one after the other. Near one island, a great crowd of natives comes swimming out to them and one turns his black buttocks up at them. The captain comments that the meaning of this action is well known in England, but he is not so sure about the language of gesture in the South Seas. They bring two of the native women aboard, who are enormously pleased at the skirts the Englishmen give them to hide their nakedness. The whites trade simple tools such as hatchets for great heaps of beaten gold ornaments.

Further out in Melanesia they make a second landing. After withstanding a heavy storm which almost forces them to slip their cables, they negotiate with the native royalty. The king is given a mirror and cuts capers as he glimpses himself in the finery the English have given him. The English are delighted in turn when they discover that the king and queen deck themselves in magnificent robes covered with spangles of real gold. The king is a handsome man except for the fact that he shows his teeth too much when he smiles. The queen is remarkable for her breasts, which do not sag like those of Indian women but remain perfectly erect. She is pretty despite her dark color.

The natives have a sort of white root from which they make an intoxicating beverage that drives the crewmen temporarily mad. A sailor thoughtlessly takes a two-year-old child and keeps it overnight, driving the mother to distraction with worry. When he returns it the next morning she runs mad with joy. The captain heartily recommends these islands as trading spots on bullionist grounds; here English merchants could replenish their supply of precious metals. The captain thinks that if only they could have made their way to the South Pole, they would have found enormous deposits of pure gold, drawn there by the magnetic power of the earth. The appearance of a huge iceberg, however, makes them veer away to the north (the square-rigged vessels can come about only with some difficulty).

Finally after many weeks of sailing they sight the Andes and land on the Juan Fernandez Islands. The men rush ashore to drink fresh water, and only those who have been careful to line their stomachs with rum avoid paralyzing stomach cramps. One of their vessels captures a Spanish ship, and the English must bribe the Spanish captain into silence about their presence in the Spanish domains.

Part two—They sail northward to Lima, where they sell the brigantine. When they reach Panama they decide that the coast is too unhealthy to allow a trek across the Isthmus. A number of the crew fall sick, and seventeen die. Fortunately there is a surgeon in the neighborhood, who happens to be an Irish Jesuit. At first they are afraid he will expose them, but there is no cause for fear; the padre is anxious to return to the British Isles. They agree to take him on the condition that he does not wear his clerical garb.

The English sail back to Juan Fernandez, where they enjoy a gam with two English ships. They capture another Spanish vessel and have the good fortune to make friends with the captain, who confides to them how thinly guarded the Spanish empire really is, with less than one Spaniard to a thousand square miles. The Spanish could be even richer than they are except for their aversion to work. The Spaniard magnanimously invites a party of the English to visit his villa, and with a picked crew the English captain begins his upcountry journey.

They are sumptuously entertained at Villa Rica, where the meanest dishes in the house are made of silver, and the English are even permitted the unheard-of courtesy of visiting with the *dona*, who is normally kept secluded and veiled with her attendants. At night they are alarmed by a sudden burst of light, which they learn comes from volcanic activity in the region. The English respond to the Spaniard's generosity with a present of three Negro slaves.

The English captain undertakes a trip into the interior through one of the passes of the Andes, despite his mistrust of the native Chileans. Four days out they come into a fertile valley and are entertained by an Indian nobleman so rich that he doesn't even bother to pick up the gold which lies scattered about on the ground. They travel just far enough to discover a large lake, on the shores of which they find a large amount of gold to be panned.

The exploring party rejoin their friends on the coast, where the captain finds that his lieutenant has been instructing their host's two sons in navigation. The captain feels that he ought not to leave the ships again, but instead dispatches a group of fifty-three men into the interior under the command of the lieutenant and the two midshipmen. This party is to pan as much gold as possible along the shore of the Golden Lake and then rendezvous with the ships on the east coast of Argentina. They agree in advance on a series of rocket signals.

On October 13, 1715, the ships set sail southward and the explorers set out across the Andes. The captain with his two remaining ships successfully rounds the Horn and celebrates Twelfth Night in the Atlantic with plum pudding. They finally anchor off the coast of Patagonia in the agreed-upon latitude. Having waited until February 16, they send a search party up one of the rivers and are finally delighted to see the rockets of the approaching explorers.

When the lieutenant arrives he tells a tale of physical privation and refractory crewmen. The men at first wanted to rob the friendly Chilean grandee and were barely prevented from doing so by their officers. At every stage the lieutenant and midshipmen had to plead with the men to travel on instead of scattering and rummaging about for gold. Finally they reached the Golden Lake, where they panned a large amount of gold from the streams flowing into it. The intense heat made daily siestas necessary, slowing down their progress. They tried to make use of a river to travel coastwards and built large rafts, but were overtaken by rising waters. They noted that the water had changed from its formerly clear state to a milky color, an indication that there had been extensive flooding somewhere upstream. One night while they were encamped ashore the rafts were carried away by the flood. They built canoes out of tree trunks, and one group of crewmen sneaked away to find more gold. But they fell to quarreling among themselves. In the confusion they upset the canoe, lost their gold, and one of the men was drowned; so disconsolately they rejoined the main body of explorers.

In order to end the disputing over the new-found gold, the captain refuses to divide it among the exploring party until he has set them ashore. The two ships sail northward to Newfoundland since they are unsure whether the war at home is over or not. (In reality, peace has already been made.) They sail to France, to the banks of the Garonne, where the captain sets the members of the exploring party ashore along with their booty. He confides that he neither knows nor cares what became of them. The Madagascar pirates discreetly leave the ship here, since they are shy of the London police.

The ships reach Dunkirk on April 12, 1716. Here the merchants and owners come over from England to receive their share of the fantastic profits which the voyage has realized. But the moving spirit behind the voyage, the rich merchant who had hoped for new discoveries, has died in the two-and-a-half years

since the ships set out, and so he can never enjoy the fruition of
his dreams.

> Jack, Will Jones, "Capt." Jean Michael Mirlotte, Sparti-
> vento, Tom.

Pamela or, Virtue Rewarded, Richardson.   Volumes I and II, 1740;
   volumes III and IV, 1741.

Volume one—Pamela Andrews, a fifteen-year-old servant girl,
writes to her mother and father that her mistress Lady B. has died.
While Pamela has been serving at B. Hall in Bedfordshire, Lady B.
taught her to read and write, to keep accounts, and to be expert at
her needle. Her parents are alarmed that she may think herself
above her natural place in society. Before dying, Lady B. urged her
son Mr. B. to care for Pamela. He is good at heart but has been so
indulged by his mother that he has never learned to restrain his
carnal appetites. He begins to pay Pamela certain alarming attentions, such as giving her intimate garments ("Dost think I don't
know pretty maids should wear shoes and stockings?"), much to the
consternation of Mr. and Mrs. Andrews.

Mr. B. makes a series of attempts on Pamela's virtue. In the
summer house, he kisses her and she runs away. In the dressing
room, he puts his hand into her bosom and she faints. Her friend,
Mrs. Jervis the housekeeper, agrees to let Pamela sleep with her but
suggests that Mr. B. is not so bad after all. Mrs. Jervis at this point
represents the servant who is overly obedient to her master, even at
the expense of compromising principle. Pamela decides to return
to her parents' home, but lingers at B. Hall to finish embroidering
a waistcoat for her master. Longman the steward and Mr. Jonathan
the butler express the greatest esteem for her and regret her imminent departure.

Pamela is visited by Lady Brooks, Lady Arthur, Lady Tower, and
a "countess of some hard name." They behave rather rudely for such
fine ladies, and their remarks insinuate that Mr. B. has designs on
Pamela. But Lady Brooks is impressed with Pamela's beauty and
comments, "she must be better descended than you have told me."

Pamela dresses in plain clothes in preparation for her return
home, and Mr. B., pretending not to recognize her, kisses her, much
to Pamela's dismay. That night Pamela comes to bed with Mrs.
Jervis, and Mr. B. rushes out of the closet at her, but the rape is
frustrated by Pamela's fainting. Mr. B. threatens to discharge Mrs.
Jervis for all her "squalling" but finally relents. When Pamela

recovers, Longman the steward praises her to Mr. B.'s face, while the master berates her. But she, because of her perfect obedience (except where a compromise of virtue is involved), does not say a word about his attempts on her.

Pamela divides her possessions into three bundles: the things she brought with her from home, gifts from Lady B., and gifts from Mr. B. She explains to Mrs. Jervis that she will leave the last two at B. Hall (Mr. B. eavesdrops on this conversation). In an interview in the library, Mr. B. offers to enrich Pamela's father if she will remain another week, but she declines. He offers to marry her to Mr. Williams, the chaplain at his other estate in Lincolnshire. Pamela asks for time to consider this offer, but her real purpose is to escape Mr. B.'s clutches. She departs in Mr. B.'s coach on what she thinks is a journey to her home. As she leaves, she is surrounded by weeping fellow servants, except for the cook, who finds Pamela uppity.

Richardson interrupts the sequence of letters with a narrative portion, explaining how Mr. B. writes to the Andrewses that Pamela has been sent away as punishment for an intrigue with Mr. Williams. Alarmed and unbelieving, Goodman Andrews walks all night to reach B. Hall and demand his daughter from Mr. B., only to be told she has been sent to the house of a bishop in London, whose name Mr. B. refuses to reveal. Mr. Andrews receives a forged letter from Pamela in which she says that she is well. He must content himself with this.

Pamela's journal commences and continues throughout the first two volumes. Robin the coachman conveys her to Mr. B.'s Lincolnshire estate, where she is met by the grotesque Mrs. Jewkes, a massive peasant woman and Mr. B.'s willing agent. John Arnold, Mr. B.'s Bedfordshire servant, arrives with directions for Pamela to transcribe the letter for her father. Pamela meanwhile has secreted writing materials about the house and contrives to smuggle letters out by Mr. Williams.

Pamela is subjected to considerable abuse. She calls Mrs. Jewkes a Jezebel and later a London prostitute, for each of which insults Mrs. Jewkes strikes her. Mrs. Jewkes also "borrows" Pamela's six pounds and keeps it. Mr. Williams' efforts to find a haven for Pamela are repulsed by the local gentry (Lady Jones and Sir Simon Darnford), and he is rebuked by Mr. Peters, the parish priest. Mrs. Jewkes hints to Pamela that Mr. B. may eventually be willing to marry her, but Pamela says she wouldn't hear of compromising her virtue for a promise of marriage and refuses to gratify Mr. B.'s request that he be allowed to visit her.

Williams writes proposing an elopement, which Pamela properly declines. Williams is robbed of his papers and money and dunked in a millpond, a deed which we later find was ordered by Mrs. Jewkes to frustrate any attempts of Pamela's to send out messages. He is then arrested for three debts of fifty pounds apiece which he owes to Mr. B. and is sent to Stamford. Pamela discovers a letter from Mr. B. to Mrs. Jewkes ("accidentally" left out) announcing his intention to send his Swiss friend Colbrand to take Pamela in hand. The ferocious, mustachioed Colbrand arrives with a long sword and a rough voice to terrify the poor girl. She feels reduced to desperate straits. Then Pamela hears that Mr. B. has been almost drowned while out hunting, and her concern for him reveals the true state of her heart.

Pamela makes a desperate attempt to escape, climbing out her window by night and throwing some of her clothes into the pond to make Mrs. Jewkes think she has drowned herself. But she is unable to climb over the brick wall around the garden, and so she hides in the woodshed where she is discovered the next morning by Nan the waiting maid. The servants have all panicked, thinking Pamela dead. Exhausted, Pamela must spend three days in bed recuperating. Mrs. Jewkes threatens Pamela with being forcibly married to the terrible Colbrand and then sold to Mr. B. When she goes for a walk, Mrs. Jewkes thinks she is trying to escape again and locks her up without shoes and stockings.

Mr. B. arrives at his Lincolnshire estate, and a new series of attempts begins. He attempts to put his hand in her bosom and then sends her the draft of a treaty (the "naughty articles," as Pamela calls them) in which he promises to set her father up as the steward of his Norfolk estate and provide for all of Pamela's children if she will become his mistress. Pamela responds as we know she will. Mr. B. disguises himself as Nan, who supposedly has drunk too much cherry brandy and fallen asleep in a chair in the bedroom shared by Mrs. Jewkes and Pamela. When Pamela and Mrs. Jewkes retire to bed, "Nan" attempts to rape Pamela with the help of Mrs. Jewkes, but Pamela again thwarts their plans by fainting, which makes Mr. B. think she is dead.

In a series of interviews, Mr. B. agrees to give Pamela a bit more freedom around the house and confesses that he is jealous of Williams. Pamela assures him that she cares nothing for Williams.

Mr. B. announces that he has dismissed Mr. Longman, Mr. Jonathan, and Mrs. Jervis from his service for sympathizing too much with Pamela.

An old gypsy woman visits the estate and prophesies that Pamela will never marry and will die of her first child. When the gypsy rubs dirt in Pamela's palm to bring out the lines, Pamela correctly interprets it as a hint that she is to look for a message under a clod of turf in the lawn. The message warns her of a sham wedding that Mr. B. allegedly will perform with her. Mr. B. demands to see the letters that Pamela has been scribbling and threatens to undress her to find them if she has them concealed about her person. To avoid this humiliation, Pamela delivers up the papers to Mr. B., who is greatly distressed to read about her sufferings during the night she attempted to escape. He proposes marriage; but Pamela, fearing the sham ceremony, refuses. Mr. B. then puts her in a coach for her home, escorted by Colbrand.

Volume two—Mr. B. becomes so upset at losing Pamela that he sends a letter after her asking her to return. She consents and travels all night to reach the Lincolnshire estate once again, only to find that Mr. B. has been so upset that the doctor has had to bleed him. The next morning Mr. B. shows Pamela an abusive letter from his sister Lady Davers forbidding him to marry his mother's serving wrench.

Mr. B. and Pamela take a long drive in the coach, during which they come to an understanding. Mr. B. is so much in love with Pamela that he decides to marry her in spite of everything. He explains the difficulties he will face for marrying someone beneath his rank. Pamela says she will not mind being excluded from high society, since she has her religious duties to occupy her time. Mr. B. confesses that he once considered the sham marriage but rejected the possibility because he would have been unable to treat Pamela's children as his legitimate heirs. When Pamela shows him the note left by the gypsy, he discovers that the handwriting is that of Mr. Longman.

Since Mr. B. has agreed to marry Pamela, Mrs. Jewkes becomes suddenly very respectful to her and is duly forgiven. Mr. B. is also reconciled with Mr. Williams. Some of the local gentry (Sir Simon Darnford, the Misses Darnford, Lady Jones and her sister-in-law, and Mr. and Mrs. Peters and their niece) visit Mr. B. and are greatly impressed with Pamela.

At this point Mr. Andrews arrives at the Lincolnshire estate, unsure about Pamela's welfare. Pamela is brought into the room, and the company are delighted with Pamela's display of filial piety. That Sunday the whole company attend church in Mr. B.'s refurbished chapel, and Mr. Andrews sings the Psalm. At dinner Mr. B. reads out Pamela's versification of Psalm 137, which she adapted to her own case during her affliction. Mr. Andrews departs for home to tell Mrs. Andrews the good news about the approaching wedding.

A hint of future trouble arrives in the form of a monitory letter from Mr. B.'s brother-in-law Lord Davers, written at the instigation of Lady Davers. However, the service is performed privately by Mr. Williams, despite Pamela's frequently expressed virgin fears. Immediately after the ceremony, three of Mr. B.'s former rakish companions arrive, and he feels obligated to go off for a ride with them, returning that evening. Before her wedding night, Pamela prays for protection and writes apprehensively to her parents. However, all goes well, and the next day she is able to write again commending Mr. B.'s delicacy.

A long series of conversations ensues, in which Mr. B. agrees to rehire Mr. Jonathan, Mr. Longman, and Mrs. Jervis, and Pamela agrees to be perfectly obedient. She will always be properly dressed for dinner and will not lie abed mornings more than half an hour after him, or until 6:30. Also she will not fret if Mr. B. should bring home unexpected guests. He bestows on her an allowance of two hundred pounds a year for her "little charities."

Mr. B. rides off to visit a sick friend, Mr. Carlton, with whom he stays overnight. He then goes to Sir Simon Darnford's and writes for Pamela to join him there. But before she can leave, she is surprised by a visit from Lady Davers and her impertinent nephew Jackey. They attack Pamela for (as they think) prostituting herself to Mr. B. in the hopes of entrapping him into marriage. Lady Davers demands that Pamela wait on table for her and Jackey, a request that Pamela refuses because of the dignity she owes to her position as Mr. B.'s wife. When Pamela tries to leave the room, Jackey terrifies her by drawing his sword half out of the scabbard. Pamela escapes out a window and flees to Sir Simon's with the help of Colbrand (now become a good character). At Sir Simon's Pamela reluctantly consents to tell the guests of her ill treatment, and Mr. B. attributes Lady Davers' impetuous behavior to her indulged childhood.

Pamela and Mr. B. return home to sleep, only to be awakened the

next morning by Lady Davers charging into the room to catch them
in bed together. Over breakfast she reveals to Pamela that Mr. B.
once fought a duel and had a previous affair with a Miss Sally
Godfrey. Mr. B. becomes very angry and justifies the duel as
fought in defense of a friend. Sally Godfrey was a girl whose
parents attempted to entrap Mr. B. into marriage; however, she
failed to hold out long enough before granting the last favor. Mr.
B. explains all of this with restraint and then stalks out into the
garden lest he be tempted to give vent to his anger. Lady Davers
is completely discomposed by her brother's anger and weeps in
Pamela's bosom. The two women now become friends. They follow Mr. B. into the garden, where each one succeeds in persuading
Mr. B. to forgive the other.

Lady Davers hears so many compliments from the neighbors
about Pamela that she feels quite satisfied with the marriage.
Pamela writes out a digest of Mr. B.'s commands and resolves to
obey all of them. She reveals to Lady Davers that her poor but
honest parents are burdened with the debts of two feckless sons.
Pamela and Mr. B. return to the Bedfordshire estate, where tearful
reunions with old servant friends and lavish bestowing of presents
take place. Mr. B. entrusts the management of his farm in Kent to
Goodman and Goody Andrews.

Mr. B. and Pamela visit a farmhouse and boarding school run by
a Mrs. Dobson, where Pamela is charmed by a child named Miss
Goodwin, who turns out to be Mr. B.'s illegitimate daughter by
Sally Godfrey. After the birth of this child, Sally was forced to leave
the country. Mr. B. pursued her in an attempt to make amends,
but, after a last tearful interview on board ship, she sailed away to
Jamaica. There she married a kind and understanding man, Mr.
Wrightson, whom she told she was a widow. Mr. B. was astonished
at the time that wind or tide or anything else could be preferred
to him and his money. He and Pamela thank God that he has now
reformed.

Pamela and Mr. B. attend church with the compliments of all the
neighbors. Alms are distributed to the poor, and Mr. B. makes a
will in which he provides amply for Pamela's parents. Mr. and Mrs.
Andrews arrive for a visit. Richardson closes this first part with a
summary of the salutary lessons which could be drawn from the
story by "the youth of both sexes."

Volume three—At the opening of the sequel, Pamela's parents
have returned to the farm in Kent. Goodman Andrews wants to

pay rent to Mr. B., but instead Mr. B. decides to employ him as steward of the farm at a salary. Pamela's heart goes flutter, flutter, flutter at Mr. B.'s goodness. She advises her father not to employ any of his relatives on the farm, since they would take advantage. Goodman Andrews describes how the country people flock to bless Pamela and Mr. B. when they ride past.

At Lady Davers' request, Pamela sends her the private papers recounting her "trial" at the Lincolnshire estate before her marriage, but she asks her not to read the delicate portions out loud to Lord Davers and Jackey. Lady Davers reads them anyway and declares that the entire household has been edified by Pamela's graceful and uplifting writing. She informs Pamela of the duties appropriate to her station: to please her sovereign lord and master, to pay and receive visits, to write Lady Davers, and to replenish the family line with a succession of brave boys.

Pamela asks permission of Lady Davers to have the rearing of Miss Goodwin. The Davers family criticizes Pamela for being so lenient to Mrs. Jewkes, but Pamela insists that Mrs. Jewkes has truly repented and that resentment would be inappropriate to a girl of Pamela's former station in life.

The Darnford episode begins. Pamela transcribes a letter from Polly Darnford in Lincolnshire describing how Sir Simon threw a book at her head in a fit of the gout. Pamela asks Sir Simon if Polly may visit and rebukes him for being so choleric. She playfully asks that the book be sent her so she can put it to a better use. Sir Simon writes angrily to Mr. B., wilfully distorting Pamela's request to make it appear she has attempted to open an illicit correspondence with him. He refuses to allow Polly to visit, ostensibly because her virtue would not be safe with Mr. B. but really because Mr. Murray of Norfolk may arrive to marry one of the two Darnford girls. Mr. B. responds with a mock-solemn letter, pretending that he has rebuked Pamela but really teasing Sir Simon, who is joshed out of his ill humor. He says Polly may visit for a month or two if Mr. Murray decides not to marry her.

We learn that Pamela is pregnant. She pays off the debts of Mrs. Jervis, evoking tearful blessings from the old fellow servant. Pamela fears that Mr. B. will be angry, but he facetiously chides her for being too niggardly and increases Mrs. Jervis's salary. Pamela writes to Mrs. Jewkes congratulating her on her reformation and explaining how happy one may be in a life of poverty, as she was in her childhood. She is thankful that she has been a humble instrument of Providence in effecting Mr. B.'s reformation. Meanwhile Mr. Murray has visited the Darnfords. Polly finds him unattractive because he is not grave enough and hopes he will marry her sister Nancy, who has a greater fortune even though she is younger.

A long section of the novel is devoted to Pamela's journal of the Daverses' visit to Bedfordshire. In each episode Pamela's good taste and sense of decorum are displayed, to the edification of the aristocrats. Clearly she is well suited to her new station in life. For instance, she urges Mr. B. not to apply to the crown for a baronetcy lest the family should appear ambitious. She urges Mr. Williams the parson to shun pluralism and exchange his lucrative living for a poorer one so that he may reform a certain dissolute lord. She edifies the entire family by her private devotions with the servants. These episodes typically conclude with the entire company dissolving in tears and piety.

The high point of the journal is the visit of crusty old Sir Jacob Swynford, who would have inherited Mr. B.'s property had B. not married. He arrogantly refuses to see Pamela because of her low birth, but the group decides to pass Pamela off as the Countess of C.'s niece "Lady Jenny." Sir Jacob is taken in by the ruse and declares that he can see the tokens of noble birth in Lady Jenny's face. When he learns Lady Jenny's true identity, he is confounded and begs forgiveness on his knees. In this affecting scene even Jackey must withdraw to shed tears.

Although he approves of Pamela personally, Sir Jacob is still critical of Mr. B.'s bad example in marrying beneath his rank. Mr. B. entraps the old gentleman into admitting that he himself has raised a poor boy, Jerry Sherwood, to be steward of his estate, and therefore has no right to be critical. Throughout the journal, there is a double attitude toward social class. The Countess of C. declares that if Sir Jacob is the product of an aristocratic breeding, she will have none of it. At the same time, Pamela proclaims that degree must be kept up.

Pamela ceremoniously visits the local poor, whose poverty she declares to be a blessing in disguise because hard work and a spare diet bring health. One afternoon she surprises her maid Polly Barlow allowing Jackey to take liberties with her person and forces her to confess that she has agreed to an illicit relationship with him. Pamela corners Jackey in the garden and forces him to send Polly back the contract he has induced her to sign, in return for which she promises not to expose him to Lord Davers. He writes her an ill-spelt letter of thanks.

The Davers ménage returns to Lincolnshire, and Pamela and Polly Darnford discuss the decorum that a wife should observe with respect to her husband. Polly wonders if Mr. B. really respects Pamela's opinions, whether he has ever allowed her to have her way in a dispute, and whether he respects her privacy. Pamela replies that he indeed waits to hear her opinions first, in matters where she is capable of judging; that a wife should have no will except her husband's; and that she should have no secrets from him.

Pamela and Mr. B. now visit Miss Goodwin, who ingenuously asks to be allowed to live with her "uncle and aunt B." Mr. B. is moved deeply by his sense of guilt and by Pamela's hopes for his eternal welfare, and gives signs of undergoing a genuine religious awakening.

Volume four—Pamela accompanies Mr. B. to his London town house, where she dislikes certain frothy friends of his but is more impressed by his learned Scottish acquaintance George Stuart. She and Mr. B. disagree over whether she should be allowed to nurse the baby when it arrives; Mr. B. is jealous of demands on Pamela's time and doesn't want her to spoil her shape. Pamela appeals to her parents for their decision, but they support Mr. B.

Polly Darnford arrives in town to visit Pamela. The correspondence at this time is filled with Pamela's evaluations of the London stage. She disapproves of Ambrose Philips' *Distressed Mother* (1712) because Hermione's love is not of that delicate sort appropriate to the female sex, and because the play treats suicide, a practice to which the English are already too much inclined. She also disapproves of Addison and Steele's *Tender Husband* because she dislikes the fact that evil characters are represented on the stage. She dislikes the opera because it is not didactic and is foreign to the spirit of the English nation.

The incident of the Countess Dowager of _____ begins when Mr. B. is accosted at a masquerade by a lady in a nun's costume, with whom he speaks in Italian. After intense fears of dying, Pamela gives birth to a son, to the rejoicing of all Mr. B.'s dependents. Polly Darnford returns to Lincolnshire, and Pamela asks Mr. B. that she be allowed to raise Miss Goodwin along with young Billy. At the same time that Pamela is undergoing childbirth, Mr. B. has begun to consort with the Countess. A Mr. Turner visits Pamela to confide that her husband has an assignation with the Countess at Oxford. Lady Davers writes at the same time that the Countess has been heard publicly to advocate polygamy.

Pamela is confounded when Mr. B. brings the Countess and her friend the Viscountess home for tea. Pamela wraps herself up in her innocence and behaves distantly, which puts Mr. B. into a huff. The next day at four a.m. he goes to Tunbridge Wells with the Countess, and Pamela receives a letter from one "Thomasine Fuller" that Mr. B. has entered into a bigamous living arrangement with her. When Mr. B. returns, Pamela arraigns herself before a mock bar of justice composed of three chairs and asks Mr. B. to decide her fate. Mr. B. convinces her that his relationship with the Countess has been entirely platonic and reveals that Mr. Turner is really a rebuffed suitor whose information is malicious and false. Pamela rejoices at their reconciliation. The Countess will go to live in Italy for several years, and Mr. B. thinks he can arrange for her marriage to a certain young lord.

Baby Billy falls ill of smallpox, and in nursing him Pamela contracts it. Luckily both recover, and Mr. B. takes Pamela to Bath to recuperate. Pamela writes Polly Darnford the news that Lady Davers has proposed Jackey as her husband, but Polly declines in favor of a Sir William G. She says that Jackey looks well but makes a fool out of himself whenever he opens his mouth. Mr. Williams receives an offer of marriage from a rich widow, and Pamela's chaplain Mr. Adams wishes to marry Pamela's maid Polly Barlow. Pamela fears that Polly's motivation may not be exclusively romantic.

Lady Davers writes that Mrs. Jewkes has died, heaping blessings on Pamela. Miss Goodwin enters the B. household, and Pamela receives a letter from Sally Godfrey, full of repentance. Pamela writes Lady Davers announcing the celebration of three weddings: Polly Darnford with Sir William G., Mr. Williams with the rich widow, and Mr. Adams with Polly Barlow. She includes a character sketch of old Miss Judy Swynford, who would be more charming were she to give up the affectation of trying to seem younger than she is. Pamela gives birth to a second child, a boy whom she names Davers.

Pamela writes a series of eight long letters containing her reaction to John Locke's *Some Thoughts Concerning Education* (1693), leaving alternate pages blank for Mr. B.'s corrections. Should children be educated at home or at school? While a home education may expose the child to the dangers of mixing with servants, and even to his parents' vicious habits, the danger of bad examples in a school is so great that Pamela favors a tutor, preferably a Scot who has learned to speak without a brogue. She feels that punishment should be administered only in anger, not after long deliberation. Locke recommends that children be taught the alphabet by dice with letters inscribed on them, a suggestion Pamela deplores since it may lead to gaming. She goes on to champion female education, since men will then respect women more and not try so hard to seduce them. Appropriately, Pamela gives birth to a daughter, whom she names after herself.

The B.s and Daverses go to France and Italy for two years, where Pamela has a fourth child, Charley, and where Jackey is almost converted to Catholicism by scheming priests, but fortunately he relapses into safe nothingness. Mrs. Jervis and Longman die, with high encomiums from Pamela. Old Mr. Jonathan the butler continues to flourish; Pamela reveres his silver hairs, and his eyes fill with tears whenever he sees her. A fifth child, Jemmy, is born.

Jackey has come of age and has assumed his title. He contracts a foolish marriage with a woman of the town who happens to be from a good family. He announces the marriage in an impertinent and ill-spelt letter to Lord and Lady Davers, who are understandably furious. Finally his wife almost bankrupts him by her extravagance, and Mr. B. arranges for a separation. When she dies, Jackey marries a prudent woman chosen for him by his aunt Davers.

The novel closes with three didactic episodes. First, Pamela tells Polly Darnford (now Lady G.) that a gentleman would do well to take a tour of England to complete his education, rather than the traditional grand tour of the Continent. In France and Italy, young Englishmen merely pick up foreign vices and acquire a contempt for their native land.

Lady Towers, Lady Arthur, and Dean L. bring four young ladies to Pamela (Miss Stapylton, Miss Cope, Miss Sutton, and the Dean's daughter Miss L.), all of whom have become entangled with gentlemen of loose character. Miss Stapylton has been led into her fault by reading novels and romances. Miss Cope is "too lively" and is involved with a libertine. Miss Sutton is too ready to pardon the sexual misdoings of gallant young men, and Miss L. is too credulous. After being instructed by Pamela, three of the ladies give up their rakes and marry discreet young men; only Miss Sutton persists in her folly and marries a gamester.

Pamela describes how she tells nursery stories to her (by now) seven children, in which good children come to good ends, but the naughty children of a poor widow comes to various evil ends. To Miss Goodwin she tells the story of Coquetilla, Prudiana, Profusiana, and Prudentia, only the last of whom is rewarded with a good marriage.

In the conclusion, we learn that Mr. B. retires into the country after serving his country well as a diplomat. Miss Goodwin marries, Lord Davers dies, and Lady Davers comes to live with her brother. Pamela's parents die at a good old age, Lady G. (Polly Darnford) dies in childbed of her fourth child. Mr. Longman has disinherited his relatives because of their evil characters and has left the bulk of his property to Mr. B. We see Pamela for the last time as she is benevolently distributing this property to Mr. Longman's now-repentant relatives.

Abraham, Mr. Adams, Elizabeth Andrews, John Andrews, John Andrews, Jr., Pamela Andrews, Thomas Andrews, William Andrews, John Arnold, Lady Arthur, Mr. Arthur, Arthur, Sir Thomas Atkyns, Aunt B., Billy B., Charley B., Davers B., James B., Lady B., Pamela B., William B.(Mr. B.), William ("Billy") B., Mary ("Polly") Barlow, Sir Jonathan Barnes, Mr. Barrow, Sir Michael Beaumont, Bell, Benjamin, Mrs. Bennet, Miss Betty, Lady Betty, Farmer Brady, Mr. Brett, Lady Brooks, Mr. Brooks, Miss Booth, Nancy Borroughs, Miss Borroughs, Miss Burdoff, Roger Burroughs, Cicely, Countess of C., Countess Dowager of _____, Mr. Carlton, Mr. Chambers, Mr. Chapman, Colbrand, Miss Cope, Nancy Darnford, Polly Darnford, Sir Simon Darnford, Lady Barbara Davers, William Lord Davers, Deb, Farmer Dickins, Mrs. Dobson, Mr. Dormer, Mr. Fanshaw, Miss Fenwick, Fielding, Mr. Floyd, Mr. Fownes, Sir William G., Sarah ("Sally") Godfrey, gypsy, Jackey H., Hannah, Sir Charles Hargrave, Mrs. Harris, Harry, Mr. Herbert, Hodge, Mr. Howard, Isaac, Jack, Jacob, Jane, Dr. Jenkins, Lady Jenny, Mrs. Jervis, Mrs. K. Jewkes, Lord John, John, Jonas, Mr. Jonathan, Farmer Jones, Lady Jones, Dean L., Miss L., Mrs. Lesley, Mr. Longman, 'Squire Martin "in the Grove," old widow Mumford, Mr. Murray, Nelthorpe, Nan, Farmer Nichols, Farmer Norton, Mrs. Norton, Miss Nugent, Mrs. Oldham, Mr. Perry, Mr. Peters, Mrs. Peters, Rachel, Bedfordshire Robin, Lincolnshire

Robin, Mr. Sedley, Jerry Sherwood, Mr. Shorter, Mr. Sidney, Mr. Simmonds, John Smith, Miss Stapylton, Mr. George Stuart, Miss Sutton, Dolly Swynford, Sir Jacob Swynford, Judy Swynford, Mab Swynford, Mrs. Thomas, Thomas, Miss Tomlins, Lady Towers, Mr. Towers, Mr. Turner, Viscountess of _____, Mr. Walgrave, John Wilkins, Arthur Williams, Col. Wilson, Beck Worden, Mr. Wrightson.

Robert Drury's Journal, Defoe, 1729. (Original title: *Madagascar: Or, Robert Drury's Journal*.)

Drury is born in 1687, his father a well-known London innkeeper. Despite the pleas of his mother on bended knee, the lad is determined to go to sea. He sails on the *Degrave*, February 19, 1701, for the East Indies. The ship is dogged by bad fortune; in Bengal, forty men die of fever, including the captain, whose son takes command. The new Capt. Yonge turns out to have very poor judgment. While leaving the roads of Calcutta, the ship goes hard aground. After it is afloat again, it is found to have sprung a severe leak and has to be pumped all across the Indian Ocean. They are forced to land on Madagascar. The ship is wrecked, but the people warp their way to shore on a raft. The captain brings ashore the heart of his father in a bottle, since he has promised to have it buried at Dover.

They fall in with another party of castaways, led by Captains Drummond and Steward. They all fall into the hands of a lean-jawed, one-eyed native king named Deaan Crindo (Deaan is the local title of respect for any noble), who obviously intends to keep them as his prisoners. The tender feet of the English are tormented by their journey. There is nothing to eat or drink but sandy beef, dirty water, and cactus plants. Drury is full of remorse for having ignored his mother's advice. Deaan Crindo's daughter falls in love with him, but he is unable to understand anything she is saying. One of the other castaways has to translate for him, and he is mortified at having forced a young lady to be so explicit.

The Englishmen make a try for liberty. They seize Deaan Crindo and his nephew as hostages and set out for Port Dauphine, where King Samuel is friendly to Europeans. Six bands of natives shadow them guardedly. They are tormented by thirst and even have to lick up the dew to survive. Capt. Yonge foolishly agrees to exchange his hostages for six muskets and three lesser nobles. An

English sailor with a wooden leg must be left behind and is stabbed to death by the natives. Finally Yonge, after repelling an attack, agrees to give up their weapons (at any rate, they are out of ammunition). The Drummond-Steward party escape under cover of darkness; but Yonge's group is slaughtered, except for Drury and three other boys, who are enslaved. On the march back to Anterndroea, Drury must eat half-raw meat (he soon grows used to it), and the black hide of his new master smells so strong that he is hardly able to sleep next to him.

Back in the village, Drury sleeps at his master's feet until it becomes clear from Deaan Mevarrow's calling him several times during the night that he is interfering with sexual intimacies, and he is removed to another hut. He is made into a cattle driver. The region is plagued by constant tribal warfare. Upon Deaan Mevarrow's return from a campaign, Drury is reluctant to perform the Salamonger Umba (foot-licking ceremony) required of all dependents. Mevarrow's brother, Deaan Sambo, persuades Drury to comply so that Mevarrow will not kill him. He narrowly escapes death a second time for refusing to bow down to the tribal totem, the Owley.

While guarding the cattle, Drury and the other white slave-boys become crazed with hunger. They kill an ox and eat it, feigning that it was gored by another of the herd. But when their masters catch them gorging themselves on a second slain beast, they seize the three other boys and castrate them. Rather than undergo this terrible punishment, Drury asks his master to stand him up against a tree and shoot him. Mevarrow fires and misses, but whether he intended to miss or not, Drury does not know. He then binds up the bleeding groins of his companions, who are unable to walk for several days.

King Samuel attacks Anterndroea, along with Capt. Drummond, to demand the release of the boys. When Drummond shouts across the battlefield to Drury, Mevarrow suspects them of plotting against him and breaks off negotiations. Later he commands Drury to reveal the plot to him; and when Drury protests that their intentions were innocent, Mevarrow places the muzzle of a musket against his breast and pulls the trigger. The weapon misfires, and Deaan Sambo berates his brother for such cruelty.

King Samuel is really a Frenchman who has become a native king. The queen at Point Dauphine mistook him (because of a birthmark under his left nipple) for her long-lost son, who had been kidnapped by the French and taken to France. He later murders one of his countrymen who tries to disillusion the blacks. Drury begins to raise bees but has a problem with robberies from his hives. He solves the problem by a trick. The Umossee (witch doctor) has put a hex on Mevarrow's hives. Drury agrees to be a guinea pig and "try out" the hex, after which he feigns terrible pains. The delighted Mevarrow applies the antidote and tells Drury what the charm is. Drury applies the hex to his own hives, and now everyone in the village is afraid to go near them.

A complicated civil war begins in Anterndroea. Drury, his white skin smeared with mud as camouflage, helps to kidnap all the women of an enemy village. Deaan Mevarrow forms a league with Deaan Murnanzack (the rightful claimant to the throne) in a ceremony that Drury compares to the early stages of European commonwealths. (Defoe here explains his social-contract theory of society.) After a second victory, Drury is sent to Mevarrow's wife with the good news. He beds down with her but assures us that nothing sinful took place during the night.

Drury gains status in the tribe by being allowed by virtue of his white skin to take over some of Deaan Mevarrow's ceremonial functions, specifically the exclusive right to slaughter cattle. He is then sent into Deaan Murnanzack's territory with part of the herd to protect it from the enemy. He dreams that Murnanzack will become angry with him, and the next day the Deaan really does have a flash of temper. That evening, to pass the time, Murnanzack (an enlightened despot) asks Drury about the religion of the English. Murnanzack finds the Old Testament stories laughable. Drury rashly offers to prove the story of the creation of Eve by counting ribs; but when the men around the campfire prove to have the same number of ribs as the women, he is laughed to scorn. Murnanzack cites the prophetic dream as proof that the Owleys are indeed guardian spirits. Despite the superstition in this country, religious persecutions are unknown, in sharp contrast to Europe.

Drury terrifies a group of Negroes who have never seen a white man, and one of the women goes into fits. As a joke he poses as one of the tribal chiefs and is able to impose on the simple folk because of the respect accorded his white skin. The tribe is reduced to desperate straits by the war, having to grub for yams to sustain life. Finally Murnanzack makes peace to relieve the suffering of his

people. Although European priests would dismiss Murnanzack as
a heathen, Drury sees him as an enlightened moralist.

An ambassador named Ry Nanno from the country of Feraighn
rebukes Deaan Mevarrow for his harsh treatment of Drury. Ry
Nanno (who speaks broken English) tries to buy Drury to take him
to Port St. Augustine, where he can be picked up by a European
ship, but Mevarrow (somewhat inconsistently) now declares that
the boy is his best slave and refuses to sell him. Drury goes out and
cries bitterly. Later the ambassador tells him to keep up his
spirits, for Providence will surely enable him to escape eventually.

In a raid, Drury captures a sixteen-year-old girl, whom he takes
for his wife. He feels he must justify to his readers his choosing a
black woman and explains that they are as loyal and affectionate
as English girls. Mevarrow suspects a village boy of adultery with
his wife and, during a hunting expedition, kills both him and his
brother. The normally merciful Deaan Sambo participates in the
execution, and so Drury thinks the charges may be grounded in fact.

The Umossee predicts that Drury will run away from his master;
therefore Deaan Mevarrow gives the boy certain potions so that
the demons will break his legs should he try to run away. Ironically, this bewitching causes Drury to run away all the sooner,
since he knows that any trivial accident that might befall him
will be interpreted by Mevarrow as the demons' tripping up an
escape attempt.

After a tearful parting with his wife, Drury runs sixty miles in
one night and throws himself on the mercy of a neighboring chieftain, Deaan Afferrer, who shelters him. The natives conclude that
demons must have no power over a white man. His eventual plan
is a journey to the Feraighners, who trade regularly with the
English; but Afferrer wants to keep him as one of his own servants
(there is enormous prestige in having a white slave). Drury fights
in the next war on Afferrer's side. The enemy soldiers get themselves ready for battle by smoking the leaves of the Jermaughler
plant, which makes their eyes red and their hearts courageous.
Drury once tried this narcotic, but since it made him ill for three
days, he never tampered with it again.

During this period Drury participates in a hunt for wild cattle,
in which one of the natives is gruesomely tossed, gored, and butted
to death by an enraged bull. One day when Afferrer's watchfulness
has subsided, Drury takes off through the bush toward the west
coast of the island. He has a number of harrowing experiences.

Upon becoming lost in the mountains, he balances his spear on its point and travels superstitiously in the direction it falls. Once he negligently lets his campfire go out and wakes to find a wild fox dragging him away by the heel. He kills the fox, but later his heel becomes swollen and he must wait for six days before continuing his journey. In crossing streams, he has to swim on his back and carry two torches to keep off the alligators.

On the twenty-sixth day out he meets some of the Feraighners and knows that he has reached his goal. They are astonished at seeing a white man. They know that he cannot have come from one of the ships, since he has no clothes and, most important, no hat. As a special mark of favor, Deaan Trongha, prince of the region, does not allow Drury to lick his feet. Great laughter is caused by the fact that Deaan Trongha speaks better English than Drury does, after so many years among the natives.

The king of the country congratulates Drury on having lost the barbarous disposition of the white man and having taken on the more civilized traits of the Negro. He wins further favor by rescuing a native woman from being dragged under water by an alligator. Deaan Trongha makes Drury his personal companion and musket-carrier. Drury makes an unguarded remark about how the country will be ruined if the war goes on much longer. Deaan Trongha warns him not to make such remarks, since the common people regard all whites as conjurers and believe that whatever they say must certainly come true.

Drury meets Eglasse, an eccentric Dutchman who has escaped from a party of unscrupulous slave traders. His companion Mr. Arnold was murdered by the natives. Eglasse has a hot temper and is critical of the tribal leaders. He is having an amour with the wife of a poor, blind Guinea Negro, one Hempshire. Hempshire's family speaks English and instructs Drury in his forgotten native tongue. During one of these visits, Drury falls ill with a fever and is given up for dead. Just as he is recovering, five natives visit Eglasse and, during a bargaining session over a cow, seize a lance and kill him. They have done so on orders from the king, since Eglasse has made a number of threatening remarks and (it later turns out) has been guilty of sharp trading practices. Drury's life is spared.

To Drury's consternation, the Feraighners join his old masters the Anterndroeans in a campaign against a common enemy, and he is maneuvered into going along. The Umossee constructs a talis-

man called the "elodge," made out of the corpse of a bird, and says
the god has ordered Drury to carry this standard three or four
stones' throw in front of the line of battle! Drury consents only
on the condition that he is preceded by a party of a hundred
skirmishers. When battle is finally joined, the gods declare they
can dispense with Drury's services. He sees his old masters again,
Deaans Mevarrow and Crindo, and suffers intense pangs of grief
on hearing how his wife is mourning for him.

He leaves the campaign early to avoid having to return to Deaan
Mevarrow, but is captured by a raiding party of Saccalauvors and
re-enslaved, along with the Hempshire family. They all undergo
a long trek to the territory of their captors. The king, Rer Trimmonongarevo, is aging and choleric (Defoe's picture of an arbitrary
ruler). He cuts the throat of one of his sons for sleeping with a
member of the harem. He has one of his wives killed for breaking
wind while he was sleeping with his head in her lap. The king's
chief wife is the biggest woman Drury has ever seen. She has to be
carried in a sort of bier, and when she sits her breasts droop down
into her lap. Drury's immediate master, Rer Vove, is a young rake
and employs Drury to arrange an assignation for him with one of
his former wives. The king's uncle, a neighboring chief named Rer
Moume, is good-natured, even though he is crippled in his legs as
a result of a poisoning attempt. He befriends Drury and eventually
arranges for his return to England.

An English ship arrives and buys off the other white slave in the
encampment, William Thornbury. Rer Vove is enraged when he
finds that Drury want to go too. An attempt to send the captain a
note written on a leaf is frustrated, because Drury's messenger
doesn't understand the art of writing and substitutes for the leaf
another one "just as good" torn from a tree. Even Thornbury
forgets about Drury when he has sailed away.

After a bout of the yaws (a skin disease), Drury escapes to Rer
Moume, who treats him as an honored guest and provides him
with a wife, a farm, and a slave boy. Disaster almost overtakes
him when he visits the old king. He is accused of plotting to steal
a Portuguese black slave named Francisco. His life is spared at
the place of execution only because of the pleas of one of the king's
wives. He is taken bound back to Rer Moume, who is indignant
at his nephew's conduct and frees Drury.

Finally a ship arrives with a letter from Drury's father (Rer
Moume has no idea what the mysterious marks on paper may

signify). Through sheer coincidence, Drury's brother has overheard Thornbury in a bar discussing Madagascar and has made
inquiries. Rer Moume reluctantly grants permission for him to
leave. Appearing to the English sailors like a wild man, Drury is
taken on board the *Drake*. Captain Macket treats him kindly, has
his hair cut, and gives him clothing. The crew laugh at his utter
ignorance of British money and his inability to hold down the
white man's liquor. He misses the mead-like "toak" of the blacks.
Drury does the captain a good turn by serving as middleman in
negotiations with the native chieftains for slaves. His experiences
have apparently given him no objections to the slave trade on
principle.

When the *Drake* arrives home on September 9, 1717, Drury has
been gone almost seventeen years. He goes to the Bell Tavern and
inquires for his father. He is crushed to learn that his father,
mother, and uncle are all dead, and the family business (the old
King's Head Tavern) is being operated by a stranger.

He works briefly in England as a clerk, but soon ships again
with a Captain White as an interpreter for a slaving voyage to
Madagascar. The native chiefs attempt to sell them slaves with
secret instructions to run away, but Drury is able to keep the captain from being swindled because of his familiarity with the island
culture. He revisits his old benefactor Rer Moume and licks his
knees in greeting. The Englishmen then sail to the Rappahannock
River in Virginia to sell their slaves. In conclusion, Drury insists
on the truth of his account and says that he can be found any day
at Old Tom's Coffeehouse to satisfy people's objections or disbelief.

Deaan Afferrer, Rer Ambarroch, Deaan Aneebeleeshy,
King of Antenosa, Anthony, Deaan Antymoor, Ry Anzack-
er, Robert Arnold, Batoengha, Robert Beardsley, Rer Be-
faugher, John Bembo, Admiral Bembo, Capt. Bloom, Capt.
Boon, Capt. Burgess, Deaan Chahary, Joseph Chamberlain,
Chemermaunda, Ry Chemotoea, Rer Chemunghoher,
Capt. Christal, Rer Chula, Rer Chulu-Mossu-Andro,
Thomas Collins, Deaan Crindo, Deude ("Dudey"), Nicho-
las Dove, Capt. Drummond, John Drury, Robert Drury
("Robin"), William Drury, Mrs. Drury, Efflep, Eglasse,
Francisco, Deaan Frukey, Rer Fungenzer, Capt. Greene,
Guy, Capt. Harvey, Mrs. Hempshire, Hempshire, Mr. Hill,
James, John, Ry Kaley, Mons. John Lapie, Ry Leffu, Lewis,

Deaan Lohefute, Capt. Henry Macket, Capt. William Mack-
et, Mechorow, Deaan Meguddummateem, Mephontey,
Deaan Mernaugha, Deaan Mernindgarevo, Capt. Mesmer-
rico, Metorolahatch, Deaan Mevarrow, Rer Mimebolambo,
Deaan Morrocheruck, Deaan Morroughsevea, Rer Moume,
Rer Mundrosser, Deaan Mundumbo, Deaan Mungazaun-
garevo, Deaan Murnanzack, Deaan Mussecorrow, Rer Myn-
bolambo, Ry Nanno, Deaan Olaavor, Ry Opheck, Mr. Prat,
John Pro, William Purser, Robin (two), Roy'nsowra, Sam,
Deaan Sambo, Sambo, John Steel, Capt. Steward, Mr.
Strahan, Deaan Termerre, Mr. Terry, William Thornbury,
Deaan Toakeoffu ("King Dick" or "Long Dick"), Toby, Rer
Towlerpherangha, Rer Trimmonongarevo, Deaan Tro-
daughe, Deaan Trongha, Rer Trortrock, Deaan Tuley-
Noro ("King Samuel"), Deaan Unghorray, Unter Morrow
Cheruck, Rer Vovvern, Capt. Ware, Capt. White, Capt.
Wilks, Deaan Woozington, Capt. Nicholas Yonge, Capt.
William Yonge, Yung-Owl, Zachary, Zaffentumppoey.

Robinson Crusoe, Defoe, 1719. (Original title: *The Life and Strange Sur-*
prising Adventures of Robinson Crusoe of York, Mariner.)
Young Robinson's two older brothers have gone to seek their
fortunes and have both lost their lives. When he evinces a similar
desire to see the world, his father beseeches him with tears to remain at home and enjoy the middle station of life instead of taking
risks for the sake of wealth. Crusoe's mother makes the same plea,
but the young man refuses to listen to advice and signs on board a
ship at Hull bound for London. The first day out a storm terrifies
the new sailor and makes him repent his disobedience, but he soon
drinks away his remorse with the captain's son. While they are
anchored in Yarmouth Roads, however, a huge storm comes and
sinks the vessel. Luckily the crew escapes in a lifeboat, but when
the captain finds out that Crusoe has run away to sea, he berates
him as a Jonas.

But Crusoe again hardens his heart and sets out for Guinea on
the coast of Africa, investing forty pounds in the voyage and
realizing three hundred. Emboldened by this success, he leaves
two hundred pounds with the captain's widow (the captain of the
Guinea expedition dies shortly after making port) and sets out
again. This time disaster strikes; the ship is overtaken by a Sallee
pirate, and the entire crew is taken captive.

Crusoe serves as a slave of the pirate captain, catching fish for his table along with a Moor and a Maresco. But one day he contrives to sail the boat out of sight of land, throws the Moor overboard, and persuades Xury, the Maresco slave boy, to run away with him. They make southward for Cape Verde. On the way they encounter naked savages and wild beasts, and shoot a lion and a leopard. Finally they are picked up by a Portuguese vessel. Crusoe sells the boat and supplies for a handsome profit and even sells faithful Xury to the Portuguese captain, who promises to free him in ten years if he will convert to Christianity.

Crusoe lands in San Salvador, Brazil, invests in land, and begins raising tobacco; but the wanderlust keeps him from being content. The planters commission him to go and fetch slaves from Guinea, promising to administer his plantation for him in his absence. He sets out with thirteen other men in a small ship on September 1, 1659. Seven degrees north of the Line a hurricane blows them far off course toward the mouth of the Orinoco River. They attempt to reach Barbados but are driven hard aground on a sandbar by a second storm. They have just abandoned ship when a huge sea upsets the longboat, and Crusoe alone makes his way to shore, almost overwhelmed by the violent surf. The next morning on the beach he finds a few tokens of his comrades: three hats, one cap, and two shoes that are not mates.

At first Crusoe is elated at being saved, but soon he is overwhelmed with despair at being marooned and sleeps in a tree for fear of wild beasts. Since the ship has been washed up within a mile of the shore, he can swim out to her. On board he is able to salvage some food, some weapons, and many tools, which he ferries ashore on a makeshift raft. He finds thirty-six pounds in cash and at first despises it, "but, upon second thought, I took it away." His despair is intensified by the discovery that he is on an island; he fires a gun, the first shot heard there since the Creation.

With enormous labor Crusoe constructs a home for himself by erecting a palisade around a ledge, high up on a hillside, and digging out a cave which he shores up with beams. A thunderstorm alerts him to the danger of sleeping near so much gunpowder, and so he secretes it in a hundred separate parcels. He kills a wild goat, but only later does he catch one and raise it up. He lacks certain crucial tools, such as a spade (he constructs one out of ironwood), a pickaxe, and a shovel. He also lacks needles, pins, and thread, but finds he can get along without underwear very well.

He makes a calendar from a post, on which each notch stands for a day (Christmas passes unobserved). He also keeps a journal, in which he draws up the advantages and liabilities of his plight in tabular form; he may be shipwrecked, but at least his life has been spared, and so on. The first stage of Crusoe's religious transformation occurs when he casually throws out some kernels of barley and rice. When he later finds barley growing near the mouth of the cave he attributes it to a miracle, but later, upon thinking of the true explanation, his glimmers of piety disappear. He husbands the grains of his little crop, but only after four years does he have enough to make bread.

A violent earthquake rocks the island, and Crusoe is so afraid of being buried alive that he decides to construct a new house in the open. The ship is washed up again on shore, and Crusoe salvages even more lumber and hardware. A captured turtle full of eggs provides him with the first meat he has had for many months.

Suddenly he discovers that he is feeling unnaturally chilly. This leads to a tertian ague and the central event of the novel, Crusoe's religious awakening. He dreams feverishly that a man wrapped in flames comes to him and says, "Seeing all these things have not brought thee to repentance, now thou shalt die." Upon awakening he turns to his Bible and undergoes a religious conversion. His shipwreck is a proper punishment for his Godless way of life and is furthermore a providential means of bringing him to know Christ. After a heartfelt prayer for deliverance he takes some rum in which tobacco has been steeping and sleeps for almost forty-eight hours.

Crusoe explores the island further and builds a bower on the northern side, which he dubs his "country house." He gathers grapes into a large pile but later finds them mysteriously scattered (the cause of this comes to light afterward). He finds penguins(!) and a parrot, which he teaches to speak. He then embarks on four new projects, which are completed after intense frustration. He masters the complicated process of baking bread; but only after much experimentation does he discover how to make a bean pot, molding it out of clay and baking it in the fire.

His most ambitious project is making a boat, since the ship's beached longboat is too heavy for him to move. After months of toil he succeeds in hewing an immense canoe out of a tree trunk, only to find that it is too heavy for him to launch. Only later does he succeed in digging out and launching a smaller canoe. As his original supplies from the ship have begun to give out, he is forced to make clothes out of furs for protection from the tropical sun. He even manages to contrive an umbrella.

On November 6, 1664, Crusoe sets out in his new canoe to circumnavigate the island. Attempting to round the eastern promontory, he is caught in a vicious current and carried far out to sea. Only by great good luck does he drift into slack water so he can paddle back to the northern side of the island. While sleeping exhausted in his bower, he is surprised by a voice calling, "Poor Robin Crusoe!" only to discover that it is only Poll Parrot. Crusoe's goats now provide him with milk, butter, and cheese, as well as meat; he imagines himself as a king with power of life and death over his subjects.

Out walking one day on the northern side of the island (the opposite side from the one he landed on), Crusoe sees the print of a man's naked foot. In terror he runs back to his cave and for three days doesn't even go out to milk his flock. At first he thinks the print may belong to the devil, but eventually decides it must be from a savage from the mainland. Then he stumbles upon a pit full of the remains of a cannibal feast and his worst fears are confirmed. He goes aside and becomes violently ill.

Crusoe's way of life becomes one of fear. For two years he spins fantasies about surprising the cannibals and massacring them, but finally he approaches a philosophical position of cultural relativism and decides that the savages are at any rate no worse than the Spaniards. Moreover, if he were to ambush them, he would draw retribution upon himself, and so he develops another hideaway in a cave. A pair of gleaming eyes in the cave alarms him, but they turn out to belong to an old dying he-goat.

During the twenty-third year of his exile, Crusoe hears a ship's guns sounding a distress signal. He builds a huge bonfire to direct the sailors to land, but in vain. The ship strikes on the rocks far offshore. All hands are lost, and only the body of a cabin boy is washed up on the strand. Crusoe's despair is profound.

He has long dreamed of liberating a savage from the cannibals to help him in escaping from the island. One day he sees five war canoes come ashore on his side of the island. The savages kill one of their four captives, but another one escapes, running frantically toward Crusoe's fortress. Crusoe runs out, stuns one of the pursuers with his gun-butt, and shoots the other. The rescued savage prostrates himself in gratitude and then cuts off the head of his remaining enemy.

Crusoe names the savage "Friday" and begins to civilize him, teaching him to speak English, to shoot, and to wear clothes. Friday offers to dig up the slain savages and eat them, but Crusoe shows his intense disgust at the suggestion. The relationship between the two from the start is one of master-slave. Friday is wooed away from the worship of Benamuckee, although he puzzles Crusoe by asking why an allegedly omnipotent God allows the devil to go on existing.

Friday tells Crusoe of some castaway Spaniards on the mainland, but before they can go to fetch them they are again invaded. This time they rescue a Spaniard and a savage from the cannibals, and the savage turns out to be none other than Friday's father. Crusoe's two new "subjects" are dispatched to bring over the other castaways, but first the Spaniard must promise not to have Crusoe delivered to the Inquisition.

Less than eight days later, an English ship finally casts anchor off the island and Crusoe sights a longboat approaching shore with three men sitting in it bound. The captives are the ship's captain, the mate, and a passenger, who are being marooned by mutineers. Crusoe helps the captain overpower his captors. Since most of the crew is still basically loyal, only the two chief conspirators are marked out for punishment. Another party of mutineers comes ashore looking for their comrades and is ambushed. The captain then enlists twelve repentant men and storms the ship. The boatswain and one other ringleader are killed, and their bodies strung up at the yardarm.

Crusoe embarks with Friday after twenty-eight years of exile. He leaves three of the most intransigent mutineers on the island (they are later joined by two others who jump ship). Crusoe arrives back in England on June 11, 1686. He finds his friend the captain's widow still living, but his parents in York are both dead. He sails to Lisbon, where his friend the Portuguese captain tells him that his Brazilian estate is being administered by the government. His Brazilian partner sends him twenty-eight years' worth of profits, making Crusoe a wealthy man.

Crusoe and a party of travelers set off overland for France, but on the way they are caught in heavy snow and attacked by wild animals. Friday amuses the company by teasing a bear, luring it after him into a tree, and then shooting it. More serious trouble materializes when the party is attacked by a ravenous band of three hundred wolves. Crusoe forms the company into a defensive triangle, and they drive the wolves off with small-arms fire.

In England Crusoe marries in a pronouncedly unromantic way, "not either to my disadvantage or dissatisfaction." The novel closes with a brief sketch of Crusoe's return to his island, narrated in detail in the *Farther Adventures of Robinson Crusoe*, published later the same year.

Will Atkyns, Robinson Crusoe, Mrs. Crusoe (his mother), Mrs. Crusoe (his wife), father of Friday, Friday, Will Frye, Mr. Kreutznaer (later called Crusoe, the hero's father), Moely, Robinson, Tom Smith, Wells, Xury.

Roxana, Defoe, 1724. (Original title: *The Fortunate Mistress*.)

The woman who later comes to be called Roxana is born in Poitiers (France) of Huguenot parents who flee the country in 1683 and settle in England. She grows up perfectly bilingual, a beautiful girl and a fine dancer, but inclined to be too satirical and forward in conversation. At age fifteen her father marries her to a brewer who turns out to be nothing but a handsome ne'er-do-well, preoccupied with hunting, and neither frugal nor diligent enough to succeed in business. After dissipating Roxana's dowry and being forced to sell his brewery, he abandons Roxana with five children. Roxana urges her female readers to marry any sort of man but a fool.

The brewer's brothers and sisters refuse to help Roxana out of her financial distress; only an elderly aunt-in-law and a former family servant come to her aid. Roxana's clever maid Amy contrives to take the five children to the home of their aunt and uncle, knock at the door, and push them inside while she makes her escape. The aunt rails and threatens to send the children to the parish, but the old family servant arrives and tells her that Roxana has run mad. The uncle prevails on his wife to take care of the children, presenting the act of charity as a business proposition with the Lord.

Roxana is befriended by her landlord, who showers her with food and drink and allows her to live in his house rent free. Amy warns her mistress that the landlord is after only one thing, but Roxana is slow to be convinced. At any rate, says Amy, it is all right to be a whore for bread, and Roxana wouldn't be one for anything else. Finally the landlord contrives a "wedding supper," after which Roxana consents to go to bed with him. After a year and a half of this affair, Amy twits Roxana for not being pregnant, in return for

which Roxana debauches Amy and puts her to bed with the landlord. She comments that once the human conscience has become
hardened, it is capable of anything. Amy has a child which Roxana
raises as her own; her own child born of the landlord dies at the
age of six months.

The landlord also deals in jewels, and he and Roxana take up
residence in Paris to carry on the business. One day he is preparing
to visit the Prince of _____ , and Roxana has a sudden vision of the
landlord first as a wasted skeleton and then covered with blood.
He ignores her entreaties to stay home. The next day she learns
that he has been murdered by thieves. Roxana has no legal claim
to his estate, since he is still legally married to another woman.
Nevertheless, she possesses herself of his jewels and writes to
Amy in London to sell everything in the house and join her in Paris.

The Prince de _____ , whom the landlord was on his way to visit,
pays his respects to the beautiful "widow" and then sends his
gentleman to her to announce that he will give her a pension of
two thousand livres a year as long as she stays in Paris. After a
series of courtly dialogues between the prince and Roxana, she
demonstrates by washing her face in his presence that she uses
no paint, and he responds by kissing her breasts. She becomes
his mistress for eight years and bears him a child, her ninth preg-
nancy. She retires to the country for her lying-in, where Amy is
seduced by the prince's gentleman. Roxana has only herself to
blame, however, for the decline in Amy's morals; she admits that
she is no longer whoring out of necessity, but rather for personal
gain.

On a visit to the French court at Meudon, Roxana is astonished
to glimpse her first husband, the brewer, as a member of the gendarmes. She sends Amy to interview him and tell him stories of
how Roxana is poverty-stricken in London. The brewer feigns sorrow and then attempts to borrow five hundred pistoles from Amy;
he must content himself finally with a single pistole. Roxana continues to have his movements traced by a private detective to prevent his discovering her.

Roxana accompanies the prince on a two years' tour of Italy,
where their second child is born, while Amy remains in Paris to
safeguard Roxana's wealth. Upon their return to France, the
prince's wife on her deathbed urges her husband to be true to his
next wife, at least. Conscience-stricken, the prince throws Roxana
over but continues to pay her rent and to provide for the two boys.

Roxana decides to return to England and goes to a Dutch merchant living in Paris to procure bills of exchange, on the security of her jewels, for transferral to a London bank. But when the merchant brings a Jew to appraise the jewels, the Jew recognizes them as the very jewels which had supposedly been stolen from the English jeweler (Roxana's landlord) eight years earlier. The Jew accuses Roxana of being the robbers' accomplice and tries to blackmail her to secure the jewels for himself, but he makes the mistake of confiding his plan to the honorable Dutch merchant. The Dutchman then arranges for Roxana's escape to Rouen, where she can take ship for Amsterdam.

At sea the ship encounters a terrible storm which frightens Amy into momentary repentance, but Roxana is so hardened in sin that she remains unmoved. They are forced to land in England, and since Amy refuses to go back aboard the ship, she remains there. Roxana goes on to Amsterdam, where the Dutch merchant joins her and tells her that the prince's gentleman has had the Jew's ears cut off. Roxana laughs heartily at the news.

The Dutch merchant entices Roxana into his bed, but to his astonishment she declines his offer of marriage. She is afraid that marriage will deprive her of her financial independence. When the Dutchman assures her that she can keep her own property, she must continue refusing in order to save face, even though she finds herself pregnant by him. She is ashamed to admit that her refusal was based on pecuniary reasons. She argues that to marry a man one has slept with is "befouling one's self and living in the smell of it."

Roxana returns to London and takes lodgings in Pall Mall, where her accumulated wealth enables her to give lavish parties, attended by members of the court and even King Charles II. Roxana puts on revealing Turkish garments and dances erotically for the court, thus gaining the sobriquet of "Roxana," a name suggesting Oriental royalty. She attracts the attention of a wicked old lord who showers her with presents and keeps her as a mistress for eight years. Roxana's fortune continues to grow because of shrewd investments made for her by her friend Sir Robert Clayton (an actual historical figure). At last the odd sexual habits of the old man cause Roxana to break off with him.

Upon returning to London at age thirty-five, Roxana sent Amy to discover the whereabouts of her first five children. Two have died, but her younger son is serving a hard apprenticeship at a "dirty trade." Using Amy as an agent, Roxana provides for his education and sets him up in business as a merchant trading with Turkey. By an astonishing coincidence, Amy discovers Roxana's oldest daughter Susan working in their own kitchen in Kensington! Roxana does not want to reveal her true identity to Susan, because her conscience has begun to trouble her for her misspent life. Fortunately Susan has passed all her time in the kitchen and has seen her mistress only on the occasion of the Turkish dance. And so Roxana's greatest triumph as a courtesan turns out to be the source of her undoing.

To avoid Susan, Roxana and Amy change lodgings. They move to a house in the Minories kept by a Quaker lady, where Roxana begins to dress in the Quaker style. One day riding in her carriage with the Quakeress, she recognizes her old friend the Dutch merchant, who seeks her out at her lodgings and asks about the welfare of their child, to whom Roxana is actually indifferent. The news arrives from Paris that Roxana's husband in the gendarmes has died; so she feels free to accept the Dutch merchant's offer of marriage. She is especially attracted to him by the fact that he has been naturalized and has found where he can purchase the patent for a baronetcy. They marry and pool their resources, but Roxana fears that her tainted money will cause God to curse the Dutch merchant's prosperity.

Meanwhile Susan has been putting two and two together. She recognizes Amy as her brother's benefactress and also recalls that Amy was the servant of the famous lady Roxana. Susan jumps to the conclusion that Amy is her real mother, or, if Amy is not the one, then it must be the lady Roxana herself. Amy is enraged and tells her mistress that she will kill Susan to put her out of the way. Roxana is horrified, although she is equally unwilling for Susan to discover her, since she fears that she would then be in Susan's power. She also wants to hide her past life from her new husband.

Roxana and the Dutch merchant decide to go to Holland and book passage, but Susan turns out to be a childhood friend of the captain's wife. As Roxana is being entertained on board, Susan arrives. She does not at this point recognize Roxana, but she later visits the Quaker lady while Roxana is there and describes the famous Turkish dance to her mother's mortification. Roxana is forced to cancel her trip to Holland and remove herself to Tunbridge Wells to avoid Susan's persistent attempts to see her.

Susan has now deduced that Roxana must be her true mother

and pursues her inexorably. Roxana is driven almost to distraction, and the Quakeress tells white lies to shield her. Amy runs across Susan on a boat trip to Greenwich and tries to lure her into the park to do away with her, but Susan takes flight. When Amy returns to Roxana and tells what she has done, Roxana throws her out of the house. She is then troubled with visions of Susan killed or drowned, and hears almost simultaneously from Susan's relations in Spitalfields that Susan was seen driving away with Amy in a coach and has not been heard of since.

Obsessed with guilt, Roxana and the Dutch merchant (who is still as ignorant as ever) remove to Holland, where Amy eventually rejoins them. The novel ends inconclusively; we are never told explicitly that Susan was murdered, but such a conclusion seems inescapable. The closing paragraph refers darkly to reverses of fortune and agonies of guilt.

> Amy, King Charles II, Sir Robert Clayton, the "Count de Clerac" (Prince de _____), the Devil, Jew, Dutch merchant, Duke of Monmouth, Quakeress, Roxana (also called Mlle. Beleau and Countess of Wintselsheim), Susan.

Sir Charles Grandison, Richardson, 1753-1754.

Volume one—Sir Charles rescues Harriet from Sir Hargrave and declines a duel with him.

Harriet Byron, a virtuous and beautiful woman of twenty, lives in Northampton with her aunt and uncle Selby. She decides to accompany her cousins the Reeveses on a visit to London. Her decision spreads consternation among her three suitors, the libertine Mr. Greville, the freethinker Mr. Fenwick, and the gentle Mr. Orme. In London Harriet meets a series of debs and beaux, most of whom she finds not sufficiently serious-minded. She writes the Selbys that she has been receiving a great deal of praise in town and receives in turn a letter from her "correcting uncle" deploring female vanity.

Harriet attracts the notice of Mr. James Fowler. The Reeveses are visited by Fowler's rich Welsh uncle, Sir Rowland Meredith, who in his blunt way pronounces Harriet overwhelmingly suitable for marriage with his nephew. Harriet overcomes Sir Rowland in a wit-combat. The next day the Reeveses visit the silly Lady Betty Williams. Among the guests is Sir Hargrave Pollexfen, a young man rather full of himself who favors Harriet with his attentions. Harriet holds her own in an argument with Mr. Walden, the college prig. This long conversation is the first in a series of discussions of sexual roles.

Upon returning to their lodgings in Grosvenor Street, the Selbys learn that Sir Hargrave is of a vengeful and miserly temper, despised by his neighbors and tenants. He has also ruined the honor of three young ladies. Sir Rowland Meredith visits again. He is unable to win Harriet's hand for his nephew, but she is so moved by his impulsive honesty that she decides to think of him henceforth as her "papa." In contrast to this tearful scene, Sir Hargrave Pollexfen pays court with a maximum of self-satisfaction and is enraged when he is refused. He storms out in a pet, and Harriet fears that he will seek revenge. Mr. Greville also comes, although he has promised Harriet not to follow her to town. He kisses her hand so hard that he leaves tooth marks.

Miss Betty Williams invites the Reeveses to accompany her to a masked ball at the Haymarket and insists on designing Harriet's costume herself. Harriet is afraid that such balls may encourage bad habits (masquerades are regularly a danger signal in eighteenth-century fiction). Meanwhile she employs a new servant, one William Wilson. The day before the ball, Sir Hargrave goes down on his knees to Harriet to beg her hand, but in vain. When she tries to leave the room, he catches her finger in the door and injures it, and then leaves the house in a rage.

After the masquerade, Harriet's sedan chair fails to bring her home, and Wilson has also disappeared. The whole family is in an uproar. The Reeveses at first suspect Mr. Greville of foul play, but the finger soon points to Sir Hargrave. The suborned chairmen are found, who reveal that they were paid to carry Harriet to Paddington. An innkeeper in that town relates that a coach arrived at six a.m. at Mrs. Awberry's house and that a second coach carried a party away at seven. Mr. Reeves calls on Sir Hargrave and decides from the porter's evasive answers that the baronet is not at home.

At this point a letter arrives from a Miss Charlotte Grandison announcing that her brother has rescued Harriet. Sir Hargrave has lost three front teeth in the encounter, while Sir Charles Grandison, the rescuer, has sustained a scratch. Harriet is resting at the seat of the Earl of L., Sir Charles's brother-in-law. When Mr. Reeves sees her, she is weak but able to consider forgiving Sir Hargrave; so Mr. Reeves concludes that "the last violence was not offered." Sir Charles puts Mr. Reeves at his ease by his gentility and lack of pretension.

The Reeves party returns to London, accompanied by the Grandisons, who are joyfully received and approved of by all. Mrs. Reeves and Lady Betty start thinking of Sir Charles as a prospective husband for Harriet. Harriet describes to Lucy Selby her terrors as she was carried over the fields to Paddington. At Mrs. Awberry's, a hireling priest appeared with Sir Hargrave and began to read the marriage ceremony, when Harriet threw a violent fit. Sir Hargrave dismissed the priest, who was glad enough to escape, fearing that Harriet was dead. Sir Hargrave mashed her body in a door and made her nose bleed, after which he carried her off in his coach to Windsor, brutally gagged and muffled up in a cloak. But on the road Sir Charles rescued her, and she threw herself gratefully into his arms, although she was humiliated by her revealing masquerade costume.

Harriet finds Sir Charles a fine man but fears he is not so open as he should be about his private thoughts. Charlotte is extremely vivacious but sometimes too witty. She and Harriet form a sisterly relationship, but their joy is disturbed by the news that Sir Charles has received a challenge from Sir Hargrave. One of his cronies, Mr. Bagenhall, writes Harriet attempting to intimidate her into marriage with Sir Hargrave. Monday morning arrives and Charlotte visits Harriet, who imagines that the duel is transpiring at that very moment. Sir Charles arrives, and Harriet learns to her joy that he declined the gage of battle.

At a party at Sir Charles's house in St. James's Square, we meet the worthy clergyman Dr. Bartlett, Sir Charles's pretty ward Emily Jervois, and the superficial Everard Grandison. During the party Sir Charles receives another challenge and daringly agrees to go alone to Sir Hargrave's house in Cavendish Square for breakfast.

When Sir Charles arrives at Cavendish Square, Sir Hargrave is accompanied by Solomon Merceda the Jew and also Mr. Bagenhall. Sir Charles's cool but courageous demeanor prepossesses everyone in his favor and discomfits the blustering Sir Hargrave. Sir Charles discharges Sir Hargrave's loaded pistols out the window. The climax of the visit occurs when Sir Hargrave leads Sir Charles into the garden and draws upon him. Sir Charles gracefully pinions his opponent's arm and leads him back inside, where he explains how he came to turn away from dueling as a way of settling quarrels.

His father, the gay and rakish Sir Thomas Grandison, had been wounded in a duel, and the shock of this affair brought on the death of Lady Grandison, the mother of Sir Charles. Sir Hargrave demands to know whether Harriet has prepossessions in favor of Sir Charles, but the latter refuses to supply this information and takes his leave. That evening, Sir Hargrave abruptly pays a visit to the astonished Harriet and again goes down on his knees to her, but to no avail.

The same day the Countess Dowager of D. visits to sound Harriet out for marriage to her son the Earl of D. She declines, but the Countess attributes her unwillingness only to the shock of her abduction. Harriet admits to Lucy for the first time that her feelings about Sir Charles may amount to more than gratitude. Lady Caroline L., Sir Charles's sister, alarms Harriet by hinting that Sir Charles may already be involved with another woman.

Volume two—History of the Grandison family; incidents of Capt. Anderson and of Mrs. O'Hara.

During a visit to the Grandisons' town house, Harriet is upset upon seeing an elegant sedan chair standing in the street, and again upon hearing Sir Charles bidding farewell to a lady. Harriet accepts the invitation of Lord L. and his lady (Sir Charles's sister Caroline) to visit them at Colnebrook. Her Aunt Selby and her reverend Grandmother Shirley urge her not to refuse an eligible suitor for the sake of a passion for Sir Charles that can never be gratified because of the smallness of her fortune. Harriet acknowledges that she is in love with Sir. Charles.

She provides further details about the history of the Grandisons. Lady Grandison's death occurred amid great piety; she "expired in an ejaculation that her ebbing life could not support." Despite this edifying example, Sir Thomas continued his evil ways, seducing Mrs. Oldham, the widow of an old drinking companion whom he had helped to bankrupt. He forbade his daughters Charlotte and Caroline to write their brother Charles (then living in Italy), lest the upright young man learn of his father's misdeeds. It later turns out that the young man is still entangled in relationships begun during this Italian visit. Concerning the prohibition of correspondence, Harriet comments that children should obey even unjust and unnatural commands of their parents.

A Scotch Lord, the Earl of L., fell in love with Caroline, but old Sir Thomas refused his consent to an alliance because the earl's estate was partially mortgaged. In an affecting scene, he denounced his two daughters for disobedience and threatened to turn them both out of the house with only five hundred pounds apiece. The old lord's estates were in the hands of dishonest stewards, and he was infatuated with an Irish fortune hunter. At the height of his folly he was taken with brain fever and died. In revenge, Everard Grandison and the Grandison girls harshly cast Mrs. Oldham out. When Sir Charles (now the heir) returned home, he set all to rights. He generously received Mrs. Oldham and gave her an annuity. He discharged the dishonest stewards and joined Caroline's hands with Lord L.'s. Finally, he brought Miss Emily Jervois and worthy Dr. Bartlett home from Florence and installed them in his household. He had received Miss Emily as a ward at the hand of her dying father. At this point the story resumes.

Under the pressure of her father's tyranny, Charlotte allowed herself to become entangled with a fortune hunter, Capt. Anderson. She rashly promised not to marry any other suitor without his consent. She first realized the captain's true character when he lost his letter-writer. "He lost his handwriting, his style, and even his orthography." Sir Charles goes to speak with Capt. Anderson and two of his blustering friends in London. They at first attempt to intimidate him; but when that gambit fails, the captain releases Charlotte from her promise in return for a sum of money.

Dr. Bartlett tells Harriet how he met Sir Charles in Italy. He had been employed as the guide of the dissolute young Mr. Lorimer on the Grand Tour. His charge actually delivered him up to the Turkish authorities in Athens, and the doctor would have been executed except for the intervention of Sir Charles and his friend, young Sir Edward Beauchamp. Mr. Lorimer later died a debauchee's death in Rome.

Charlotte steals a letter of her brother's containing high praise of Harriet, but Harriet refuses to read it or hear it described. She learns only that Sir Charles has proposed that she take over the duties of being guardian to his young ward. Harriet perceives that Emily is in love with Sir Charles, but her fortune is only fifty thousand pounds, and so she is no eligible bride for him. Harriet agrees to be a "second mamma" to Emily.

Emily's mother, the profligate Mrs. Jervois, visits Sir Charles, intimates that he is up to no good with his ward, and demands that she be restored to her own custody. Sir Charles refuses, especially in view of the fact that Emily's mother has married an Irish army officer, Maj. O'Hara. She, her husband, and his friend Capt. Salmonet pay a shocking visit to Lord and Lady L. at Colnebrook, trying to obtain a glimpse of Emily, but she flees in terror. Mrs. O'Hara's (i.e., Jervois's) scheme is to marry her daughter off at a bargain price and keep half the family fortune herself.

Sir Charles goes to visit his maternal uncle Lord W., who is plagued by his mistress Mrs. Giffard, now grown hateful to him. Sir Charles pays off Mrs. Giffard to get rid of her. Lord W. is overwhelmed with his nephew's generosity and decides to reform and marry any woman whom Sir Charles sees fit to pick out for him. In London once again, the baronet is visited by Mrs. O'Hara and her two bravos. The visitors lose their temper, and in the ensuing scuffle Sir Charles disarms them and sends them packing. The next day their attorney visits him to serve notice of legal proceedings, but privately confides not only that the two men are not truly officers but also that "Major" O'Hara may not even be really married to Emily's mother.

Sir Charles queries Charlotte about her intentions regarding young Lord G., who is clearly in love with her. Charlotte uses the opportunity to employ her caustic wit at the expense of Lord G.'s failings. Her brother becomes angry with her for trifling and compares her conduct unfavorably with Harriet's candor.

Sir Charles is executing the will of Mr. Danby, a merchant who died estranged from his niece and two nephews. The baronet distributes the fortune to the young people, remarking that "the merchants of Great Britain are the most useful members of the community." He tells Harriet how he once saved Mr. Danby from assassins hired by his brother and won his eternal gratitude.

Volume three—Story of the Porretta family; marriage of Charlotte Grandison.

The story of Sir Charles's Italian entanglement is told partly by himself and partly in letters from Dr. Bartlett. From his seventeenth to his twenty-fifth year, Sir Charles lived in Italy. Having staved off the advances of Signorina Olivia, he befriended Jeronymo della Porretta. Signor della Porretta was involved with a crowd of loose-livers and failed to respond to Sir Charles's admonitions. The two friends broke off, until Sir Charles accidentally happened to save Jeronymo from a set of assassins. Jeronymo received a shoulder wound in this encounter that has not yet healed. While visiting the noble Porretta family in Bologna, Sir Charles instructed two of the brothers and their lovely sister Clementina in the English tongue.

Clementina was charmed by the handsome foreigner. Sir Charles obtusely acted as intermediary for the Count of Belvedere's suit to Clementina, which only caused the girl to fall more in love with the intermediary. When Sir Charles went away to Vienna, Clementina was plunged into despondency. She was sent to Rome to stay with Miss Hortensia Beaumont, who soon found out the true source of the trouble and recommended marriage with Sir Charles as the only cure. He was recalled to Bologna, where marriage negotiations were opened.

Sir Charles refused to accede to the demands of the Porrettas, that is, to forsake England and give up the Protestant faith. Clementina felt despised and went mad with grief, while her family felt that their honor had been besmirched. (Harriet admires Clementina for her loyalty to her religion and to her country.) There was a stormy encounter between Sir Charles and the oldest son of the family, Giacomo della Porretta, called "The General." Sir Charles offered a compromise, but the General was enraged that a foreigner and a heretic would dare to make conditions about a daughter of the casa della Porretta. Sir Charles decided to leave Italy. Clementina donned servant's garb to see him, and he reassured her that he had not despised her because of her religion.

The Porrettas decided to push Clementina toward marriage with the Count of Belvedere. (The dramatic situation of *Clarissa* is re-enacted, with the Marchioness consenting against her better judgment to the harsh measures of her husband and sons.) Clementina ran mad, dreamed of finding a corpse in the orange grove, and had to be reassured that the family would not have Sir Charles assassinated. Her attempted escape over the garden wall was thwarted, and she attempted to throw herself into the great cascade (cf. *Pamela*, volume one). Mrs. Beaumont visited the Porrettas and blamed them for not allowing Clementina a final interview with Sir Charles, with the result that her depression intensified. Sir Charles and Mr. Edward Beauchamp went to Paris, where the latter still remains, waiting for his father and spiteful stepmother to allow him to return to England. Upon the death of Sir Thomas, Sir Charles returned to his native country. Harriet doubts now that Sir Charles can ever love a second woman.

It turns out that Mrs. O'Hara is married after all to the major and hopes to make amends for her shabby conduct so that Sir Charles will not cut her annuity in half. When the baronet increases it to four hundred pounds, all the members of the O'Hara party tearfully acknowledge their unworthiness. Sir Charles goes to see the Mansfields, a genteel family fallen upon hard times. He hopes to negotiate a match for Miss Mansfield with Lord W., which would retrieve the family fortunes.

He also visits Sir Harry and Lady Beauchamp to prevail on them to allow young Edward to return home. Lady Beauchamp formerly fancied young Edward but had to content herself with the father. Now she fears that Sir Charles will marry Edward to Charlotte Grandison and make financial demands on the Beauchamps. But Sir Charles teases her out of her ill humor, showing a gallant side of his personality that we have not seen before. He reconciles the Beauchamps to each other and secures their permission for Edward to return.

Sir Charles also marries off the Danby children to suitable mates in a triple ceremony, after which he sings and dances at the reception.

Harriet is back in London with the Reeveses when Sir Charles arrives for a momentous interview with her. He tells her that the Porrettas are anxious for him to visit Bologna once more, since Clementina's depression continues, and he wants to have her advice. She magnanimously approves of the project. Taking her hand, Sir Charles says he wants to have a relationship with her more tender than that of friendship. However, they must wait to see the issue of his visit to the stricken Clementina.

Harriet is distressed when Sir Charles tells her of the harsh treatment Clementina has been subjected to at the hands of her aunt Juliana Sforza and her cousin Laurana. The poor girl has been confined in a strait jacket. Sir Charles will take with him to Italy a skilful surgeon, Mr. Lowther, for Jeronymo's still-unhealed shoulder wound. Edward Beauchamp is mentioned as a possible mate for Miss Jervois, but Sir Charles will not force any choice upon her. Harriet promises to help persuade Charlotte to marry Lord G.

The Reeves group dines the following day at Sir Charles's, where Charlotte is prevailed upon by her brother to give her hand to Lord G. no later than the following Tuesday. The Earl of G., Lord G., and Lady Gertrude arrive, and Sir Charles places his sister's hand in that of Lord G. Charlotte doubts privately that she can be obedient to Lord G., while Harriet tries to persuade her to give up her habit of raillery. She balks at the idea of being married in a church because that makes the arrangement too solemn; but Harriet and Sir Charles talk her into the idea, and Dr. Bartlett refuses to conduct the ceremony if it is held anywhere else.

Lord W. arrives and Harriet finds him more spry than she had imagined; she wishes that his modesty were as great as his intelligence. He mortifies Harriet by publicly expressing the wish that she may be united to his nephew. The day of Charlotte's wedding at St. George's dawns. She remarks that she really can't be satisfied with any man, since she is accustomed to the excellence of her brother. During the ceremony, she still refuses to be serious, and that night she is reluctant for the guests to leave. She even wants Harriet to sleep with her.

In a few days, Charlotte invites Harriet to come to the house in St. James's Square to vindicate her in the first marital quarrel. But Harriet condemns Charlotte for not showing proper deference to her husband. Dr. Bartlett and Sir Charles present their proposal for Protestant nunneries, where young ladies could spend a few years safe from the entrapments of men.

Unexpectedly, Lady Olivia arrives from Florence with her aunt, Mrs. Maffei, to seek to entrap Sir Charles. She is enraged to find that he is about to depart for Bologna to try to restore Clementina's mental health. She is a passionate woman who carries a dagger and who once stabbed a man who had offended her. Harriet sees in her the bad effects of a young woman's having an independent fortune and being deprived of the guidance of her parents in selecting a mate.

Sir Charles entrusts Lady Olivia to his sisters. His last evening in England is spent with all his friends. All are in tears at the contemplation of the baronet's many benevolent actions. He takes solemn leave of Harriet, who is certain that she sees signs of love in his conduct toward her.

Volume four—Clementina decides at last not to marry Sir Charles.

Harriet learns that Lady Olivia made an attempt with a poniard on the life of Sir Charles, the Thursday evening before he was to leave England. He disarmed her, injuring her wrist slightly. Lady D. visits again, still promoting the suit of her son. She is so moved at Harriet's and Sir Charles's mutual renunciation that she wishes their hands may finally be joined.

Harriet returns to Northampton, where there is a moving reunion with that ornament to old age, Grandmother Shirley. Mr. Greville pays a call and blusters against Sir Hargrave and Sir Charles, should either of those gentlemen be favored with Harriet's hand. Meanwhile, back in London, Charlotte has begun to feel affection for Lord G., even though he accidentally sticks his sharp nose into her eye, and even though he collects all sorts of odds and ends. She is pleased when he decides to give his shell collection to Emily Jervois.

Near Abbeville, France, Sir Charles rescues two gentlemen who

are being beaten by seven others. These two are Sir Hargrave and
Solomon Merceda, who are being justly chastised for attempting
the virtue of a young lady. Mr. Lowther, Sir Charles's surgeon,
writes to his brother an account of their journey through the Alps,
a region which he calls "one of the worst countries under Heaven."
At Bologna, Sir Charles learns the true motive of Laurana Sforza
and her mother, Signora Juliana, in their mistreatment of Clementina. Clementina's two grandfathers willed her a large fortune, but
only on condition that she not enter a nunnery. Laurana thought
if she could drive Clementina into a convent, the vast inheritance
would revert to the Sforzas and she could entice the Count of Belvedere to marry her.

Jeronymo's shoulder wound is still festering, but Mr. Lowther
hopes it can be drained. Sir Charles pacifies the haughty General
by promising that any marital arrangement must be approved by
all three Porretta brothers. Only then is he allowed to see Clementina, who is suffering from a rooted melancholy. Only in the second
interview is she brought to converse freely. Gradually her mental
health returns, under the influence of the English baronet.

Lady Olivia visits Harriet at home in Northampton. Harriet
deplores her hot temper but admires her spontaneity. Charlotte
confides that her old Aunt Eleanor, the Methodist maiden lady,
is in love with Dr. Bartlett. Charlotte asks Harriet to conceal the
fact that Sir Charles is a virgin, since, if that fact were generally
known, it would make him "the jest of one sex and the aversion
of the other."

Even though Charlotte has been brought to sign herself "Lady
G.," her marriage continues stormy. She wins Aunt Eleanor over to
her side by hinting that her haughtiness is necessary to prevent
his making sexual demands on her. He rents a house without con-
sulting her, and when she chides him, he flies into a rage and
smashes her harpsichord. But when Lord G. is taken with one of
his fits, Charlotte discovers that she loves him after all. She makes
peace with him so that he won't get the reputation of being hen-
pecked.

The silly Sir Everard Grandison has compromised himself with
gambling debts and a written promise to marry the castoff mistress
of that blustering bully, Lord B. Sir Charles advises him to pay
the debts of honor but not to be bullied into marrying the trollop.
Affairs in Bologna approach a crisis. The family agree to take Sir
Charles up on his offer of matrimony (as long as the Pope approves),

since they feel that Clementina will recover fully only if her every wish is gratified.

In England we observe the anguish of each member of both families when they hear that Sir Charles is to marry Clementina. Only Harriet and Grandmother Shirley receive the news with resignation. Harriet's Uncle Selby rails against the man who could prefer an Italian to a Harriet Byron. When the Lady Olivia hears the news, she leaves in a rage for Italy. Sir Harry Beauchamp is ailing, and his son Edward is obviously falling in love with Emily Jervois. Perhaps she can be wooed away from her unacknowledged love for her guardian.

Back in Bologna, Sir Charles receives a visit from the irate Count of Belvedere, who feels that the English baronet is the only obstacle between him and his love. He demands a meeting with rapiers before the gates of the city, but Sir Charles refuses to oblige him. Belvedere leaves, threatening suicide. Later they learn that the count was provoked to issue the challenge by Lady Juliana Sforza, who is still scheming to grab the family fortune.

Sir Charles has an interview with Clementina to prefer his suit. She says she is obligated to him for helping her regain her reason, but cannot marry him because her love for a heretic might endanger her faith. She throws herself at his feet to implore forgiveness. She wants to enter a convent to show her contempt for money (i.e., the grandfathers' legacy). The family gradually becomes more and more glad that the marriage negotiations are likely to be broken off, although they are naturally appalled by the convent scheme.

Sir Charles must walk a tightrope. If he allows Clementina to think he is angry, it will unsettle her mind again. But if he allows himself to appear glad that she has rejected him, she will feel spurned and be unsettled for the opposite reason. His own emotions are far from simple. He left England torn between esteem for Clementina and love for Harriet. Now that he is in Italy, he reveres Clementina even more for her greatness of mind; at the same time he is nettled by the pride of the family. The Marquis, for example, bridles at the slightest hint that Clementina is the rejected one and not Sir Charles. To make Sir Charles's task even more difficult, he must pacify the mercurial Belvedere, who oscillates between suicidal and homicidal moods.

After four days of this psychological minuet, the baronet decides to condition Clementina to his absence. He undertakes a journey to visit friends in Florence. In England, the families of Lord G. and of Harriet rejoice that the marriage has been called off, but they long for a final resolution. Harriet wonders whether Sir Charles will ever be able to consider another woman. She thinks that, had Sir Charles been Adam, he would not have been tempted by Eve to eat the forbidden fruit.

Clementina asks Sir Charles to be her advocate for the convent scheme, but he responds that retiring into a nunnery would look too much like disappointment. Furthermore, the will of her parents should be seen as the will of God. In Florence, he has a passionate interview with Lady Olivia. She upbraids him with ingratitude; he refuses to give her grounds for hope. She declares that if he had married the "proud bigot," she would have had him killed, and that at one point she even thought of setting the Inquisition on him. Later Sir Charles must repulse an attempt by a gang of her bravos to abduct him.

Before leaving Italy, Sir Charles invites Clementina and Jeronymo to visit him in England. Clementina rushes into her closet to pray for strength to endure the parting. While saying farewell to Jeronymo, the baronet is unable to restrain his tears. In Milan, he has a bitter scene with Signora Juliana Sforza, who is full of spite at Clementina and tells Sir Charles that he has been badly used. In Paris, he meets with his dissolute cousin Everard, who is shy and evasive about a certain request he wants to make. Sir Charles suspects that he is angling for the hand of Emily Jervois, hoping to repair his fortune with hers. Naturally this scheme must be thwarted. The next day he leaves Paris for England.

Volume five—Harriet's wedding with Sir Charles.

Emily Jervois faints upon Sir Charles's arrival. While he has been gone, Lord W. has married Miss Mansfield and they rejoice in their new-found happiness. The Mansfields had been defrauded of their inheritance by the evil steward Bolton, but he has fallen upon hard times and is anxious to compromise. They have also discovered an old will that provides them with an indisputable title.

The evil characters begin to meet their just deserts. Sir Hargrave Pollexfen, still suffering from his wounds, asks Dr. Bartlett's help in framing a prayer for forgiveness. At Sir Charles's request, Harriet agrees to be reconciled to him. Solomon Merceda has died, and Mr. Bagenhall is miserable with his new bride, whom he later deserts. The lightheaded girls whom Harriet met in London during the winter have come to a bad end, having all eloped with army officers.

Harriet rebukes Charlotte for her hypocrisy in first being reluctant to enter the married state and then deriding old maids for having successfully avoided it. Harriet is shocked at Charlotte's preference of wicked wit to plain decent cheerfulness.

The plot begins to revolve around the approaching wedding. Harriet becomes faint with joy upon hearing of the baronet's arrival, and her Uncle Selby is glad to consent to the proposed match. Harriet's godfather Mr. Deane draws up the legal documents, which are summarized in full detail. Sir Charles generously declines the proffered dowry. He is extremely delicate about tendering his love to Harriet; and she, understanding his entanglement with Clementina, hints her willingness to accept his suit.

One morning Sir Charles is accosted by Mr. Greville, who forces him to draw his sword. He wounds and disarms Greville, and then gives him his life. He meets with Fenwick and the injured Greville to make up their differences. Greville attempts to save face by announcing that his arm is bandaged because of a fall from his horse. In church, Sir Charles behaves generously to Greville and edifies the congregation by his exemplary piety. After the service, Greville draws Harriet aside, and she expects him to upbraid her. But instead, after a passage of his usual strained wit, he gives her his blessing and rushes out sobbing, barely stopping for his hat and sword.

On the way to Mr. Deane's, Sir Charles (in all things perfect) demonstrates his superlative horsemanship and voices sentiments in the neoclassical mode about how art should be the handmaid to nature. An extremely complex process of negotiations now goes on about setting the wedding date. Decorum requires Harriet to be superlatively reluctant; she cannot even listen to talk of a particular date. Sir Charles, on the other hand, must have an early date to forestall trouble from Lady Olivia and to oblige the Porrettas in their attempt to nudge Clementina toward marriage with Count Belvedere.

A momentary crisis blows up. In one of her letters to Charlotte, Harriet bemoans the fact that Emily Jervois is hopelessly in love with her guardian and hopes that she may be allowed to live with them at Grandison Hall. She inadvertently drops this crucial page in the garden and later learns that Sir Charles picked it up. What if he should find out the true state of Emily's heart? But Sir Charles magnanimously declines to read the page and returns it to Harriet. At this time Everard Grandison is scheming to marry the widow of a rich vintner and so set himself up again in life.

Sir Charles and Mr. Selby disagree about the merits of the Dis-

senters, with Sir Charles upholding their right to be respected.
At this very juncture Maj. and Mrs. O'Hara become Methodists,
and Emily gives them a coach so they may travel from their home
in Soho to the Methodist chapel in Moorfields. She then discovers
that she has overspent her allowance and writes her guardian a
trembling letter asking for a supplement, which he gladly grants.
The O'Haras are overwhelmed with his generosity.

Harriet has a series of nightmares and is tormented with anxiety
lest Clementina decide to marry Sir Charles after all. To her great
joy, he forwards to her a newly arrived letter from Jeronymo, en-
closing Clementina's blessing on the Grandison-Byron alliance. An
anonymous letter arrives at Selby House saying that Mr. Greville
has set off with a party of armed men to make an attempt on the
life of Sir Charles. Harriet falls into hysterics and the whole family
is up all night. But the next morning brings the baronet to Selby
House perfectly safe. He goes to Mr. Greville, reconciles himself
to him, and brings him back to Selby House for dinner.

Harriet edifies the whole company by her reverent attentions
to venerable Grandmother Shirley. The dilemma about the wedding
date is resolved by allowing Harriet's grandmother to set it; she
chooses the following Thursday. Now another round of delicate
palpitations ensues, since Harriet wishes for a private ceremony,
while her family are all for a public one. Sir Charles warns Harriet
against a false shame and reconciles her to the public rites. After
the ceremony, everyone will travel to Grandison Hall for the celebration, so that Harriet's old beaux in Northamptonshire will not
be subject to too much heartburning. Three public houses in the
neighborhood will be set open for the celebrations of the local folk.
Harriet practically faints away when she comes to sign the marriage
articles, and Sir Charles has to hold her pen hand.

The great day dawns, and Harriet must be sustained by hartshorn
and salts. A procession of eight coaches makes its way over the
half mile to the parish church, where all the peasants of the neighborhood are gathered in respectful reverence. Harriet manages
to stammer through the ceremony. A gala wedding dance is held.
At the end of the evening, Harriet retires to her bedchamber. Aunt
Selby takes her leave of Harriet in tears, and Charlotte refers to
brides in "virgin-white, like milk-white heifers led to sacrifice."
Finally Sir Charles also discreetly takes leave of the company.

The next morning, Sir Charles deflects Uncle Selby's jokes at
Harriet's expense. Everyone tearfully congratulates her, and money

is distributed to those among the poor who are deserving. A debate occurs in the family about the justice of sexual roles, and Sir Charles upholds the divinely ordained natural superiority of the male sex.

Volume six—Clementina visits England and decides against a life of celibacy.

Sir Harry Beauchamp dies, and Sir Charles returns to London for the opening of the will. Edward will allow his stepmother to continue living in the Berkeley Square house for as long as she likes. Sir Rowland Meredith and his nephew Mr. Fowler visit Grandison Hall, and Sir Rowland presents Harriet with a set of magnificent jewelry. The usual tearful scene ensues. Mr. Fowler is mooted as a possible mate for Lucy Selby, but she thinks him a milksop. She is more friendly to the idea of Mr. Greville, when she learns that he is interested in her hand. But Harriet warns her that Mr. Greville has a libertine past and free principles. Harriet also knows that Greville wants to marry Lucy only so that he can be closely allied to Harriet.

In an important conversation with Emily Jervois, Harriet shows her that the emotion she feels for her guardian is really romantic love and not "filial reverence," as Emily, still unaware of the state of her own heart, insists on calling it. Harriet tries to prepare Emily for the prospective courtship of Edward Beauchamp. In a later scene, Emily tearfully unburdens her heart to Harriet. She decides to go and live with the Selbys to avoid further involvement of her feelings with Sir Charles.

Mr. Lowther arrives from Italy with the news that Jeronymo is improved in his health and that Clementina by this time has probably been pressured into marrying the Count of Belvedere. Harriet bitterly disapproves when she learns that the General has behaved in an imperious manner to his sister. If Belvedere really loved her, he would not want her to be compelled. Then Sir Charles receives electrifying news from Jeronymo: Clementina has slipped away to Leghorn and has taken ship for England, apparently to avoid marrying the Count of Belvedere. The entire Porretta family along with the count is following. Sir Charles departs for London, where he finds that Clementina arrived ten days ago.

In London Edward Beauchamp asks Sir Charles's permission to pay court to Emily, but the baronet suggests that she is still too young. Mr. Everard Grandison is putting on a great deal of swagger, and his new middle-class bride is exceedingly proud of the Grandison lineage. Sir Charles disapproves of such snobbery in a nation whose greatness is based on trade. Charlotte discovers to her chagrin that she is pregnant.

Harriet follows Sir Charles to London and has a moving interview with Clementina. Overwhelmed by the Italian lady's greatness of mind in wishing well to the new Lady Grandison, Harriet urges that Clementina not be forced into marriage. The Porretta family arrives in London and stays in the G.s' Grosvenor Square house, where they converse in French with the Reeveses. Belvedere seems to be genteel and makes a favorable impression on Harriet. Clementina has not yet been informed of the arrival, especially as her mind is again giving signs of being deranged.

Sir Charles acts as go-between and draws up terms of a treaty between Clementina and her parents, by which Clementina is to decline the veil and her parents are not to mention marriage. Clementina agrees to the treaty, especially since she can now use her grandfathers' fortune to do good works. Belvedere expresses his resentment at being sacrificed to family amity. Clementina comes to the Grosvenor Square house to sign the articles. The reunion is marked by tearful embraces on all sides. When the articles are signed, Clementina tears off the portion with her parents' names, to indicate that they are bound only by their good will. All are invited to visit Grandison Hall, while the Count of Belvedere plans to visit Madrid.

News arrives that Charlotte G. has given birth to a baby girl, whom she has named Harriet. She was shocked when her husband walked in on her while she was nursing the baby, but Lord G. declares himself enamored of her in her new role of mother and apologizes for resenting her vivacity. From now on Lord and Lady G. are an indissolubly happy couple. Lucy Selby rejects the addresses of the libertine Greville; she later becomes engaged to Lord Reresby.

Clementina is gradually weaned away from her romantic plans of carrying a torch for Sir Charles. Charlotte indiscreetly reveals to her the story of how Emily removed herself from her guardian's household to avoid a romantic involvement. This revelation has a lucky result, since Clementina applies the story to her own case. As Lady Olivia has been making unkind remarks that Clementina is still enamored of Sir Charles, everyone fears that taking the veil would reinforce this impression. Charlotte's witty letter about silly young things who insist on their first love is read to her. Her resolution to remain single is further weakened by a hint from Sir Charles that Count Belvedere may have his eye on a Spanish lady.

A letter comes from the General recounting the suicide of Clementina's cousin Laurana. She fell into despair when the Count of Belvedere followed Clementina to England. The financial grounds for Clementina's marrying are now removed; but even before learning of Laurana's death, Clementina had decided to throw herself at her parents' feet and submit to their judgment. She promises not to take the veil and proposes a one-year waiting period before making up her mind about the count. She will leave him free to do as he wishes; he, of course, pledges eternal fidelity. The entire Italian party now makes plans to return home, except for Jeronymo, who will visit an English spa for his shoulder wound.

Love takes its course in Northamptonshire, and Emily finds Edward Beauchamp more and more agreeable. She wonders if her guardian would consider such an alliance at the end of three years' time. The final incident in the novel is the death of the repentant Sir Hargrave Pollexfen, with Sir Charles keeping watch by his deathbed. He dies blessing Harriet and leaves a large legacy to the Grandisons. Harriet comments that true heroism consists in being a TRULY GOOD MAN!

Sir John Allestree, Miss Allestree, Mr. Allestree, Count Altieri, Capt. Anderson, Andrew, Anne, Antony, Mrs. Penelope Arby, John Arnold, Deb Awberry, Sally Awberry, Mr. Awberry, the widow Awberry, Cicely Badger, James Bagenhall, Miss Barclay, Mr. Barnet, Miss Barnevelt, Mr. Barnham, Rev. Dr. Ambrose Bartlett, Daniel Bartlett, Edward Beauchamp, Sir Harry Beauchamp, Lady Beauchamp, Hortensia Beaumont, Beckford, Count of Belvedere, Mr. Bever, Blagrave, Bolton, Sally Bramber, Miss Bramber, Sir Arthur Brandon, Burgess, Harriet Byron, Mr. Calvert, Camilla, Miss Cantillon, Sir Samuel Clarke, Miss Clarkson, Pulcheria Clements, Henry Cotes, Mons. Creutzer, Dr. Curtis, Mrs. Curzon, Countess Dowager of D., Earl of D., Anthony Dagley, Edward Danby, John Danby, Thomas Danby, Miss Danby, Mr. Danby, Miss Darlington, Mr. Dawson, Charles Deane, Thomas Deane, Maj. Dillon, Mr. Dobson, Mrs. Dobson, Miss Dolyns, Capt. Duncan, Mrs. Eggleton, Mr. Elford, Ellen, Sir Thomas Falconbridge, Mr. Falconbridge, Mrs. Farnborough, Richard Fennel, Richard Fenwick, Mr. Filmer, Lady Finlay, James Fowler, Lady

Frampton, Frank, Frederick, Lady Gertrude G., Harriet
G., Earl of G., Lord G., Mr. Galliard (Sr.), Mr. Galliard (Jr.),
Father Geraldino, Gibson, Mrs. Giffard, Mr. Godfrey, Sir
Charles Grandison, Sr., Sir Charles Grandison, Charlotte
Grandison (later Lady G.), Aunt Eleanor Grandison ("Aunt
Nell"), Everard Grandison, Sir Thomas Grandison, Lady
Grandison, John Greville, Arthur Gunning, Halden, Mrs.
Harrington, Hartleys (two), Hawkins, Alexander Hender-
son, Mr. Hervey, Sir John Holles, Kitty Holles, Patty Holles,
Mr. Holles, Dr. Holmes, Miss Horste, James, Farmer Jen-
kins, Jenny, Jerry, Emily Jervois, John, Johnson, John Jordan,
the Keelings, Countess of L. (née Caroline Grandison), Earl
of L., Sir John Lambton, Mrs. Lane, Laura, Sir Joseph Law-
rence, Mr. Lorimer, Mr. Lowther, Sir Christopher Lucas,
Lieut. Col. Mackenzie, Macpherson, Lady Maffei, Lady
Mansfield, Miss Mansfield, Sir Thomas Mansfield, Fanny
Mansfield, Miss Mansfield, Fr. J. P. M. Marescotti, Col.
Martin, Martina, Count Marulli, M'Dermot, Solomon Mer-
ceda, Sir Rowland Meredith, Mr. Milbourne, Dr. Mitchell,
Lady Frances N., Lady N., Lord N., Dolly Nedham, Miss
Nedham, Nelthorpe, Sir Alexander Nesbitt, Bishop of
Nocera (family name: della Porretta), Miss O'Brien, Maj.
O'Hara, Mrs. Helen O'Hara (first called Mrs. Jervois), Mr.
Oldham, Mrs. Oldham, Oliver, Lady Olivia, Kitty Orme,
Robert Orme, Sir Arthur Poinings, Sir Hargrave Pollexfen,
Clementina della Porretta, Giacomo della Porretta ("the
General"), Jeronymo della Porretta, Juliana della Porretta,
Sebastiano della Porretta, Conte della Porretta, Marchesa
della Porretta ("the Marchioness"), Marchese della Por-
retta ("the Marquis"), Mr. Poussin, Mrs. Preston, Archi-
bald Reeves, Mrs. Reeves, Lord Reresby, Richard, Mr.
Roberts, Lady Anne S., Sally, Capt. Salmonet, Richard
Saunders, George Selby, James Selby, Lucy Selby, Mrs.
Marianne Selby, Nancy Selby, old Mrs. (Grandmother)
Selby, Signora Juliana Sforza, Signorina Laurana Sforza,
Mrs. Henrietta (Grandmother) Shirley, Mr. Singleton, Mr.
Somner, Mr. Steele, Miss Steevens, Mr. Sylvester, Mr. Tol-
son, Sir William Turner, Mrs. Turner, General W., Lady
W., Lord W., Mr. Walden, Sir William Watkyns, Miss
Watson, Lady Betty Williams, Miss Williams, William
Wilson, Mrs. Wimburn, Col. Winwood.

The Six Notorious Street-Robbers, Defoe, 1726. (Original title: *A Brief Historical Account of the Lives of the Six Notorious Street-Robbers Executed at Kingston, viz., William Blewet, Edward Bunworth, Emanuel Dickenson, Thomas Berry, John Higges, and John Legee.*)

The most detailed treatment in this narrative is devoted to the robberies of Blewet, who has collected sixteen silver-hilted swords from his own thefts (many of which he fails to bring off). Of particular interest is a little manual of instructions about how to unhook a man's sword and scabbard in a crowd without his noticing it. During his days as a pickpocket, Blewet is admonished by a gentleman that he will someday be hanged. He is soon after captured by the mob and ducked in a horse trough.

Blewet's most productive day is at the Court of St. James, where he steals a gold snuffbox, a gold-headed cane, and two gold watches. Since he refuses to co-operate with Jonathan Wild, he has to go over to Holland to find a market for these items. Having returned to England, Blewet joins a gang of thieves who stop coaches going through deserted streets in the London area. They even resort to murder to conceal their deeds, a practice which up until now has been very rare. A number of their tricks are clever, such as luring footmen off on wild-goose chases so that they can rob the coach carrying the master.

Blewet is caught and transported with three of his cronies, but he soon returns to England to take up his career again. He even springs aboard moving coaches and snatches gentlemen's wigs off their heads. Citizens are attacked in broad daylight, and even courtiers must go under armed guard. Popular indignation reaches a high pitch when the gang murders one Thomas Ball in cold blood. Ball has sworn to run down the gang; so they go to his house, and Edward Bunworth shoots him through the left pap with a pistol.

After this outrage, which caps a series of murders, the gang is finally run to earth. Blewet, Dickenson, and Berry are apprehended in Holland. One of the gang, Marjoram, decides to turn state's evidence, and a certain Barton attempts to murder him in broad daylight in the open street. In prison Bunworth, who like Sheppard was apprenticed to a buckle maker, almost breaks free and must be chained down to the floor in the condemned hold. A rebellion among the prisoners comes to nought. Bunworth himself refuses to plead until he is almost pressed to death. Finally the six ringleaders of the gang are hanged.

Thomas Ball, Mrs. Ball, Barton, Thomas Berry, Justice

Blackerby, William Blewet, Emanuel Dickenson, Edward
Frazier (alias Bunworth), John Higges (or Higgs or Higgi-
dee), Sir John, John, John Legee, Lennard (or Leonard),
Marjoram, William, Wilson.

A Tale of a Tub, Swift, 1704.

The *Tale* is a satiric medley concerned with two main subjects:
corruptions in religion and abuses in modern learning.   Swift
gives us a thumbnail history of Christianity in the allegory of the
three brothers, Peter (the Roman Catholics), Jack (the Calvinists),
and Martin (the middle way between extremes, as in the Church of
England).   Alternating with the chapters on the brothers are
deliberately chaotic "digressions," which can best be seen as a
parody of a book written in the modern style by a Grub Street
author writing for quick sales.   The religious allegory is easily
grasped, but the heart of the satire is in the digressions, which are
filled with irony.   An integral part of the digressions is the welter
of mock references to Greek and Roman authors, which make up
an elaborate parody of the dry-as-dust scholarly treatise.

The *Tale* opens with a mass of prefatory matter, which con-
stitutes a slap at the way modern books are swollen to an inordinate
length.   First comes a list of "Treatises wrote by the same Author,"
then a long "APOLOGY for the, &c."   In the apology (first printed
in the fifth edition, 1710) Swift answers in his own voice, albeit
anonymously, two criticisms leveled at the earlier editions, especially by William Wotton.   Swift insists that the *Tale* is not im-
pious and that he has not borrowed ideas from anyone else.   In the
fifth edition, Swift impishly borrowed material from Wotton's
book and used it in his footnotes.

The dedication to John, Lord Somers (a Whig nobleman), contains sideswipes at modern dedicators.   There follows a second
"Epistle Dedicatory to his Royal Highness Prince Posterity," in the
voice of the modern hack author.   He asserts that Posterity's
governor, Time, is conspiring to make everyone believe there are
no important books written nowadays, so fast do the best sellers
drop out of sight.

The preface explains the title *A Tale of a Tub*.   Formerly when a
ship was attacked by a whale, the crew would throw out an empty
tub to distract it so that the ship could get away.   The author says
he will write a satire on abuses in religion to draw the fire of the
atheists, who otherwise might direct their attacks against the

poor old church herself. He apologizes for not making the usual ritualized objections to the number of authors jamming the book market today but observes that the crowd would be lessened by the simple expedient of fewer people's rushing into print. He attacks modern authors' demands for sympathy for themselves and closes with observations on the art of satire. His main target here is John Dryden.

Before the *Tale* begins, an introduction explains the three most notable modern devices for obtaining a hearing in a crowd: the pulpit, the ladder (leading up to the scaffold), and the stage-itinerant (carnival wagon). Swift implies that the English Dissenters, with their emphasis on inspired preaching, are no better than mountebanks and that their career may well lead to the gallows. He then parodies symbolic and cabalistic writing. Too many modern readers are content with superficial appearances and don't realize what symbolic meanings are contained in seemingly childish stories such as Tom Thumb or Reynard the Fox. Finally Swift attacks the martyr complex of party writers such as Dryden and Sir Roger L'Estrange.

Section two begins the allegory of the three brothers. Their father (Christ) wills to each of them a coat which will last forever and which changes shape automatically with the wearer (the doctrines of Christianity are adaptable for any culture). He also leaves a will with explicit instructions for their conduct (Holy Scripture). After seven years the three brothers come to town and take part in fashionable amusements such as drinking, whoring, and beating up the watch. They fall in love with the Duchess d'Argent (money), the Madame des Grandes Titres (position), and the Countess d'Orgeuil (pride), but cannot win any favors, because they are unfashionably dressed.

Swift here introduces the "clothes philosophy." The religion of modern man is nothing but an adoration of the tailor-god. The soul of man today consists only of what he wears. That is, modern society is concerned with superficial appearances and ignores values that may not catch the eye. Swift then discusses a series of corruptions in apostolic Christianity, each one symbolized by some new ornament that the brothers want to add to their coats. For example, epaulettes stand for the introduction of pageantry. When the brothers cannot find authorization for this innovation in the will, they distort the text to rationalize their behavior. Under Peter's leadership, item after item is added to the coats (flame-colored satin is the doctrine of purgatory, embroidery with Indian figures the use of images). Finally the will is locked up, and the brothers proceed on oral tradition. Peter gets a position as tutor to a nobleman but upon the gentleman's death turns the young heirs out of the house and usurps the inheritance (the official establishment of the Christian church in Rome).

Section three is the first of the digressions, a "Digression Concerning Critics" (critics are examples of modern "learning"). A critic used to mean a man who wrote about faults in art only to avoid them, like a gentleman walking down the street in Edinburgh, careful not to step in human ordure. But modern critics find fault for the sheer joy of it, and so their writings are as boring as those they pretend to condemn. This section is soaked in mock erudition, pretending to prove from ancient texts that criticism is the oldest of the sciences.

Section four takes us back to the three brothers. Peter demands that he be addressed with dignified titles. He purchases a continent and tricks people into buying the same lots over and over again (purgatory). He sets up a "whispering-office" (the confessional) and a fire insurance company (sale of indulgences). He stages puppet shows (religious processions) and sells a fluid for pickling (holy water). He also raises two fire-breathing bulls (papal bulls) and sells fraudulent pardons to criminals just going to execution. He becomes paranoid, wears three hats stacked one on top of the other, and imagines himself to be God. He kicks his and his brothers' wives out-of-doors and forces them to take up with streetwalkers (clerical "celibacy"). The final straw is that he no longer serves meat and wine to his brothers but instead dry crusts of bread which he insists contain the essence of all foods (transubstantiation). They respond by breaking into the wine cellar and dismissing their concubines. When a request comes from a thief seeking a pardon, they send him directly to the king (God). Peter then comes with the police (co-operation of civil with church power) and expels the two from his house.

Section five, "A Digression in the Modern Kind," is a mock assertion of the superiority of modern learning to ancient. The author claims to have discovered an elixir into which all the arts and sciences have been distilled and which can be snuffed into the nostrils. The author attacks Homer, who, far from being a universal genius, was deficient in his knowledge of alchemy and ignorant of modern candlesticks.

In section six the two brothers take on names (Martin and Jack) and set about removing the accretions of fringe and embroidery from their coats (the Reformation). Martin proceeds with caution. He observes that the fabric of the coat has been damaged by a series of workmen, and so he is willing to leave some of the embroidery to hold the coat together. (That is, the Church of England has respect for the traditions of Christianity.) But Jack is motivated more by hatred of Peter than by respect for his father's commands, and so he rips off the fringe with such zeal that he rends the fabric. Jack now envies the good state of repair of Martin's coat. He runs mad with rage and moves into other lodgings, where the village boys give him a string of nicknames (rise of the various sects within Calvinism).

Section seven is a "Digression in Praise of Digressions," attacking the methods by which modern books are put together. Modern literature consists chiefly of bits and pieces of former works cooked up together as though they were new, and can be compared to a stew of leftovers. Scholars of the modern age drop the names of learned authors instead of reading their books.

Section eight explains the sect of the "Aeolists." Just as clothes are the essence of the personality, so the essence of the mind is wind. The Dissenters' inspiration is nothing but hot air. They have a tube up their anus by which they are pumped full of wind (female preachers receive the tube in the vagina). They then dispense sermons in the form of belches to the congregation. Their religion is characterized by an exaggerated fear of various devils.

Section nine is the key to the whole *Tale*, the famous "Digression concerning the Original, the Use and Improvement of Madness in a Commonwealth," divided into three sections. 1. Swift uses madness as a metaphor for the plans of conquerors, system builders, and religious reformers. Convulsions in world politics can be traced to bilious gases in the anus or sex organs of monarchs, as in Henry IV and Louis XIV of France. 2. Madmen are the happiest people in the world, since happiness consists of the "perpetual possession of being well-deceived." Reasonable people, argues Swift ironically, shouldn't go spoiling the happiness of others by curing them of their delusions. 3. So-called reformers may be seen as benefactors of the state or as candidates for Bedlam, depending on historical accident. Hence the city Whigs in Parliament might well go directly to the madhouse to find candidates for public positions. A raving lunatic would make a fine officer in the army. Other members of the "academy of Bedlam" would distinguish themselves as city merchants, politicians, lawyers, scientists, or even as king.

Section ten allegedly continues the allegory, but is really another digression warning against spurious imitators or authors of "Second Parts" of the *Tale*. Swift asserts that many great truths are hidden in the symbolism of the *Tale*. The Rosicrucians will find cabalistic secrets by multiplying the number of O's in the text and dividing by seven.

In section eleven, the author promises to finish the narrative without more digressions. Jack now speaks using only the words of the will (excessive veneration for scripture) and fouls his pants rather than ask the way to the bathroom, since there is no formula for such a request contained in the will. He walks about the streets with his eyes closed (the Dissenters' distrust of secular learning) and frequently runs into posts and falls into the sewer, explaining that these accidents were predestined. While saying his prayers in the gutter, he opens his pants and urinates in the eyes of spectators (the Puritans used piety as a cover for their crimes in 1642-1649). He asks passers-by on the street to strike or kick him, and then claims he is persecuted for his religion. But unluckily for Jack's zeal, the more extreme his behavior becomes, the more frequently he is mistaken for his brother Peter (the totalitarianism of the Puritans is similar to that of the Papists).

The author goes abruptly into an account of the importance among the Dissenters of having large ears (the close-cropped hair of the Roundheads made their ears appear prominent). The real reason is that large ears are supposed to correspond to the presence of large sexual organs. The section closes with veiled references to recent English history.

The conclusion is another attack on modern literature. Booksellers know that modern books are sold more by prevailing fads than by literary merit; so the author has conspired with his publisher to have the *Tale* attributed to whichever wit happens to be popular at the moment. (In fact, the book was published anonymously.)

> Duchess d'Argent, author of the *Tale*, Dr. Richard Bentley, Richard Blackmore, Sir John Bowls, Charles Boyle (Lord Orrery), Wm. Congreve, John Dryden, Sir Humphry Edwin, Madame de Grands Titres, Harry the Great of France, John How, Jack, Sir Roger L'Estrange, Martin, Sir Christopher Musgrave, Countess d'Orgueil, Peter, Prince Pos-

terity, Ravillac, Tom Rymer, Sir Edward Seymour, Nahum Tate, Sir William Temple, Time, William Wotton.

A True Relation of the Apparition of Mrs. Veal, Defoe. See *The Apparition of Mrs. Veal*.

CHARACTERS

Key to short titles used in the character list:

Battle—Battle of the Books, Swift.
Campbell—Duncan Campbell, Defoe.
Carleton—Captain Carleton, Defoe.
Cavalier—Memoirs of a Cavalier, Defoe.
Clarissa—Clarissa, Richardson.
Crusoe—Robinson Crusoe, Defoe.
Drury—Robert Drury's Journal, Defoe.
Due Preparations—Due Preparations for the Plague, Defoe.
Farther Adventures—Farther Adventures of Robinson Crusoe, Defoe.
Gow—John Gow, Defoe.
Grandison—Sir Charles Grandison, Richardson.
Gulliver—Gulliver's Travels, Swift.
Jacque—Colonel Jacque, Defoe.
King—The King of Pirates (Captain Avery), Defoe.
Life of Sheppard—Life of John Sheppard, Defoe.
Moll—Moll Flanders, Defoe.
Narrative—A Narrative of the Proceedings in France, Defoe.
Pamela—Pamela, Richardson.
Philosopher—The Dumb Philosopher, Defoe.
Pirates—A General History of the Pirates, Defoe.
Plague Year—A Journal of the Plague Year, Defoe.
Roxana—Roxana, Defoe.
Sheppard's Narrative—Narrative of John Sheppard, Defoe.
Singleton—Captain Singleton, Defoe.
Street-Robbers—Six Notorious Street-Robbers, Defoe.
Tale—A Tale of a Tub, Swift.
Veal—The Apparition of Mrs. Veal, Defoe.
Voyage—A New Voyage Round the World, Defoe.
Wild—Jonathan Wild, Defoe.
NB: Generally speaking, the textual reference is only for the character's first appearance. For further explanation, see the preface.

Abraham. *Due Preparations* XV 55, 62. Porter employed by the grocer to run errands; dies in service.

Abraham. *Pamela* II 17. Succeeds John Arnold as Mr. B.'s personal valet; attends him as he is suffering from a fever.

Accabo, the. *Pirates* 549. King of Magadoxa; keeps the mulatto in his service for sixteen years.

Ackland, Mr. *Clarissa* VII 235. Solicitor whom Bella asks to take down particulars of Clarissa's case for a prosecution; see Derham, Counsellor.

Adams, Mr. *Pamela* III 250. Sober young clergyman whom Pamela engages to read morning prayers.

"Adeodata" (in *Campbell*). See Amanda.

Aesculapius. *Battle* I 158. Physician in Greek mythology, protector of Blackmore in his battle with Lucan.

Aesop. *Battle* I 150. Putative author of the *Fables*, praised by Temple as one of the best ancient writers; ambushed by Bentley while sleeping.

Afferrer, Deaan. *Drury* 129. Brother of Deaan Murnanzack, lives on the mountains of Yong-gorvo; gives Drury asylum from his first owner, Deaan Mevarrow.

Afra (Behn, Aphra, 1640-1689). *Battle* I 158. Lady novelist and author of Pindarics; an Amazon in the battle.

Agrippa. *Gulliver* Part III chap. 8. Admiral of Octavius's fleet at Actium; admits to Gulliver that the real hero of the battle was an obscure captain.

Airs, Capt. *Pirates* 313. Commands sloop from Connecticut captured by Lowther, 1722.

Alberoni. *Carleton* 182. Accompanies the Duke de Vendosme through Spain during the Peninsular campaign, 1706.

Alcade Major. *Jacque* XI 124. The intendant of the Havana, where Col. Jack and his companions are carried as criminals.

Alderman of Portsoken Ward. *Plague Year* IX 183. Appoints the saddler an examiner in his parish, to detect plague victims.

Aldrovandus (Ulisse, 1522-1605). *Battle* I 161. Bolognese biologist;
    Bentley and Wotton pass his tomb in their night attack.

Alfelt, Count D'. *Carleton* 152. Besieges city of Denia, 1705.

Allen, William. *Pirates* 280. One of the witnesses against William
    Davis in Roberts' crew, 1722.

Allestree, Sir John. *Grandison* I 90. Harriet's London friend who
    warns her against Sir Hargrave Pollexfen.

Allestree, Miss. *Grandison* I 20. One of Harriet's new friends in
    town, "pretty, gentle, easy, free."

Allestree, Mr. *Grandison* V 361. Sir John Allestree's nephew, en-
    gaged to Miss Dolly Needham; guest at Harriet's wedding.

Allisons, the. *Clarissa* VIII 94. The Harlowes' distant relatives who
    attend Clarissa's funeral.

Alston, Fanny. *Clarissa* VIII 116. Friend of Clarissa's; mentioned
    in her will.

Alston, Mr. *Clarissa* VII 215. "Grave old farmer-looking man";
    sent by Morden to inquire about Clarissa's health.

Altieri, Count. *Grandison* IV 410. Count with whom Sir Charles
    had a duel at Verona on his first Italian visit.

Altringer, Gen. *Cavalier* V 97. Imperial commander killed at the
    crossing of the Lech, 1632.

Amabella. *Campbell* IV 207. Wife of Amandus in the incident of
    "Adeodata's" mysterious identity.

Amanda (called "Adeodata"). *Campbell* IV 207. Natural daughter
    of Amandus, whose origin is discovered by Duncan.

Amandus. *Campbell* IV 206. Consults Duncan about the identity
    of "Adeodata."

Ambarroch, Rer. *Drury* 167. A petty prince on Madagascar; Deaan
    Mevarrow takes Drury along to make war on him.

Amy. *Roxana* XII 14. Roxana's maid, depraved by her; presumably
    murders Roxana's daughter Susan.

Anderson, Sally. *Clarissa* VI 369. Marries a shoemaker's appren-
    tice to spite her uncle; commits suicide by taking laudanum.

Anderson, Capt. *Grandison* II 181. Sprightly officer and fortune
    hunter to whom Charlotte Grandison almost falls prey.

Anderson. *Clarissa* VIII 47. Surgeon whom Lovelace wants to em-
    balm Clarissa.

Andrew. *Clarissa* V 177. One of Lovelace's servants; waits on him
    at Hampstead.

Andrew. *Clarissa* VII 152. Footman of the lady in the Smiths' shop;
    bursts his fingers through a pair of gloves.

Andrew. *Grandison* V 97. Servant of the Shelbys.

Andrews, Elizabeth. *Pamela* I 1. Pamela's mother, beginning to go blind.

Andrews, John. *Pamela* I 1. Pamela's father; originally a schoolmaster, now a ditchdigger.

Andrews, John, Jr. *Pamela* III 7. Pamela's brother, who has gone bankrupt; Mr. Andrews has assumed his debts.

Andrews, Pamela (later called Lady B.) *Pamela* I 1. Servant girl who marries Mr. B.; aged fifteen at the opening of the novel. She has seven children in all, named (in order of birth) William, Davers, Pamela, Charley, and James, plus two more whose names we are not told.

Andrews, William. *Pamela* III 7. Pamela's other brother.

Aneebeleeshy, Deaan. *Drury* 243. Ancestor of Deaan Mernaugha of Feraighn; now prayed to as a god.

Ann (in *Pamela*). See Nan.

Anne, Queen. *Gulliver*, Letter to Sympson. Ruler of England, 1702-1714; greatly revered by Gulliver.

Anne. *Grandison* II 323. Servant to Emily Jervois.

Annesly, Mr. *Pirates* 375. Engages Roche to transport his goods; thrown overboard by the rogues, 1721.

Anstis, Capt. Thomas. *Pirates* 288. Pirate who breaks off from Roberts' crew; murdered in his hammock by his own men, 1722.

Antenosa, King of. *Drury* 101. Killed by the French in Madagascar ninety years before the opening of the narrative.

Anthony, Mr. *Moll* VIII 55. Journeyman of the merchant who accuses Moll falsely.

Anthony. *Drury* 284, 294. Slave boy given to Drury by Rer Moume to help him work his farm.

"Anthony" (in *Jacque*). See Jack, Maj.

Antonio, Don. *Pirates* 444. Portuguese taken off a Moorish ship by Kid; used as an interpreter, 1697.

Antonio, Padre ("Father Anthony"). *Singleton* VI 10. Priest on the Portuguese ship; keeps Singleton from being sold into slavery as a Turk by pointing out that the boy is uncircumcised.

Antony, Uncle (in *Clarissa*). See Harlowe, Antony.

Antony. *Grandison* III 312. Former servant of Mr. Jervois, now a servant of Sir Charles in St. James's Square.

Antymoor, Deaan. *Drury* 243. Ancester of Deaan Mernaugha in Feraighn; now revered as a deity.

"Anything, Mr." (in *Jacque*). See Jack, Col.

Anzacker, Ry. *Drury* 267. Second wife of Rer Moume, sister of Deaan Toakeoffu; made Drury's foster mother.

Apollo. *Battle* I 162. Greek god of poetry; prevents Wotton's drinking from Helicon.

App---ee, Mr. (Appleby?). *Life of Sheppard* XVI 197. Turnkey in Newgate.

Aquinas (St. Thomas, c. 1225-1274). *Battle* I 152. Italian theologian, part of the "confused multitude of moderns."

Arby, Mrs. Penelope. *Grandison* VI 221. Old maid who refused to marry for fear of being dominated; now ruled by a favorite servant.

Arcos, Duke of. *Carleton* 88. Enemy commander, tricked by Peterborough into thinking that one of his fellow commanders has been suborned by the English.

Argent, Duchess d'. *Tale sect.* II. Allegorical representation of money, one of the town ladies with whom the brothers fall in love; see Grands Titres, Orgeuil.

Argyll, Earl of. *Campbell* IV 35. Leads abortive rebellion against James II, 1685.

Aristotle (384-322 B. C.) *Battle* I 146, *Gulliver* Part III chap. 8. Ancient philosopher; summoned from the dead on the island of Glubbdubdrib.

Armstrong. *Pirates* 242. Deserter from the Royal Navy; informs Roberts of the approach of the *Swallow*; hanged on board the *Weymouth*.

Arnheim, Gen. *Cavalier* V 61. Commander of the Swedish cavalry at Leipzig, 1631.

Arnold, John. *Grandison* IV 106. Mr. Lowther's brother-in-law, to whom he sends an account of Sir Charles's second visit to Italy.

Arnold, John. *Pamela* I 2. Servant at Mr. B.'s Bedfordshire estate, part of the plot to seduce Pamela; later repents.

Arnold, Robert. *Drury* 230. Co-owner of a sloop trading at St. Augustine Bay, Madagascar; murdered by the natives.

Arnold, Mr. *Clarissa* VIII 118. Clergyman with whom Clarissa used to maintain a correspondence.

Arthur, Lady. *Pamela* I 59. Neighbor of Mr. B.'s; gives herself airs.

Arthur, Lord (also Mr.) *Pamela* I 60, III 218. Vexed visibly when a footman drops a china dish; he and his wife make cutting remarks at each other's expense.

Arthur. *Pamela* I 131. Gardener at Mr. B.'s Bedfordshire estate.

Ashburnham, Mr. *Cavalier* V 292. Accompanies Charles I in his flight from Oxford to Newark, 1646.

Ashby, Sir Jacob. *Cavalier* V 284. Attempts to recruit a force to help Charles I; defeated at Stow-on-the-Wold.

Ashplant, Valentine. *Pirates* 194. Judge in the trial of Harry Glasby; procures his acquittal.

Ashton, Sir Arthur. *Cavalier* V 192. Royalist wounded at Reading, 1643.

Astley, Sir Jacob. *Cavalier* V 146. Royalist commander posted at Newburn-upon-Tyne to keep out the Scots.

Atkins, Mrs. Mary (in *Clarissa*). See Harlowe, Clarissa.

Atkins, Will. *Crusoe* I 299, *Farther Adventures* II 119. One of the most virulent of the mutineers; later reforms.

Atkins, Mr. *Pamela* II 51. Gentleman living within two miles of the Andrewses; is supposed to deliver a letter to them.

Atkinson, Mr. *Pirates* 609. Pressed by Fly into serving as a pilot; overcomes Fly in a mutiny, 1726.

Atkyns, Sir Thomas. *Pamela* II 346, III 218, IV 5. An affected beau; puts on airs in a visit to Pamela.

Aubigny, D' (in *Pirates*). See Caraccioli, Seignior.

Augur, John. *Pirates* 42. Pirate who returns to his life of crime after being pardoned; hanged, 1718.

Austin, William. *Life of Sheppard* XVI 190, *Sheppard's Narrative*, XVI 224. Sheppard's jailer in Newgate.

Author of the *Tale*. *Tale, passim*. Pedantic hack living in Grub Street; his voice coalesces intermittently with that of Swift himself.

Auverquerque, Mons. D'. *Carleton* 23. Prevents the Prince of Orange from being shot at the Battle of St. Dennis, 1678.

Avery, Capt. Henry. *King of Pirates* XVI 7, *Pirates* 49, *Singleton* VI 205. Founder of a pirate colony on Madagascar; encountered briefly by Singleton.

Awberry, Deb. *Grandison* I 228. Daughter of Mrs. Awberry; participates in Harriet's abduction, is apparently in love with Wilson.

Awberry, Sally. *Grandison* I 228, 246. Sister of above; forces Harriet to wear a capuchin (a cloak-and-hood for women).

Awberry, Mr. *Grandison* I 264. Son of Mrs. Awberry, employee in the customs office.

Awberry, the widow. *Grandison* I 228. Owns the house to which Sir Hargrave has Harriet carried away.

B., "Charley." *Pamela* IV 383. Pamela's fourth child, born while the family is abroad.

B., Davers. *Pamela* IV 288, 349. Pamela's second child.

B., James ("Jemmy"). *Pamela* IV 395. Pamela's "fourth dear boy," her fifth child.

B., Lady Pamela (in *Pamela*). See Andrews, Pamela.

B., Pamela. *Pamela* IV 372. Pamela's daughter, her third child.

B., Mr. William (generally called "Mr. B.") *Pamela* I 3. Pamela's master; attempts to seduce her, later marries her.

B., William ("Billy"). *Pamela* IV 127. Pamela's first child; falls ill with smallpox but recovers.

B., Aunt. *Pamela* III 186. Relation of Mr. B.'s (already dead when the novel opens), who once asked what Lady B. intended to do to help Pamela.

B., Lady. *Pamela* I 1. Pamela's employer before the novel opens; has taught her to write, keep accounts, and sew.

Bacon (Sir Francis, 1561-1626). *Battle* I 156. English philosopher; antagonist of Aristotle in the battle.

Badger, Cicely. *Grandison* IV 269. Companion of Aunt Eleanor Grandison.

Bagenhall, James. *Grandison* I 259. Previous employer of Wilson living near Reading, crony of Sir Hargrave's; IV 85, forced to marry a woman he tried to seduce.

Bains, Mr. *Life of Sheppard* XVI 175, *Sheppard's Narrative* XVI 215. Cloth seller in Whitehorse Yard, Sheppard's first victim.

Baldrick, Ralph. *Pirates* 253. Boatswain of the *Swallow*; testifies against Roberts' crew, 1722.

Baldwin, Mr. *Pirates* 236. Agent of the Royal African Company; warned of the approach of Roberts by Gen. Phips, 1722.

Baldwin, Mr. *Pirates* 541. Third mate of the *Albemarle*, sent to negotiate with the Magadoxans; torn apart by wild beasts, 1700.

Balfour, Sir William. *Cavalier* V 173. Commands Parliamentary cavalry at Edgehill, 1642.

Ball, Thomas. *Street-Robbers* XVI 374. Apprehends one of the robbers; later murdered by the gang.

Ball, Mrs. *Street-Robbers* XVI 376. Wife of above.

Ballard. *Life of Sheppard* XVI 199. Turnkey at the trial of Joseph Blake.

Balmuff. *Gulliver* Part I chap. 7. Grand Justiciary of Lilliput; joins in the impeachment of Gulliver.

Bamzau, the. *Pirates* 562. Priest at the Moorzacks (royal tombs) who instructs the mulatto in his duties.

Baner, Sir John. *Cavalier* V 104. Left by the Swedes to guard Augsburg, 1632.

Barbarouse. *Pirates* 30. Pirate from Mitylene on the island of Lesbos; becomes so powerful he surprises Selim Eutemi, the king of Algiers, in his bath.

Barclay, Miss. *Grandison* V 354. Friend of Harriet's, wedding guest.

Bargrave, Mr. *Veal* XV 227. Treats his wife barbarously.

Bargrave, Mrs. *Veal* XV 225. Witnesses the ghost of Mrs. Veal.

Barker, Cousin. *Clarissa* VII 318. Manteaumaker who sees Clarissa talking with Belford; helps sully her reputation.

Barlow, Anthony. *Philosopher* XV 202. An old, contemplative Welsh gentleman; forms close friendship with Dickory.

Barlow, Mary ("Polly"). *Pamela* III 49, IV 257. Genteel new servant whom Mr. B. has taken on for his Kentish estate.

Barnard, Mr. *Campbell* IV 203. Jokingly proposes a ramble to Sevenoaks in Kent to test the validity of Duncan's "second sight."

Barnes, Betty. *Clarissa* I 92. Bella's maid, assigned to Clarissa to watch over her; very impertinent to her.

Barnes, Sir Jonathan. *Pamela* IV 435. Marries Miss Stapylton, but only after she relinquishes her passion for reading romances.

Barnet, Capt. *Pirates* 150. Commissioned by the governor of Hispaniola to capture John Rackam, 1720.

Barnet, Isaac (later editions: Burnet). *Pirates* 273. Testifies that he has overheard Scudamore plotting with the blacks to mutiny, 1722.

Barnet, Mr. *Grandison* I 21. Nephew of Lady Allestree; very juvenile, hums Italian airs and talks only about clothes.

Barnevelt, Miss. *Grandison* I 56. Amazonian visitor at Lady Betty's.

Barnham, Mr. *Grandison* III 43. Friend of Sir Charles near Grandison Hall.

Barnwell, Anthony. *Carleton* 17. Gentleman killed in the assault on Maestrich, 1676.

"Barone, the" (in *Grandison*). See Porretta, Jeronymo della.

"Barrow, Col." (in *Clarissa*). See Lovelace, Robert.

Barrow, Mr. *Pamela* III 351 (IV 51 "Mr. Barlow"). Apothecary whom Pamela engages to treat her poor neighbors.

Bartlett, Rev. Dr. Ambrose. *Grandison* I 345. Worthy clergyman with curling silver locks whom Sir Charles brings back from Italy.

Bartlett, Daniel. *Grandison* VI 36. Nephew of above, aged eighteen, employed by Sir Charles as accountant and secretary.

Barton, Johnny. *Clarissa* I 252. Young carpenter with whom Rosebud is in love; Lovelace furthers their romance.

Barton, Mr. *Life of Sheppard* XVI 179. Robbed by Sheppard and Charles Grace while he is asleep.

Barton. *Street-Robbers* XVI 367. One of the rogues; attempts to shoot Marjoram, the state's witness.

Basset, Gen. *Carleton* 125. Spanish governor of Xativa, 1705.

Bateman, Lieut. Col. *Carleton* 135. His scandalous neglect causes his whole company to be wiped out by the enemy.

Bates, James. *Gulliver* Part I chap. 1. Gulliver's "Master Bates," an eminent surgeon in London.

"Bath gentleman." *Moll* VII 107. Gentleman with whom Moll has a long liaison after her return from Virginia; after she has borne him four children, he has a fit of repentance and leaves her.

Batoengha. *Drury* 121. Son of Deaan Mephontey; during a war persuades his father and Deaan Mevarrow not to counterattack, since he fears an ambush.

Beachcroft, Sir Robert. *Clarissa* VI 419. Man whose servant carries a letter from Mrs. Norton to Clarissa.

Beal, Capt. John. *Pirates* 595. Merchant skipper who lures John Cornelius ashore at Trinity Harbor, Newfoundland, to capture him.

Beardsley, Robert. *Drury* 303. Man who inherits the Drury family home in Stoke Newington after Drury's long exile.

Beauchamp, Edward. *Grandison* II 267. Son of Sir Harry; persuades Sir Charles to bail Dr. Bartlett out of prison; in love with Emily Jervois.

Beauchamp, Sir Harry. *Grandison* II 271. Crusty old gentleman; Sir Charles resolves his estrangement from his son.

Beauchamp, Lady. *Grandison* II 271. Stepmother of Edward; originally in love with him.

Beaumont, Mrs. Hortensia. *Grandison* III 29. English lady living at Florence, to whose care Clementina is entrusted.

Beaumont, Laetita (in *Clarissa*). See Harlowe, Clarissa.

Beaumont, Sir Michael. *Pamela* IV 435. Marries Miss Cope.

Beavis, Capt. William. *Pirates* 540. Master of the *Albemarle*, part of whose crew is captured by the Magadoxans; later records the mulatto's adventures.

Beck (in *Pamela*). See Worden, Beck.

Beckford. *Grandison* II 83. Housekeeper at Grandison Hall in Hampshire.

Bedall, Arthur. *Clarissa* VIII 124. One of the witnesses to Clarissa's will.

Beer, Capt. *Pirates* 587. Master of a sloop captured by Bellamy; receives a lecture on his own pusillanimity.

Befaugher, Rer. *Drury* 192. Brother of Deaan Trongha; assists in the command of the army of the Feraighners.

Beleau, Mlle. de (in *Roxana*). See Roxana.

Belford, John (alias "Capt. Sloane"). *Clarissa* I 210. Lovelace's friend, "so rough and so resolute"; quickly becomes an advocate of Clarissa's cause.

Bell, Miss. *Clarissa* III 203. Friend of Anna Howe's.

Bell. *Pamela* III 339. Maid of the Darnfords.

Bella (in *Clarissa*). See Harlowe, Arabella.

Bellamont, Lord. *Pirates* 440. Governor of Barbados; grants William Kid a commission for privateering, 1698.

Bellamy, Capt. *Pirates* 585. Pirate captain of the *Whidaw*; captured and hanged after running aground on the New England coast, 1717.

Bellarmine (Roberto, 1542-1621). *Battle* I 152. Italian cardinal; one of the leaders of the confused multitude of moderns.

Bellasis, Col. *Cavalier* V 293. Royal governor of Newark; ordered by the king to surrender the town, 1646.

Belton, Hal. *Clarissa* IV 140, 147. Son of Thomasine and the hostler; Belton thinks he is his own child.

Belton, Thomas ("Tom"). *Clarissa* I 220. Libertine friend of Lovelace's, "so pert and so pimply"; dies of consumption.

Belton, Tom. *Clarissa* IV 140, 147. Bastard son of Thomasine and the hostler, allegedly son of Thomas Belton.

Belvedere, Count of (alias "Signor Marsigli," VI 176). *Grandison* III 21. Suitor of the Lady Clementina, aged twenty-five or twenty-six.

Belvin, James. *Gow* XVI 298. Boatswain of sloop captured by Gow; joins the pirates.

Bembo, John. *Drury* 41. Fourth mate, later second mate on the *Degrave*, 1701; escapes from Deaan Crindo.

Bembo, Admiral. *Drury* 41. Uncle of John Bembo; the *Degrave* passes his squadron while leaving the Downs, 1701.

Benbrooke, James. *Pirates* 611. Seaman pressed into service on a pirate ship by Fly, 1726.

Benjamin. *Pamela* I 58. Groom and assistant of Arthur at Mr. B.'s Bedfordshire estate.

Bennet, Mrs. *Pamela* IV 60. Neighbor of Mr. B.'s who indelicately refers to the "former condition" of Pamela's parents.

Bennet, Rev. Dr. *Sheppard's Narrative* XVI 231. Chaplain who visits Sheppard before his execution.

Bennet. *Cavalier* V 278. Parliamentary officer who disputes the Royalist entry into Huntingdon, 1645.

Benson, Mrs. *Clarissa* VI 253. Neighbor of Anna and Clarissa, at whose house they saw Betsey Sadlier before Betsey's death.

Benson. *Life of Sheppard* XVI 177. Accomplice of Sheppard.

Bentley, Dr. Richard. *Tale* Epistle Dedicatory, sect. V; *Battle* I 159. Royal librarian at St. James's Palace, author of the *Dissertation on the Epistles of Phalaris* and target of Swift's satire; enters the battle with a manure pot.

Bernard, Jonathan. *Pirates* 72. Owner of three sloops from Jamaica which are captured by Blackbeard, 1718.

Bernhard, Duke of Weimar. *Cavalier* V 107. Lieutenant of Gustavus Adolphus in Bavaria, 1632.

Berry, Thomas. *Street-Robbers* XVI 377. One of the six robbers.

Berwick, Dr. *Plague Year* IX 37. Mentioned as being one of the legitimate doctors practicing in London.

Berwick, Duke of. *Carleton* 110. Captures Peterborough's supply train at Huette, 1705; defeats Galway at Almanza, 1707.

Besace, Jean. *Pirates* 392. Made third mate on the *Victoire* after Misson assumes command.

"Bess, Edgworth" (in *Life of Sheppard, Sheppard's Narrative*). See Lyon, Elizabeth.

Bett, Miss. *Pamela* III 426. Young governess of Miss Goodwin at the school near Mr. B.'s Bedfordshire estate.

Betterton, Miss. *Clarissa* III 183. Girl from Nottinghamshire whom Lovelace formerly ruined; James Harlowe revives the story.

Betty, Lady. *Pamela* II 280, III 31, IV 41. Woman whom Lady Davers would like Mr. B. to marry; sister of Lord John and Lady Jenny.

Betty, Mrs. *Moll* VIII 71. Child of twelve or thirteen years whose watch Moll steals after pretending she is acquainted with her family; see also Flanders, Moll.

Betty. *Clarissa* VII 179. Maid at Belton's house.

Bever. *Grandison* II 100. Sir Thomas Grandison's dishonest English steward.

Bevis, Mrs. (the widow). *Clarissa* V 145. A lively young woman at

Mrs. Moore's in Hampstead; impersonates Clarissa in order to intercept Anna's letter; see Rogers.

Biddle, John. *Gulliver* Part I chap. 8. Captain of the ship which picks Gulliver up after his escape from Blefuscu.

Biddulph, Rachel. *Clarissa* I 11, VI 444, VIII 116. Friend of Clarissa's, guest at Col. Ambrose's party.

Biddulph, Sir Robert. *Clarissa* V 114. Acquaintance of Charlotte Montague and Lady Betty Lawrance, at whose house Lady Betty once saw Clarissa.

Bird, Capt. *Pirates* 237. Reports the presence of Roberts to the *Swallow* and *Weymouth*, 1722.

Bird, Mr. *Life of Sheppard* XVI 200. Keeps a turner's shop near Newgate; through his house Sheppard completes one of his famous escapes.

Bizeau (or Bisseau), Joseph (alias "Gratien Devanelle," XVI 157). *Narrative* XVI 97. Most hard-bitten of the highwaymen.

Black prince (in *Singleton*). See Prince, black.

"Blackbeard" (in *Pirates*). See Teach, Edward.

Blackburn. *Carleton* 42. One of the conspirators in the Assassination Plot against William III, 1696; see Cassels and Porter, Capt.

Blackerby, Justice. *Life of Sheppard* XVI 198, *Street-Robbers* XVI 378. London justice of the peace who issues warrant for Sheppard's arrest; commits the six robbers to Newgate.

Blackmore, Sir Richard (c. 1650-1729). *Tale* sect. X, *Battle* I 158. Modern writer of immense epics; opposed to Lucan in the battle.

Blagrave. *Grandison* II 380. An attorney mediating between the O'Haras and Sir Charles.

Blake, Joseph (alias "Blueskin"). *Life of Sheppard* XVI 176, *Street Robbers* XVI 359. London robber; stabs Jonathan Wild while Wild is testifying against him.

Bland, Robert. *Pirates* 601. Helmsman in Cornelius's crew; beats Joseph Williams.

Blefuscu, Emperor of. *Gulliver* Part I chap. 8. Ruler of the other empire of tiny people (France); invites Gulliver to stay in his kingdom.

Blewet, William. *Street-Robbers* XVI 349. Most hardened of the thieves.

Bliffmarklub, the. *Gulliver* Part III chap. 9. High Chamberlain of Luggnagg; ordered to give Gulliver a lodging at court.

"Blueskin" (in *Life of Sheppard, Street-Robbers*). See Blake, Joseph.

Blome, Dr. *Clarissa* VIII 118. Clergyman with whom Clarissa carries on a correspondence.

Blomer. *Clarissa* VII 203. Friend of Belton's, reported to have said there is nothing but pickpocket and parade in the physician's art.

"Bloodyhand, Capt." (in *King*). See Nichols.

Bloom, Capt. *Drury* 293. Commander of the *Sarah*, which, with the *Drake*, comes to rescue Drury.

Blunt. *Clarissa* V 59. Man for whose chariot Lovelace sends, to take him to Hampstead to recapture Clarissa.

Bohemia, King of. *Cavalier* V 85. Son-in-law of James I of England; visits Gustavus Adolphus in his winter camp at Hoechst.

Bolton. *Grandison* III 245, IV 355. Unscrupulous steward of Mr. Calvert; at length brought to make a composition with the Mansfields, whom he has swindled.

Bonnet, Maj. Stede (alias Edwards, alias Thomas). *Pirates* 72. Pirate captain deposed by Blackbeard because of his half-heartedness.

Bonny, Anne (or Bonn). *Pirates* 156. Female pirate, not so reserved in point of chastity as Mary Read.

Bonny, James. *Pirates* 623. Husband of above, whom she deserts after he catches her in a hammock making love with another man.

Boon, Capt. *Drury* 43. Pirate met by the *Degrave* at Mauritius.

Boone, Charles. *Pirates* 121. Governor of Bombay for the East India Company; sends for help from England, 1720.

Booth, George. *Pirates* 474. Former gunner of the *Dolphin*; stages a surprise takeover of Capt. Fourgette's ship.

Booth, William. *Gow* XVI 339. Pirate who turns state's evidence.

Booth, Miss. *Pamela* II 331. Pretty brunet girl with fine eyes; attends Mrs. Dobson's boarding school.

Borroughs, Nancy ("Nanny"). *Pamela* II 227. Younger of the two Borroughs sisters, very much taken with Pamela.

Borroughs, Miss. *Pamela* II 227. Older of the Borroughs girls.

Bouflers. *Carleton* 39. Commands French dragoons at Namur, 1695.

Bourgard, Brigadier. *Carleton* 134. English officer in Spain, pleased with Carleton's engineering skill.

Bow, Daniel (alias Black). *Campbell* IV 130. Foretells the imminent death of a woman in Minginis, Scotland.

Bowen, Capt. John. *Pirates* 452. Captures the *Speedy Return*, for which Capt. Thomas Green is unjustly hanged; warns his crew in vain against eating the poisonous red snapper fish.

Bowler, Capt. *Gow* XVI 309. Commander of the British navy vessel *Argyle*, which receives the pirate Williams on board.

Bowles, Capt. *Pirates* 217. Master of ship taken by Roberts, 1720.

Bowls, Sir John. *Tale* sect. IX. Whig MP whom the author advises to visit Bedlam for candidates for office.

Boyd, Maj. *Carleton* 140. Ludicrous figure whom Carleton sees riding under an immense poncho on a tiny donkey.

Boyle, Charles, fourth earl of Orrery (1676-1731). *Tale* Apology, *Battle* I 139. Author of *Dr. Bentley's Dissertation . . . Examin'd*, 1698; revenges Temple in the battle.

Bradley, Capt. George. *Pirates* 294. Deserts from Roberts' party off the coast of Africa, 1721.

Brady, Farmer. *Pamela* I 85. Neighbor of Mr. B.'s; has a chaise which Pamela might borrow to return to her parents.

Bramber, Sally. *Grandison* I 21. Younger of the Bramber sisters, aged seventeen; kept down by the vivacity of her sister.

Bramber, Miss. *Grandison* I 20. A witty lady, "too talkative," one of Harriet's friends in town.

Brand, Elias. *Clarissa* II 327. Pedantic young clergyman who collects gossip on Clarissa and smears her reputation.

Brandenburg, Duke of. *Cavalier* V 42. Comes in reluctantly on the side of Sweden in the Thirty Years' War.

Brandon, Sir Arthur. *Grandison* VI 273. Emissary of Lady D. to Sir Charles in Italy.

Brennan, Murtough. *Carleton* 184. Rascally cleric who tries to convert Carleton to Catholicism.

Brereton, William. *Cavalier* V 244. Parliamentary commander from Cheshire, defeated at Lichfield.

Breton, old Mr. *Veal* XV 235. Has been giving Mrs. Veal ten pounds a year.

Brett, Mr. *Pamela* I 172. Postal employee in the pay of Mr. B.; not to be trusted.

"Brewer, the." *Roxana* XII 3. Roxana's first husband, who deserts her.

Bridds. *Pirates* 327. Master of a snow (a sort of brig) going from Jamaica to London; captured by Edward Low, 1723.

Brobdingnag, King of. *Gulliver* Part II chap. 3. The enlightened despot who holds English cultural institutions up to scorn.

Brobdingnag, Queen of. *Gulliver* Part II chap. 3. Gulliver wins her
   favor by fulsome flattery.
Brody. *Carleton* 29. Highlander whose nose Carleton blows off with
   a hand grenade.
Brookland, Sir Josias. *Clarissa* VIII 123. Clarissa's mother's uncle;
   has given Clarissa a diamond necklace, solitaire, and buckles.
Brooks, Dr. *Plague Year* IX 37. One of the legitimate London physicians.
Brooks, Lady. *Pamela* I 59. Lady with a "malicious sneering countenance" who comes to laugh at Pamela.
Brooks, Mr. *Pamela* I 60, III 218. Has one of the aristocratic marriages Mr. B. deplores; makes jokes on serious subjects.
Brother of the saddler. *Plague Year* IX 12. Sends his wife and children
   down into Bedfordshire, advises the saddler that the best
   physic against the plague is to run away from it.
Brother, older. *Due Preparations* XV 93. Skeptical about his sister's
   religious preachments.
Brother, older. *Moll* VII 14. Young gentleman in the Colchester
   family where Moll is a servant; the first to seduce her.
Brother, younger. *Due Preparations* XV 93. Prepares himself for
   the plague by heeding the pious admonitions of his sister.
Brown, Capt. John, Jr. *Pirates* 320. Ordered to capture Low by the
   governor of Rhode Island, 1722.
Brown, Mr. *Clarissa* VI 89. Peruke maker in St. Martin's Lane,
   Westminster, where "Tomlinson" claims to board.
Brown, Mr. *Life of Sheppard* XVI 175. Beadle, cares for the St.
   Giles roundhouse.
Brown, Mrs. *Life of Sheppard* XVI 175. Wife of above; both are
   beaten up by Sheppard.
Bruce. *Pirates* 287. Young pirate of twenty-six, hanged with
   Roberts' crew, 1722; makes the best gallows speech of
   the lot.
Brutus. *Gulliver* Part III chap. 8. Roman patriot; summoned from
   the dead on Glubbdubdrib.
Buchanan (George, 1506-1582). *Battle* I 152. Scottish humanist
   and historian; commander of modern infantry in the battle.
"Bullet-head." *Jacque* X 152. Slave in Maryland who gets drunk
   and tries to murder an overseer.
Bunce, Phineas. *Pirates* 628. Under the pretense of a friendly
   palaver, takes over Augur's sloop along with Macarty, 1718.
Bruce, Stephen. *Pirates* 318. Celebrated criminal executed at
   Tyburn along with Jack Hall and Ned Low's brother.

"Bunworth" (in *Street-Robbers*). See Frazier, Edward.

Burdoff, Miss. *Pamela* II 331. Girl with a great deal of sweetness in her countenance who visits Pamela.

Burford, John. *Singleton* VI 274. Chief mate of the *Anne*; commands the ship after the *Dissauva* captures Capt. Knox.

Burgess, Capt. Josias (Thomas?). *Pirates* 41, 615. Pirate in the West Indies; later commissioned as a privateer and wrecked south of Green Key.

Burgess, Capt. Samuel. *Drury* 230, *Pirates* 476. Trader at St. Augustine's Bay, Madagascar; as mate of the *Neptune*, betrays the ship into the hands of John Bowen.

Burgess. *Grandison* III 43. Sir Charles's steward at Grandison Hall.

Burnet, Isaac (in *Pirates*). See Barnet, Isaac.

Burroughs, Roger. *Pamela* III 10. Son of a cousin of Mr. Andrews; his father asks Mr. Andrews to employ him.

Burton, Edmund. *Gulliver* Part I chap. 1. Hosier in Newgate St., London, and Gulliver's father-in-law.

Burton, Hannah. *Clarissa* I 45. Clarissa's beloved maid, whom she is not allowed to see.

Burton, Mary. *Gulliver* Part I chap. 1. Gulliver's bride; at the end of the book he can hardly bear to be with her.

Bush, Capt. *Carleton* 149. English soldier buried in Spain; since he is a heretic, the peasants disinter his body from the cornfield where he is buried so he won't blight the crop.

Butler, Deb (alias "Dorcas Wykes," "Dorcas Martindale"). *Clarissa* III 311. Clarissa's maid in the evil house; feigns illiteracy.

Butler, Nicholas. *Pirates* 276. In the trial of Roberts' crew, testifies that George Wilson complained to him of the wretchedness of a pirate's life, hence presumably was compelled to go along.

Byng, Sir George. *Carleton* 93, *Jacque* XI 60. English admiral; pursues the Chevalier de St. George in his attempted invasion.

Byron, Sir John. *Cavalier* V 162. Raises a party of five hundred cavalrymen; captures Oxford for the king, 1642.

Byron, Mr. *Clarissa* I 94. A former suitor of Clarissa's.

C., Lord. *Pamela* IV 295, 382. Mr. B.'s neighbor; the Countess Dowager refuses to marry him because he thinks B.'s marriage with Pamela is dishonorable.

Caesar (Julius, 102?-44 B.C.) *Gulliver* Part II chap. 8, *Pirates* 18. Called up from the dead on Glubbdubdrib; captured by pirates, later extirpates the whole gang.

Callander, Earl of. *Cavalier* V 239. Leads second Scottish army of ten thousand men into England, 1644.

Calvert, Mr. *Grandison* III 245. Gentleman who, influenced by his steward, leaves his money to his mistress instead of to the Mansfield girls; see Bolton.

Calvo, Mons. *Carleton* 15. French defender of Maestrich; distinguished by his raillery.

Cambden (Camden, William, 1551-1623). *Battle* I 152. English antiquary and historian; commands modern infantry in the battle.

Camilla. *Grandison* III 60. Clementina's servant, Sir Charles's faithful correspondent in Bologna.

Campbell, Archibald. *Campbell* IV 2. Duncan's father; abducted to Lapland.

Campbell, Miss Cartwright. *Clarissa* VIII 116. Friend of Clarissa's who receives five guineas for a ring in her will.

Campbell, Duncan (Sr.). *Campbell* IV 6. Duncan's grandfather.

Campbell, Duncan. *Campbell* IV 1. The deaf-and-dumb Scottish seer.

Campbell, Mrs. *Campbell* IV 9. Duncan's Lapp mother, also has the "second sight."

Campion, Miss. *Clarissa* I 276. Friend of Anna's; too easily attracted by the physical appearance of men.

Canning, Capt. (or Kanning). *Pirates* 274. Testifies against the pirate George Wilson, 1722.

Cantillon, Miss. *Grandison* I 56, V 43. Pretty but affected girl at Lady Betty Williams' party; runs away with a "nominal" captain.

Cantle (or Cantlow). *Campbell* IV 74. Magician who causes a bell to toll in the vicar's house.

Caraccioli, Seignior (alias D'Aubigny). *Pirates* 385. Lewd priest who corrupts Misson's principles; killed on Madagascar after becoming secretary of state of the pirate colony.

Carberry, Betty. *Clarissa* V 18. Prostitute at Mrs. Sinclair's who breaks to Lovelace the news of Clarissa's escape.

Carleton, Capt. George. *Carleton* 1. Serves under the Prince of Orange and the Earl of Peterborough; alleged author of the *Memoirs*.

Carlton, Mr. *Pamela* II 189. Man whose death prompts Mr. B. to make his will.

Carnarvon, Earl of. *Cavalier* V 207. Royalist killed at Newbury, over whose death the king weeps.

Caroline. (in *Grandison*). See L., Caroline, Countess of.

Caron, Mary Frances Beausse de. *Narrative* XVI 98. Keeps a tavern at Beauval, hides some of the robbers.

Carpenter, Gen. *Carleton* 172. English cavalry officer; not allowed to join Staremberg at Villa Viciosa.

Carr, James. *Pirates* 628. Loyal member of the crew of the *Batchelor's Adventure*; marooned on Green Key by Bunce and Macarty.

Carravallas, Don Garcia de Pimentesia de. *Singleton* VI 5. Commander of the ship in which Bob's Portuguese pilot ships.

Carter, Mr. *Life of Sheppard* XVI 179. A mathematical instrument maker in Wych St., master of Sheppard's accomplice Anthony Lamb.

Carter, Mrs. *Clarissa* VIII 54. Sister of Mrs. Sinclair, keeps a bagnio in Bloomsbury.

Cartouche, Col. (also Capt.). *Narrative* XVI 98. Leader of the band of French highwaymen; attracts Bizeau to him.

Cary, Capt. *Pirates* 217. Master of the *Samuel*, captured by Roberts, 1720; testifies for Harry Glasby, 1722.

Cassels. *Carleton* 40. Conspirator, arrested by Carleton for his part in the Assassination Plot against William III, 1696; see Blackburn and Porter, Capt.

Catharine (also Katharine). *Clarissa* VI 313, VIII 117. Maid at Mrs. Smith's who assists Clarissa on her deathbed.

Catinat, Mons. *Jacque* XI 45. French commander in the Italian campaign, 1701.

Cavalier, the. *Cavalier* V 1. Soldier of fortune in the Thirty Years' War, supporter of the king in the English Civil Wars.

Cavendish, Lt. Gen. *Cavalier* V 203. Royalist killed at Grantham by Cromwell, 1643.

Ceylon, King of. *Singleton* VI 260. Seeks to lure whites ashore so he can make captives of them; see Knox and Dutchman.

Chahary, Deaan. *Drury* 87. Prince of Anterndroea; steals some of Deaan Mevarrow's cattle.

Chamberlain, Joseph. *Drury* 41. Member of the barge crew that goes to put Mons. Lapie ashore at Ft. St. George.

Chambers, Thomas. *Singleton* VI 272. English agent at Ft. St. George, India.

Chambers, Mr. *Pamela* II 324. Gentleman lately settled in Bedfordshire; invited to dinner at Mr. B.'s.

Chambers, Mrs. *Pamela* II 350. Wife of above.

Chandler, Capt. *Pirates* 323. Commander of an English vessel captured by Low, 1722.

Chaponan, Mr. *Pamela* III 219. He and his wife are fond of one another, but not with a "censurable fondness."

Chaponan, Mrs. *Pamela* III 219. Wife of above.

Charles I of England. *Cavalier* V 88. The "unfortunate monarch," who was served faithfully by the Cavalier until executed, 1649.

Charles II of England. *Carleton* 7, *Cavalier* 285, *Philosopher* XV 189, *Roxana* XII 203. Forced to make peace with the Dutch, 1674; narrowly escapes the Parliamentary forces after the Battle of Worcester; rumored to be present at Roxana's party.

Charles III of Spain. *Carleton* 53. Austrian candidate for the Spanish crown during War of the Spanish Succession, 1702-1713.

Charles, Mr. *Life of Sheppard* XVI 177. Householder in May Fair; robbed by Sheppard.

Charles, Prince. *Cavalier* V 120. Son of the king of Bohemia; restored to the throne of the Lower Palatinate by the Peace of Westphalia, 1648.

"Charnot, Mons." (in *Jacque*). See Jack, Col.

Cheeseman, Edward. *Pirates* 346. Carpenter pressed into service by the pirate John Phillips; stages a successful revolt, 1724.

Chemermaundy. *Drury* 88. Son of Deaan Woozington; prince of Mefaughla on Madagascar.

Chemotoea (Chemetoe), Ry. *Drury* 263. Head wife of Rer Trimmonongarevo, grandmother of Rer Vove; immensely fat; keeps Drury from being capriciously executed.

Chemunghoher, Rer. *Drury* 268. Cousin of Rer Vove, with whose wife Vove wants to have an affair.

Chevalier de St. George. *Jacque* XI 59. The "Old Pretender"; Jacque joins his expedition to invade England, 1702.

Chichely, Sir John. *Carleton* 4. English commander of the *Katherine* at the naval action off Sole Bay, 1672.

Child, Mr. *Pirates* 272. Deposes against Scudamore in the trial of Roberts' crew, 1722.

Chimave. *Pirates* 605. Son of Chimenatto; has become king of Mathelage by the time of Cornelius' return from the Persian Gulf.

Chime, Mrs. *Moll* VIII 71. Governess of Mrs. Betty, whose gold watch Moll steals.

Chimenatto, Andian (or Deaan). *Pirates* 602. Native prince in Mathelage, near Port St. Augustine; with the help of Cornelius' crew, wrests the kingdom away from his elder brother.

Christal, Capt. *Drury* 308. Succeeds Capt. White as skipper during Drury's second voyage to Madagascar, 1719.

Christallina. *Campbell* IV 97. A London toast, in love with Secretarius; seeks out Duncan's help.

Chula, Rer. *Drury* 200. Tribal leader on Madagascar, nephew of Deaan Woozington; killed in battle.

Chulu-Mossu-Andro. *Drury* 165. Tribal leader on Madagascar, son of Rer Moume; diverts himself with hunting alligators.

Cicely. *Pamela* I 131. Housemaid at Mr. B.'s estate in Bedfordshire; weeps when Pamela leaves, promises they will all pray for her.

Clark, Mrs. Rachel (in *Clarissa*). See Harlowe, Clarissa.

Clark, Robert. *Pirates* 85. Commands a ship captured by Blackbeard, 1718.

Clarke, Sir Samuel. *Grandison* III 43. Friend of Sir Charles at Grandison Hall.

Clarkson, Miss. *Grandison* V 238. Friend of Miss Orme; wants to meet Harriet.

Clayton, Sir Robert. *Roxana* XII 186. Eminent London merchant; invests Roxana's fourteen thousand pounds for her.

Clementina (in *Grandison*). See Porretta, Clementina della.

Clements, Pulcheria. *Grandison* I 56. Plain girl, acquaintance of Harriet's; has a fine understanding improved by reading.

Clements. *Clarissa* VII 288. Servant at Lord M.'s.

Clemson, Lady Betty. *Grandison* IV 216. Exaggerates so much no one believes her.

"Clerac, Count de." *Roxana* XII 85. Roxana's name for the French prince, who keeps her handsomely as a mistress but leaves her after the death of his wife.

Cleveland, Earl of. *Cavalier* V 246. Royalist captured by the Parliament men at Donnington Castle, 1644.

"Closterhoven, Emanuel." *Farther Adventures* II 216. Assumed name of the Dutchman who sells Crusoe a stolen ship.

Clustril. *Gulliver* Part I chap. 6. One of Flimnap's informants against Gulliver in the plot; see Drunlo.

Coates, Mr. *Campbell* IV 198. Mentioned as a tobacco merchant living in Fenchurch St., 1713.

Cock, Capt. *Pirates* 100. Master of a vessel captured by Stede Bonnet, 1717.

Cock, John. *Plague Year* IX 262. Barber in St.-Martin's-le-Grand; returns too soon to London, and so his entire family except for the maid dies.

Cocklyn (Cocklin). *Pirates* 41. Pirate with whom Howel Davis joins forces off the coast of Africa, near Sierra Leone.

Cog, Count. *Campbell* IV 41. Edinburgh gamester who makes a fortune by following Duncan's advice.

Coggershall. *Pirates* 136. Commander of an Ipswich vessel captured by Charles Vane, 1718.

Colalto, Count de. *Cavalier* V 26. Imperial general in Italy, 1630.

Coletheart. *Life of Sheppard* XVI 199. Surgeon who assists Jonathan Wild after he is stabbed by "Blueskin."

Collier, Maj. *Carleton* 75. English officer; criticizes Carleton for attempting to change an exposed artillery placement before Barcelona.

Collins, Simon. *Clarissa* III 326. "Honest higgler" who carries Anna's letters to Clarissa.

Collins, Thomas. *Drury* 298. Ship's carpenter; elected governor of the little group cast away with Eglasse on Madagascar.

Colmar, "honest" Sir George. *Clarissa* IV 48, 191. One of the rakes who almost captivated Anna Howe.

Commercy, Prince de. *Jacque* XI 54. General under Prince Eugene of Savoy; killed in battle, 1701.

Comry, Adam. *Pirates* 272. Surgeon of the *Elizabeth*; compelled by George Wilson to go along with the pirates.

Condent, Capt. *Pirates* 581. Pirate who makes a captured Portuguese captain say mass at the mainmast.

Constable of Walthamstow. *Plague Year* IX 157. Has long conference with John the baker about allowing the refugees to pass.

Conway, Lord. *Cavalier* V 146. Posted at Newburn to resist the Scots.

Cook, Mary. *Life of Sheppard* XVI 176. Linen draper in Clare Market, robbed by Sheppard.

Cope, Miss. *Pamela* IV 403. An "inconsiderately soft" young lady who fancies herself in love with a rakish lord.

Cornelius, John. *Pirates* 598. Irish quartermaster captured by the authorities at Trinity Harbor; later assists Chimenatto.

Corregidore of Havana. *Jacque* XI 55. Captor of Jack in Havana; totally bound up by his regulations.

Cotes, Henry. *Grandison* I 343. Secretary who transcribes the conversation between Sir Charles and Sir Harcourt.

Countess Dowager of _____. *Pamela* IV 129. A free-living lady; poses as a nun at the masquerade, flirts with Mr. B.

Countess "of some hard name." *Pamela* I 59. Neighbor who visits Pamela while she is still a servant; admires Pamela's beauty.

Courser, Mr. *Pirates* 542. Fourth mate on the *Albemarle*; the Magadoxans throw him to the wild beasts.

Cowley (Abraham, 1618-1667). *Battle* I 158. Poet known for his
love lyrics as well as for his "Pindaric odes"; cut in two by
Pindar.

Cox, Capt. *Pirates* 218. A Bristol man whose ship is fired on by
Roberts in the roads of St. Christopher.

"Crackers." *Pirates* 226. Former pirate who now runs a pub at
the mouth of the Sierra Leone River.

Craggs, Mr. Secretary. *Clarissa* IV 257. Politician-friend of Lord
M.'s.

Cratz, Col. *Cavalier* V 122. Sent to reinforce the Protestants at
Nördlingen, 1632.

Craven, Lord. *Cavalier* V 85. Accompanies the king of Bohemia in
reinforcing Gustavus Adolphus with Dutch cavalry, 1632.

Crawford, Lord. *Cavalier* V 244. Loyalist Scottish commander
defending Newcastle, 1644.

Creech (Thomas, 1659-1700). *Battle* I 158. Translator of Lucretius
and Horace; in the battle, hidden by Dulness in the shape
of Horace.

Crequi, Marquis. *Jacque* XI 55. French commander in Italy; killed,
1702.

Creutzer, Mons. *Grandison* II 262. Profligate governor of Sir Charles
on his European tour.

Crindo, Deaan ("the Dean"). *Drury* 48. One-eyed, lean-jawed
Negro king at Cape St. Mary, Madagascar; held hostage by the
English, finally killed in battle with Deaan Woozington.

Crisp, Edward. *Pirates* 267. Prisoner of the pirate Roberts; testifies
in favor of Harry Glasby, 1722.

Crisp, Sir Nicholas. *Cavalier* V 204. Accompanies the Cavalier at
the Battle of Cirencester, 1643.

Criticism. *Battle* I 153. A malignant deity called up by Momus to
aid the moderns.

Cromwell, Oliver. *Cavalier* V 203. Parliamentary commander,
first mentioned as a private cavalry captain, 1643.

Cronke, Dickory. *Philosopher* XV 189. Born dumb, but regains
the power of speech and becomes a prophet during his last
days alive.

Cross, Capt. *Gow* XVI 304. Commander of a New England ship
carrying staves, captured by the pirates.

Crow, Mr. *Carleton* 55. English emissary in Spain; persuades
Queen Anne of the wisdom of taking Barcelona, 1705.

Crusoe, Robinson. *Crusoe* I 1, *Farther Adventures* II 1. Mariner from York, born 1632 of a German family; after roaming the world, he settles in England in 1705.

Crusoe, Mr. (in *Crusoe*). See Kreutznaer, Herr.

Crusoe, Mrs. (née Robinson). *Crusoe* I 1. Crusoe's mother, marries Herr Kreutznaer in York.

Crusoe, Mrs. *Crusoe* I 341, *Farther Adventures* II 4. Woman married by Crusoe after his return from the island; her devotion to him moves him to resist the wanderlust for a while.

Cullembach, Col. *Cavalier* V 63. Swedish cavalry commander; killed at Leipzig, 1631.

Cullen, Andrew. *Pirates* 373. One of Roche's gang; poses as supercargo of the ship to deceive honest merchants, 1721.

Cullen, Pierce. *Pirates* 373. Brother of above, crony of Roche.

Culliford, Capt. *Pirates* 447. Pirate captain of the *Resolution*; has a gam with Kid at Madagascar, 1697.

Cullum. *Jacque* X 48. Collier in Billingsgate from whom Jack and Robin steal a bag of money.

Curtis, Dr. *Grandison* V 245. Minister of a Dissenting congregation; assists in Harriet's wedding ceremony.

Curtisos. *Carleton* 50. Jew who loans the Earl of Peterborough a hundred thousand pounds for his expedition to Spain.

Curzon, Mrs. *Grandison* VI 22. Housekeeper at Grandison Hall.

"Cutler, the" (later called "the silversmith"). *Singleton* X 32. Makes trinkets with which the travellers beguile the natives.

Cutts, Lord. *Carleton* 40. Commissions Carleton to arrest the conspirators in the Assassination Plot against William III, 1696.

D., Countess of. *Pamela* III 218. Dinner guest at Mr. B.'s.

D., Countess Dowager of (initials: M. D.) *Grandison* I 324. Hopes Harriet will consent to marry her son, the Earl of D.

D., Earl of. *Pamela* III 218. Dinner guest at Mr. B.'s.

D., Earl of. *Grandison* I 328. Young man who hopes to marry Harriet; has an estate of twelve thousand a year.

Dagley, Anthony. *Grandison* VI 109. English youth, servant of Lady Clementina; manages her escape to England.

Dampier (William, 1652-1715). *Gulliver*, Letter to Sympson. Cited as Gulliver's cousin; adventurer and author of *Voyages* (1697), referred to by Gulliver as *A Voyage Round the World*.

Danby, Edward. *Grandison* II 250. Younger son of Mr. Danby;

apprenticed to a French wine merchant, marries Miss Galliard; see Poussin.

Danby, John. *Grandison* II 248, 438. Wicked brother of Mr. Danby; tries to have him assassinated.

Danby, Thomas. *Grandison* II 250. Older son of Mr. Danby; apprenticed to a West India merchant at Enfield, marries his master's niece; see Hervey, Mr.

Danby, Miss. *Grandison* II 249. Pretty and genteel girl who marries Mr. Galliard.

Danby, Mr. *Grandison* II 160. Merchant whose life Sir Charles saved and whose executor he has become.

Daniel, Councillor. *Wild* XVI 243. Staffordshire man who brings Wild up to London as a servant.

Darling, William. *Pirates* 276. Witness in the trial of Roberts' crew who testifies in favor of George Wilson.

Darlington, Fanny. *Clarissa* VIII 221. Lady whom the gossips disparage but whom Clarissa defends from loose talk.

Darlington, Miss. *Grandison* I 23. Poetess who wrote "On the Parting of Two Lovers," "On the Morning-dawn," "On the Death of a Favorite Linnet," and other efforts.

Darnford, Lady. *Pamela* I 171. Wife of Sir Simon.

Darnford, Nanny (or Nancy). *Pamela* I 171, II 187. Girl with a waspish temper; Pamela hopes Mr. Murray will marry her.

Darnford, Polly (later "Lady G."). *Pamela* I 171, II 186. Older of the Darnford girls; writes admiring letter to Pamela on Mrs. Jewkes's reformation.

Darnford, Sir Simon. *Pamela* I 171. Neighbor of Mr. B.'s in Lincolnshire; refuses to protect Pamela from him.

Daventry, Jack. *Clarissa* VII 19. Drunken friend of Lovelace's who has to run all the way home, because if he tried to walk he would fall.

Davers, Barbara ("Captain Bab"). *Pamela* I 9. Mr. B.'s sister; at first hostile to Pamela but later endeared to her.

Davers, William Lord. *Pamela* II 337, III 45. Illiterate nobleman, Mr. B.'s brother-in-law; called "the titled ape."

Davies, Mr. *Narrative* XVI 152. One of the murdered English gentlemen.

Davila (Enrico Caterino, 1576-1631). *Battle* I 152. Italian historian; commands the modern infantry.

Davis, Howel. *Pirates* 115. Pirate distinguished by clever stratagems against the Portuguese.

Davis, Lumley. *Life of Sheppard* XVI 185. Sheppard's crony in Newgate.

Davis, William. *Pirates* 280. One of Roberts' crew; once sold his Negro wife into slavery in order to buy liquor.

Davison. *Carleton* 42. Watchmaker arrested at the time of the Assassination Plot, 1696.

Dawson, Mr. *Grandison* I 326. Nottingham attorney; gives Sir Charles a favorable recommendation to the Selbys.

Deal, Robert. *Pirates* 138. Vane's chief mate; opposes the attack on the French man-of-war.

Dean, Mary (née Brown). *Wild* XVI 258. Widow of Skull Dean; becomes Wild's sixth wife.

Dean, "Skull." *Wild* XVI 258. Skilled housebreaker who works for Wild.

Dean, the. *Pamela* II 347. Clergyman near Mr. B.'s Bedfordshire estate; declares that Pamela's piety has edified the whole church.

Deane, Charles. *Grandison* V 174. Nephew of Thomas Deane; escorts Harriet to Deane's Grove after the wedding.

Deane, Thomas. *Grandison* I 7. Harriet's godfather, whom she calls "papa"; a former lawyer with a good estate.

Deb. *Pamela* IV 48. Servant of Polly Darnford's on her trip to London to visit Pamela.

Delbridge, Andrew. *Pirates* 326. Commander of the pink *Stanhope*, captured by Low, 1722.

Delphina, Lady. *Campbell* IV 207. Beautiful lady who visits Duncan in the incident of "Adeodata's" true parentage.

Dempaino. *Pirates* 500. Madagascar chief who demands that David Williams be turned over to him by the king of Maritan.

Denbigh, (Basil Feilding, second) Earl of (also spelled "Denby"). *Cavalier* V 241, 262. Parliamentary commander and great-grandfather of Henry Fielding the novelist; besieges Darley Castle, 1644; helps the Cavalier's father to retain his estate by paying a certain sum to the rebels, 1645.

Denham (John, 1615-1669). *Battle* I 157. Author of *Cooper's Hill*, 1642; slain by Homer in the battle.

Dennis, John. *Pirates* 194. One of Roberts' crew who testifies for the crown but is hanged anyway.

Derby, Countess of. *Cavalier* V 213. Defends Latham House against the rebels, 1644.

Derby, Earl of. *Cavalier* V 159. Commands royalist cavalry from Lancashire.

Derham, Counsellor. *Clarissa* VII 235. Solicitor whom Bella sends up to London to take down particulars of Clarissa's case; see Ackland, Mr.

Derwentwater, Lord. *Jacque* XI 108. Leads abortive invasion of Lancashire on behalf of the Pretender in which Jack rashly takes part.

Descartes (René, 1596-1650). *Battle* I 146. French philosopher, associated with the theory of vortices; commands modern archers.

Despréaux (Nicolas Boileau, 1636-1711). *Battle* I 152. French neoclassical critic, usually known as Boileau; commands modern light cavalry.

Deude (p. 72, "Dudey"). *Drury* 51. Wife of one of the castaways of the Drummond-Steward party; escapes to King Samuel.

Devil, the. *Moll* VIII 9. Puts evil thoughts into the head of Moll; referred to throughout Defoe's works.

Diamond, Capt. *Pirates* 338. Master of the *Dove*; captured by Evans, 1722.

"Dick, King," or "Lord Dick" (in *Drury*). See Toakeoffu, Deaan.

Dickenson, Emanuel. *Street-Robbers* XVI 368. A dexterous housebreaker.

Dickins, Farmer. *Pamela* III 9. Tenant of Mr. B.'s; Mr. Andrews asks to be allowed to pay the same rent as he does.

Digby, George Lord. *Cavalier* V 283. Royalist commander at Newark.

Digby, Sir Kenelm. *Campbell* IV 263. Inventor of the "sympathetic powder" for curing sword wounds.

Digby, the widow. *Campbell* IV 167. Widow with a handsome jointure who becomes one of Duncan's best customers.

Diggs, Mr. *Clarissa* I 1. Surgeon whom Anna Howe sends to enquire after James, following his encounter with Lovelace.

Dill, Capt. *Pirates* 100. Master of a sloop captured by Charles Vane, 1718.

Dillon, Major. *Grandison* II 223. Officer friend of Capt. Anderson's; present at the meeting with Sir Charles.

Dios, Pedro de. *Carleton* 194. Dean of the Inquisition; at Carleton's request, bars Murtough Brennan from celebrating Mass.

Dissauva, the. *Singleton* VI 273. General of the king of Ceylon; captures Capt. Knox and the Dutchman.

Dittwitt, Capt. *Pirates* 235. Master of the *Hardey*, a slaver; asks Roberts for a receipt for the protection money he has to pay.

Dobbins, Mr. *Life of Sheppard* XVI 199. A surgeon who assists Jonathan Wild after Blueskin stabs him.

Dobson, George. *Gow* XVI 339. Seaman who escapes with the pirates' longboat and turns crown witness.

Dobson, Mr. *Grandison* III 43, VI 75. Clergyman at Grandison Hall, "a credit to his cloth."

Dobson, Mrs. *Grandison* VI 76. Wife of above.

Dobson, Mrs. *Pamela* II 330. Keeps a farm and boarding school near Mr. B.'s Bedfordshire estate.

Doctor of Belton. *Clarissa* V 204. Attends him on his deathbed.

Doe, Sir Charles. *Plague Year* IX 53. Sheriff of London, 1665.

D'Oily, Nelly (in *Clarissa*). See Oily, Nelly D'.

Doleman, Thomas. *Clarissa* III 193, VII 332. Libertine friend of Lovelace's, part of the plot to get Clarissa into the evil house.

Doleman, Mrs. *Clarissa* III 194. Wife of above; helps find lodgings for Clarissa in London.

Dolins, Mrs. *Clarissa* VI 102. Manteaumaker of Mabell's acquaintance; figures in Clarissa's second escape.

D'Ollyffe, Biddy (in *Clarissa*). See Ollyffe, Biddy D'.

Dolyns, Miss. *Grandison* I 45. A "young lady of merit," one of Harriet's new town friends.

Donne, John. *Campbell* IV 67. Noted English clergyman and poet; sees a vision of his wife with a dead child in her arms.

"Dorcas" (in *Clarissa*). See Butler, Deb.

Dormer, Mr. *Clarissa* VI 343. Hickman's friend at whose house the meeting with Lovelace takes place.

Dormer, Mr. *Pamela* II 352, III 219. Visits Pamela and Mr. B., with Mr. Martin; always speaks well of "the sex."

Dorrell, Mr. *Clarissa* VI 434. Belford's attorney, whom Belford consults about the affairs of poor Belton.

Dorrington, Miss. *Clarissa* VI 369. Young lady who ran away with the groom because her father would not let her marry a half-pay officer.

Douglas, James. *Pirates* 308. Master of the *Charles* of Boston; captured by Lowther, 1721.

Douglas, Sir Robert. *Carleton* 32. At the Battle of Steenkirk, retrieves the regimental colors at the cost of his life.

Dove, Nicholas (often called "Nick"). *Drury* 296. One of the castaway white men from the island of St. Mary's.

Downeton, Sir Harry. *Clarissa* II 65. Tells Anna that Mr. Solmes plans to keep Clarissa in a state of fear after the wedding.

Drayton, Miss. *Clarissa* II 82. Her mother fails to make allowances for her youth and immaturity.

Drayton, Mrs. *Clarissa* II 82. Clarissa writes her a letter, allegedly from an older woman, advising her that children should be led rather than driven.

Drummond, Capt. *Drury* 49, *Pirates* 453. Scottish captain; marooned by his crew at Mattatan Roads, Madagascar, eventually escapes to King Samuel's domain. Bowen takes command of his ship, the *Speedy Return*.

Drunlo. *Gulliver* Part I chap. 6. One of Flimnap's spies; see Clustril.

Drury, John. *Drury* 39. Father of Robert; operates a beefsteak house, "The King's Head," in the Old Jury, Cheapside.

Drury, Sir Robert. *Campbell* IV 67. Has a vision of Dr. John Donne while in a trance.

Drury, Robert ("Robin"). *Drury* 39. Shipwrecked on Madagascar; author of the *Journal*.

Drury, William. *Drury* 303. Robert's uncle; runs the beefsteak house after the death of John Drury.

Drury, Mrs. *Drury* 40. Robert's mother; beseeches him not to go to sea.

Dryden, John (1631-1700). *Battle* I 146, *Tale* Dedication. English poet, playwright, and critic; figures in the battle as Virgil's epigone.

Dubalt, Col. *Cavalier* V 109. Sent to seize and destroy an Imperial garrison at Freynstadt, 1632.

Dulness. *Battle* I 158. Child of Criticism, who lures Creech away from the battlefield with an image of Horace.

Duncan, Capt. *Grandison* I 96. Lucy Selby conquers her passion for him after he proves to be of a bad character.

Duns Scotus. (1265?-1308). *Battle* I 144, 152. Combines with Aristotle to throw Plato out of his place among the divine authors in St. James's library.

Durfey, Capt. *Pirates* 295. From Rhode Island; captive of the pirate Fenn, 1721.

Dutchman. *Gulliver* Part III chap. 1. Crony of the Japanese pirates; seeks to have all the English captives put to death.

Dutchman. *Singleton* VI 257. From Delft; seeks to lure Europeans into the hands of the king of Ceylon.

Dwarf at court of Brobdingnag. *Gulliver* Part II chap. 2. Malicious rival of Gulliver; sticks him in a marrow bone, drops him into the cream pitcher.

Dyvel, Baron. *Cavalier* V 63. Commands the guards of Gustavus Adolphus at Leipzig.

Eagle, Solomon. *Plague Year* IX 118. Madman; runs about London with a pan of hot coals on his head, announcing God's imminent judgment on the city.

Eastlake, Capt. Thomas. *Pirates* 476, 689n. Rashly attacks the pirates on the island of St. Mary's in his ship, the *Speaker*; is in turn captured by them.

Eastwick, Capt. *Pirates* 328. Master of the *Kingston*; captured by Low, 1723.

Eden, Charles. *Pirates* 76. Governor of North Carolina; acts in collusion with Blackbeard.

Edwards, Benjamin. *Pirates* 312. Master of the *Greyhound*; gives battle to Lowther but is captured and sunk, 1722.

Edwards, Rev. Mr. *Sheppard's Narrative* XVI 231. Visits Sheppard while he is awaiting execution.

Edwin (or Edwyn), Sir Humphry. *Tale* sect. XI. Presbyterian Lord Mayor of London who had the effrontery to attend a conventicle in the regalia of his office.

Effiat, Maréchal D'. *Cavalier* V 20. Sent with reinforcements to the French army in Italy, 1630.

Efflep. *Drury* 229. A West Indian Negro, abandoned on Madagascar by pirates; speaks only English.

Eggleton, Mrs. *Grandison* VI 222. Old maid, embittered by two abortive engagements.

Eglasse. *Drury* 229. Dutch castaway living near St. Augustine's Bay; an unscrupulous loose-talker put to death by the king, Deaan Mernaugha.

Elford, Mr. *Grandison* I 33. Earliest of Harriet's suitors, three and a half years before the opening of the novel.

Ellen. *Grandison* I 27. Grandmother Shirley's servant, married to Oliver.

Empson. *Clarissa* IV 247. Servant of Charlotte Montague who carries her letters to town.

England, Edward. *Pirates* 41. Commands a sloop salvaging sunken Spanish plate, turns pirate, is pardoned by the king of Spain, 1717.

English, Lieut. *Cavalier* V 141. Dies of a broken heart after his unit is defeated by the Scots.

Ericeira, Conde de. *Pirates* 130. Master of a Portuguese man-of-war of sixty guns; captured near the island of Bourgon by England, 1721.

Essex, Earl of. *Cavalier* V 159. Parliamentary commander-in-chief, 1642.

Estwell. *Pirates* 168. Acquitted of piracy in Holland for lack of evidence.

Euclid (323-283 B.C.) *Battle* I 152. Greek geometer, chief engineer in the army of the ancients.

Eugene of Savoy, Prince. *Jacque* XI 47. Imperial commander in Italy, 1701.

Eutemi, Selim. *Pirates* 31. King of Algiers, murdered in his bath by the pirate Barbarouse.

Evander. *Battle* I 152. Ancient astronomer whose "arrows turn to meteors" in the battle.

Evans, John. *Pirates* 337. A Welshman; turns pirate.

Evans, Sir Stephen. *Jacque* X 21. Goldsmith from whom Jack steals a bill for three hundred pounds.

Evans, Capt. *Pirates* 65. Master of a galley, the *Greyhound*, captured by Capt. Martel.

Evelyn, Sir John. *Cavalier* V 180. Parliamentary commissioner of peace, taken exception to by the king.

F., H. *Plague Year* IX 1. The saddler, keeper of the *Journal*; it has been suggested that H. F. stands for Defoe's uncle, Henry Foe.

F., Lord. *Pamela* IV 5. Old schoolfellow of Mr. B.'s at Eton who comes to pay his respects in London.

Fahy, Father. *Carleton* 193. Chief of the Irish college at Madrid; consulted by Carleton for advice, concerning his accusation by Brennan.

Fairfax, Sir Thomas. *Cavalier* V 246. Parliamentary commander, in action at Marston Moor.

Fairfax, Lord ("Old Fairfax"). *Cavalier* V 264. Garrisons Hull for the Parliament men, 1642; the Cavalier respects him more than any other general of his era except for Gustavus Adolphus.

Falconbridge, Mr. *Grandison* V 361. Nottingham neighbor of Mr. Selby.

Falkland, Lord. *Cavalier* V 207. Royalist killed at Newbury.

Fanshaw, Mr. *Pamela* IV 6. Lawyer, disliked by Pamela; welcomes her to town.

Farley, poor. *Clarissa* VIII 154. Woman whom Belford once seduced, and to whom he now sends an annual allowance.

Farmer in Brobdingnag. *Gulliver* Part II chap. 1. Gulliver's mercenary first owner; shows him about for pay.

Farnborough, Mrs. *Grandison* II 49. Mistress of Sir Thomas Grandison; he repents his evil deeds after her death of smallpox.

Father of the Cavalier. *Cavalier* V 1. Wealthy gentleman in Shropshire; raises a regiment for the Cavalier.

Father of Friday. *Crusoe* I 265. Saved by Crusoe and Friday from being devoured by the savages.

Father of Moggy. *Jacque* XI 86. Jack employs him in hauling goods from Liverpool and Whitehaven.

Fea, Mr. *Gow* XVI 318. Owner of the estate on the isle of Rossness which is attacked by Gow.

Fea, Mr., of Whitehall. *Gow* XVI 327. Helps his kinsman in his defense against the pirates.

Fea, Mrs. *Gow* XVI 320. Wife of the estate owner; in terrible fright at the approach of the pirates.

Fenn, George. *Pirates* 260. Mate of Capt. John Trahern; testifies against Scudamore, 1722.

Fenn, John. *Pirates* 289. Put in command of the brigantine *Morning Star* by Roberts, 1721.

Fennell, Richard. *Grandison* I 196. Servant of Archibald Reeves who carries the news of Harriet's rescue to Mr. Selby.

Fenwick, Sir John. *Carleton* 17. Commander of the regiment in which Carleton becomes an ensign; later executed for high treason.

Fenwick, Richard. *Grandison* I 2. Second of Harriet's three lovers, less determined than Mr. Greville; also threatens to follow her to town; see Greville and Orme.

Fenwick, Miss. *Pamela* IV 436. Friend of Polly Darnford who tells her about Pamela's making up nursery stories to entertain her children.

Ferdinand, the Emperor. *Cavalier* V 33. Holy Roman Emperor during the Thirty Years' War.

Ferdinando, Antonio. *Pirates* 455. Indian boy on whose false testimony Capt. Thomas Green is hanged.

Fern, Thomas. *Pirates* 342. Attempts to run away with one of the ships when Phillips replaces him as quartermaster.

Ferneau, Oliver. *Gow* XVI 288. Honest captain against whom Gow plans the mutiny.

Fetherstone, pious Mrs. *Clarissa* V 153. A prude at Oxford; Lovelace takes Belford to Oxford just to see her.

Field, Will. *Life of Sheppard* XVI 176, *Sheppard's Narrative* XVI 218. Notorious London robber.

Fielding, "Captain." *Cavalier* V 5. The Cavalier's companion at Oxford, a poor younger son who accompanies him to the Continent.

Fielding. *Pamela* IV 396. Cousin of Lady G. who tells her about the book Pamela has written on education.

Fiennes, Col. Nathaniel. *Cavalier* V 194. Parliamentary governor of Bristol to whom Prince Rupert surrenders; he is condemned by a revolutionary court; but his execution is suspended.

Figg, Mr. *Life of Sheppard* XVI 204. Famous prize fighter who visits Sheppard in prison.

Filmer, Mr. *Grandison* II 97. Dishonest steward of Sir Thomas Grandison's Irish estates.

Filmer. *Clarissa* III 41. Husbandman in Finch Lane; agrees to receive Clarissa's letter to Anna, addressed to "Mr. John Soberton."

Fin, Capt. *Pirates* 175. Master of the sloop *Morrice*, captured in Anamboe, 1717.

Finch, Mr. *Grandison* II 97. The Montagues' goldsmith.

Finlay, Lady. *Grandison* VI 275. Has a parrot and marmoset admired by Lord G.

Flanders, Moll (during her first employment, called "Lady Betty"). *Moll* VII 1. Prostitute, thief, and penitent; the name is actually a criminal pseudonym.

Flecker, James. *Pirates* 279. Master of the *Rebecca*, from Charlestown in New England; captured by Lowther, 1722.

Flestrin, Quinbus (in *Gulliver*). See Gulliver, Capt. Lemuel.

Fletcher, Samuel. *Pirates* 286. A captured pirate, condemned to be hanged but reprieved.

Fletcher, Capt. *Pirates* 235. Master of the *Porcupine*, a slaver burned to the waterline with eighty Negroes on board, 1722.

Flimnap, Lady. *Gulliver* Part I chap. 6. Gulliver indignantly denies the reports that he has had an affair with her; presumably a reference to Catherine Walpole (née Shorter), who did have numerous liaisons.

Flimnap. *Gulliver* Part I chap. 3. Treasurer at the court of Lilliput, generally believed to be a satiric portrait of Sir Robert Walpole.

Flood, Rev. Mr. *Sheppard's Narrative* XVI 231. Attends Sheppard before his death.

Floyd, Mr. *Pamela* III 379. A rake who drops in to see Mr. B.; enjoys "drinking, hunting, and lewdness."

Fly, Capt. William. *Pirates* 606. Pirate distinguished by his profanity; murders his captain, later steered onto a shoal by Mr. Atkinson.

Fontenelle (Bernard le Bovier de, 1657-1757). *Battle* I 157. Chief supporter of the moderns in France; has his brains dashed out by Homer in the battle.

Forbes, Sir Frances. *Life of Sheppard* XVI 188. Alderman; commits Edgworth Bess to the poultry compter (a prison).

Forbes, Capt. *Cavalier* V 98. Commands a Scottish scouting party at the crossing of the Lech, 1632.

Forbes, Col. *Cavalier* V 257. Parliamentary commander at the siege of Pontefract Castle.

Force, Maréchal de la. *Cavalier* V 20. Ally of Schomberg in Italy, 1630.

Ford. *Plague Year* IX 151. Leader of the party of thirteen Londoners who joined John, Thomas, and Richard, their first night out.

Fortescue, Mrs. *Clarissa* I 71. Friend of Lady Betty Lawrance's and source of information about Lovelace.

Fourbin, Claude, Comte de. *Pirates* 383. Master of the *Victoire*; takes Misson on board, killed fighting a Sallee rover.

Fourgette, Capt. *Pirates* 474. Master of a French vessel captured by Booth, North, and White on Madagascar.

Fowler, James. *Grandison* I 39. Suitor of Harriet's, nephew of Sir Rowland Meredith.

Fowles, Stephen. *Life of Sheppard* XVI 186. Helps Sheppard escape from the condemned hole.

Fownes, Mr. *Pamela* I 195. Parish priest in Lincolnshire; Mr. Williams has been promised his place when he dies.

Frampton, Lady. *Grandison* I 3, V 74. Promotes the interest of Mr. Greville with Harriet.

Francisco. *Drury* 286. Negro of Portuguese origin, born in the East Indies; Drury is accused of plotting to help him escape from Rer Trimmonongarevo.

Frank. *Grandison* I 246. Servant of Sir Hargrave who helps take

Harriet from Paddington toward Windsor.

Franklin, Charles. *Pirates* 170. Monmouthshire man in Davis's crew; eventually settles down on St. Nicholas, Cape Verde Islands.

Frazier, Edward (alias "Bunworth"). *Street-Robbers* XVI 368, 379. Bred a buckle maker, becomes a housebreaker.

Frazier, William. *Pirates* 328. Ship captain whose crewmen have the flesh burned off their fingers by Edward Low.

Frederick. *Grandison* I 211. Servant of Sir Charles during his rencounter with Sir Hargrave.

Freeman, Sir Ralph. *Campbell* IV 64. One of the masters of the requests at the court of James I; brings Parker to warn the Duke of Buckingham of his impending murder.

Frelock, Clefren. *Gulliver* Part I chap. 2. Takes an inventory of Gulliver's pockets.

Frelock, Marsi. *Gulliver* Part I chap. 2. Aids in the inventory.

"Fretchville, Mrs." *Clarissa* III 343. Alleged widow whose house Lovelace is trying to rent for Clarissa.

Friday. *Crusoe* I 226, *Farther Adventures* II 11. Crusoe's servant, about twenty-six years old, "tall and well-shaped."

Friedland, Duke of. *Cavalier* V 117. Imperial commander who besieges Coburg Castle while the Cavalier is a prisoner of war.

Frukey, Deaan. *Drury* 87. Son of Deaan Crindo and prince of Anterndroea.

Frye, Will. *Crusoe* I 299. Mutineer wounded in the captain's fusillade.

Fugger. *Cavalier* V 99. Commands the popish garrison at Augsburg.

Fulker, Capt. *Pirates* 609. Master of the *John and Hannah*; whipped at the geers by Capt. Fly, 1726.

"Fuller, Thomasine." *Pamela* IV 175. Assumed name of person who writes Pamela telling her that her husband and the Countess Dowager of _____ are having an affair.

Fullers, the. *Clarissa* VIII 94. Distant relations of the Harlowes who attend Clarissa's funeral.

Fulworth, Anne. *Pirates* 624. Accomplice of Anne Bonny, passing herself off as Anne's mother; summoned to a hearing by Gov. Rogers.

Fungenzer, Rer. *Drury* 200. Son of Deaan Woozington; killed in battle.

Furness, Sir Henry. *Jacque* X 59. London merchant; issues bills of exchange.

Fynnet, Jenny. *Clarissa* II 2. Anna's cousin; Jenny's visit prevents her being able to write Clarissa.

G., Lady Gertrude. *Grandison* III 238. Sister of the Earl of G., a maiden lady advanced in years who intends to leave her fortune to Lord G.

G., Harriet. *Grandison* VI 230. Daughter of Lord G. and Charlotte (née Grandison).

G., Sir William. *Pamela* IV 258, 263. Polite young gentleman of Lincolnshire, proposed as a suitor for Polly Darnford.

G., Earl of. *Grandison* I 275. Father of Lord G., has estate in Berkshire.

G., Lady (in *Pamela*). See Darnford, Polly.

G., Lady (in *Grandison*). See Grandison, Charlotte.

G., Lord. *Grandison* I 275, 345. In love with Charlotte Grandison, referred to as "a very Mr. Hickman"; eventually happily married to her.

Galen (A.D. 129-199). *Battle* I 156. Ancient Roman physician; antagonist of Paracelsus in the battle.

Galliard, Mr. (Sr.). *Grandison* II 257. Gives his daughter in marriage to Edward Danby.

Galliard, Mr. (Jr.). *Grandison* II 257. Son of a Turkey merchant, in love with Miss Danby.

Galway, Lord. *Carleton* 103. Supplants Peterborough in command of the Peninsular expedition, 1706.

Ganmore. *Clarissa* IV 270. Commander of the vessel which Lovelace plans to use in abducting Miss Howe.

Garon, Mons. *Clarissa* VIII 60. Physician, a venal pedant; tells Mrs. Sinclair she may escape dying of her fractured leg if she will only have patience.

Garret, Mr. *Sheppard's Narrative* XVI 214. Sheppard's schoolmaster.

Gassendi (Pierre, 1592-1655). *Battle* I 152. French philosopher; cited favorably in Wotton's *Reflections*, attempted to refute Aristotle, commands modern archers.

Geary, Capt. *Life of Sheppard* XVI 200, *Sheppard's Narrative* XVI 221. Keeper of New Prison.

Gee, Capt. *Pirates* 228. Commands frigate-built ship at Sestos seized by Roberts.

Gell, Sir John. *Cavalier* V 274. From Derbyshire, Parliamentary commander at Lichfield, 1643; pursues the king in his move from Worcester to Chester, 1645.

"General, the" (in *Grandison*). See Porretta, Giacomo della.

George I of England. *Jacque* XI 121, *Pirates* 39. Pardons the rebels who took part in Lord Derwentwater's invasion, including Col. Jack.

George the reformade. *Singleton* VI 299. Accompanies Capt. Bob and Quaker William in their escape from the pirate vessel.

George. ' *Cavalier* V 71. Servant of the Cavalier who obtains a great deal of plunder for him.

George. *Jacque* X 83. Member of the boys' gang; when captured, he peaches on Will, the gang's leader.

Geraldino, Father. *Grandison* III 70. Priest at Bologna; Clementina suggests that he hold a theological discussion with Sir Charles.

Gerard, Col. *Cavalier* V 283. Royalist who makes a private peace treaty with the Parliamentary forces.

Gibson. *Grandison* III 45. Lucy Selby's servant; carries letters to her from Harriet.

Giffard, Mrs. *Grandison* II 350. Housekeeper and mistress of Lord W.; Sir Charles bribes her into going away.

Gilliman, Capt. Jack. *Jacque* X 129. Pretending to be a collier master, he abducts the three deserting soldiers and carries them away to Virginia.

Giudici, Cardinal. *Carleton* 206. Important figure in the Spanish regime; seen by Carleton.

Glasby, Harry. *Pirates* 222. Master of the pirate vessel *Royal Fortune*; tried for deserting the pirate flotilla, eventually acquitted of piracy by a court of justice.

Glemham, Sir Thomas. *Cavalier* V 292. Royalist commander of the garrison at York, 1644.

Glumdalclitch. *Gulliver* Part II chap. 2. The Brobdingnagian word for "little nurse"; Gulliver's keeper and friend.

Glyn, Mr. *Pirates* 251. Trader at Sierra Leone; testifies that the pirates went on shore leave and thus that they all could have escaped if they had had a mind to. His testimony scuttles their defense that they were "compelled" to be pirates.

Goddard, Mr. *Clarissa* VI 318. Honest and skillful apothecary who treats Pamela on her deathbed.

Godfrey, Sarah ("Sally," later Mrs. Wrightson). *Pamela* II 266, IV 276. Girl set on to entrap Mr. B. into marriage; after the birth of her illegitimate daughter, she goes to Jamaica.

Godfrey, Mr. *Grandison* V 361. Wedding guest from Northampton.

Godfrey, Mrs. *Pamela* II 335. Mother of Sally; schemes to entrap
Mr. B. into marriage.

Goignet, Capt. *King* XVI 12. Earlier pirate commander of Avery's.

Golbasto Momaren Evlame Gurdilo Shefin Mully Ully Gue. *Gulliver*
Part I chap. 3. Emperor of Lilliput, a pompous little tyrant.

Golding, Johanetta. *Clarissa* V 298. Courtesan, lively yet modest
looking; impersonates Lovelace's cousin Charlotte Montague.

Gondibert. *Battle* I 156. Title of a modern heroic poem by Sir William Davenant; personified by Swift as a cavalryman in the
army of the moderns.

Goodwin, Sally. *Pamela* II 331. Illegitimate child of Mr. B. and Sally
Godfrey, adopted by him and Pamela.

Gordon. *Singleton* VI 192. A Scotsman whom Singleton puts in
command of a captured sloop.

Gorge, Gen. *Carleton* 122. English besieger of Alicant; swindles
the residents out of their valuables, 1705.

Goring, Col. Charles. *Cavalier* V 161. Royalist commander who
captures Portsmouth.

Gough, Mr. *Life of Sheppard* XVI 200. Official of the Gatehouse in
Westminster.

Goulding, Capt. *Pirates* 325. Master of the *Liverpool Merchant*, captured by Low, 1722.

Gourdon, Capt. *Cavalier* V 52. Scottish captain who persuades
Captain Fielding to enlist under the Swedish banner.

Governor of Porto Santo. *Gow* XVI 301. Portuguese official; when
taken prisoner by Gow, he is so frightened he befouls
himself.

"Governor, the." *Clarissa* VI 404. Mrs. Ambrose's brother; will
be at the party given by the colonel.

"Governess, my" (also called Mrs. B. and "Mother Midnight").
Moll VII 167. Helps Moll dispose of an unwanted child, later
becomes the manager of her criminal career.

"Governess, our." *Due Preparations* XV 93. Older sister of the London
family, their pious instructress.

Gow, John (alias John Smith). *Gow* XVI 287. Pirate; leads a life of
brigandage until subdued by Mr. Fea in Scotland.

Grace, Charles. *Life of Sheppard* XVI 179. A "graceless cooper" and
crony of Sheppard's.

Grandison, Caroline (in *Grandison*). See L., Caroline, Countess of.

Grandison, Sir Charles (Sr.). *Grandison* II 29. Frugal grandfather
of the hero of the novel; left the family an estate of eight
thousand a year.

Grandison, Sir Charles. *Grandison* I 195. The good man, aged twenty-six or twenty-seven; declines duels, marries Harriet.

Grandison, Charlotte (later Lady G.). *Grandison* I 194, 272. Sir Charles's sister, aged about twenty-four; perfectly genteel but too full of wit.

Grandison, Aunt Eleanor ("Aunt Nell," "Aunt Prue"). *Grandison* II 85, IV 62. Methodist maiden sister of Sir Thomas; lives in Yorkshire.

Grandison, Everard. *Grandison* I 345. Weak-minded cousin of Charles, always in scrapes.

Grandison, Sir Thomas. *Grandison* I 195, II 29. Father of the hero; has estates in Hampshire and Essex, trains Sir Charles in the arts of defense.

Grandison, Lady. *Grandison* II 29. Sir Charles's mother, who has trained him in Christian principles; dies of shock when her husband is wounded in a duel.

Grandmother of Rosebud. *Clarissa* I 250. Wins Lovelace's favor by asking him to spare her granddaughter's innocence.

Grands Titres, Madame de. *Tale* sect. II. One of the three ladies courted by the brothers; she stands for worldly honor; see Argent and Orgeuil.

Grant, George. *Pirates* 297. Master of a sloop from Philadelphia which Worley the pirate captures.

Graves, Capt. *Pirates* 215. Sent from Barbados with a sloop to capture Bartholomew Roberts.

Graves, Capt. *Pirates* 334. Master of a ship from Virginia; when captured by Low, he is forced to drink a quart of punch.

Gray, Col. *Cavalier* V 266. Parliamentary commander captured at siege of Leicester, 1645.

Greatrix, Mr. *Campbell* IV 198. A stroker who keeps the Earl of Ormond's Irish butler from being carried away by spirits.

Green, Capt. Thomas. *Pirates* 454. Executed by mistake for Bowen's capture of the *Worcester*, 1704.

Green, Capt. *Pirates* 606. Master of the *Elizabeth* of Bristol; murdered by William Fly, 1726.

Greenaway, William. *Pirates* 627. Master of the *Lancaster*, overwhelmed and marooned by Bunce and Macarty, 1718.

Greene, Capt. *Drury* 299. Master of an East India vessel; unjustly hanged in Scotland for the alleged murder of Capt. Drummond.

Gréme. *Clarissa* III 7. Lord M.'s steward at The Lawn, Hertfordshire.

Greme, Mrs. *Clarissa* III 7. Housekeeper at Lord M.'s Hertfordshire seat; asks Clarissa to come stay there.

Grenville, Sir Bevil. *Cavalier* V 161. Royalist commander in southwestern England.

Grenville, Sir Richard. *Cavalier* V 285. Parliamentary commander; besieges Plymouth.

Greville, John. *Grandison* I 1. Welshman of free principles, one of Harriet's suitors; see Fenwick and Orme.

Grey, Col. *Cavalier* V 212. Joins forces with the Scots as soon as they invade England, 1644.

Grildrig (in *Gulliver*). See Gulliver, Capt. Lemuel.

Grimes. *Clarissa* V 144. A "gossiping, sottish rascal," whom Clarissa sends to Anna with her letter from Hampstead.

Guiccardine (Guicciardini, Francesco, 1483-1540). *Battle* I 152. Florentine historian, commander of heavy-armed infantry among the moderns.

Guillaume, Capt. *King* XVI 41. New England captain who carries Avery to England.

Guilotte. *King* XVI 22. Comrade of Avery's who leads a desperate expedition across Central America to reach civilization.

Guiscard, Count. *Carleton* 39. French commander who surrenders Namur, 1695.

Gulliver, Betty. *Gulliver* Part I chap. 8. Gulliver's daughter.

Gulliver, John. *Gulliver* Part I chap. 1. Gulliver's uncle, who gives Gulliver the money to study medicine at Leyden.

Gulliver, Johnny. *Gulliver* Part I chap. 8. Gulliver's son at grammar school.

Gulliver, Capt. Lemuel (also called Quinbus Flestrin, "the Man-Mountain," in Lilliput, and Grildrig, "Mannikin," in Brobdingnag). *Gulliver* Part I chap. 1. The voyager of the *Travels*.

Gulliver, Mr. *Gulliver* Part I chap. 1. Gulliver's father; sends him to Cambridge.

Gunner's mate (later, "our gunner"). *Singleton* VI 29. A good mathematician and astronomer, invaluable in the trek across Africa; predicts young Bob will make an eminent thief.

Gunning, Arthur. *Grandison* VI 111. Master of a frigate at Leghorn which will bring the della Porretta family to England.

Gustavus Adolphus. *Cavalier* V 28. King of Sweden, Protestant champion in the Thirty Years' War; the Cavalier's ideal soldier.

Guy. *Drury* 259. Drury's master among the Saccalauvors.

Gwatkins, Capt. *Pirates* 314. Master of the *Amy*; killed in an attack on the pirate Lowther, 1722.

Gypsy. *Pamela* I 304. Tells Pamela's fortune at the Lincolnshire estate; plants a note for her.

H., Jackey. *Pamela* I 16, II 196. Lord Davers' ill-bred nephew who comes unannounced with Lady Davers to torment Pamela; always says, "I'll be hanged."

H., Mother. *Clarissa* VI 12. A madam; Lovelace plots to pass her off as an elderly gentlewoman in order to trick Clarissa.

Hacker, Capt. *Cavalier* V 266. Parliamentary officer captured at the siege of Leicester, 1645.

Halden. *Grandison* II 350. Steward of Lord W.

Hale, Dr. *Clarissa* VIII 47. Lovelace's physician ("my good Astolfo") during his period of insanity.

Hales, Col. *Carleton* 24. English officer severely wounded at the Battle of St. Dennis.

Hall, Fayrer. *Pirates* 99. Master of the *Sea Nymph*, captured by Stede Bonnet, 1718.

Hall, Jack. *Pirates* 318. Celebrated chimney sweeper, executed with Stephen Bunce and Ned Low's brother.

Hall, Capt. *Pirates* 175. Master of the *Hind*, captured at Anamboe in Africa by pirates, 1717.

Hall, Col. *Cavalier* V 63. English officer slain commanding the rear at the Battle of Leipzig, 1631.

Halsey, Capt. John. *Pirates* 465. Pirate on Madagascar; buried in a watermelon patch with the full rites of the Church of England.

Haman, John. *Pirates* 624. Owner of the fastest ship in the Bahamas, which is stolen by Rackam and Anne Bonny.

Hamilton, Capt. *Pirates* 313. Master of a sloop from Jamaica, captured by Lowther, 1722.

Hamilton, Gen. *Pirates* 66. Commander of English forces stationed in the Caribbees, 1716.

Hamman, the. *Pirates* 574. Tyrannical native governor of the town of Saeni, near Magadoxa; murdered by the townspeople, 1716.

Hammond, Col. *Cavalier* V 295. Officer to whom Charles I surrenders in the Isle of Wight.

Hampden, Mr. *Cavalier* V 181. Parliamentary commander; raises

a regiment of infantry in Aylesbury, Buckinghamshire.
Hance, John. *Pirates* 320. Master of the *Amboy*, captured by Low,
1722.
Hands, Israel. *Pirates* 72. Member of Blackbeard's crew; shot by
Blackbeard capriciously, escapes the gallows by accepting
the king's pardon.
Hannah. *Pamela* I 99. Fellow servant of Pamela's; cries heartily
when Pamela leaves Buckinghamshire.
Hannah (in *Clarissa*). See Burton, Hannah.
Harding, Maj. *Carleton* 158. English officer; narrowly escapes being
blown up by the Spanish at the siege of Alicant.
Hardy. *Pirates* 285. Pirate; surprised when at his execution his
hands are tied behind him, 1722.
Hargrave, Sir Charles. *Pamela* II 185, III 379. Bedfordshire gentle-
man; drops in to see Mr. B. on his wedding day.
Hargrave, Sir (in *Grandison*). See Pollexfen, Sir Hargrave.
Harlowe, Antony ("Uncle Antony"). *Clarissa* I 3. Younger of Cla-
rissa's two uncles; has grown rich through the East India
Trade.
Harlowe, Arabella ("Bella"). *Clarissa* I 6. Clarissa's older sister,
"plump, high-fed"; in love with Lovelace; jealous of Clarissa.
Harlowe, Mrs. Charlotte, nee Lovell. *Clarissa* I 4. Clarissa's mother,
dominated by Mr. Harlowe.
Harlowe, Clarissa. *Clarissa* I 1. Beautiful daughter of an English
country family; about twenty years old, the sum of all that
is perfect; dies after being raped by Lovelace. Pen-names:
Laetitia Beaumont, Harriet Lucas, Mrs. Rachel Clark, Mrs.
Mary Atkins.
Harlowe, James (Sr.). *Clarissa* I 13. Clarissa's father, a gloomy
tyrant; suffers from gout.
Harlowe, James (Jr.). *Clarissa* I 2. Clarissa's brother, an ill-tempered
young man.
Harlowe, John (Sr.). *Clarissa* I 6. Clarissa's grandfather; has left
her his estate, "The Dairy-House" (formerly "The Grove").
Harlowe, John (Jr.). *Clarissa* I 14. Clarissa's older uncle, rich
through new-found mines; calls her his "daughter-niece."
Harman, Aunt. *Clarissa* VI 346. Anna's aunt on the Isle of Wright;
Anna visits her while Clarissa is dying.
Harradine, Andrew. *Pirates* 348. Captured ship captain; joins
Cheeseman in the revolt against Phillips, 1724.
Harrington, Mrs. *Grandison* III 332. Miss Danby's aunt; does
everything but worship Sir Charles when he visits her.

Harriot, David (also Hariot). *Pirates* 102. Master of the *Adventure*, captured by the pirate Richards; eventually turns pirate himself, is shot down by Col. William Rhet, 1718.

Harris, Charles. *Pirates* 313. Second mate of the *Greyhound*; joins Lowther's crew, eventually commands a brigantine under Low, 1722.

Harris, George. *Carleton* 41. Involved in the Assassination Plot, turns crown witness, 1696.

Harris, James. *Pirates* 273. Persuaded by Scudamore to help run away with the vessel in which he has shipped.

Harris, Mrs. *Pamela* IV 115. Midwife, brought to Mr. B.'s house to help Pamela in childbirth, under the pretense of being simply Polly Darnford's friend.

Harris. *Singleton* VI 158. Bob's shipmate on the voyage to Cadiz, and the first to suggest the idea of a mutiny to him; later the pirates' second-in-command.

Harry the Great of France (Henri IV). *Tale* sect. IX. Swift attributes his military ambitions to his desire for a certain young lady.

Harry. *Pamela* I 10. Servant in Bedfordshire who makes a pass at Pamela but later reforms; weeps when she departs.

Harry. *Clarissa* VII 129. Servant of Belford's who carries letters to Lovelace.

Hartley, Lady. *Clarissa* III 206. Lady who is referred to as managing "affairs that do not belong to her sex to manage."

Hartley, Mr. *Clarissa* VII 236. Has a widowed sister in Pennsylvania, where Bella hopes Clarissa can hide out till the scandal dies down.

Hartleys, the two. *Grandison* V 25. Lawyers helping the Mansfields.

Hartop, Johnny. *Clarissa* IV 367. Punster of Belford's acquaintance.

Harvey (William, 1578-1657). *Battle* I 152. Discovered the circulation of the blood; commands modern dragoons.

Harvey, Capt. *Drury* 301. Master of the *Henry*; joins Capt. Macket during his trading with the natives.

Harvey, Gen. *Carleton* 170. English cavalry commander under Stanhope at Breuhiga.

Hastings, Col. *Cavalier* V 274. Royalist, surrenders Leicester, 1645.

Hatton, Miss. *Clarissa* VII 320. Lovelace once made Mowbray an object of ridicule to her.

Hawkins, Capt. *King* XVI 9. Privateer captain with whom Avery first sails.

Hawkins. *Grandison* V 339. The well-respected steward of Mr. Selby.

Hayward, John. *Plague Year* IX 102. Under-sexton of the parish of St. Stephen, Coleman St.; after being a gravedigger during the plague, he lives on for twenty-six years.

Hayward, Mrs. *Plague Year* IX 103. Wife of above; washes her head in vinegar to keep off plague.

Headland, Capt. John. *Pirates* 320. Sent out by the governor of Rhode Island to apprehend Low, 1722.

Heath, Dr. *Plague Year* IX 88. Physician friend of the saddler's; thinks the plague bacillus may be carried by sick people's breath.

Hempshire, Mrs. *Drury* 232. Wife of the Guinea Negro; Eglasse is having an amour with her, sends her many presents.

Hempshire. *Drury* 232. A poor, blind, Guinea Negro living in Feraighn; speaks English and has a pretty wife.

Henderson, Alexander. *Grandison* VI 109. Master of the *Scanderoon*, which brings Clementina to England.

Henderson, Sir John. *Cavalier* V 204. Royalist, defeated by Cromwell, 1645.

Hennelet, Laurence. *Narrative* XVI 160. Servant killed by the robbers near Bapaume.

Henrietta Maria. *Cavalier* V 195. Daughter of Charles I, born at Exeter, 1643.

Hepburn, Sir John. *Cavalier* V 52. Scottish colonel in the service of Gustavus Adolphus; Fielding enlists in his regiment.

Herbert, Cousin. *Clarissa* VII 358. Anna's cousin on the Isle of Wight.

Herbert, Lady. *Pamela* IV 150. Wife of Mr. Herbert.

Herbert, Mr. *Pamela* IV 150. Accompanies Mr. B. to Oxford along with the Countess Dowager.

Herbeville, Gen. *Jacque* XI 54. French commander in Italy, 1702.

Herodotus (c. 480-425 B.C.) *Battle* I 152. Greek historian; commands ancient infantry.

Hertford, Marquis of. *Cavalier* V 171. Marches to relieve Goring at Portsmouth.

Hervey, Dolly. *Clarissa* I 311. Clarissa's cousin, secretly in sympathy with her.

Hervey, Mrs. Dorothy (Aunt Hervey). *Clarissa* I 10. Half-sister of Mrs. Charlotte Harlowe; favors the match with Solmes.

Hervey, Mr. *Grandison* III 112. A merchant trading to Turkey, master of Mr. Thomas Danby.

Hervey, Uncle. *Clarissa* I 17. Asks Lovelace to write a description of the courts and countries he has visited.

Hesse, Prince of. *Carleton* 51. Peterborough's contentious ally in Spain; shot at Barcelona.

Hickman, Charles. *Clarissa* I 64. Miss Howe's admirer; prim and proper but good at heart.

Higges, John (or Higgs or Higgidee). *Street-Robbers* XVI 378. Attempts to elude the law by enlisting in the Royal Navy at Spithead.

Hill, Capt. *Pirates* 242. Master of the *Neptune*, captured by Roberts off the African coast, 1722.

Hill, Mr. *Drury* 293. Steward on board the *Drake*, the ship which rescues Drury.

Hind, Joseph. *Sheppard's Narrative* XVI. 215. Buttonmold maker, keeper of the Black Lion alehouse in Drury Lane; corrupter of Sheppard's youthful morals.

Hingstone, Capt. *Pirates* 223. Master of a ship bound for Jamaica, plundered by Roberts, 1721.

Hippocrates (c. 460-357 B.C.) *Battle* I 152. Greek physician; commands dragoons in the battle.

Hobbes (Thomas, 1588-1679). *Battle* I 146. Notorious atheistical political scientist; commands the modern archers.

Hodge. *Pamela* II 311. Former manager of the farm in Kent that Mr. Andrews is to manage after the wedding.

Hodges, Mrs. Sarah. *Clarissa* V 36, VI 134. Housekeeper of Uncle Harlowe; they have an illicit relation.

Hodges, Dr. *Plague Year* IX 37. Reputable London physician, 1665.

"Holden, Sir Edward." *Clarissa* III 351. Pretended guardian of the heiress Priscilla Partington.

"Holden, Lady." *Clarissa* III 351. Pretended wife of above; always admired Mamma Sinclair's good management.

Holford. *Pirates* 140. Privateer captain who surrenders Charles Vane to the authorities.

Holland, Earl of. *Cavalier* V 133. Royalist officer sent on reconnaissance in Scotland during the Northern War.

Holles, Sir John. *Grandison* VI 2. Father of the Misses Holles; Sir Charles visits him after the wedding.

Holles, Kitty. *Grandison* IV 54. Cousin of Harriet Byron; receives her on her return to Selby House.

Holles, Patty. *Grandison* IV 54. Sister of above; both "*good* young creatures."

Holmes, Sir Antony. *Clarissa* III 344. Gentleman whose nieces are invited to a party with Sally Martin and Polly Horton.

Holmes, Dr. *Grandison* I 197, 200. Treats Harriet for shock at the Earl of L.'s house, Colnebrook.

Homer. *Gulliver* Part III chap. 8, *Battle* I 152. Summoned from the dead on Glubbdubdrib; commands the ancient cavalry in the battle.

Honnyman, Mr. *Gow* XVI 316. Sheriff of Grahamsey County, captured by Gow's men.

Honnyman, Mrs. *Gow* XVI 317. Wife of above.

Hood, John. *Pirates* 315. Master of the *Swift*, captured by Lowther, 1723.

Hopton, Sir Ralph. *Cavalier* V 186. Commands royal forces in Cornwall, 1642.

Horn, Gustavus. *Cavalier* V 87. One of the chief Swedish commanders during the Thirty Years' War, captured at Nördlingen.

Hornigold, Capt. Benjamin. *Pirates* 41. Pirate who, after being pardoned, is cast away upon the rocks, 1718.

Horton, Mary ("Polly"). *Clarissa* III 319. Prostitute at Mrs. Sinclair's; Clarissa trusts her more than she does Sally Martin.

Hotham, Sir John. *Cavalier* V 155. Appropriates the king's train of artillery at Hull, 1641.

How, John (1657-1722). *Tale* sect. IX. Whig MP and former Lord Mayor (also an antagonist of Defoe) whom Swift advises to search Bedlam for candidates for public office; see Musgrave and Seymour.

Howard, Capt. Thomas. *Pirates* 459. Thames lighterman who becomes a pirate with Bowen; murdered by the natives in India.

Howard, Mr. *Pamela* IV 150. Along with his daughter, accompanies Mr. B. to Oxford with the Countess Dowager.

Howe, Anna ("Nancy"). *Clarissa* I 1. Clarissa's most intimate friend and correspondent; a witty lady.

Howe, Mrs. Annabella. *Clarissa* I 3. Anna's domineering and money-loving mother; essentially good-hearted.

Hume, Capt. *Pirates* 66. Master of his majesty's ship-of-war *Scarborough*; disperses Martel's band of pirates, 1716.

Humphry. *Moll* VII 76. Moll's half-brother, whom Moll inadvertently marries.

Humphry. *Moll* VIII 140. Moll's son by her incestuous marriage
with her brother; Moll is reunited with him at the end.

Hunt, Capt. *Pirates* 336. Master of the *Delight*, captured by Low,
1723.

Hunt, Mr. *Clarissa* II 256. Neighbor to whom Mrs. Howe sends
Robin with a letter.

Hungary, King of. *Cavalier* V 124. Turns the tide at the Battle
of Nordlingen by charging the Swedes.

Hunter. *Pirates* 266. He was the chief surgeon of Roberts' pirate
crew before Scudamore's arrival.

Huntingford, Robert (in *Clarissa*). See Lovelace, Robert.

Hurste, Miss. *Grandison* IV 271. Chief figure of one of Richardson's cautionary tales; she responds too quickly to compliments.

Hutcheson, Archibald. *Clarissa* IV 257. Friend of Lord M.'s,
referred to approvingly as having always supported the
administration.

Ignorance. *Battle* I 153. Father and husband of the goddess Criticism.

Ill-Manners. *Battle* I 154. Child of Criticism.

Impudence. *Battle* I 153. Child of Criticism.

Ireton, Commissary-Gen. *Cavalier* V 267. Commands the Parliamentary left wing at Naseby.

Ireton, Mr. *Life of Sheppard* XVI 188. Bailiff in Drury Lane.

Irwin, Mrs. *Campbell* IV 95. Tavern keeper in London, 1698; Duncan foretells the execution of her son at Tyburn.

Isaac. *Pamela* I 48. Footman at Mr. B.'s Bedfordshire estate.

Ishmael ("Moely"). *Crusoe* I 20, 22. Moorish slave with Crusoe in
Sallee; Crusoe makes him swim for shore when he escapes.

Jack, Capt. *Jacque* X 3. One of the three beggar boys, the true
son of their nurse, a year older than Col. Jack; strongly
made but brutish and sullen.

Jack, Col. (alias "Mr. Anything," "Don Ferdinand de Villa Moresa,"
"Mons. Charnot"). *Jacque* X 1. Hero of the tale; after many
adventures, he finally attains the coveted status of a gentleman.

Jack, Maj. (alias "Anthony"). *Jacque* X 3. Third of the three beggar boys; merry, facetious, and pleasant.

Jack. *Farther Adventures* II 193. Roguish Englishman left on the Island of Despair.

Jack. *Pamela* III 310. Servant of Sir Jacob Swynford, ordered to fetch his horse; see Jonas.

Jack. *Tale* sect. II, VI. One of the three brothers, representing Calvinism; has a long list of nicknames, end of sect. VI.

Jack. *Voyage* XIV 41. A crewman who initially joins the mutiny but then goes over to the captain's side.

Jackey (in *Pamela*). See H., Jackey.

Jacob. *Pamela* I 168. Gardener at Mr. B.'s Lincolnshire estate; good and honest but reserved.

James. *Drury* 229. Oldest son of Efflep; acts as interpreter since he speaks both English and Malagasy.

James. *Grandison* I 26. Harriet's servant in town; wants to return to Selby House because he "has a sweetheart in his head."

Jane. *Pamela* I 131. Cook in Bedfordshire, sniffy about Pamela but later softens up; doesn't say her prayers often enough.

Japan, Emperor of. *Gulliver* Part III chap. 11. Allows Gulliver to dispense with the usual ceremony of trampling on the crucifix.

Jeffery, Thomas. *Farther Adventures* II 193. Crewman who rapes a native girl and has his throat cut for it.

Jeffreys, Benjamin. *Pirates* 278. Seaman given six lashes from each pirate in the crew for insulting them.

Jemmy, or Jemy ("Lancashire Jemmy"). *Moll* VII 147. Moll's fourth husband; Moll marries him thinking he is a rich Irish noble; after a career as a highwayman, he is reunited with her.

Jenkins, Thomas. *Pirates* 609. Mate of the *Elizabeth*, murdered by William Fly, 1726.

Jenkins, Dr. *Pamela* IV 436. Marries the Dean's daughter, Miss L., after she has discovered that her rake is untrue to her.

Jenkins, Farmer. *Grandison* I 94. Brings a letter from Lucy Selby to Harriet in Grosvenor St.

Jennings, Capt. *Pirates* 36. Pirate who surrenders to Woodes Rogers, 1718.

Jenny, Lady. *Pamela* IV 41. Oldest child of "the Earl," friend of Lady Davers; admires Pamela's letter.

Jenny. *Grandison* I 274. Maidservant at Lord L.'s, attending Charlotte; a clergyman's daughter.

Jenyns, Tony. *Clarissa* IV 145. Relation of Belford's who advocates keeping mistresses and who comes to a bad end.

Jerry. *Grandison* I 211.   Sir Charles's coachman; assists in the
   rescue of Harriet.

Jervis, Mrs. *Pamela* I 9.   Servant in Bedfordshire, although she
   is a gentlewoman born; loves Pamela.

Jervois, Emilia ("Emily"). *Grandison* I 345.   Sir Charles's ward,
   aged fourteen but looks sixteen or seventeen; in love with
   Sir Charles.

Jervois, Mr. *Grandison* II 148.   Emily's father, an Italian merchant,
   deceased at the opening of the novel.

Jervois, Mrs. (in *Grandison*). See O'Hara, Mrs.

Jew. *Roxana* XII 126.   Merchant who accuses Roxana unjustly of
   theft when she attempts to sell her jewels to him.

Jewkes, Mrs. K. *Pamela* I 83.   Mr. B.'s mannish housekeeper in
   Lincolnshire; tries to intimidate Pamela.

Joel. *Clarissa* VII 333.   Servant carrying Lovelace's letters to Belford while Clarissa is dying.

Johanna, Queen of. *Pirates* 407.   Friend of Capt. Misson; aided
   by the pirates in her war with the king of Mohilla.

John, Lord. *Pamela* IV 41.   Noble friend of Lady Davers' who
   admires Pamela's letters.

John, Sir. *Pamela* IV 205.   Uncle to Lord C.; would like to arrange
   a marriage between his nephew and the Countess Dowager,
   except for her misbehavior with Mr. B.

John, Sir. *Street-Robbers* XVI 364.   A gentleman on a journey
   westward, robbed by the band of rogues.

John. *Drury* 240. Second son of Efflep.

John. *Grandison* I 246.   Servant of Sir Hargrave during the abduction.

John. *Pamela* II 259.   One of Lady Davers' footmen on her first
   visit to Pamela.

John. *Plague Year* IX 66.   Former soldier in the Low Countries,
   now a biscuit maker in Wapping; leaves the city with his
   brothers to escape the plague; see Richard and Thomas.

John. *Street-Robbers* XVI 364.   Servant of the gentleman headed
   west; decoyed by the gang so they can rob his master.

Johnson, Anthony. *Moll* VIII 100.   Master of the shop in which
   Moll is finally apprehended.

"Johnson, Capt. Charles." *Pirates* title page.   Alleged author of the
   General History of the Pirates.

Johnson, Col. Robert. *Pirates* 111.   Governor of South Carolina;
   personally captures Lowther off Charleston, 1718.

Johnson, Robert. *Pirates* 242. Pirate with Roberts; when joining the gang, he was so drunk he had to be hauled aboard ship with a block and tackle.

Johnson, Susanna. *Campbell* IV 174. Lady who lives near Romford in Essex; is bewitched by a hateful old woman.

Johnson. *Grandison* I 200. Servant of Sir Charles who carries the news of Harriet's rescue to the Reeveses in London.

Jonas. *Clarissa* III 129. Servant of Lord M., serving Lovelace for the time being.

Jonas. *Pamela* III 310. Servant of Sir Jacob Swynford; see Jack.

Jonathan, Mr. *Pamela* I 54. Good old butler in Bedfordshire; keeps Pamela informed of what he overhears.

Jonathan. *Clarissa* VII 186. Belford's sluggish and disobedient servant.

Jones, Will. *Voyage* XV 39. Crewman on the side of the mutineers.

Jones, Col. *Carleton* 82. English officer relieved in Santo Mattheo (Spain) by Peterborough, 1705.

Jones, Col. *Cavalier* V 284. Commands Parliamentary forces at Chester, 1645.

Jones, Farmer. *Pamela* II 329. Mr. Andrews' employer; Pamela presents him with a Bible, a *Common Prayer*, and a *Whole Duty of Man*.

Jones, Lady. *Pamela* I 171, IV 391. Lincolnshire lady who refuses to give Pamela sanctuary; dies upon Pamela's return from the Continent.

Jordan, John. *Grandison* II 379, V 249. Speaks with a lisp, attends the meeting between Sir Hargrave and Sir Charles.

Joseph. *Clarissa* VII 145. One of John Smith's journeyman bodice makers; Lovelace threatens to cut out his teeth.

Jossee, Seignior. *Pirates* 251. Man to whom William Davis is sold as a slave.

Joyce, Cornet. *Cavalier* V 295. Parliamentary officer; brings the king from Holmby House in Northamptonshire to Hampton Court.

Judith, Mrs. *Moll* VIII 71. Little sister of Betty, whose watch Moll steals.

Jupiter. *Battle* I 152. King of the gods; summons a council on Olympus but refuses to reveal the issue of the battle.

Juxon, Bishop. *Cavalier* V 146. Treasurer of Charles I; stores up a million pounds for him.

Kaley, Ry. *Drury* 264. Wife of Rer Vove, whom Drury guards.

Kasboo, the. *Pirates* 552. Jailer at Magadoxa; guards the mulatto.

Katharine (in *Clarissa*). See Catharine.

Keelings, the. *Grandison* IV 355. Family with whom the Mansfields are having a lawsuit.

Kendrick, Mrs. *Life of Sheppard* XVI 176. Lodger in Phillips' house, robbed by Sheppard.

Kennedy, Lt. Walter. *Pirates* 195. Pirate subordinate commander; abandons Roberts to his fate and goes off with the ship.

Kid, Capt. William. *Pirates* 217. Master of the *Adventure*; commissioned as a privateer but turns pirate; executed in London, 1700.

"Kidd, young Capt." *Singleton* VI 160. Young crewman made into gunner on the pirate vessel.

Killigrew, Sir Peter. *Cavalier* V 180. Carries the king's answer to Parliament, which has proposed a treaty of peace, 1642.

Killigrew, Col. *Carleton* 128. Carleton's regimental commander, 1705.

King, Moll. *Wild* XVI 265. Thief in Wild's service.

Kirby, Capt. *Pirates* 118. Master of the man-of-war *Greenwich*; deserts his comrade Capt. Mackray during a fight with Edward England, 1720.

Kit. *Clarissa* V 70. Hostler, referred to as drinking in the taproom of the Upper Flask, Hampstead.

Kitty. *Clarissa* I 185, II 256. Anna's maid; reports that Solmes's tenants hate their landlord, and the servants don't speak well of him.

Klienfurt, Mons. *Clarissa* VIII 263. Host in Munich with whom Morden stays while waiting for Lovelace to find him.

Kneebone, Mr. *Life of Sheppard* XVI 180, *Sheppard's Narrative* XVI 214. Linen draper near New Church in the Strand, Sheppard's first master; later robbed by him.

Knight, Tobias. *Pirates* 76. Secretary of Gov. Eden, part of the plot to divide the plunder with Blackbeard.

Knollys, Mrs. *Clarissa* I 178, II 341. Lady at whose house Clarissa once saw Miss Patty Montague.

Knot, Capt. *Pirates* 207. Master of a ship from Virginia.

Knox, Capt. Robert. *Singleton* VI 272. Sea captain beguiled and taken captive by the natives on Ceylon.

Knox, Robert. *Singleton* VI 273. Son of above; after being held captive by the Ceylonese, he finally makes his escape.

Kreutznaer, Herr. *Crusoe* I 2. Born in Bremen, father of Crusoe; advises him to adhere to the middle station in life.

Kronenburg, Baron. *Cavalier* V 64. Commands Tilly's cuirassiers at Leipzig.

L., Caroline, Countess of, née Grandison ("the countess"). *Grandison* I 308. The older of Sir Charles's two sisters, well adapted to the role of wife and mother.

L., Dean. *Pamela* III 219. Attends the B.s' dinner party during the visit of the Davers; "has a genteel vein of raillery."

L., Earl of. *Grandison* I 200. Scottish nobleman, Grandison's brother-in-law; has estate at Colnebrook.

L., Miss. *Pamela* III 219. Daughter of the dean; receives warnings from Pamela about not believing everything young men say.

La Bouse (or La Bouche). *Pirates* 174. French pirate; joins forces with Davis in the harbor of Gambia, 1721.

Laing, James. *Gow* XVI 319. Sent by Mr. Fea with a message for Gow.

Lalcon. *Gulliver* Part I chap. 7. Chamberlain in Lilliput, one of Gulliver's accusers.

Lamb, Anthony. *Life of Sheppard* XVI 179. Transported along with Sheppard.

Lambert, Col. *Cavalier* V 258. Parliamentary general, 1644.

Lambton, Sir John. *Grandison* IV 102, 355. Disinterested neighbor of the Keelings and Mansfields who will mediate between them.

"Lancashire Jemmy" (in *Moll*). See Jemmy.

Lane, Mrs. *Grandison* II 298. Discreet widow gentlewoman taking care of Miss Jervois.

Langdale, Sir Marmaduke. *Cavalier* V 285. Marches with the Cavalier into Staffordshire to raise a body of men for the king, 1645.

Langhorn, Maj. Gen. *Cavalier* V 286. Parliamentary commander; overruns Wales, 1645.

Langley. *Life of Sheppard* XVI, 189. Turnkey at Newgate.

Lapie, Mons. John. *Drury* 41. A jeweler, traveling with his son to Ft. St. George in the East Indies.

Laputa, King of. *Gulliver* Part III chap. 2. Ruler of the flying island; absorbed in abstract speculations.

Lardner, Miss. *Clarissa* V 34. Informant of Anna's who finds out that Mrs. Sinclair's establishment is a house of ill repute.

Larkin, Grandmother. *Clarissa* II 2. Grandmother of Jenny Fynnet; wants Mrs. Howe to help her make her will.

Laud, Archbishop. *Cavalier* V 144. Charles I's high-handed primate; all men blame him for provoking the Scots.

Laura. *Grandison* III 145. Clementina's maid, whose clothes Clementina borrows.

Lawrance, Lady Betty. *Clarissa* I 7. Lord M.'s half-sister and Lovelace's aunt; lives at Glenham Hall in Oxfordshire; see Sadleir, Lady Sarah.

Lawrance, Sir. Joseph. *Grandison* III 347. Friend of Lord W.'s; his house is only fifteen miles from the Mansfields'.

Lawrence, Sir John. *Plague Year* IX 53. Diligent Lord Mayor of London during the plague year.

Laws, Nicholas. *Pirates* 45. Royal governor of Jamaica; presides over the trial of Rackam; Capt. Massey reports depredations of Lowther to him.

Laws, Capt. *Pirates* 310. Master of the sloop *Happy*; goes to hunt down Lowther with Capt. Massey on board.

Lawton, Capt. *Pirates* 65. Master of the *Kent*, captured by Martel, 1716.

Leake, Sir John. *Carleton* 93. Admiral of the English fleet before Barcelona, 1705.

Leathes, Capt. *Campbell* IV 128. Commands a ship from Belfast, loses thirteen men in a violent storm.

Le Barre, Capt. *Pirates* 597. French accomplice of Capt. Lewis, scuttled by him; his men later murder Lewis.

Lee, Sir Charles. *Campbell* IV 64. His daughter has a strong presentiment of her death.

Leeson. *Clarissa* V 111. Lady Betty Lawrance's alleged cousin, whom the pretended Lady Betty goes to visit the night of the rape.

le Febvre, Jean Baptist. *Narrative* XVI 123. One of the murderous trio of brothers, allegedly an alehouse keeper.

le Febvre, Lewis. *Narrative* XVI 123. Second of the brothers, a sutler by profession.

le Febvre, Peter. *Narrative* XVI 97. Third of the brother-bandits.

Leffu, Ry. *Drury* 203. The guardian demon of a particular Owley, who orders a man in a dream to have his brother shoot at him.

Legee, John. *Street-Robbers* XVI xvii. One of the six robbers, mentioned only in the title.

Leman, Joseph. *Clarissa* I 23. Relation of a discharged bailiff of Lord M.'s; a double agent, really in the pay of Lovelace to spy on the Harlowes.

Lennard (or Leonard). *Street-Robbers* XVI 374. Member of the band of thieves apprehended by Mr. Ball.

Le Noy, Mr. *Carleton* 210. Comes to visit Col. Salter about a debt.

Leonard, Robert. *Pirates* 326. Master of a snow bound from New York to Curacoa, captured by Low, 1722 (a snow is a sailing vessel much like a brig).

Lesley, Sir James. *Carleton* 26. Assumes command of Carleton's regiment when the original commander, Col. Tufton, refuses to swear allegiance to William III, 1688.

Lesley, Mrs. *Pamela* III 253. The Countess of C.'s woman's woman; attends Pamela's little chapel service.

Leslie, Gen. (later Earl of Leven). *Cavalier* V 151. Scottish officer; receives the surrender of the king at Newark, 1646.

L'Estrange, Sir Roger (1616-1704). *Tale* sect. X, *Battle* I 152. Court pamphleteer and journalist; leads a disorderly rout in the battle.

Le Tondu, Matthieu. *Pirates* 392. Quartermaster of the *Victoire* after Misson assumes command.

Leven, Earl of (in *Cavalier*). See Leslie, Gen.

Levingston, Sir Thomas (later Earl of Tiviot). *Carleton* 27. Sent to attack the Highlanders, 1689.

Lewen, Dr. Arthur. *Clarissa* I 26. A worthy divine; often visits Clarissa, disapproves of the Solmes marriage project.

Lewis, Capt. *Pirates* 593. Multilingual pirate captain who makes a pact with the devil; murdered in his cabin by his own men.

Lewis. *Drury* 269. An English-speaking slave who, along with Drury, pimps for Rer Vove.

Lexington, Lord. *Clarissa* IV 129, 255. Nobleman whom Lord M. once accompanied on an embassy to Spain.

Lichfield, Earl. *Cavalier* V 282. Captured at a battle near Ludlow in Chester, 1645.

Lilburne, Mr. *Clarissa* V 105. Acquaintance of Tomlinson who allegedly hears Clarissa is married to Lovelace.

Lilliput, Prince of. *Gulliver* Part I chap. 4. Observed to have a hobble in his gait (he is believed to have leanings toward the High-Heel party).

Lilliput, Queen of. *Gulliver* Part I chap. 4. Mortally offended when
Gulliver puts out a fire in the palace by urinating on it.

Lilly, Capt. *Pirates* 325. Master of a sloop captured by Low, 1722.

Limtoc. *Gulliver* Part I chap. 7. General of Lilliput, who accuses
Gulliver of high treason.

Lindsey, Earl of. *Cavalier* V 170. Commander of the king's infantry, 1641.

Littleton, Commodore James. *Pirates* 507. Brings the king's
amnesty to the pirates on Madagascar, 1700.

Littleton, Capt. *Carleton* 73. At the siege of Barcelona, has the
artillery drawn into position by the soldiers themselves,
after making harness for a team of two hundred men, 1705.

Livy (59 B.C.-A.D. 17). *Battle* I 152. Latin historian; commands
the ancient infantry.

Lloyd, Biddy. *Clarissa* I 55, VIII 116. Friend of Clarissa's, mentioned in her will.

Loane, Capt. *Pirates* 268. Master of a ship captured by pirates at
Calabar.

Lock, Mr. *Narrative* XVI 153. The first English gentleman to be
murdered on his way back from Paris.

Lockyer, Miss. *Clarissa* IV 62. One of Lovelace's earlier victims.

Loftus, John. *Clarissa* VIII 154. Belford gives him an annuity to
make up for having disabled him in a duel.

Lohefute, Deaan. *Drury* 271. Deceased father of Rer Trimmonongarevo, now venerated.

Longman, Mr. *Pamela* I 56. Steward at Mr. B.'s Bedfordshire
estate.

Lorimer, Mr. (Sr.). *Grandison* II 266. Learned father of the young
wastrel (see below).

Lorimer, Mr. (Jr.). *Grandison* II 261. Wicked young man whom
Dr. Bartlett accompanies abroad on the Grand Tour.

Lorimer, Mrs. *Clarissa* IV 184. Go-between for Mrs. Howe and
Antony Harlowe.

Lovelace, Robert (alias "Col. Barrow," "Robert Huntingford").
Clarissa I 2. The rake, of Sandoun Hall, Lancaster; abducts
and rapes Clarissa; killed by Col. Morden.

Loveland, John. *Singleton* VI 273. English merchant on the *Anne*;
foolishly goes ashore to see the Ceylonese king, 1657.

Lovell, Grandmother. *Clarissa* I 30. Clarissa's maternal grandmother; left estates in Scotland and Yorkshire to James
Harlowe.

Lovereigne, Capt. *Pirates* 328. Master of the ship *Crowne*, captured by Low, 1723.

Lovick, Mrs. *Clarissa* VI 212. A busybody lodging at Mrs. Smith's in Hampstead.

Low, Edward ("Ned"). *Pirates* 312. Pirate captain, sadistic in his treatment of prisoners.

Lowther, George. *Pirates* 304. Pirate; absconds with a ship of the Royal Africa Company, 1721.

Lucan (39-65 A.D.) *Battle* I 158. Writer of epics; antagonist of Blackmore.

Lucas, Sir Charles. *Cavalier* V 219. Leads the main wing of the royalists at Marston Moor, 1644.

Lucas, Sir Christopher. *Grandison* I 259. Wilson's second master, a profligate; reduces himself and his victims to misery.

"Lucas, Harriet" (in *Clarissa*). See Harlowe, Clarissa.

Luggnagg, King of. *Gulliver* Part III chap. 9. Requires visitors to lick the floor on the way to his throne.

Lumsdale. *Gow* XVI 314. Master of a Scottish vessel from which the pirates buy wine.

Lumsdell, Col. *Cavalier* V 52. Scottish colonel in the service of Gustavus Adolphus.

Lundsford, Col. *Cavalier* V 176. Royalist captured at Edgehill, 1642.

Luxemburg, Duke of. *Carleton* 23. French general attacked by the Prince of Orange at St. Dennis, 1678.

Lyfouchy, Andian (or Deaan). *Pirates* 602. Father of Chimenatto and Timanangarivo; former king of the area between Mathelage and Port St. Augustin.

Lynx. *Wild* XVI 264. Thief of Wild's acquaintance (really in his employ).

Lyon, Elizabeth (alias "Edgworth Bess"). *Life of Sheppard* XVI 174, *Sheppard's Narrative* XVI 215. Prostitute with whom Sheppard cohabitates.

Lyon, Mr. *Life of Sheppard* XVI 174, *Sheppard's Narrative* XVI 215. First husband of Edgworth Bess; quarrels with Sheppard.

M., Dr. *Pamela* IV 241. Pamela's physician while she has the smallpox.

M., Lady. *Clarissa* IV 254. Lovelace's hot-tempered aunt, deceased at the time of the novel.

M., Lord. *Clarissa* I 6. Lovelace's rich and proverb-spouting uncle.

Mabell. *Clarissa* IV 295, VI 94. Servant at Mrs. Sinclair's, involved in Clarissa's second escape.

Macarty, Dennis. *Pirates* 43. Condemned pirate; before the trap door is sprung he kicks off his shoes so that those who predicted he would "die with his boots on" will be proved liars.

Macaulay. *Gow* XVI 287. Scottish murderer and pirate; executed.

Macdonald, Archibald. *Campbell* IV 131. Citizen of St. Mary's parish, Isle of Skye; famous for his gift of "second sight."

Macdonald, Sir Donald. *Campbell* IV 131. Sentences two rogues to death on the Isle of Man.

Mackenzie, Lt. Col. *Grandison* II 223. Officer who accompanies Capt. Anderson during the confrontation with Sir Charles.

Macket, Capt. Henry. *Drury* 295. Master of a ketch fitted out to cruise along the coast of Madagascar.

Macket, Capt. William. *Drury* 291. Master of the *Drake*; rescues Drury from Madagascar.

Mackray (or Macrae), Capt. *Pirates* 118. Master of the *Cassandra*, defeated by Edward England in the Indian Ocean, 1720.

Macleod, Sir Norman. *Campbell* IV 129. Instructed by his clairvoyant butler how to play his hand at cards.

Macmow. *King* XVI 76. Irishman who leads a group of pirates in an escape from Madagascar to Mocha.

Macpherson. *Grandison* I 185. One of the rogues hired by Wilson to carry Harriet off to Paddington.

Mafaly. *Pirates* 473. King of Elexa (south end of Madagascar); extends hospitality to Thomas White's pirate crew.

Maffei, Lady. *Grandison* III 392. Lady Olivia's aunt; accompanies her to England.

Magnes, William. *Pirates* 246. Captured pirate; plans insurrection on board the *Swallow*, 1722.

Mahoni, Brigadier. *Carleton* 80. Commander of Spanish garrison at Molviedro; Peterborough tries to induce him to defect, 1705.

Mallory. *Clarissa* IV 351. Lawyer-friend of Lovelace who helps him obtain the marriage license.

Malpa. *Pirates* 462. Dutch merchant at Cochin, prevented by his colleagues from trading with the pirates.

Man, Elizabeth. *Wild* XVI 257. Wild's third wife; "a sensible and agreeable woman, though a whore."

Manchester, Earl of. *Cavalier* V 246. Parliamentary commander in the north against the Earl of Newcastle, 1643.

Mansfield, Fanny. *Grandison* III 251. Second daughter of the Mansfield family (slightly decayed gentility).

Mansfield, John. *Pirates* 279. Pirate with Roberts; is so drunk during the fight between the *Swallow* and the *Ranger* that he doesn't know his mates have surrendered.

Mansfield, Sir Thomas. *Grandison* III 244. A peer who has had reverses at law; Sir Charles aids his family.

Mansfield, Lady. *Grandison* III 251. Wife of Sir Thomas.

Mansfield, Miss. *Grandison* III 247. Older daughter of the family.

Manso. *Campbell* IV 76. Friend of Tasso's who is by his side when he sees a spirit.

Mantua, Duke of. *Cavalier* V 20. Supported by the Spaniards against the French at the time of the Cavalier's arrival, 1630.

Manwaring, Peter. *Pirates* 99. Master of the sloop *Frances*, captured by Bonnet, 1718.

"Marchioness, the" (in *Grandison*). See Porretta, Marchesa della.

Mare, Michael. *Pirates* 246. Captured pirate who plans an insurrection on board the *Swallow*.

Marescotti, Father J. P. M. *Grandison* III 118. Father confessor of Clementina and supporter of the Count of Belvedere's suit.

Margaret ("Peggy"). *Clarissa* V 259. Maid at Mrs. Moore's in Hampstead, wooed by Will to be on Lovelace's side.

Margate, Mons. *Clarissa* VIII 271. Col. Morden's valet.

Maria. *Cavalier* 190. Daughter of Carleton's landlady in San Clemente, almost raped by Brennan.

Mariana (Juan de, 1537-1624). *Battle* I 152. Spanish historian; officer in the modern infantry.

Maritan, King of. *Pirates* 500. Madagascar king, forced to surrender David Williams to Dempaino.

Marjoram. *Street-Robbers* XVI 368. One of the rogues; peaches on the others.

Marks, Mr. *Pirates* 74. Prisoner of Blackbeard off Charleston; goes to convey Blackbeard's demand for a medicine chest, 1718.

"Marquis, the" (in *Grandison*). See Porretta, Marchese della.

Marquis, the. *Jacque* XI 64. Officer of the Guards du Corps; has an affair with Jack's wife.

Marrow, Col. *Cavalier* V 245. Gallant Cavalier colonel, killed at Chester, 1644.

"Marsigli, Signor" (in *Grandison*). See Belvedere, Count of.

Marston, Capt. *Pirates* 288. Master of a ship from New York, captured in the West Indies by Bradley, 1721.

Martel, Capt. *Pirates* 41. Privateer-turned-pirate, finally chased into the jungle on St. Croix by a man-of-war.

Marten, Mr. *Life of Sheppard* XVI 199. Surgeon who assists Wild after he is stabbed by Blueskin.

Martin, Sarah ("Sally"). *Clarissa* IV 149. Prostitute at Mrs. Sinclair's; is particularly vile to Clarissa in the sponging house.

Martin, Col. *Grandison* II 230. Sir Charles's friend, whom he met abroad; present at the confrontation with Capt. Anderson.

Martin, Mr. *Clarissa* VIII 285. Father of Sally, a mercer living in a manner inappropriate to his social rank.

Martin, Mr. *Life of Sheppard* XVI 193. Sheppard steals watches from him.

Martin, 'Squire, "in the grove." *Pamela* I 89. Rakish neighbor of Mr. B.'s; has had three illegitimate births recently on his estate.

Martin. *Tale* sect. II, VI. One of the three brothers; represents the moderate element in the Reformation (Martin Luther and the Church of England).

Martina. *Grandison* III 144. Maidservant at the Porrettas', sent to inform the Marchioness that Clementina has been found.

"Martindale, Dorcas" (in *Clarissa*). See Butler, Deb.

Marulli, Count. *Grandison* III 60. Soldier of fortune in Naples who attempts to obtain access to Clementina.

Mary. *Farther Adventures* II 143. Native wife of Atkins; decides to be baptized.

Mary. *Pirates* 162. Mr. Bonny's maidservant, mother of Anne Bonny; accompanies Bonny to Carolina, where she dies.

Massey, Capt. John. *Pirates* 304. Commands detachment of soldiers sent to Gambia; persuaded to join Lowther as a pirate.

Massey. *Cavalier* V 197. Parliamentary governor of Gloucester, 1643.

Masters, Capt. John. *Pirates* 99. Master of the *Henry*, which joins the hunt for Stede Bonnet.

Mathelage, Andian (or Deaan). *Pirates* 602. Madagascar king attacked by Chimenatto.

Matthews, Capt. *Carleton* 125. Carleton's superior officer, "of more courage than conduct."

Maurice, Prince, of England. *Cavalier* V 159. Older brother of Prince Rupert; commands royal forces in the west.

Maurice, Prince, of Holland. *Cavalier* V 127. Fights a war of attrition against the Spanish imperialists.

Maxwell, Lord. *Cavalier* V 244. A loyal Scot defending Newcastle against the rebels.

May, Charles. *Pirates* 455. Surgeon on board the Worcester; testifies against Capt. Thomas Green, 1704.

Maynard, Lieut. Robert. *Pirates* 78. First lieutenant of the *Pearl*, the valiant conqueror of Blackbeard, 1718.

Mayor of Colchester. *Moll* VII 5. Comes to the orphange to visit when he hears that one of the girls wants to become a "gentle-woman."

McDermot. *Grandison* I 185. Rogue hired by Wilson to carry off Harriet.

McDonald, Patrick (alias "Capt. Antony Tomlinson"). *Clarissa* IV 302. A solemn rascal; pretends to mediate between Clarissa and her Uncle Harlowe.

McLaughlin, Daniel. *Pirates* 253. Mate of the *Swallow*; testifies against Roberts' crew, 1722.

Mead, Mr. *Carleton* 156. English paymaster at Barcelona during the Peninsular campaign.

Mecherow. *Drury* 278. Cook to whom Drury is assigned as assistant among the Saccalauvors.

Meek, Capt. *Campbell* IV 87. From Kirkcaldy; carries young Duncan to London with letters of recommendation to the Earl of Argyll.

Meguddummateem, Deaan. *Drury* 243. Ancestor of Deaan Mernaugha, now venerated as a god.

Melville, Mr. *Clarissa* VIII 82. Curate who reads Clarissa's funeral eulogy, Dr. Lewen being deceased.

Melvin. *Gow* XVI 293. Scottish mutineer and pirate, finally executed.

Mendez, Capt. Pedro de. *Gulliver* Part IV chap. 11. Portuguese captain who forcibly retrieves Gulliver from the savages.

"Mennell, Capt." (in *Clarissa*). See Newcomb, Antony.

Mephontey. *Drury* 119. Uncle of Drury's owner, Deaan Mevarrow; appealed to for aid in the civil war.

Merceda, Solomon. *Grandison* I 261. Portuguese Jew, one of Wilson's former masters; wounded in an attempt on a lady's honor.

Merchant, Dutch. *Roxana* XII 125. Helps Roxana escape from the clutches of the Jew, later marries her.

Mercury. *Battle* I 152. Messenger-god who brings Jupiter the book of fate in three folio volumes.

Meredith, Sir Rowland. *Grandison* I 39. Elderly Welsh gentleman; has a series of tearful interviews with Harriet trying to negotiate a marriage treaty for his nephew James Fowler.

Mernaugha, Deaan. *Drury* 192. Succeeds Rer Vovvern as king of Feraighn, near Port St. Augustine; Drury flees to his protection.

Mernindgarevo, Deaan. *Drury* 156. Copper-colored Negro, the father of Deaan Crindo.

Mesmerrico, Capt. *Drury* 101. French captain chosen by lot to remain on Madagascar and trade with the natives.

Metcalfe, Tom. *Clarissa* VII 184. Killed by Belton in defense of his sister's honor; his ghost appears to Belton.

Methuen, Paul. *Carleton* 64. Trusted lieutenant of Gen. Stanhope.

Metorolahatch. *Drury* 200. A younger son of Deaan Woozington, killed in battle.

Mevarrow, Deaan. *Drury* 79. Drury's cruel first master, grandson to Deaan Crindo.

Middleton, Sir Thomas. *Cavalier* V 234. Parliamentary cavalry commander who hunts down fleeing Cavaliers after Marston Moor, 1644.

Middleton, Maj. Gen. *Campbell* IV 136. Royalist in the Civil Wars; has several experiences of the "second sight."

"Midnight, Mother" (in *Moll*). See "Governess, my."

Milbourne, Mr. *Grandison* V 245. Minister of a Dissenting congregation in Northampton; impresses Harriet by being friendly to a priest of the Church of England.

Miles, "the caitiff." *Clarissa* VIII 45. Rake who ruins and abandons a farmer's daughter, allegedly a worse crime than Lovelace's.

Miller, Capt. James. *Pirates* 469. Master of the *Neptune*, handed over to Halsey by Samuel Burgess.

Milliner, Mary. *Wild* XVI 244. Prostitute and thief, sent to the Compter (a prison).

Mills, Capt. *Pirates* 338. Master of the *Lucretia and Catherine*, captured by Evans, 1722.

Milton (John, 1608-1674). *Battle* I 152. Commands modern cavalry in the battle.

Mimebolambo, Rer. *Drury* 129. Youngest brother of Deaan
Murnanzack; lives five miles east of Deaan Mevarrow.

Mirlotte, Jean Michael. *Voyage* XIV 24. French "captain" of the
voyage, really one of the privateers.

Misson, Capt. *Pirates* 383. French pirate; treats his prisoners
liberally, founds colony of Libertalia on Madagascar.

Mitchel, Alexander. *Pirates* 606. Accomplice of William Fly;
persuades him not to shoot Mr. Atkinson, 1726.

Mitchell, Dr. *Grandison* I 18. London doctor who attends Nancy
Selby.

Mitton, Col. *Cavalier* V 251. Captures Shrewsbury for the Parliamentary forces, 1644.

"Moely" (in *Crusoe*). See Ishmael.

Moffat, Catharine. *Narrative* XVI 98. A "widow" in Funes; conceals the thieves along with their girl friends.

Moggy (also called Mrs. Margaret). *Jacque* XI 86. Jack's fourth
wife, an innocent country wench in Lancaster, aged thirty-
three.

Mohilla, King of. *Pirates* 408. Attacks the island of Johanna while
Misson is visiting there.

Moiang Andro (in *Drury*). See Mynbolamb , Rer.

Molins, Thomas. *Due Preparations* XV 65. Second porter of the
grocer's family, also carried away by the plague.

Moll, Herman. *Gulliver* Part IV chap. 11. Chartmaker who ignores
Gulliver's advice about the true position of New Guinea.

Mompesson. *Narrative* XVI 152. One of the murdered English
gentlemen.

Momus. *Battle* I 153. God of Dulness and patron of the moderns.

Monmouth, Duke of. *Carleton* 23, *Roxana* XII 206. Fights on the
side of the Prince of Orange at St. Dennis; attends one of
Roxana's balls.

Montague, Charlotte. *Clarissa* II 313. Lovelace's pretty cousin;
finally marries Belford.

Montague, Martha ("Patty"). *Clarissa* I 178. Charlotte's sister; at
first charmed by Lovelace, later denounces him.

Montery, Count de. *Carleton* 13, 207. Ally of the Prince of
Orange, 1674; later takes holy orders, is seen by Carleton
in Madrid.

Montgomery, Capt. *Pirates* 95. Master of the *Ann*, captured by
Bonnet, 1717.

Montmorency, Duke of. *Cavalier* V 20. French commander

ordered to relieve the city of Casale, 1630; the Cavalier joins his army.

Montrose, Earl of. *Cavalier* V 280. Royal commander in Scotland, 1645.

Moody. *Pirates* 246. Pirate planning an escape from the *Swallow*, 1722.

Moor. *Pirates* 446. Gunner brained by Capt. Kid with a bucket for accusing him of ruining them all.

Moore, Mrs. ("Goody"). *Clarissa* V 54. Widow who keeps a lodging-house at Hampstead, to which Clarissa flees.

Morasab. *Pirates* 554. Old man in Magadoxa who befriends the mulatto in prison, bringing him news.

Mordant, Mrs. Mary. *Philosopher* XV 192. Second person whom Dickory serves, after Mr. Owen Parry.

Morden, Col. William. *Clarissa* I 169. Clarissa's cousin; kills Lovelace at the end of the novel.

Morden, Mr. *Clarissa* VIII 234. Father of above; used to love to display Clarissa's needlework.

Morley, Sir John. *Cavalier* V 244. A loyalist Scot at the siege of Newcastle, 1644.

Morris, Thomas. *Pirate* 43. Condemned pirate; blames his comrades for not savi ng him from the gallows.

Morrison, John. *Campbell* IV 134. Wears a sprig of the plant called *fuga daemonum* sewed into the neck of his coat to prevent his seeing specters.

Morrison, Susan. *Clarissa* V 298. A tenant farmer's daughter, servant to the pretended Lady Betty.

Morrocheruck, Deaan. *Drury* 234. Petty king in the mountains near Port St. Augustine, Madagascar.

Morroughsevea, Deaan. *Drury* 306. Native king with whom Drury trades for slaves during his second voyage to Madagascar, 1719; killed in battle.

Morwell, Samuel. *Pirates* 276. Testifies in favor of George Wilson at his trial for piracy, 1722.

"Mother Midnight" (in *Moll*). See "Governess, my."

Mother of the Cavalier. *Cavalier* V 1. Has two prophetic dreams about his future career while she is pregnant with him.

Mother of Moll. *Moll* VII 2. Condemned to death for stealing three pieces of fine Holland cloth but "pleads her belly"; turns up later in Maryland.

Mouchat. *Jacque* X 160. Negro slave whom Jack induces to reform by merciful treatment instead of beating.

Moume, Rer. *Drury* 266. King of the Virzimbers on Madagascar, and eldest son to Trimmonongarevo and uncle to Rer Vove; brings about Drury's escape from the island.

Mowbray, Richard. *Clarissa* I 220. Lovelace's friend, "so fierce and so fighting," aged thirty-three or thirty-four, from Yorkshire; attempts to provoke a quarrel with Morden.

Mulatto, the. *Pirates* 541. Actually a Chinese from Canton; goes ashore to negotiate with the Magadoxans; kept there for sixteen years.

Mullins, Mr. *Clarissa* I 27. Former suitor of Clarissa's; attends her funeral muffled up.

Mumford, old widow. *Pamela* I 5. Neighbor of the Andrewses; re-assures them that it was proper for Lady B. to have given some things to Pamela.

Mundrosser, Rer. *Drury* 192. Brother of Deaan Mernaugha; assists in the command of the army of Feraighn.

Mundumbo, Deaan. *Drury* 98. Prince of Anterndroea (Madagascar), where Drury is a slave.

Mungazaungarevo, Deaan (also spelled Munguzungarevo). *Drury* 156, 195, 243. An early king of Feraighn, grandfather of the present ruler, Deaan Mernaugha; alleged to have married a white man's daughter; made the original treaty of peace with the English.

Munodi, Lord. *Gulliver* Part III chap. 4. The only landowner on Balnibarbi who has resisted the rush to modern methods; often believed to represent Swift's friend Robert Harley.

Murnanzack, Deaan. *Drury* 63. Held hostage by the English, later the leader of one side in the civil war; a noble ruler of the people of Anterndroea.

Murphy, Timothy. *Gow* XVI 339. Pirate who becomes a crown witness.

Murray, Mr. *Pamela* III 142. Suitor to Polly Darnford, a fine, prim young fellow from Norfolk.

Musgrave, Sir Christopher (1632?-1704). *Tale* sect. IX. Whig MP, enjoined to draw on Bedlam for his personnel needs; see How and Seymour.

Mussecorrow, Deaan. *Drury* 129. Brother of Deaan Murnanzack; marches with him to attack the usurper, Deaan Crindo.

Mynbolambo, Rer (alias Moiang Andro). *Drury* 235. King of Morandavo, bordering the territory of the Saccalauvors, whose crown has been usurped by his brother Trimmonon-garevo.

N., Lady Frances. *Grandison* II 95, 135. Noblewoman proposed as a wife for Sir Charles.

N., Earl of. *Grandison* VI 273. Recommended to the favor of Sir Charles when he visits Italy.

N., Lady. *Grandison* II 95. Mother of Lady Frances N.

N., Lord. *Grandison* II 95. Father of Lady Frances N.

Nan (also called Ann). *Pamela* I 238. Housemaid at Mr. B.'s Lincolnshire estate, "a little apt to drink, if she can get at liquor"; finds Pamela's clothes in the pond.

Nanno, Ry. *Drury* 161. Ambassador of Rer Vovvern, King of Feraighn; is a good judge of human nature, assures Drury he will eventually escape.

Neal. *Pirates* 373. A fisherman from Cork, confederate of Roche.

Nedham, Dolly. *Grandison* V 361. Wedding guest, engaged to Mr. Allestree.

Neels, Grave. *Cavalier* V 80. Swedish officer, affronted when the king gives the Cavalier a command over his head.

Nelthorpe. *Grandison* IV 95. Servant of Lady G.'s.

Nelthorpe. *Pamela* IV 214. Maidservant of the Countess Dowager.

Nesbitt, Sir Alexander. *Grandison* IV 358. Englishman anxious to meet Dr. Bartlett; brings letters from Sir Charles.

Nevers, Duke of. *Cavalier* V 19. Driven out of Mantua by the Germans, 1630.

Newcastle, Earl of. *Cavalier* 160. Commands royal forces in the north, 1642.

Newcomb, Antony (alias "Capt. Mennell"). *Clarissa* IV 43. Pretends to negotiate new lodgings for Clarissa with Mrs. Fretchville.

Newton, Justice. *Life of Sheppard* XVI 180. Sentences Charles Grace to transportation.

Nicholas, Capt. John. *Gulliver* Part II chap. 8. Commander of the *Adventure*; picks Gulliver up at sea after his sojourn in Brobdingnag.

Nichols (alias "Capt. Bloodyhand," "Capt. Redhand"). *King* XVI 12. Most ruthless of the pirates, preying on all nations alike; his shipmates rejoice when he is killed.

Nichols. *Pamela* I 50. Farmer from whom Pamela procures dark cloth to make unbecoming clothes for herself.

Nicholson, Daniel. *Campbell* IV 132. Minister of St. Mary's, Isle of Skye; a vision of a corpse is seen in front of his pulpit.

Noakes, William. *Pirates* 504. Member of David Williams' pirate crew; shot by a group of hostile blacks whom he rashly allows to come on board.

Nocera, Bishop of. *Grandison* III 15. Second son of the Marchese della Porretta; opposes Clementina's marriage with the English heretic, Sir Charles.

Noise. *Battle* I 153. Child of Criticism.

North, Nathaniel. *Pirates* 469. Evenhanded pirate king on Madagascar; has a number of children by native wives.

Norton, Judith ("Goody"). *Clarissa* I 280. Clarissa's nurse, responsible for many of her good qualities.

Norton, Tommy. *Clarissa* VI 126. Son of Judith Norton; his fever prevents her from rushing to Clarissa's side.

Norton, Farmer. *Pamela* I 136. Tenant on Mr. B.'s Lincolnshire estate; Pamela stays at his house on her journey.

Norton, Miss. *Pamela* I 136. Farmer's daughter; gives Pamela a letter from Mr. B.

Norton, Mrs. *Pamela* I 136. Farmer Norton's wife, sympathetic with Pamela's plight.

Norton. *Pirates* 221. Master of a Rhode Island brigantine, captured by Roberts, 1721.

Nugent, Miss. *Pamela* II 331. Very fair young lady at Mrs. Dobson's boarding school.

Nun, Judith. *Wild* XVI 257. Wild's fifth wife.

Nurse of Col. Jack. *Jacque* X 1. Paid extra for teaching Jack that he is a gentleman born.

Nurse, Mistress. *Moll* VII 3. A good old woman who keeps a school for orphans in Colchester; dies when Moll is fourteen.

Nyn, Mr. *Pirates* 545. First mate of the *Albemarle*; sent ashore by Capt. Beavis at Magadoxa with a white flag.

O'Brien, Miss. *Grandison* II 97. Fortune hunter and Mr. Filmer's tool, who hopes to ensnare Sir Thomas Grandison; finally gets smallpox and marries a tradesman near Golden Square.

Odell, Samuel. *Pirates* 83. Accidentally on board Blackbeard's sloop when it is captured; hence, acquitted of piracy.

Offkirk, Baron D'. *Cavalier* V 122. Rashly precipitates the Protestants into the Battle of Nordlingen.

Ogle, Chaloner. *Pirates* 236. Master of the ship of the line *Swallow*; captures Roberts' crew, 1722.

Ogleby (or Ogilby, John, 1600-1676). *Battle* I 158. Notorious translator of Virgil and Homer, referred to as the spiritual father of Creech.

O'Guaza, Col. *Carleton* 125. Governor of Monteza, 1705.

O'Hara, Mrs. Helen (first called Mrs. Jervois). *Grandison* II 148, 298. Emily Jervois's wayward mother; lives in Dean St., Soho, would be handsome if her vices did not render her odious.

O'Hara, Maj. *Grandison* II 299. Mrs. Jervois's new husband, an Irish bully.

Oily, Nelly D'. *Clarissa* I 200 (VI 444, called "Kitty"). Proposed bride for James Harlowe; he doesn't like her.

Olaavor, Deaan. *Drury* 177. Madagascar chief; cites the wishes of the demon Lulu-bay when he wants anything for himself.

Oldham, Mr. *Grandison* III 237. First son of Mrs. Oldham; well-inclined and well-educated.

Oldham, Mrs. *Grandison* II 43. Mistress of Sir Thomas Grandison; bears him two sons, is forgiven by Sir Charles.

Oldham, Mrs. *Pamela* IV 268. Sister of Beck Worden, a widow, recommended to the service of Mr. B.

Oldham (John, 1653-1683). *Battle* I 158. Satirist, writer of Pindarics; slain by Pindar in the battle.

Oliver. *Grandison* I 27. Servant of Grandmother Shirley; marries Ellen and becomes an innkeeper.

Olivia, Lady. *Grandison* II 240. Florentine lady in love with Sir Charles; pursues him to England.

Ollyffe, Biddy D'. *Clarissa* VI 444. Guest at Col. Ambrose's party.

Opheck, Ry. *Drury* 99, 199. Nephew of Deaan Woozington; invades Anterndroea, killed in battle.

Opinion. *Battle* I 153. Sister of the goddess Criticism.

Orgueil, Countess d'. *Tale* sect. II. One of the three ladies wooed by the brothers; represents pride; see Argent and Grands Titres.

Orleans, Duke of. *Carleton* 20. French commander at Cambray, 1677.

Ormond, Earl of. *Cavalier* V 209. Royal governor in Ireland during the Civil Wars.

O'Roirk, Maj. (also O'Rourk). *Carleton* 125. Irishman in the service of the Duke of Anjou, 1705.

Ortega, Don Pedro. *Carleton* 176, 192. Gallant toreador at San Clemente; Carleton's ally in the Brennan affair.

Osgood, Mr. *Clarissa* III 19. Belford's cousin, a man of reputation living near Soho Square, to whom Anna is to direct her letters to Clarissa.

Osgood, Mrs. *Clarissa* III 183. Wife of above, Belford's landlady.

Ossory, Earl of. *Carleton* 23. Commander of the English and Scottish troops at St. Dennis, 1678.

Osta, Commissary. *Cavalier* V 103. Commands the Imperial forces at the siege of Biberach, 1632.

Owen, Mrs. *Moll* VIII 141. Old woman in Virginia who points out to Moll her brother-husband Humphry.

Oxenstiern, Axel. *Cavalier* V 107. Gustavus Adolphus's chancellor; commands the Swedish forces in the Palatinate while the king is advancing into Bavaria.

P., Lord. *Pamela* IV 406. Rakish peer carrying on an affair with Miss Cope.

P., Mrs. *Pamela* IV 392. Widow of Mr. J. P., marries Jackey H.; former mistress of the Duke of _____; is a shrew, has a bastard child.

Pacheo, Don Felix. *Carleton* 159. Friend of Carleton's, distinguished by his irreverence.

Pallas. *Battle* I 152. Greek goddess of wisdom; patron of the ancients.

Palmer, Joseph. *Pirates* 96. Master of a brigantine captured by Bonnet, 1717.

Pannel, Abraham. *Gulliver* Part I chap. 1. Commander of young Gulliver's very first ship.

Panton, Mr. *Life of Sheppard* XVI 176. Carpenter for whom Sheppard works; the job gives Sheppard a chance to stage a robbery.

Panton. *Gow* XVI 316. Pirate used as sentinel at Mr. Honnyman's house.

Pappenheim. *Cavalier* V 117. Imperial lieutenant at Lützen, 1632.

Paracelsus (Phillippus Aureolus Theophrastus Bombastus ab Hohenheim, 1493-1541). *Battle* I 152. Modern chemist; brings to the battle a squadron of stinkpot flingers.

Pargitter, John. *Life of Sheppard* XVI 181. Chandler in Hampstead, robbed by Sheppard.

Parker. *Campbell* IV 61. Officer of the king's wardrobe, Windsor Castle; sees ghost of old Sir George Villiers.

Parker. *Pirates* 444. Englishman taken by Kid from a Moorish ship to serve as pilot, 1697.

Parrin, Sarah. *Wild* XVI 257. Wild's fourth wife.

Parry, Owen. *Philosopher* XV 191. Takes the dumb Dickory under his protection.

Parry, Justice. *Life of Sheppard* XVI 177, *Sheppard's Narrative* XVI 220. Commits Sheppard to St. Giles's roundhouse.

Parsons, Simon. *Clarissa* V 363. Lord M.'s Berkshire bailiff; brings Lovelace news of Lord M.'s illness, is obsequious to the new heir.

"Partington, Priscilla." *Clarissa* III 344. Allegedly an heiress in honor of whom the dinner party is held.

Partrick, Peter. *Clarissa* V 160. Messenger sent by Will with news that Clarissa is at Mrs. Moore's in Hampstead.

Payne. *Pirates* 313. Mate of a brigantine captured by Lowther, 1722.

Pease, James. *Pirates* 325. Master of a sloop bound for Brazil, captured by Low, 1722.

Pedantry. *Battle* I 154. Child of Criticism.

Pell, Ignatius. *Pirates* 102. Boatswain of Bonnet's ship; promises to become a crown witness, 1718.

Penner, Maj. *Pirates* 41. Pirate, surrenders to Capt. Woodes Rogers, 1718.

Pennico. *Jacque* XI 113. Negro slave girl whom Jack gives to his wife on the plantation in Maryland.

Percival, Maj. *Carleton* 152. Surrenders his post at Denia to preserve his own cache of money.

Perkin. *Campbell* IV 203. Servant of the Earl of Dorset at Sevenoaks in Kent, in the incident of Mr. Saxon's house.

Perkins, Dr. *Clarissa* VI 75. One of Lord M.'s personal London physicians.

Perrault (Charles, 1628-1703). *Battle* I 157. Chief supporter of the moderns in France; unhorsed by Homer.

Perry, Mr. *Pamela* II 224. Lover of Miss Borroughs; is visiting the Darnfords when Pamela arrives.

Peter. *Clarissa* IV 186. House servant at Mrs. Sinclair's.

Peter. *Tale* sect. II, IV. Eldest of the three brothers; represents the Roman Catholic Church.

Peterborough (Charles Mordaunt, third) Earl of. *Carleton* 49. Brilliant commander of the English Peninsular expedition (1705-1706) during the War of the Spanish Succession.

Peters, Mr. *Pamela* I 179. Parish priest in Lincolnshire; refuses to protect Pamela from Mr. B.

Petersen. *Gow* XVI 287. Ruthless Swedish pirate, executed in the end.

Phalaris. *Battle* I 162. Tyrant of ancient Syracuse, alleged author of the spurious *Epistles of Phalaris*; in the battle, surprised in his sleep by Bentley.

Philip of Anjou. *Carleton* 54. French claimant to the throne of Spain during the War of the Spanish Succession.

Philips, James. *Pirates* 217. Master of the *Little York*, captured by Roberts, 1720.

Philips, William. *Pirates* 265. Boatswain of the *King Solomon*; surrenders the ship and joins Roberts, 1721.

Phillips, Frederick. *Pirates* 506. New York merchant, early employer of Samuel Burgess.

Phillips, John. *Pirates* 341. Pirate captain; has a leg sawed off; subdued by his own captives, 1724.

Phillips, William. *Life of Sheppard* XVI 176. Houseowner robbed by Sheppard.

Phinnes, John. *Gow* XVI 339. One of the pirates, who turns state's evidence.

Phipps, Sir William. *Jacque* XI 142. Man alleged to have salvaged the wreck of the Spanish plate fleet in the Caribbean.

Phips, Gen. James. *Pirates* 236. Writes a letter to the agent of the Royal African Company, warning of the proximity of Roberts.

Pight, Mrs. *Campbell* IV 75. Woman in Water Lane who has a familiar spirit.

Pilot, Dutch. *Voyage* XIV 87. Persuaded to guide the ship through the Straits of Molucca by virtue of a noose hung around his neck.

Pindar. *Battle* I 152. Greek author of the *Odes*; commands the ancient light cavalry.

Pinkham, John. *Pirates* 328. Master of a ship sailing from Biddiford to Jamaica, captured by Low, 1723.

Piper, the. *Plague Year* IX 103. Old man who falls asleep on a bulk and is inadvertently put into one of the dead-carts.

Pitt, Mr. *Life of Sheppard* XVI 191, *Sheppard's Narrative* XVI 223. Newgate turnkey to whom Sheppard demonstrates his agility in slipping out of chains.

Plato (c. 427-348 B.C.) *Battle* I 147. Greek philosopher; laughs at the modern efforts at mobilization.

Playford, Miss. *Clarissa* VI 445. Guest at Col. Ambrose's to whom Lovelace pays a genteel compliment.

Plumb, Capt. *Pirates* 175. Master of the *Princess*, captured by Davis in Anamboe, 1717.

Plummer, Capt. *Pirates* 237. Master of the *Jason*, out of Bristol; gives Capt. Ogle information about Roberts' whereabouts, 1721.

Plune, Calin Deffar. *Gulliver* Part I chap. 7. Former emperor of Lilliput who declared it illegal to make water in the palace precincts.

Plunket, Mr. *Pirates* 280. Governor of the Royal African Company, stationed at Sierra Leone.

Pocock, Capt. *Gulliver* Part IV chap. 1. Accompanies Gulliver's ship part way; later founders in a storm.

Poinings, Sir Arthur. *Grandison* VI 236. Suitor of a girl whose father (secretly favoring the match) maneuvers her into eloping.

Pollexfen, Sir Hargrave. *Grandison* I 58, 61. A rakish dandy, aged twenty-eight; abducts Harriet, provokes fight with Sir Charles.

Pollexfen, Mr. *Grandison* VI 322. Relation of above; summons Sir Charles to Sir Hargrave's deathbed.

Pompey the Great. *Pirates* 29. Roots out the Cilician pirates.

Popoli, Duchess of. *Carleton* 76. Spanish noblewoman saved from a mob in Barcelona by the gallant Earl of Peterborough.

Porretta, Clementina della. *Grandison* III 15. Sir Charles's pupil; falls in love with him, corresponds in England under the name "George Trumbull."

Porretta, Giacomo della ("the General"). *Grandison* III 15. Haughty oldest son of the family; has estate in Naples.

Porretta, Jeronymo della ("the Barone"). *Grandison* III 15. Sir Charles's friend, suffering from a shoulder wound.

Porretta, Juliano della. *Grandison* III 179. Young nephew of the Marchese, present at Sir Charles's farewell interview.

Porretta, Sebastiano della. *Grandison* III 168. Older nephew of the Marchese; treats Clementina with pity bordering on contempt.

Porretta, Conte della. *Grandison* III 15. Head of the Urbino branch of the family, father of Sebastiano and Juliano.

Porretta, Marchesa della ("the Marchioness"). *Grandison* III 15. Mother of the Bologna branch of the family.

Porretta, Marchese della ("the Marquis"). *Grandison* III 15. Father of the Bologna branch of the family.

Porter, Thomas. *Pirates* 96. Master of a brigantine from New England captured by Bonnet, 1717.

Porter, Capt. *Carleton* 41. One of the conspirators in the Assassination Plot, 1696; See Blackburn and Cassels.

Porter, Maj. Gen. *Cavalier* V 219. Royalist commanding the main wing at Marston Moor, 1644.

Porter. *Pirates* 221. Master of a pirate sloop; visits Roberts in Hispaniola.

"Poser, William" (in *Drury*). See Purser, William.

Positiveness. *Battle* I 154. Child of Criticism.

Posterity, Prince. *Tale* Epistle Dedicatory. Noble lord, having Time as his governor; assured by the Author that such writers as Dryden and Tate really exist.

Pouillard. *Narrative* XVI 160. Servant killed by the robbers near Bapaume.

Poussin. *Grandison* III 333. French wine merchant, master of Edward Danby.

Poyntz, Maj. Gen. *Cavalier* V 274. Parliamentary commander who pursues the king in his northward march, 1645.

Prat, Mr. *Drury* 46. Chief mate of the *Degrave* after the death of Capt. Yonge; shipwrecked on Madagascar, 1701.

Preston, Mrs. *Grandison* I 189. Lady in New Bond St. who reports that Mr. Greville has not left town as he was supposed to do.

Price, Mr. *Life of Sheppard* XVI 177. Constable in St. Giles's parish to whom Sykes betrays Sheppard.

Prichard, William. *Gulliver* Part I chap. 1. Captain of the *Antelope*, the ship in which Gulliver travels to Lilliput.

Pride. *Battle* I 153. Mother of Criticism.

Prince, black. *Singleton* VI 64. Captured by the pirates; becomes their slave and guide through the heart of Africa.

Prince de _____ (in *Roxana*). See "Clerac, Count de."

Pritchard. *Clarissa* IV 246. Lord M.'s steward.

Pro, John. *Drury* 296, *Pirates* 503. A Dutchman, one of the castaway white men from the island of St. Mary's.

Punt. *Pirates* 462. Dutch merchant at Cochin; persuades Malpa not to trade with Bowen's pirate crew.

Purefoy, Robert. *Gulliver* Part IV chap. 1. Ironically-named surgeon on board the *Adventure*.

Purney, Mr. *Life of Sheppard* XVI 198, *Sheppard's Narrative* XVI 231. Ordinary of Newgate (clergyman on the staff).

Purser, William (called "William Poser" by the blacks). *Drury* 240, 293. English-speaking Negro at St. Augustine's Bay; acts as interpreter for Drury, who has forgotten his native tongue.

Quaker lady ("the Quakeress"). *Roxana* XIII 28. Landlady and friend of Roxana's who puts her to bed with her Dutch merchant and tells white lies to shield her from Susan.

"Quaker William" (in *Singleton*). See Walters, William.

"Queen, the" (Henrietta Maria of England). *Cavalier* V 157. Consort of Charles I; sends military supplies from France.

Quilt. *Life of Sheppard* XVI 182. Domestic servant of Jonathan Wild; captures Sheppard.

"Quinbus Flestrin" (in *Gulliver*). See Gulliver, Capt. Lemuel.

Rachel. *Pamela* I 75, IV 206. Maid in Bedfordshire, jealous of Pamela; wants Mr. Andrews brought into the house right away when he comes seeking his daughter.

Rachel. *Plague Year* IX 126. Wife of the waterman of Blackwall Stairs; she is already sick of the plague; see Robert.

Rackam, John (alias "Calico Jack"). *Pirates* 138. Succeeds Vane as commander of the pirate crew; in love with Anne Bonny; captured and hanged on Hispaniola.

Ramos, Gen. *Carleton* 52. Ally of the English, left by Peterborough in command of Denia.

Ramsey, Harry. *Pirates* 396. Master of an English privateer, surprised and boarded by Misson.

Ramsey, Sir James. *Cavalier* V 74. Leads a party of Scots in an attack on the Marienburg at Würzburg.

Ramsey, Commissary-Gen. *Cavalier* V 176. Scot in command of the Parliamentary forces left at Edgehill, 1642.

Ravillac (Ravaillac, François, 1578-1610). *Tale* sect. IX. Assassin who stabbed Henry IV of France in his coach.

Rawlins, Miss. *Clarissa* V 72. Prude lodging near Mrs. Moore, consulted by the neighbors on all important undertakings.

Rawlins, Mr. *Clarissa* V 90. Brother of above; behaves with impertinent curiosity toward Lovelace.

Rawlins, the Mr. (two brothers). *Sheppard's Narrative* XVI 230. Pawnbrokers in Drury Lane into whose shop Sheppard breaks.

Read, Mary. *Pirates* 153. Woman pirate with Rackam; dies of jail fever.

Read, Robert. *Gow* XVI 339. Young man forcibly brought along with the pirates; escapes from them in the Orkneys.

Read, Thomas. *Pirates* 99. Master of the sloop *Fortune*, captured by Bonnet, 1718.

Read, Mr. *Pirates* 153. Husband of Mary Read's mother; she passes Mary off as her son by him.

Read, Mrs. *Pirates* 153. Mary Read's mother, who raises her as a boy.

Reay, Lord. *Cavalier* V 52. Friend of the Cavalier in the Swedish army.

Redding, George. *Pirates* 634. Pirate who mercifully equips Turnley and the other castaways with a tinder box.

"Redhand, Capt." (in *King*). See Nichols.

Reeves, Archibald. *Grandison* I 27. Harriet's cousin; takes her to London with him.

Reeves, Mrs. *Grandison* I 1. Wife of above.

Regiomontanus (Latin name of Johann Muller, 1436-1476). *Battle* I 152. German mathematician and astronomer; commander of the modern engineers.

Reldresal. *Gulliver* Part I chap. 3. Principal Secretary for Private Affairs in Lilliput, Gulliver's friend at court.

Reresby, Lord. *Grandison* V 361. Irish lord; marries Lucy Selby.

Rhet, Col. William. *Pirates* 99. Receives the commission of the governor of South Carolina to hunt down Stede Bonnet, 1718.

Rhinegrave, the. *Cavalier* V 126. Hastens to relieve the Protestants at the Battle of Nordlingen.

Richard. *Grandison* III 121, 332. Servant at Sir Charles's house in St. James's Square.

Richard. *Pamela* II 317. Servant of Mr. B. in Bedfordshire.

Richard. *Plague Year* IX 66. A joiner, one of the three brothers who escape from the city; lives near Shadwell in Stepney; See John and Thomas.

Richards, John. *Pirates* 217. Master of the *Phoenix*, captured by Roberts, 1720.

Richards, Gen. *Carleton* 157. English officer blown up by a mine at the siege of Alicant.

Richards. *Pirates* 72. Pirate, set in command of a sloop captured by Blackbeard, 1718.

Richards. *Pirates* 136. Master of a sloop from "Curacoa" (Curaçao), captured by Vane, 1718.

Richardson, Capt. *Farther Adventures* II 285. Scot who helps Crusoe destroy the idol at Cham-chi-Thaungo near Tobolsk, Russia.

Richelieu, Cardinal. *Cavalier* V 9. Virtual ruler of France at the time of the Cavalier's visit, 1630.

Risburg, Marquis of. *Carleton* 70. Spanish defender of Monjouick (near Barcelona) at the time of Peterborough's surprise attack, 1705.

Rivers, Earl. *Campbell* IV 151. Happens to be looking out a window when his servants accost the fleeing Duncan.

Rivet, Col. *Carleton* 42. Officer who arrests Blackburn during the Assassination Plot, 1696.

Roach, Capt. *Pirates* 323. Master of a French vessel captured by Low after leaving Lisbon, 1722.

Robert (Robin). *Clarissa* I 56. Anna's servant; carries letters to and from Clarissa's house.

Robert. *Plague Year* IX 121. Waterman at Blackwall Stairs; has remained in London during the plague because of his wife and two small children; see Rachel.

Roberts, Bartholomew. *Pirates* 6. Succeeds Howel Davis as Pirate captain, raids the coast of Africa, killed in battle on board the *Ranger*, 1722.

Roberts, Mr. *Grandison* V 361. Wedding guest, admirer of Miss Barclay.

Robin, Black. *Pirates* 298. Negro commanding a sloop from Philadelphia, captured by Worley, 1718.

Robin (in *Clarissa*). See Robert.

Robin. *Drury* 94. White slave of the blacks in Anterndroea.

Robin. *Drury* 231. English-speaking Negro; swims ashore from Capt. Burgess' ship to join Arnold on Madagascar.

Robin. *Moll* VII 15. Younger brother of the rich family where Moll (as "Mrs. Betty") is a servant; eventually becomes her first husband.

Robin (in *Jacque*). See Will.

Robin ("Bedfordshire Robin"). *Pamela* I 131. Coachman; parts from Pamela with tears in his eyes.

Robin (or Robert; "Lincolnshire Robin"). *Pamela* I 115. Accomplice of Mr. B. who spirits Pamela off to his other estate rather than carrying her to her parents' house.

Robins, Mr. *Life of Sheppard* XVI 194. The city smith; Sheppard commends his work as worthy of an escape artist like himself.

Robinson, William. *Gulliver* Part III chap. 1. Master of the *Hopewell*, Gulliver's ship in his third voyage.

Robinson, Mrs. *Clarissa* IV 167. Has a ridiculous grotto with a statue of Neptune in it.

Robinson. *Crusoe* I 298. A mutineer who yields to the captain.

Roch (or Roche), Philip (alias John Eustace). *Pirates* 372. Irish pirate; murders a crew of Frenchmen and then "goes on the account."

Rodrigues. *Pirates* 326. Master of the *Nostra Signora de Victoria*, captured by Low; has his lips cut off and broiled before his face, 1722 (name included in first edition, omitted from the fourth).

Roger. *Pamela* II 317. Servant of Mr. B. in Bedfordshire.

Rogers, Woodes (Sr.). *Pirates* 595. Captures John Cornelius in Trinity Harbor, Newfoundland.

Rogers, Capt. Woodes. *Pirates* 39. Governor of the Bahamas; cleans out pirate colony on Providence Island, 1718.

Rogers, Capt. *Pirates* 215. Master of a galley sent out to capture Roberts, 1717.

Rogers, Mr. *Farther Adventures* II 31. Bristol relation of the starving youth from the disabled ship, to whom a bill of lading for eleven hogsheads of sugar is sent.

Rogers. *Clarissa* VI 209. Young farmer who unwittingly gives up Anna's letter to the widow Bevis, thinking she is Clarissa.

Rolls, Capt. *Pirates* 271. Allegedly forced Scudamore to join Roberts' pirate crew.

Ronquillo, Don. *Carleton* 190. Official at Madrid, to whom the corregidor complains of Carleton's behavior in the Brennan affair.

"Rosebud" (real name Betsy, but always called Rosebud). *Clarissa* I 250. Maid at the White Hart whose virtue Lovelace spares in order to enhance his reputation.

Rossiter, Col. *Cavalier* V 254. Attacks the Parliamentary forces on their way to relieve Newark, 1645.

Rounsivil, George. *Pirates* 640. Reprieved from execution, 1718; goes back to perish with his captain on board a sinking ship.

Rouse, Mr. *Sheppard's Narrative* XVI 223. Newgate jailer to whom Sheppard demonstrates his art of slipping out of chains.

Rowland, Mr. *Clarissa* VI 277. Bailiff who arrests Clarissa for debt.

Rowland, Mrs. *Clarissa* VI 285. The bailiff's wife; encourages Clarissa to eat.

Rowling, Charles. *Pirates* 139. Master of the *Pearl*, captured by Rackam, 1718.

Rowlinson. *Gow* XVI 293. One of the mutiny conspirators, executed.

Rowry, Mr. *Pirates* 371. Master of an English vessel seized by her crew off the coast of Africa.

Roxana (referred to only on the title page as Mlle. Beleau and the Countess de Wintselsheim; apparently her real name is Susan, XIII 21). *Roxana* XII 1. Woman of French descent; after an extravagant and wicked life, she is hounded by her own daughter, Susan.

Roy'nsowra. *Drury* 112. One of Drury's fellow cattle herders working for Deaan Mevarrow.

Rue, Mr. de la. *Carleton* 41. One of the conspirators in the Assassination Plot, 1696.

Rupert, Prince. *Cavalier* V 163. Nephew of Charles I and his chief cavalry commander; habitually throws victories away by his impetuous behavior.

Russel, Charles. *Pirates* 304. Master of the *Gambia Castle*, in which Lowther ships for Africa, 1721.

Rutland, Stephen. *Singleton* VI 277. Companion of young Robert Knox in Ceylon; escapes with him back to civilization.

Ruyter, De. *Carleton* 1. Dutch admiral at the Battle of Sole Bay, 1672.

S., Lady Anne. *Grandison* II 150. Only daughter of the Earl of S.; the Grandison girls hope Sir Charles will marry her.

S., Dr. *Clarissa* VI 60. Lovelace takes him to Berkshire to treat Lord M.'s gout.

S., Lord. *Pamela* III 169. Agrees to have Mr. B. made a baronet in response to Lord Davers's request.

Saddler, the (in *Plague Year*). See F., H.

Sadlier, Betsy. *Clarissa* VI 253. Agreeable daughter of Lady Sarah; she dies an untimely death.

Sadlier, Lady Sarah. *Clarissa* I 7. Lord M.'s half sister, from whom Lovelace has great expectations; see Lawrance, Lady Betty.

St. John, Lord. *Cavalier* V 176. Parliamentary commander captured at Edgehill, 1642.

Sale, Mr. *Pirates* 543. Purser of the *Albemarle*; thrown to wild animals at Magadoxa, 1700.

Sally. *Grandison* I 26, VI 91. One of Harriet's servants in town and at Grandison Hall.

Salmonet, Capt. *Grandison* II 304. A bully who speaks broken English, married to Mrs. O'Hara's sister.

Salter, Col. *Carleton* 209. Gen. Stanhope's secretary, in hiding because of an amour with a Spanish woman.

Salter, Col. *Clarissa* VIII 36. Man who treats Mrs. Sinclair to too much punch, causing her to fall and break her leg.

Sam. *Drury* 48, 53. English castaway at Cape St. Ann; tells the story of the Steward-Drummond party to Drury and his friends.

Sambo, Deaan. *Drury* 83. Brother of Drury's master, Deaan Mevarrow.

Sambo. *Drury* 254. Slave given to Rer Befaugher to compensate him for Drury's disappearance from the army.

Sambre, Mrs. *Clarissa* VII 205. Belton's sister; he leaves her some money invested in the funds.

Samuel, King (in *Drury*). See Tuley-Noro, Deaan.

Sanderson, young widow. *Clarissa* VI 369. Drowns herself when slighted by a younger brother of a noble family.

Sandwich, Earl of. *Carleton* 2. English naval officer; killed at Battle of Sole Bay, 1672.

Sandys, Col. *Cavalier* V 163. Parliamentary commander who attacks Sir John Byron at Worcester; routed by Prince Rupert and killed, 1642.

Sarah, Mrs. *Grandison* I 184. Housekeeper of the Reeves.

Sarah. *Life of Sheppard* XVI 205. Young woman in prison with both eyes beaten black and blue.

Saunders, Richard. *Grandison* II 223. Servant used to carry letters.

Saunders, Capt. *Pirates* 64. Master of the galley *Berkley*, plundered by Martel, 1716.

Savage, Miss. *Clarissa* VI 369. Marries her mother's coachman because she was refused a trip to Wales.

Savoy, Duke of. *Cavalier* V 18. Lays siege to Montferrat, 1630.

Savoy, Duke of. *Carleton* 109, *Jacque* XI 18. Peterborough is sent to his aid, 1706; opposes the French army in which Jack is serving, 1701.

Saxe-Weimar, Duke of. *Cavalier* V 104. Left to guard Ulm and Meningen by Gustavus Adolphus, 1632.

Saxon, Mr. *Campbell* IV 102. Duncan announces clairvoyantly that his wife is to inherit a house in Kent with four trees around it.

Saxon, Mrs. *Campbell* IV 200. Duncan tells her what became of her six pounds' worth of Flanders lace.

Saxony, Elector of. *Cavalier* V 36. Protestant prince allied with Gustavus Adolphus, 1631.

Say, Lord. *Cavalier* V 163. Parliamentary commander at Oxford, 1642.

Scaliger (Joseph Justus, 1540-1609). *Battle* I 161. Son of the famous Renaissance critic; rebukes Bentley for presuming to claim the armor of every foe he slays (that is, a critic is of less stature than the author he criticizes).

Schomberg, Duke. *Carleton* 19. Comes to relieve Maestrich at the head of the French troops, 1676.

Schomberg, Duke. *Cavalier* V 20. Commands the Imperial forces at Genoa, 1630.

Scollary. *Gow* XVI 327. Master of a vessel near Calf Island, in Scotland; allows himself to be held as a guarantee for Gow's safety.

Scot, Capt. *Pirates* 95. Master of the *Endeavor*, captured by Bonnet, 1717.

Scot. *Pirates* 325. Master of a ship from Liverpool, captured by Low, 1722.

Scudamore, Peter. *Pirates* 247. Surgeon of Roberts' crew; plans an uprising among the blacks; pious at his execution.

Seabright. *Narrative* XVI 153. One of the murdered English gentlemen.

Secretarius. *Campbell* IV 99. Young man on whom Christallina has set her heart.

Sedley, Mr. *Pamela* III 379. A rake, friend of Sir Charles Hargrave, who drops in to see Mr. B.

Seigensius, Dr. *Cavalier* V 37. Lutheran minister who draws up the Conclusions of Leipzig, the Protestant treaty of unity, 1631.

Selby, George. *Grandison* I 2. Harriet's uncle, affectionately severe with her.

Selby, James. *Grandison* III 51. The Selbys' son, in love with Emily Jervois.

Selby, Lucy. *Grandison* I 1. The Selbys' niece, Harriet's intimate friend; marries Lord Reresby.

Selby, Marianne. *Grandison* I 2. Sister of Harriet's father, wife of George.

Selby, Nancy. *Grandison* I 14. Mrs. Selby's niece, Lucy's sister; is "weak and low" at the opening of the novel.

Selby, Aunt. *Grandison* I 2. Sister of Harriet's father.

Selby, Grandmother. *Grandison* I 2. Lucy's grandmother, pleased with Mr. Greville's chatter.

Sexton in Aldgate Church. *Plague Year* IX 69. Allows the saddler in to see the great burial pit.

Seymour, Sir Edward (1633-1708). *Tale* sect. IX. Tory Speaker of the House; invited to use Bedlam as a recruiting source for talented personnel; see How and Musgrave.

Sforza, Signora Juliana. *Grandison* III 179. Sister of the Marchesa della Porretta; a widow, mother of Signora Laurana.

Sforza, Signora Laurana. *Grandison* III 179. Clementina's cousin; torments her in a strait jacket; finally commits suicide.

Sharp, Bat. *King* XVI 9. Privateer captain with whom Avery sails.

Sharp, Capt. John. *Pirates* 274. Master of the *Elizabeth*, prominent witness in the trial of Roberts' crew, 1722.

Shattock, John. *Pirates* 138. Master of a brigantine from Jamaica, captured by Vane, 1718.

Shelbourne, Anne. *Clarissa* VII 385. Clarissa's nurse in her final illness.

Sheppard, John. *Life of Sheppard* XVI 173, *Sheppard's Narrative* XVI 213, *Street-Robbers* XVI 359. Notorious London thief and escape artist; executed, 1724.

Sherwood, Jerry. *Pamela* III 332. Steward of Sir Jacob Swynford, taken on as an act of charity.

Shirley, Henrietta ("Grandmother Shirley"). *Grandison* I 308. Harriet's grandmother, tearfully revered throughout the novel.

Shivers, Capt. Richard. *Pirates* 517. Pirate master of the *Soldado*; joins forces with North to plunder the Moors, 1695.

Shorey. *Clarissa* I 102. Mrs. Harlowe's maid.

Shorter, Mr. *Pamela* I 219. Mr. B.'s attorney; has Parson Williams thrown in jail for debt.

Shovel, Cloudsley. *Carleton* 51. Commands the English fleet that carries Peterborough's expeditionary force to Spain.

Shubander, the. *Pirates* 544. Prince of Magadoxa; promises the Englishmen a present if they will visit him.

Sidney, Mr. *Pamela* III 253. Servant of Lord Davers.

Simmonds, Mr. *Pamela* III 351. Surgeon whom Pamela engages to help her sick neighbors.

Simon, Father. *Farther Adventures* II 246. Jolly French missionary at Quinchang and at the Imperial Court of China.

Simpkins. *Pirates* 325. Master of a sloop captured by Low, 1722.

Simpson (alias "Sim. Tugmutton"). *Pirates* 235, 286. When he is led out to be executed, he recognizes a woman in the crowd and shouts that he "had lain with that bitch three times."

Sims, John. *Pirates* 638. Sent by Gov. Rogers with a ship to rescue Turnley, Carr, and the others from Green Key.

"Sinclair, Mrs. Magadalen" ("Widow Sinclair," "Mamma Sinclair," alias "Aunt Forbes"). *Clarissa* III 201. Assumed name of the madam in whose house Clarissa is raped.

Singleton, Capt. Bob. *Singleton* VI 1. Hero of the trek through Africa; kidnapped as a child of two and raised at sea.

Singleton, Capt. *Clarissa* III 202, 231. Employed by James to carry Clarissa off to Hull or Leith; never enters the action.

Singleton, Mr. *Grandison* I 57. Simple-minded but harmless gentleman; laughs at all Sir Hargrave's jokes.

Sister of William Walters. *Singleton* VI 311. Widow with five children; keeps a shop in the Minories; Singleton finally marries her.

Skiff, Nathan. *Pirates* 333. Skipper of a whaler out of Nantucket; tortured and shot by Low's crew, 1723.

Skinner, Capt. *Pirates* 115. Master of the snow *Cadogan*, captured and murdered by the pirate crew of Edward England, 1717.

Skippon, "brave old." *Cavalier* V 267. Parliamentary commander near Exeter, 1644.

Skymmington, Mrs. Tabitha. *Life of Sheppard* XVI 209. Sheppard hides out with her in Hammersmith.

Skyrme (or Skyrm). *Pirates* 241. Commands the Royal Fortune in the fight with the *Swallow*; loses a leg and fights on with only the stump.

Slanning, Sir Nicholas. *Cavalier* V 161. Royal partisan in Cornwall, 1642.

"Sloane, Capt." (in *Clarissa*). See Belford, John.

Slunt. *Carleton* 149. Englishman refused a Christian burial by the Spaniards because he is a heretic.

Smith, John. *Clarissa* VI 116. Glovemaker in King St., Covent Garden, who takes Clarissa in after her second escape.

Smith, John. *Pamela* III 354. Breaks a leg while thatching a barn; aided by Pamela's charity.

Smith, Tom. *Crusoe* I 298. One of the mutineers.

Smith, Capt. *Cavalier* V 174. Retrieves the king's standard at Edgehill, 1642.

Smith, Mrs. *Clarissa* VI 212. Wife of the glovemaker, plain-hearted and prudent.

Smith, Mrs., of Kentish Town. *Jacque* X 72. Robbed by Jack on her way home; he later has a guilty conscience and returns the money.

Snelgrove. *King* XVI 41. Shipwright; sells the *Griffin* to Avery.

Solcombe, Col. *Clarissa* III 344. Gentleman who gives a party that Sally Martin and Polly Horton must attend.

Solgard, Capt. Peter. *Pirates* 331. Master of the *Greyhound*, which captures the *Ranger*, commanded by Harris, 1723.

(Solmes), Sir Oliver. *Clarissa* I 62, 128. Roger Solmes's grasping predecessor.

Solmes, Roger. *Clarissa* I 46. Admirer of Clarissa, favored by her family; a tyrant and miser.

Solmes, Count. *Carleton* 8. Carleton serves in his regiment in the Low Countries.

Somerville, John. *Gow* XVI 300. Gentleman from Port Patrick, master of a ship out of Glasgow.

Somner, Mr. *Grandison* I 21. An affected gentleman who despises the female sex; has recently married a rich widow.

Sorlings, Betty. *Clarissa* III 65. Older daughter of the farm family; Lovelace flirts with her.

Sorlings, Miss. *Clarissa* III 65. Younger daughter of the family.

Sorlings, Mrs. *Clarissa* III 23. Sister of Mrs. Greme; owns a farmhouse near The Lawn in Hampshire where Lovelace and Clarissa stay.

Souches, Count. *Carleton* 13. Ally of the Prince of Orange whose sluggishness obliges the Prince to raise the siege of Oudenarde.

Southwell, Col. *Carleton* 66. One of Peterborough's subordinates during the attack on Monjouick, 1705.

Sparr, Maj. Gen. *Cavalier* V 111. Sent with six thousand men to cut off the Cavalier's retreat, 1632.

Spartivento. *Voyage* XIV 28. The captain's Negro cabin boy; overhears the mutiny plans.

Spencer, Col. *Cavalier* V 205. Commands regiment of royalist cavalry quartered at Cirencester, 1643.

Spenlow, Thomas. *Pirates* 150. Master of a sloop captured off Hispaniola by Rackam, 1720.

Spezuter, Col. *Cavalier* V 116. The Cavalier's captor while he is a prisoner of war at Neustadt, near Coburg Castle.

Spilsworth, the two cousins. *Clarissa* VII 358. Relations who come to visit Mrs. Howe when she is ill.

Spinckes, Jack. *Pirates* 588. Undergoes a mock trial on board Bellamy's ship the *Whidaw*; a drunken gunner mistakes the trial for the real thing.

Spindelow. *Narrative* XVI 97. Mr. Seabright's servant, seriously
wounded by the French brigands.

Spinola, Marquis. *Cavalier* V 26. Spaniard besieging Casale, 1630.

Spotswood, Alexander. *Pirates* 77. Governor of Virginia; issues
proclamation for the arrest of Blackbeard, 1718.

Sprage. *Carleton* 1. Master of the *London*, on which Carleton sails
to fight the Dutch, 1674.

Spriggs, Capt. Francis. *Pirates* 352. Splits off from Low's gang;
notoriously cruel to prisoners; driven ashore in the Florida
swamps by the man-of-war *Spence*.

Spurrier, Mr. *Clarissa* V 105. Steward of Lady Betty Lawrance.

Stanhope, Gen. *Carleton* 58. Chief lieutenant of Peterborough at
Barcelona; annihilated at Breuhiga.

Stanny, Richard. *Pirates* 315. Master of the *John and Elizabeth*, captured by Lowther, 1723.

Staples. *Pirates* 325. Master of a sloop captured by Low, 1722.

Stapleton, Sir Philip. *Cavalier* V 173. Commands Essex's guards
in the Parliamentary army at Edgehill, 1642.

Stapylton, Miss. *Pamela* IV 403. Flirtatious young lady of eighteen,
given to reading romantic fiction.

Staremberg, Gen. *Carleton* 170. Imperial commander at Villa Viciosa,
Spain.

Stedman. *Clarissa* V 303. Lady Betty Lawrance's solicitor in her
chancery affair.

Steel, John. *Drury* 40. Cousin of Drury's at Bengal; works for the
New East India Company.

Steele, Mr. *Grandison* V 361. Wedding guest from Northampton.

"Stella." *Clarissa* III 308. Former mistress of Lovelace, recipient of
his verses on the joys of cohabitation.

Stephens, Mrs. Anne. *Campbell* IV 188. Lives in Spitalfields; has a
vision of a corpse in her living room.

Stephenson, Capt. *Pirates* 336. Master of the *Squirrel*, captured by
Low near the coast of Guinea, 1723.

Stephenson. *Pirates* 243. Member of Roberts' crew; discovers
the captain shot through the throat with grapeshot.

Stetham, Katherine. *Wild* XVI 273. Woman testifying against Wild
at his trial.

Stevens, Miss. *Grandison* I 22. Daughter of Col. Stevens; well read,
but makes no parade of learning.

Steward, Capt. *Drury* 49. Companion of Capt. Drummond; set
ashore at Mattatan Roads on Madagascar by pirates.

Stiffrump, Alderman. *Campbell* IV 100. Beloved by Urbana, who inquires of Duncan whether or not she will obtain him.

Stradling, Sir Edward. *Cavalier* V 176. Cavalier killed at Edgehill, 1642.

Strafford, Earl of. *Cavalier* V 152. Commander of the royal forces at York; attainted and executed by the Long Parliament, 1641.

Strahan, Mr. *Drury* 299. Surgeon on board the *Drake*; accompanies Capt. Mackey to the natives' town.

Stuart, George. *Pamela* IV 8. Learned Scottish gentleman Mr. B. met on his travels; has a very shy nephew.

Summers, Will. *Clarissa* III 58. Lovelace's servant and factotum; lacks teeth because of a blow from his master.

Sun, Isaac. *Pirates* 240. Lieutenant on board the *Swallow*; testifies against Roberts' crew, 1722.

Susan. *Farther Adventures* II 25. Maid on the disabled ship; marries Crusoe's Jack-of-all-trades.

Susan. *Roxana* XII 15, XIII 21. Maid in Roxana's household who turns out to be her long-lost daughter.

Sutor, Archibald. *Gow* XVI 339. Farmer to whom Robert Read makes his escape from the pirates.

Sutton, Miss. *Pamela* IV 407. Young lady too much given to witty sallies but not severe enough in her disapproval of rakes.

Sutton, Thomas. *Pirates* 246. Member of Roberts' crew who signs the waggish name of "Aaron Whifflingpin" to a receipt for the extortion money.

Swanton, Elizabeth. *Clarissa* VIII 124. One of the three witnesses to Clarissa's will.

Sweetapple, Sir John. *Jacque* X 66. Goldsmith between Gracechurch St. and Lombard St., where Will and Jack stage a robbery.

Swynford, Dolly. *Pamela* III 322. Daughter of Sir Jacob.

Swynford, Sir Jacob. *Pamela* III 267. Crusty old relative of Mr. B.'s father, inclined to disapprove of Pamela.

Swynford, Judy. *Pamela* IV 283. Sir Jacob's sister; pretends to be younger than she is.

Swynford, Mab. *Pamela* III 322. Daughter of Sir Jacob; plays the harpsichord.

Syburg, Col. *Carleton* 158. Despite the warnings of the Spanish besiegers, he persuades the English to remain in the castle at Alicant; as a result, the mine destroys them all.

Sykes, James (alias "Hell and Fury"). *Life of Sheppard* XVI 176. London chairman and robber.

Sylvester, Mr. *Grandison* II 246. Honest attorney for Mr. Danby.

Symmes, Edward. *Clarissa* I 27. Brother of Clarissa's former suitor; the fight between James and Lovelace takes place at his house.

Symmes, Mr. *Clarissa* I 27. Former suitor of Clarissa; see Wyerley, Alexander.

Sympson, Richard. *Gulliver* Letter to Sympson. Gulliver's cousin and his agent for the publication of his travels.

Tarlton, John. *Pirates* 275. George Wilson's captain before Wilson defects to the pirates, 1722.

Tarlton, Thomas. *Pirates* 275. Brother of above; captured by Roberts and savagely beaten at Wilson's instigation.

Tartoue, Peter. *Pirates* 373. Frenchman who charters Roche's ship to Nantes; murdered and thrown over the side.

Tasso, Torquato (1544-1595). *Battle* I 152, *Campbell* IV 77. Italian epic poet; modern cavalry commander in Swift's satire; had visionary experiences, according to Defoe.

Teach, Edward (alias Edward Thatch, called "Blackbeard"). *Pirates* 41. Blockades Charleston Harbor; ousts Bonnet from his command; killed by Lieut. Maynard at Ocracoke Inlet, 1718.

Temple, Sir William (1628-1699). *Battle* I 147. Swift's patron, a famous diplomat and essayist; his works are shelved with the moderns but desert to the side of the ancients.

Termerre, Deaan. *Drury* 126. Former enemy of Deaan Mevarrow (Drury's master), aided by Deaan Murnanzack.

Terry, Mr. *Drury* 294. Friend of Drury's father and agent for his rescue from Madagascar.

Tesse (Thesse), Count de. *Carleton* 90, *Jacque* XI 45. French commander in Spain, 1706; in Savoy, 1701.

Tew, Capt. Thomas. *Pirates* 58, 419. Joins Misson's colony of Libertalia; killed by a cannon shot near the Red Sea, 1696.

Thoiras. *Cavaliar* V 20. Commands the French garrison of Montferrat, 1630.

Tholouse, Count de. *Carleton* 97. French admiral; the English fleet drives him away from relieving Barcelona, 1705.

Thomas, Capt. *Pirates* 217. Master of a brigantine captured by Roberts, 1720.

"Thomas, Mrs." *Clarissa* IV 146. Assumed name of Tony Jenyns's mistress.

Thomas, Mrs. *Pamela* IV 116. Assistant midwife for Pamela in London at the birth of Billy.

Thomas ("Tom"). *Pamela* II 13. Mr. B.'s Lincolnshire groom, robs Mr. Williams at the instigation of Mrs. Jewkes.

Thomas. *Plague Year* IX 66. Former sailor who walks with a limp, now a sailmaker in Wapping; richest of the three brothers who strike out into the country; see John and Richard.

Thomas. *Singleton* VI 299. Boatswain on board Singleton's pirate ship.

Thomasine. *Clarissa* IV 131. Belton's perfidious mistress; has been carrying on for years with her father's hostler.

Thompson, Capt. *Pirates* 100, 136. Man whose Negroes are stolen by the pirate Vane but restored by Yeats when Yeats accepts the king's pardon.

"Thompson, Goody." *Cavalier* V 232. Joke name for one of the Cavaliers fleeing from Marston Moor disguised as a woman.

Thompson, Mr. *Clarissa* V 36. Poor parish schoolmaster over seventy; lives five miles from Uncle Harlowe.

Thompson, Mr. *Farther Adventures* II 217. Crusoe's mate on his voyage to Siam to obtain rice.

Thomson, Goodman. *Cavalier* V 229. Farmer whom the Cavalier robs after Marston Moor, thinking he is a Parliamentary sympathizer.

Thornbury, William ("Will"). *Drury* 263. White slave of Rer Trimmonongarevo; forgets about Drury as soon as he makes his own escape.

Tidman, Mr. *Wild* XVI 275. Corn chandler in Giltspur St.; has a pocketbook stolen with a banknote for £116.

Tilly, Count. *Cavalier* V 43. Commander of the Imperial forces in the Thirty Years' War; destroys Magdeburg, is killed resisting the Swedish attempt to ford the Lech, 1632.

Tilyard, Maj. Gen. *Cavalier* V 221. Cavalier captured at Marston Moor, 1644.

Time. *Tale* Epistle Dedicatory. Malignant deity who destroys the works of modern authors; governor of Prince Posterity.

Tisdell, Hosea. *Pirates* 148. Tavern keeper at Jamaica; Rackam entrusts a captured ship to him.

Titus. *Clarissa* III 245. Joseph Leman's Nottinghamshire cousin, a witness in Lovelace's affair with Miss Betterton.

Tiviot, Earl of (in *Carleton*). See Levingston, Sir Thomas.

Toakeoffu (or Toakoffu), Deaan ("King Dick" or "Long Dick").

Drury 267, 296n. King of Munnongaro or Masseelege.

Toby. *Drury* 230. Black slave serving Eglasse, the Dutchman, having escaped from Capt. Burgess.

Toler, Toland. *Campbell* IV 205. Lawyer involved in the incident of Mr. Saxon's house at Sevenoaks, Kent.

Tolson, Mr. *Grandison* I 40. Old bachelor in Derbyshire with strict stipulations for his future mate, all of which his eventual bride violates; see Turner, Mrs.

Tom. *Jacque* X 74. Manservant who gets drunk and spoils the chances of the gang for a housebreaking in Chelsea.

Tom. *Voyage* XIV 40. Crewman who joins the captain's side during the mutiny after being spoken kindly to by him.

Tomkins, Mr. *Clarissa* VII 118 (VIII 225, spelled "Tompkins"). Deceased clergyman-friend of Clarissa's.

Tomkins. *Clarissa* V 36. Day laborer living four miles from Uncle Harlowe.

Tomlins, Miss. *Pamela* II 319. Heiress proposed as wife for Mr. B.; has too masculine an air.

"Tomlinson, Capt. Antony" (in *Clarissa*). See McDonald, Patrick.

Tommy. *Pamela* I 131. Scullion at Mr. B.'s in Bedfordshire.

Torres, Conde de los. *Carleton* 82. Besieges Santo Mattheo; tricked by Peterborough into withdrawing, 1705.

Tortenson. *Cavalier* V 113. Swedish colonel captured at the Battle of Altemberg.

Tour, F. J. de la. *Clarissa* VIII 248. Lovelace's traveling valet; writes the letter announcing his death to Belford.

Tourville, James. *Clarissa* I 220. Friend of Lovelace from Nottinghamshire, "so fair and so foppish"; introduces French and Italian words constantly into the "beastly English."

Towers, Lady. *Pamela* I 59. Maiden lady, "called a wit"; makes fun of Pamela, formerly flirted with 'Squire Martin.

Towlerpherangha, Rer (in *Drury*). See Vove, Rer.

Townsend, Mrs. *Clarissa* IV 162. Friend of Anna's who deals in contraband fabrics; Clarissa can hide out with her.

Trahern, Capt. Joseph. *Pirates* 231. Master of the *King Solomon*, attacked by Roberts, 1721.

Trengrove, Elizabeth. *Pirates* 266. Passenger in the *Onslow*; testifies in favor of Harry Glasby, 1722.

Trengrove, Capt. *Pirates* 267. Testifies in favor of Glasby, 1722.

Trevor, Capt. *Pirates* 399. Captain of the man of war *Severn*, almost fired on by mistake by the *Kingston*.

Trimmonongarevo, Rer (in *Pirates* spelled Timanangarivo). *Drury* 221, *Pirates* 602. Arrogant and arbitrary king of the Saccalauvors; threatens to kill Drury for conspiring to steal the slave Francisco.

Trodaughe, Deaan. *Drury* 87. A prince of Anterndroea, where Drury is first enslaved.

Trongha, Deaan. *Drury* 192. Nephew of Rer Vovvern; commands the army of the Feraighners; Drury's protector.

Trortrock, Rer. *Drury* 165. First native king to the north of Anterndroea.

Trot, Nicholas. *Pirates* 103. Judge before whom Bonnet is tried in Charleston, 1718.

Tucker, Capt. *Pirates* 593. Commander of a brigantine of ten guns at the Bay of Campeachy; wants to give battle to William Lewis.

Tuckerman. *Pirates* 185. Master of a pirate vessel; visits Roberts at Hispaniola, 1721.

Tufton, Col. *Carleton* 25. Must relinquish his regimental command when he refuses to swear allegiance to William III, 1689.

"Tugmutton, Sim." (in *Pirates*). See Simpson.

Tuley-Noro, Deaan ("King Samuel"). *Drury* 93. Frenchman who by an accident of fate has become a native king in Antenosa, Madagascar; demands satisfaction from Deaan Crindo for murdering white people.

"Turn Joe." *Pirates* 637. Spanish privateer who formerly worked for the English; smashes Phineas Bunce's attack.

Turner, Sir William. *Grandison* VI 37. One of Sir Charles's neighbors at Grandison Hall.

Turner, Sir William. *Jacque* X 12. Alderman and president of Bridewell; lectures Capt. Jack on his evil ways while watching him being whipped.

Turner, Mr. *Pamela* IV 6. Lawyer of Gray's Inn; makes Pamela insincere frothy compliments when she comes to town.

Turner, Mrs. *Grandison* I 40. Laughs constantly, has disagreeable red hair; marries Mr. Tolson, who hates red hair.

Turnley, Richard. *Pirates* 625. Seaman hated by Rackam and Anne Bonny; marooned by Bunce and Macarty on Green Key, 1718.

"Tutor, my." *Jacque* X 183. Transported felon who teaches Jack Christian doctrine and Latin; later becomes his sotweed factor.

Tyzard, Capt. *Pirates* 115. Master of the *Pearl*, captured by Capt. England, 1717.

Unghorray, Deaan. *Drury* 243. God of the Malagasy religion.

Unter Morrow Cheruck. *Drury* 306. Madagascar king from whom Deaan Morroughsevea hopes to capture slaves to sell to Drury, 1719.

Upton, Anthony. *Life of Sheppard* XVI 185. Rogue condemned to be executed along with Sheppard, 1724.

Upton, Dr. *Plague Year* IX 37. Listed as one of three reputable London physicians, 1665.

Urbana. *Campbell* IV 97. A young widow who asks Duncan's help in finding a mate.

Ursini, Princess of. *Carleton* 206. Powerful figure at the Spanish court, 1713; later betrayed by Alberoni.

Valasco, Don. *Carleton* 75. Harsh Spanish governor of Barcelona; almost mobbed by the citizens after Peterborough captures the town.

Vandergest. *Singleton* VI 261. Pilot of a Dutch ship which Singleton's crew captures.

Vane, Charles. *Pirates* 41, 135. Declines to accept the king's pardon brought by Woodes Rogers; deposed by his own crew for cowardice, 1718.

Vane, Sir Walter. *Carleton* 7. Carleton hopes to join his regiment in Holland, 1674.

Van Ghent, Admiral. *Carleton* 2. Commands the Amsterdam squadron at Sole Bay, 1674.

Vangrult, Theodorus. *Gulliver* Part III chap. 17. Master of the Dutch ship *Amboyna* which brings Gulliver away from Japan.

Vanity. *Battle* I 154. Child of Criticism.

Van Tyle, Ort. *Pirates* 492. New York merchant and ship captain living on Madagascar; plundered by Howard's gang.

Vaudemont, Prince. *Carleton* 35. Executes a "glorious retreat" from Arseel, 1695.

Vaughan, Hodge. *Carleton* 4. Wounded at Sole Bay, devoured by hogs in the hold of the ship.

Vaughan, Sir William. *Cavalier* V 282. Sent to relieve Chester, routed by the Roundheads, 1645.

Veal, Mr. *Veal* XV 228. Brother of Mrs. Veal; obtains a place in the customhouse at Dover.

Veal, Mrs. *Veal* XV 227. Her ghost appears to Mrs. Bargrave.

Vendosme, Duke de. *Carleton* 168, *Jacque* XI 45. French com-

mander in Spain and Savoy; tall, fair, and fat, with an eye
patch; dies of eating too much fish.

Venus. *Battle* I 159. Roman goddess of love; protector of Cowley
in his battle with Pindar.

Vergil, Polydore (1576-1631). *Battle* I 152. Italian historian; modern
infantry commander.

Verney, Sir Edward. *Cavalier* V 176. The king's standard-bearer,
killed at Edgehill, 1642.

Villa Moresa, Don Ferdinand de (in *Jacque*). See Jack, Col.

Villars, Lucy. *Clarissa* V 273. Former paramour of Lovelace's.

Villeroi, Duke de. *Carleton* 35, *Jacque* XI 41. French commander
who bombards Brussels as a diversion from the siege of
Namur, 1695; commands in Italy, 1701.

Villiers, Sir George. *Campbell* IV 62. Father of the first Duke of
Buckingham; his ghost appears to the faithful family servant
Parker with a warning about the Duke's impending murder.

Villiers, George (first Duke of Buckingham). *Campbell* IV 64.
Warned of his death through a supernatural agency.

Virgil (70-19 B.C.) *Battle* I 146. Roman poet; in the battle, tricked
into exchanging armor with Dryden.

"Viscountess, the." *Pamela* IV 163. Sister of the Countess Dowager
of _____; makes a great fuss over Pamela's baby.

Vossius (Gerard John, 1618-1689). *Battle* I 152. Dutch scholar;
with Temple, one of the ancients' allies.

Vove, Rer (alias Rer Towlerpherangha). *Drury* 258. Madagascar
chieftain of the Saccalauvors who captures Drury.

Vovvern, Rer. *Drury* 161. King of Feraighn who attacks Deaan
Woozington, thus accidentally resolving the civil war in
Anterndroea.

W., Gen. *Grandison* II 42. Brother of Lord W.; recommends a governor to accompany Sir Charles on his travels.

W., Lady. *Grandison* II 43. Wife of Lord W.; adopts Caroline and
Charlotte after Lady Grandison's death.

W., Lord. *Grandison* I 220. Licentious old uncle of Sir Charles, persuaded by the baronet to reform; brother of Lady Grandison.

Wagstaff, Rev. Mr. *Life of Sheppard* XVI 176, *Sheppard's Narrative* XVI
231. Magistrate who examines Sheppard.

Waldeck, Prince. *Carleton* 11. Dutch commander shot through the arm
at Seneff, 1674.

Walden, Mr. *Grandison* I 57. Pedantic Oxford scholar at Lady Betty's.

Walden, John. *Pirates* 231. One of Roberts' men; objects to heaving up the anchor on a ship they are going to burn anyway, 1721.

Walgrave, Mr. *Pamela* III 379. Rake who drops in to see Mr. B. at his Bedfordshire estate.

Wallden, Capt. *Pirates* 109. Master of a Jamaica sloop captured by Rackam, 1718.

Wallenstein. *Cavalier* V 104. Becomes Imperial commander after the death of Tilly, 1632.

Waller, Sir William. *Cavalier* V 161, 193. Parliamentary commander; defeated at Roundway Down, 1642.

Wallis, Bab. *Clarissa* V 297. Crony of Lovelace's; impersonates Lady Betty Lawrance with a particularly grand air.

Wallis, Dr. *Campbell* IV 19. Professor at the University of Glasgow who has perfected a method of teaching the deaf to read, write, and speak.

Walter, Robert. *Pirates* 331. Mayor of New York; makes Peter Solgard free of the city in gratitude for his capturing the pirate Harris, 1723.

Walters, William (usually "Quaker William," alias "Signor Constantine Alexion of Ispahan" at Venice). *Singleton* VI 163. Crony of Singleton's, taken out of a ship from Pennsylvania.

Walters, Justice. *Life of Sheppard* XVI 178. Justice of the Peace at St. Ann's Roundhouse, Soho.

Walton, John. *Clarissa* VII 320. Milliner who conveys malicious gossip about Clarissa to Brand; also petty officer in the excise and Brand's former schoolfellow.

Walton, Mrs. *Clarissa* VII 320. Wife of above.

Ward, Joseph. *Life of Sheppard* XVI 185. Comrade of Sheppard in prison; both are condemned to be executed.

Ware, Capt. *Drury* 306. Presumably a pirate; Drury's crew meets an Irishman who has run away from his band.

Warneton, Maj. *Clarissa* VI 221. Acquaintance of Lovelace, visited after church by the rake.

Waterman, Sir George. *Plague Year* IX 53. Sheriff of London, 1665.

Watkyns, Sir Walter. *Grandison* I 274. Somersetshire landowner, suitor of Miss Charlotte Grandison.

Watson, Capt. *Veal* XV 233. Mrs. Veal's cousin, to whom she gives two gold pieces.

Watson, Miss. *Grandison* V 327. Friend of the Selbys in Northampton.

Watson, Mrs. *Veal* XV 234. Wife of the captain.

Weaver, Capt. Daniel. *Carleton* 158. Accidentally blown up at the siege of Alicant, having just come on guard duty.

Welby, Dolly. *Clarissa* VII 347. Mistress of Lovelace's; describes the experience of childbirth to him.

Welch, James. *Gulliver* Part IV chap. 1. Mutinous crewman who informs Gulliver that he is to be marooned.

Wells. *Crusoe* I 37. Portuguese neighbor of Crusoe's in Brazil, to whom Crusoe entrusts the administration of his plantation.

Welwood, Miss. *Campbell* IV 89. Duncan predicts her death by smallpox.

Welwood, Mrs. *Campbell* IV 89. Doctor's wife in London; follows her daughter to the grave, 1698.

Wesley (Samuel, 1662-1735). *Battle* I 157. Father of the evangelists and minor poet; slain by Homer in the battle.

Whalley. *Cavalier* V 268. Parliamentary officer stationed on the right wing at Naseby, 1645.

Wheatly, Paul. *Clarissa* IV 55. Will Summers' cousin; Lovelace sends Paul to Anna posing as Capt. Singleton's mate in order to alarm her.

"Whifflingpin, Aaron" (in *Pirates*). See Sutton, Thomas.

White, Henry. *Pirates* 627. Master of the *Batchelor's Adventure*, taken over by Bunce and Macarty, 1718.

White, James. *Pirates* 267. Pirate musician; testifies on Glasby's humane conduct during the fight with the *Swallow*, 1722.

White, Capt. Thomas. *Pirates* 464, 472. A Plymouth man, one of the Madagascar pirates; assists in the capture of the *Speaker*, 1700.

White, Capt. *Drury* 295, 301. Master of the *Mercury*; anchors at Yong-Owl at the time of Drury's rescue.

White. *Carleton* 212. Irish priest in Spain who tells Carleton the origins of the Carthusian order.

Whitfield, Jonathan. *Pirates* 217. Master of the *Richard* out of Biddiford, captured by Roberts, 1720.

Whitney, Col. *Pirates* 304. Governor of James's Island, Gambia, 1721.

Wicksted, Capt. *Pirates* 315. Master of the *Princess* out of Guinea, captured by Lowther, 1723.

Wilcocks, Thomas. *Gulliver* Part II chap. 8. A Shropshire man, captain of the ship which picks Gulliver up after his sojourn in Brobdingnag.

Wild, Andrew. *Wild* XVI 241. Brother of Jonathan; a buckle maker.

Wild, John. *Wild* XVI 241. Brother of Jonathan, a rioter at the time of the Preston rebellion, 1715.

Wild, Jonathan. *Life of Sheppard* XVI 184, *Street-Robbers* XVI 357, *Wild* XVI 241. Notorious London fence and "thieftaker," stabbed by Joseph Blake during a trial, hanged to great popular rejoicing, 1725.

Wilkins, John. *Pamela* III 332. Deceased steward of Sir Jacob Swynford.

Wilkins (John, 1614-1672). *Battle* I 152. One of the founders of the Royal Society; commander of the modern engineers.

Wilks, Capt. *Drury* 278. Master of the galley *Clapham*; comes to trade with the Saccalauvors but pays no attention to Drury.

Will (in *Clarissa*). See Summers, Will.

Will (in *Drury*). See Thornbury, William.

Will (also "Robin" and "the diver"). *Jacque* X 51. Rogue six years older than Jacque, his tutor in the ways of crime (his name changes from Robin to Will in the course of the novel).

Willard, Capt. *Pirates* 328. Master of the *Amsterdam Merchant*; Ned Low slits his nose and cuts off his ears because he is a New England man.

"William, Duke." *Cavalier* V 112. Lieutenant of Gustavus Adolphus in Bavaria, 1632.

William, Mr. *Moll* VIII 55. Journeyman whose master falsely accuses Moll of theft.

William, Prince of Orange (later William III of England). *Carleton* 7. Valiant defender of his country against the French; joined by Carleton, 1674.

William. *Street-Robbers* XVI 363. Servant of the gentleman robbed in his coach.

Williams, Arthur. *Pamela* I 113. Clergyman in Lincolnshire; keeps a little Latin school, becomes Pamela's ally.

Williams, Lady Betty. *Grandison* I 23. Widow of forty-odd, relation of Mr. Reeves; disapproves of book learning.

Williams, Capt. David. *Pirates* 495. Bad-tempered and illiterate Welsh shepherd who turns pirate; two of his men are tortured to death by the Arab governor of the Boyne, Madagascar.

Williams, Dolly. *Clarissa* VII 243. Daughter of the housekeeper; wants to go to Clarissa on her deathbed.

Williams, John. *Clarissa* VIII 124. Witness to Clarissa's will.

Williams, Joseph. *Pirates* 599. Seaman on an English slaver; mounts a brave defense against Cornelius.

Williams, Peter. *Gulliver* Part I chap. 8. Old companion of Gulliver's who recommends Gulliver favorably after his escape from Blefuscu.

Williams, William. *Pirates* 279. Receives two lashes from everyone in the ship's company for trying to desert.

Williams, Capt. Paul. *Pirates* 41. Pirate who surrenders to Woodes Rogers and receives the king's pardon, 1718.

Williams, Paul. *Pirates* 585. Pirate crony of Capt. Bellamy, 1717.

Williams, Counsellor. *Clarissa* IV 260. Lawyer allegedly appointed to draw up the marriage settlements between Lovelace and Clarissa.

Williams, Lieut. *Gow* XVI 305. Gow's lieutenant, unspeakably brutal.

Williams, Miss. *Grandison* I 24. Younger daughter of Lady Betty, aged fifteen; has been kept in ignorance because of her mother's views on education.

Williams, Master. *Grandison* I 24. Son of Lady Betty, aged seventeen.

Williams, Mrs. *Clarissa* VII 243. Former housekeeper at Harlowe Place; wants to go to Clarissa on her deathbed.

Willoughby. *Cavalier* V 171. With the Marquis of Hertford, commands the left wing of the Parliamentary forces at Edgehill, 1642.

Wilmot, "Capt." *Singleton* VI 159. English sailor who helps plan the mutiny and accompanies Singleton around the world.

Wilson, George. *Pirates* 273. Gives the alarm about the planned uprising on board the *Swallow*; receives a stay of execution, 1722.

Wilson, William. *Grandison* I 145. Harriet's new servant, twenty-six years old; turns out to be Sir Hargrave's agent.

Wilson, Capt. *Pirates* 64. Master of the *John and Martha*, captured by Martel, 1716.

Wilson. *Clarissa* IV 45. Servant at Mrs. Sinclair's who carries Clarissa's letters to Anna.

Wilson. *Street-Robbers* XVI 375. Member of the revenge conspiracy against Thomas Ball.

Wimburn, Mrs. *Grandison* I 152. Miss Clements' aunt; took her away from her selfish mother in York, treats her now as a daughter.

Wincon. *Pirates* 272. Pirate who quarrels with Scudamore about the surgeon's instruments.

Windham, Gen. *Carleton* 105. Officer sent by Peterborough to attack Requina, 1705.

Windisgratz, Baron. *Clarissa* VIII 261. Proprietor of the Favorita, Lovelace's inn in Vienna.

Wingfield, John. *Pirates* 263. Witness for Harry Glasby, 1722.

Wintselsheim, Countess de (in *Roxana*). See Roxana.

Winwood, Col. *Grandison* IV 101. Charlotte Grandison's informant who reports on Everard Grandison's rakish activities.

Wise, Francis. *Pirates* 373. Seemingly unwilling confederate of Philip Roch.

Wise, Thomas. *Gow* XVI 298. Master of a ship from Poole sunk by Gow.

Withers (really Wither, George, 1588-1667). *Battle* I 146. Regarded as a typically bad poet; Virgil's works are hemmed in between his and Dryden's; cavalry commander.

Wood, Owen. *Life of Sheppard* XVI 173, *Sheppard's Narrative* XVI 214. Carpenter to whom Sheppard is apprenticed.

Wood, Mrs. *Life of Sheppard* XVI 175, *Sheppard's Narrative* XVI 214. Pious woman, felled by Sheppard with a lath.

Wooley, Capt. George. *Pirates* 460. Master of the *Pembroke*; forced by Thomas Howard to serve as a pilot; later set ashore in India, 1703.

Woozington, Deaan. *Drury* 88. Wily and treacherous king of Mefaughla; constant enemy of Drury's various masters.

Worcester, Earl of. *Cavalier* V 197. Gives Charles I the disastrous advice to attack Gloucester and Hertford before capturing London.

Worden, Beck. *Pamela* II 195, 203. Lady Davers's woman.

Worley, Capt. *Pirates* 297. Pirate from New York; sets sail with eight men in an open boat; captured and hanged at Norfolk, Va., 1718.

Wotton, William (1666-1727). *Battle* I 155. Author of *Reflections on the Ancient and Modern Learning* (1694), attacking Temple's essay; in the battle, Criticism crams a book into his brain to prepare him for combat.

Wragg, Samuel. *Pirates* 75. Councilman of Charleston, S.C.; falls into Blackbeard's hands, 1718.

Wright, Dr. *Clarissa* VII 127. Parson of the parish at M. Hall in Berkshire; comes to say prayers while Lovelace is raving.

Wrightson, Mr. *Pamela* II 338, IV 274. Kind and understanding man in Jamaica who finally marries Sally Godfrey.

Wrightson, Mrs. Sarah (in *Pamela*). See Godfrey, Sarah.

Wroughton, George. *Campbell* IV 74. Owns the home adjoining the churchyard in which Cantlow makes the bell ring.

"Wry-neck." *Jacque* X 9. Thief who lives with the young ragamuffins near Dallow's Glasshouse in Rosemary Lane.

Wyar, Capt. *Pirates* 72. Master of the *Protestant Caesar*, captured by Blackbeard, 1718.

Wycherley. *Clarissa* IV 128. Friend of Lord M.'s who married in old age only to plague his nephew; Lord M. threatens to do likewise.

Wyerley, Alexander. *Clarissa* I 2. Suitor rejected by Clarissa because of his habit of jesting about sacred things; see Symmes, Mr.

"Wykes, Dorcas" (in *Clarissa*). See Butler, Deb.

Xury. *Crusoe* I 20, 24. A Maresco boy who accompanies Crusoe on his escape from Sallee; Crusoe later sells him into slavery.

Yeats, Tobit. *Campbell* IV 165. Barber in Hampton Town; helps Duncan find his way home after his return from France.

Yeats. *Pirates* 100. Comrade of Charles Vane, 1718.

Yonge, Capt. Nicholas. *Drury* 42. Son of above; succeeds his father in command; his poor judgment leads the party into disaster.

Yonge, Capt. William. *Drury* 41. Master of the *Degrave*, on which Drury sails as a passenger; dies of a fever in Bengal.

York, Duke of (later James II of England). *Carleton* 1. Commands English fleet at Sole Bay, 1672; distinguishes himself for courage.

Yung-Owl. *Drury* 130. Uncle of the wife of Mundumber; out of respect for him, Deaan Murnanzack releases her and her daughter.

Zachary. *Drury* 296. One of the castaway white men from the island of St. Mary's.

Zaffentumppoey. *Drury* 165. Native king at the head of the Oneghayloghe River, Madagascar.

Zerda, Don Joseph de la. *Pirates* 398. Spanish governor of Carthagene; conspires with Misson to capture the *St. Joseph*.

Zoulicafre, Mons. *Carleton* 156. Banker in Spain, ordered to pay Carleton fifty pistoles.